C000215972

The Conquest of Death

The Conquest of Death

Violence and the Birth of the Modern English State

Matthew Lockwood

Yale

UNIVERSITY PRESS

New Haven & London

Published with assistance from the Kingsley Trust Association Publication Fund established by the Scroll and Key Society of Yale College, and from the foundation established in memory of Amasa Stone Mather of the Class of 1907, Yale College.

Yale University Press books may be purchased in quantity for educational, business, or promotional use. For information, please e-mail sales.press@yale.edu (U.S. office) or sales@yaleup.co.uk (U.K. office).

Set in Bulmer type by Newgen North America.
Printed in the United States of America.

Library of Congress Control Number: 2016958014

ISBN 978-0-300-21706-3 (cloth : alk. paper)

A catalogue record for this book is available from the British Library.

This paper meets the requirements of ANSI/NISO Z39.48-1992 (Permanence of Paper).

10 9 8 7 6 5 4 3 2 1

For my parents, Jack and Nancy

Contents

Acknowledgments

THE PROCESS OF RESEARCHING AND writing a book would be impossible, or at least far more difficult and much less enjoyable, without the help of numerous people. I would like to thank my colleagues at Yale University and the University of Warwick for their welcoming collegiality and enthusiastic support. Particular thanks are due to Amanda Behm, William Bulman, Christian Burset, Mara Caden, Haydon Cherry, Megan Cherry, Leslie Cooles, Justin du Rivage, Carlos Eire, Paul Griffiths, Steve Gunn, Elizabeth Herman, Rab Houston, Richard Huzzey, Emma Kaufman, John Merriman, Jamie Miller, Sara Miller, Noah Millstone, Wendy Moffat, Ariel Ron, Dave Tengwall, Courtney Thomas, Matthew Underwood, Jennifer Wellington, and Alice Wolfram, for advice, encouragement, and many productive and stimulating discussions.

Steve Hindle and Bruce Gordon read much of what follows with careful eyes and open minds. I will be profoundly proud if my work reflects their incisive and insightful comments and suggestions. Special thanks are owed to Keith Wrightson, who not only read and commented on the entire work in its various stages and iterations, but has also been a friend and mentor of the greatest distinction for close to a decade. I hope that in some small way this serves as recompense for the hours, days, months, and years he spent toiling over my work. Perhaps that effort has not been entirely in vain.

Supportive institutions and funding bodies are the life-blood of academic research. As such, gratitude is due to the Yale Center for the Study of Representative Institutions, the Jack Miller Center, the Whitney and Betty Macmillan Center for International and Area Studies at Yale, and the Yale Boswell Editions for providing the funding necessary to complete this project. The Historic County Borders Project provided the open source data on early modern borders necessary for my creation of the maps featured in this book.

Yale University Press has proved to be a wonderful publisher. My editors, Jaya Chatterjee and Laura Davulis, deserve special praise for their championing of this book and their guidance throughout the publication process. Harry Haskell has been a sensitive and incisive copyeditor. Thanks are also due to the anonymous reviewers for their perceptive and constructive critiques.

My family has lived with this book for as long as I have been writing it. My parents, Jack and Nancy; my brothers Jack, Kaleb, John, Joey, and Josh; my sister Caitlin; and the extended Lockwood and Heid families have always supported my endeavors in whatever ways they could. I greatly appreciate their unflagging generosity and their forbearance of my ranting and rambling. My in-laws, Wendy, Donald, Emma, Eric, Barbara, and Tracy, have likewise shared the research and writing process in all its ups and downs, emotionally and intellectually.

Lucy Kaufman has been my intellectual sounding board, writing coach, and wellspring of support throughout this process and far beyond. Any thanks I give will never be sufficient recompense for her time, effort, and perseverance on my behalf. Quite simply, I would not be where I am today without her.

The Conquest of Death

Figure 1. Map of the counties of early modern England

Introduction

"Revenge is a kind of wild justice; which the more man's
nature runs to, the more ought the law to weed it out."
—Francis Bacon, "On Revenge" (1625)

THE EYES OF THE STATE WERE everywhere in early modern England (Fig. 1). When the body of Thomas Chennell was discovered drowned in a Surrey pond in 1591, the gaze of the leviathan fixed with rapt attention on the poor man's corpse. The discovery was marked by the presence of multiple layers of surveillance. Like so many vultures, the heirs and creditors, local officials, and central agents of the crown circled the body, all intent on their own ends and interests. Among those who surveyed the scene with covetous eyes were John Derrick, one of the coroners for Surrey; a Mr. Morgan, in whose pond the body was found; Chennell's widow; 14 coroner's jurors; several neighbors; and a number of agents of the almoner.[1]

All of these parties had a financial stake in the outcome of the coroner's inquest and the verdict it assigned. If the death was ruled to be a homicide, John Derrick would stand to receive a fee as coroner; a verdict of accident or suicide, however, would mean Derrick's pains would go unrewarded. If the death was found to be an accident, Mr. Morgan could potentially lose the value of any piece of movable property that was deemed to have caused the accident. As the crown appointee who was granted the right to all forfeit goods, the almoner, whose agents were on the ground in Surrey, stood to gain Chennell's goods and chattels if the verdict was suicide. Thomas Chennell's widow, however, would lose all her inheritance if her husband's death was ruled to be suicide. Finally, one of Chennell's

1

neighbors claimed that before he died, Chennell had given him wardship of his son and possession of his goods. If the inquest verdict was death by homicide or accident, this neighbor would have a claim to a portion of Chennell's property.[2]

With so many competing interests it is no surprise that not every party present was fully satisfied with the process and outcome of the coroner's inquest. As so often transpired in early modern England, dissatisfaction led inexorably to a lawsuit, and the dispute over Thomas Chennell's death shifted venue to the Court of Star Chamber, where crown officials perused the records of coroner, almoner, witness, and heirs to determine the proper redistribution of the deceased's property. The almoner brought suit against three members of the coroner's jury, claiming that, in collusion with Chennell's heirs, these men had bribed a local pauper to flee the county as if he were responsible for Chennell's death, thus paving the way for a verdict of death by homicide. The men denied this charge, claiming that the almoner was pushing for a suicide verdict so as to gain the dead man's forfeit property. John Derrick, the coroner, was also sued for failing to return a verdict of any kind.[3] Neighbors, witnesses, local agents of the almoner, and others were called to provide evidence, and the records produced by the coroner and his jury were examined, all to settle the matter of how a Surrey yeoman's property was to be redistributed after his violent death.

While on the surface these events might seem mundane or routine, such litigation over the forfeit property of felons and the violently deceased performed an important function in early modern England. As the financial interests of heirs, creditors, coroners, and crown all rested on the outcome of the coroner's inquest, few violent deaths went unnoticed, unexamined, or unexplained. Furthermore, these contestations over inquest verdicts created a new level of written documentation that allowed the representatives of the state new avenues and novel opportunities for the oversight of violent death in the early modern period. In turn, the advent of a new system of surveillance allowed the state to obtain a true monopoly of violence for the first time in English history. This is the story of how that monopoly came to exist and the judicial official whose primary purpose was its enforcement.

Violence and State Formation in Early Modern Europe

The control or restriction of violence has long been at the center of definitions of the state. In perhaps the earliest complete formulation of this conception of the state, Max Weber declared that "in the final analysis the modern state can be defined only sociologically by the specific means that are particular to it, as to every political organization: namely, physical violence."[4] For Weber, it was clear that throughout history states had engaged in a variety of activities and undertaken numerous tasks. The use of violence, however, was and is the only common feature of all states. Thus, at its most basic, the modern state can be defined as "the form of human community that (successfully) lays claim to the monopoly of legitimate physical violence within a particular territory."[5]

This conception of the function of a state was not lost on political theorists of early modern England. Prefiguring the work of Weber, Thomas Hobbes argued that in a state of nature, war, strife, and discord reigned. With "the continual fear and danger of violent death" the life of man, according to Hobbes's famous dictum, was "solitary, poor, nasty, brutish, and short."[6] In order to protect themselves, individuals agreed to give up their natural right to govern themselves to an individual or assembly of men. Among the 12 principal rights given to the sovereign in this exchange were the exclusive right to make war, to act as judge, to define justice, and to appoint magistrates and officers. As individuals thus give up their power to make war, to adjudicate disputes, and to punish lawbreakers—and because they forfeit the right to punish, change, or execute their sovereigns—one can conclude that, for Hobbes, a key aspect of the social contract was the granting to the state of the sole right to use force or violence.[7]

In a similar vein, John Locke conceived of political power as "a right to make laws—with the death penalty and consequently all lesser penalties—for regulating and preserving property and to employ the force of the community in enforcing such laws and defending the commonwealth from external attack."[8] For Locke, in a state of nature, each individual had an equal natural right to protect his person and property, as well as a right to enforce the law against those who threatened these. In other words, "the enforcement of that law of nature (in the state of nature) is in every man's hands, so that everyone has a right to punish law-breakers as severely as is needed to hinder the violation of the law."[9] However, because individuals are not always capable of fairly adjudicating disputes in which they have an interest, and because "the state of nature often lacks a power to back up and support a correct sentence, and enforce it properly," individuals are forced to band together in a collective state to protect their interests.[10] Thus for Locke, the state is defined as an entity that possess the right to use violence to restrain the "partiality and violence" of individuals. Locke suggests that this power is based in the will of the majority and is to be used solely to advance interests of the commonality; however, this definition of the makeup of the state does not change what Hobbes, Locke, Weber, and others see as its primary function: the regulation of violence.

Most scholars of modern state formation have incorporated some aspects of Weber's definition of the state as an entity that exercises a monopoly of violence in a circumscribed territory into their examination of state growth. Michael Mann, for instance, defines the state as "a centralized, differentiated set of institutions enjoying a monopoly of the means of legitimate violence over a territorially demarcated area."[11] In a similar formulation, Charles Tilly defines states as "coercion-wielding organizations that are distinct from households and kinship groups and exercise clear priority in some respects over all other organizations within substantial territories."[12] More recently, Philip Gorski has conceptualized the state as an "organization that claims clear priority (if not complete monopoly) over the legitimate means of socialization within a given territory."[13] Whether the terminology used prioritizes the means of socialization or the means of coercion, these definitions are consistent with Weber's monopoly of legitimate violence.

Using Weber's definition as a starting point, these scholars and others, such as Perry Anderson and Immanuel Wallerstein, have reached a variety of conclusions about the process of state formation.[14] With few exceptions, however, historians of the state have neglected significant aspects of state formation that are central to Weber's definition. First of all, most accounts focus on the positive or active use of physical violence by the state, rather than on the negative aspects of the state's attempts to restrict violence. According to Weber, the two prerequisites for "every ruling apparatus" are the requirements that "human action should be predisposed to obedience toward the rulers who claim to be the agents of legitimate force" and that "rulers should have at their disposal the material resources necessary to make use of physical force where required."[15] In other words, a true monopoly of violence entails both the ability to use violence *and* the power to restrict violence that is deemed illegitimate. On the whole, however, the state-formation literature focuses almost exclusively on the use of physical force by the state and ignores the restriction of the violence of nonstate actors.

Michael Mann, John Brewer, Charles Tilly, and Geoffrey Parker are all primarily concerned with the ways in which the prospective modern state marshaled the resources necessary to engage in warfare and the effects these efforts had on the growth of political institutions. This single-minded concentration on the means necessary to use force led Mann, for example, to focus his examination of the English state on the finances of the Exchequer, and in particular on how the revenue of the Exchequer fluctuated in times of international war. This privileging of the means of making war led Mann to conclude that the function of the English state was largely military and international.[16] The outward projection of violence is surely a central function of a modern state and, as historians have shown, the marshaling of resources to engage in international military competition had an enormous impact on the creation of bureaucratic government. However, privileging the international sphere and ignoring the internal, domestic aspects of the monopolization of violence have led historians astray by distorting both the process and chronology of state formation. Only when we examine the monopoly of violence in both its internal and external aspects can we truly understand how and when the modern English state was created.

Historians have provided a variety of potential time frames for the creation of the modern English state. Focusing on the growth of bureaucratic institutions of central government, G. R. Elton, for instance, makes a case for the importance of governmental reforms in the 1530s in the birth of the modern English state.[17] Thomas Ertman places his emphasis on the revolutions of the mid-seventeenth century, when he argues the English state was finally purged of its patrimonial aspects and bureaucratic reforms were finally forced on the monarchy.[18] Others, such as John Brewer, have pointed to the period after the Glorious Revolution of 1688 as the period of state formation driven by fiscal-military concerns.[19]

These are certainly important developments, but historians who privilege the use of physical violence forget that Weber's definition of the state requires a *monopoly* of violence, a definition that implies the exclusive right to use physical violence rather than the simple ability to extract the resources necessary to commit acts of violence. Central to Weber's conception of the modern state, then, are both the power to use violence and the power to restrict the violence of nonstate actors. Too often, this latter aspect of the modern state has been overlooked in favor of explanations of state growth that examine the apparati of warfare rather than the means by which nonstate warfare, or nonstate violence more generally, is restricted.

The monopoly of violence, even when taken in both its positive and negative, restrictive senses, should not be limited to warfare alone. A modern state must have exclusive control not only over warfare, but also over physical violence more generally. In order to control violence and establish a definition of legitimate and illegitimate violence, a state must have the sole power to use judicial violence and the ability to restrict and regulate interpersonal violence. In general, the regulation and monopolization of interpersonal and judicial violence have been neglected by historians of the state, creating a skewed and incomplete view of the development of the early modern state.

More recently, scholars influenced by developments in social history have begun to theorize new definitions of the state and thus of state formation, stressing the importance of local domestic developments. Steve Hindle has argued that the driving force behind the growth of governance in the early modern period was not the high officers of state or central institutions but rather parish governors who filled the ranks of local offices, such as churchwardens, constables, jurors, and vestrymen. For Hindle, the state is not so much an entity or set of institutions as it is "a series of multi-

lateral initiatives to be negotiated across space and through the social order." Because governance of necessity involves the negotiation of authority
at the local level, Hindle concludes that state formation is not so much "a
matter of centralization," as has often been argued, but rather a matter of
"the social dynamics of the localization of state power."[20]

The key actors in this localization of state power in the early modern
period were the middling sort of people in their roles as parish officials
and village governors. The primary goal of this growth of governance in
the localities was to ensure social stability and maintain order in a period
that was rife, or so it was perceived, with chaos and disorder. Because most
aspects of the English system of law enforcement and criminal justice were
voluntary and relied on widespread popular participation, the increase in
litigation and the growing influence of the state were not simply the result
of central desires for greater control; they were also, and perhaps primarily, a consequence of popular pressure for greater central participation in
local governance. Thus, the growth of the state in early modern England
could be said to be the result of the intersecting interests of central and local
authorities.[21]

A similar theory of state formation has been posited by Michael Braddick. In addition to the fiscal-military state, the confessional state, and the
dynastic state, Braddick examines the role of the "patriarchal state" in the
process of state formation. At the heart of Braddick's argument is a definition of the state not as a set of institutions created by bureaucrats as in the
Eltonian model, but rather as a network of local officeholders with a reciprocal, and at times ambiguous, relationship with the central authorities.
In other words, the state for Braddick is defined as "a coordinated and
territorially bounded network of agencies exercising political power, and
this network was exclusive of the authority of other political organizations
within those bounds."[22] Thus, the growth of governance was in reality a
response to local needs and local concerns in a time of social crisis rather
than an unwanted imposition from above.[23]

Like Hindle, Braddick argues that the legal system was of critical importance to this reciprocal process of state formation. The law, and the legal
system that enforced it, was not simply an instrument used by the central

authorities "to discipline and regulate social life from the outside," nor was it seen as such. Instead, the law was "a resource and a tool that could be manipulated, even for those of fairly humble status."[24] Courts served a useful function as a means of resolving disputes, maintaining order, and preventing or ameliorating social strife. As a result, government itself gained a more precise legal definition, as well as a growing semblance of regularity.

Defining the state in a more expansive, inclusive way as Braddick and Hindle have done does not, however, diminish the importance of Weber's conception of the monopoly of violence. While it is surely correct to expand the definition of the state to include local institutions and officers as well as a sense of the negotiated aspects of the growth of governance, the function of the state at its most basic level remains the exclusive power to define legitimate and illegitimate violence. Nor should we overstate the level of negotiation present in the early modern justice system. Social historians' recent obsession with giving agency to the disenfranchised, while admirable and compelling, occludes the very real imbalances of power as well as the totalizing nature of exploitation and repression in all its forms. The weapons of the weak are rather weak weapons in the face of actual political, social, legal, and economic inequality. By focusing on the agency of the repressed or instances of negotiation between the powerful and the powerless, we excuse, ignore, or mitigate the very real repression of the law. The early modern justice system did leave some room for action on the part of the poor and powerless, but this space was heavily circumscribed. The legal system was unequal, and was a key aspect of the state's apparatus of power and control. That sometimes the interests of the state could align with those of the poor and powerless should not blind us to the realities of its true nature and purpose. Thus, while Braddick and Hindle do a remarkable job of explaining the local institutions of the state and the local causes and functions of state growth, the practical process of the monopolization of violence, the core means and function of the modern state, has still not been explained satisfactorily.

Social historians have certainly provided a useful corrective to a historical literature too focused on central authority. Illuminating the local processes of state formation is invaluable, but we should not confuse the coopting of local officials and local communities with an equal relationship in governance between the state and the individual. People were indeed increasingly bound to the state and its institutions because they offered real, tangible benefits, such as pay, protection, dispute resolution, and law enforcement. A grudging acceptance of the growing importance and power of the state, however, is not the same thing as negotiation, much less negotiation between equals. The unequal balance of power between state and individual makes even the possibility of real negotiation difficult to imagine. By acting as officials and using courts, individuals and communities helped to sow the seeds of state formation, but while the benefits of participation were real, room for alternate action was severely circumscribed. Likewise, while local officials had some autonomy in the performance of their duties, their actions were always made within the bounds set by the state and by higher officials. Repression and enforcement were of necessity selective, but when it chose, the state could bring its full force to bear on anyone at anytime, and this power could be terrible. Thus, the early modern English state was a surveillance state, but one made of paper and neighbors. Private individuals and legal records, those great repositories of information, were tapped by agents of the state to create a complex, detailed, and usable picture of the English polity.

    As we have seen, there has long been a general agreement among scholars, from Locke to Weber and beyond, that the most elemental aspect of state formation and a vital function of a modern state is the monopolization of violence. What this monopolization looks like in practice is much less clear and requires that one posit a number of further questions. First of all, it is crucial to establish which individuals are encompassed by "the state." For our purposes, a simple, loose definition is most useful: the state can be said to encompass the central officers and institutions of government as well as their appointees in the provinces. Locally appointed parish officials, although often used as agents of the state and often acting on the state's behalf, are excluded from this definition. This conception of the state differs from previous definitions that have sought to include both ruler or regime *and* realm or commonwealth. While such a definition may accurately reflect how people speak about the state, the conception is too broad to be historically or theoretically useful. For our purposes, the state is very much synonymous with rule or ruling regime and all its coercive connotations.[25]

Given the widespread acceptance that a monopoly of violence is a prerequisite for the development of a modern state, we might also ask, why would a state want a monopoly of violence in the first place? On the face of it, the desire to restrict violence seems laughably intuitive. Violence is bad, therefore preventing and punishing violence are good. In reality, however, there are much deeper reasons why states might want to control violence — order, political economy, and legibility, the restructuring of society to enable surveillance of its constituents.

In the first place, the most basic social contract between rulers and governed is an exchange of freedom for protection. One of the basic functions of any state is the protection of its population and the mediation of disputes. By violating this protection and challenging the state's exclusive right to define justice, interpersonal violence, and especially lethal violence, undermines the very foundation of a state's claim to legitimacy and authority. Furthermore, when a state's ability to protect its population from physical harm is so undermined, the possibility of extrajudicial violence, in the form of vendetta, feud, and popular punishment, grows. Extrajudicial violence of these types in and of itself begets more violence, creating a cycle that destabilizes order and thus the fundamental legitimacy of the state. Unchecked violence among the populace could also be turned against the state itself, with similarly destabilizing consequences. Thus, for the sake of order and the stability of the polity at large, it is in a state's best interest to maintain both an exclusive right to use violence and an exclusive right to define what violence is legitimate and illegitimate.

Second, lethal violence undermines and erodes the very lifeblood of any country, its population, or human resources. Historians tend to view concerns over population as a strategic, economic, and political resource as a byproduct of international competition in the nineteenth and early twentieth centuries. However, the importance of population as an asset was widely accepted in the early modern period. From Machiavelli and Thomas More to Jean Bodin and William Petty, the human resources of a nation were deemed to be a vital aspect of its strength. As the political economist Charles Davenant put it in the late seventeenth century, "The Bodies of Men are without a doubt the most valuable Treasure of a Country."[26] As such, the individual who caused depopulation, according to another seventeenth-century commentator, was a "man of bloud" or a "matricide" because the reduction of population prevented the performance of "service and liege obedience, immediately to their Prince, and mediately to the Common-weale."[27] Because population was viewed in this light, interpersonal violence was seen as a threat to the maintenance of a viable, competitive political and economic community. It was thus widely believed that "the People being the first Matter of Power and Wealth, by whose Labour and Industry a Nation must ne Gainers in the Balance, their Increase and Decrease must be carefully observ'd by any Government that designs to thrive; that is, their Increase must be promoted by good Conduct and wholesome Laws, and if they have been Decreas'd by War or any other Accident, the Breach is to be made up as soon as possible, for it is a Maim in the Body Politick affecting all its Parts."[28]

Finally, the regulation of violence was an aspect of related attempts to create a legible society. If order was to be maintained and population resources marshaled to their fullest extent, it was necessary for the state to know the number and location of its populace. According to the sixteenth-century French jurist and political philosopher Jean Bodin, a census of a country's population had innumerable benefits including knowledge of "what numbers they [the state] could draw foorth, either to go to the wars, or to remain at home; either to be sent abroad to colonies or to bee imployed in publike works."[29] Bodin's argument for legibility was taken up in England by influential political economists such as Charles Davenant, Francis Brewster, and William Petty. As a result, the early modern period saw the English state launch a myriad of programs designed to give authorities a better sense of the extent of its citizenry. Mandatory recording of births, marriages, and deaths was instituted by order of Thomas Cromwell in 1538. The London bills of mortality, designed to enumerate the details of deaths in the capital, were first compiled between 1592 and 1595 and were published annually from records of burials made by parish clerks from 1603. In response to demographic growth and fears of mobility and vagrancy, restrictions on movement within and from England were put in place in the sixteenth and seventeenth centuries, with those moving required to obtain passes and, in the case of foreign travel, swear an oath of allegiance and have recorded their name, place of birth, occupation, status, and reason for leaving the country.[30] Fears of a religious fifth column prompted the creation of the Compton census of 1676, a national numbering of the nonconforming population.

All of these new measures were created in an effort to establish the extent of the population and their location, which in turn made such governmental functions as tax gathering and conscription much easier and more efficient. Because the state's ability to read its population was important, the restriction of violence played a vital role not only in limiting violence itself, but also in helping to detect and explain changes in population that resulted from violence. In England the responsibility for investigating violence and making death legible to the state fell to the coroner, a critically important but oft-ignored judicial officer. The story of the monopolization of violence is also, then, the story of the coroner.

If we conclude that a state seeks a monopoly of violence for reasons of order, political economy, and legibility, only one important question remains before we can examine how such a monopoly was created in practice, namely, how do we measure the successful creation of a monopoly of violence? In other words, how do we know when a state has achieved a monopoly of violence? For a state to possess a monopoly of violence, there must be almost universal acceptance that the state holds the exclusive right to use violence as well as the sole ability to define and punish illegitimate violence. In practice, this means, first, that no citizens have the ability to wage private warfare, either against the state or against each other; second, that extrajudicial violence such as feud, vendetta, lynching, and other violent forms of nonstate dispute resolution cease to exist and that such disputes are settled primarily through state apparati; and finally, that

levels of interpersonal violence decrease. As we will see, all of these criteria
were met in England over the course of the early modern period. All that
remains is to detail when this successful monopoly of violence was created, and how such a monopoly was created in an era before the advent of
professional policing and widespread bureaucratic institutions.

Histories of Violence

In recent years there has been something of a vogue for histories of violence. Most of these studies span centuries in their scope and view the history of violence through the lens of the present. Scholars such as Steven
Pinker and Robert Muchembled examine violence, or aspects of it, in the
longue durée in an attempt to answer questions about modern society. Is
the modern world especially violent when compared to previous times? If
the present is less violent than the past, what caused the long-term trend of
declining levels of violence? With few exceptions these studies incorporate
aspects of Norbert Elias's well-known theory that declining levels of violence resulted from a "civilizing process," a widespread cultural shift that
saw values of politeness and restraint replace older values of strength and
force. In this conception, changes in elite behavior and culture that placed
a new premium on self-control trickled down to the lower orders through
a combination of education, emulation, and popular print culture.[31] Although this cultural revolution certainly occurred, many scholars have neglected to adequately explain two key aspects of the civilizing process: the
timing of this change and the mechanism responsible for it.

Criminologists and historians have convincingly shown that violence
(or at least lethal violence) began to decline from at least the late Middle
Ages.[32] Historians examining the rise of polite society, on the other hand,
describe a civilizing process that only reached its apogee in the late seventeenth and early eighteenth centuries. It must be granted that Elias himself
chose Erasmus as one of his early exemplars and proponents of self-control.
Erasmus certainly seems a likely candidate, and it is also true that there
were notable advocates of self-control and moderation from Greco-Roman

times to Thomas More in the sixteenth century and beyond. However, while there were certainly outliers and precursors before the eighteenth century, a socially deep and culturally broad adherence to the values of politeness and self-control as the markers of masculinity did not displace the more violent form of popular masculinity before the end of the seventeenth century at the very latest. Thus, any contention that the rise of polite society led to the decline in violence is fundamentally flawed because levels of violence began to decline a century or more before widespread acceptance of a polite, self-abnegating masculinity. Given these conflicting timelines, proponents of a cultural explanation for declining levels of violence must explain how it is that violence began to decline long before the cultural changes they outline had emerged, and certainly centuries before such changes were able to trickle down to the populace at large. Put another way, why did violence begin to decline in the late medieval period if the culture of restraint and politeness did not emerge until much later?

The answer to this question—one proposed by Elias himself and echoed by Pinker—accounts for the timing of decline in violence through an explanation of the mechanism responsible for catalyzing the cultural revolution in the first place. For Elias, the direct cause of the declining levels of violence in the early modern period was cultural change, but this cultural shift was in turn the product of changes in the nature of governance. Elias theorized that the growth of the state in the late medieval period began to restrain the violence of feudal lords and other elites whose power rested on their ability to use violence and project force. As the violence of these elites was restricted, a culture of strength and force had to be replaced, which in turn led to the advent of new social norms based on self-control.[33] These new social cultural norms, for Elias, Pinker, and others, were the most important factor in the long-term decline in violence.

While the general schema of state growth causing cultural change is convincing, other aspects of this argument are more problematic. First of all, such theories presuppose that expanding states were concerned solely or primarily with elite violence. Given the potential threat posed by overmighty subjects, it is reasonable to argue that the control of elite violence was a priority for late medieval and early modern states. However, we should not assume that attempts to restrict elite violence precluded a similar effort to regulate violence in its totality. Late medieval and early modern states went to great and growing lengths to control the violence of all of their subjects, whatever their status. A narrow focus on the regulation of elite violence thus obscures the extent of state efforts to monopolize violence. Second, by honing in on aspects of cultural change, proponents of the civilizing process have mistakenly focused on the *products* of the decline of violence rather than its cause. Concerned with detailing the characteristics of civilized society and the cultural productions of modernity, such studies have neglected the mechanism ultimately responsible for initiating cultural change. As a result, the details of the process of state monopolization of violence have been sorely lacking. We may concede that the long trend of declining violence resulted from a civilizing process which was in turn caused by the growth of the state; however, what remains to be explored is how states made this transition to modernity—in other words, how states created a monopoly of violence. By examining the English state during this process, the present book shifts the focus from the products of change to the cause of change, and in so doing demonstrates the state's central role in the control and decline of violence.

The Stages of the Monopoly of Violence

The monopoly of violence has, to my mind, a variety of necessary facets. The first requirement of a monopoly of violence is for the prospective state to possess or acquire the institutions, capital, and resources necessary to engage in warfare. This aspect of the monopoly of violence has been adequately described elsewhere. For our purposes it is sufficient to say that so-called bellicist models of state formation tend to see the process of state growth as a function of the need to extract resources for the purpose of engaging in warfare; according to this argument, different models of resource extraction led to differential outcomes in state structure.[34] The exact process of state formation and the timelines provided by such interpretations of course differ; however, generally speaking, theories that link the growth of the state to international warfare tend to see the critical period for the birth of the modern states sometime in the sixteenth, seventeenth, or eighteenth century.[35]

The second requirement of a monopoly of violence is the ability or power to restrict the warfare of nonstate actors. As mentioned previously, this facet of state formation has been less fully explained or explored than have the various apparati of war. While it is true that the restriction of private warfare has been somewhat overlooked, it has not been neglected entirely. The details of the process have not been sufficiently established, but the general outline of the restriction of private warfare is clear enough. In the sixteenth century the Tudor monarchs engaged in a series of actions that were designed to reduce the traditional military power of the great nobility by restricting private armies through statutes limiting the maintenance of armed retinues, by eliminating the private fortresses of the magnates, and by restricting aristocratic violence more generally. The process of restricting retaining and private warfare was piecemeal, and although statutes against retaining had been introduced as early as 1468, the practice did not fully disappear until the late sixteenth century.[36] Whatever the cause, and however circuitous the route, it is clear that private warfare was effectively restricted in England at some point in the mid- to late sixteenth century.

The final prerequisites of a monopoly of violence are the restriction of interpersonal violence and the monopoly of judicial violence. Historians of early modern Europe have long recognized that the period between 1500 and 1800 witnessed the gradual displacement of extrajudicial forms of dispute resolution in favor of state-controlled law courts.[37] Although this trend has been identified in the abstract, no sufficient explanation of how this process worked in practice has been provided. Bruce Lenman and Geoffrey Parker have pointed to a vague combination of economic polarization, urbanization, and religious reform to explain early modern Europeans' growing use of formal law courts.[38] While this may indeed, in part, explain the growth in prosecutions for property crimes and moral or sexual crimes, it is insufficient to explain the growing monopoly of lethal violence, and the increased detection and prosecution of crimes by state and society were not affected by economic fluctuations or religious change.

Restricting Violence in England

Attempts were first made to restrict the interpersonal lethal violence of the English people in the Middle Ages with the establishment of the office of the coroner by Richard I in 1194.[39] The coroner's role was to investigate violent death in order to determine its legitimacy. Practically speaking, this entailed the investigation of potential homicides, suicides, and accidental deaths in order to punish offenders and procure for the crown any goods or property found to be forfeit.[40] Coroners were thus responsible for holding inquests on the bodies of any person whose death was thought to be violent or otherwise suspicious and for providing verdicts that were the initial step in the forfeiture and indictment processes. Therefore, the coroner should be seen as the judicial official with the most direct and fundamental role in the maintenance of the monopoly of interpersonal and judicial violence.

Historians of the medieval period have long recognized the importance of violence and disorder for the governance of England. J. G. Bellamy has contended that "the preservation of public order was often the biggest problem the king had to face," a problem fundamentally concerned with "royal authority and the structure of the state." According to R. A. Griffiths, "crime was endemic" in medieval England, "and a regime's success in controlling it may be gauged by the ability to curb its most violent forms." Thus, for many medieval historians, the ability to control violence was a central measure of a monarch's effectiveness.[41]

While there is much disagreement about which periods and which monarchical reigns witnessed the most violence and disorder, most historians agree that violence was relatively common throughout the medieval era, and certainly more prevalent than in the eras that followed.[42] The causes of this elevated level of violence are complex; some historians have suggested bastard feudalism and competition among local elites for "the limited resources of local society" as a causal factors, while others have focused on "undermighty" kings who failed to control their elite subjects. Others have suggested that rampant violence was caused by inadequate policing, widespread weapon carrying, and social norms of community action in the face of crime.[43] Some have even suggested that violence was simply one tool in a range of social strategies of dispute resolution, and as such was not necessarily indicative of disorder or disruption, but was rather a legitimate aspect of local social relations.[44] Violence may well have been only one part of a range of strategies that included arbitration, litigation, and other formal and semiformal means of nonviolent dispute resolution. The question remains, however, how and why did violence cease to become a legitimate strategy of dispute resolution, an action reserved to the state and its agents alone? Whatever the cause, the reality of frequent violence, and the perception of rulers and subjects alike that violence was a dangerously destabilizing force, was a salient feature of the medieval world, one that necessitated action and reforms, primary among them the creation and supervision of the office of the coroner.

The historical literature relating to the early modern coroner is limited and insufficient. There has been no systematic academic study of the office, and most treatments of the coroner in more general works rely on studies focusing on either an earlier or a later period.[45] The result of this dearth is that most conclusions made about the early modern coroner are drawn either from a medieval literature that stresses a decline in the importance of the office or from a modern literature that stresses the rise of medico-legal science.[46] As a consequence, we have a skewed view that places the early modern coroner at the nadir of his importance—sadly declined from his medieval prestige and responsibility, but not yet the technically advanced medico-legal professional of the modern world.

This lack of a systematic study has in turn led to a number of ill-founded assumptions about the importance and competence of the early modern coroner. The first misapprehension about the early modern coroner found in the available literature is that the years between 1500 and 1836 were a static period for the office, free of innovation or reform. According to J. D. J. Havard, whose *The Detection of Secret Homicide* remains one of the most frequently cited sources for the history of the coroner, "for nearly two and a half centuries after the Act of 1508, there were no developments of any importance affecting the coroner or his investigation of sudden death."[47] Even in the restricted realm of statute law this statement is patently false. To cite just two important examples, the Marian statutes of

1554–1555 made coroners responsible for examining witnesses and liable to fines for negligence, and the reforms of 1752 changed the payment structure for coroners in such a way as to incentivize greater action.[48]

The second common claim made in the historiography is that since the coroner lacked medical training and forensic medicine was in its infancy, a large proportion of early modern deaths went unsolved or unexplained. Havard is again typical of this type of thinking, arguing that "throughout this period the investigation of sudden death was almost entirely unencumbered by the evidence of medical men, and the verdicts were arrived at by a process of guesswork."[49] Despite the fact that Havard's cursory examination of the early modern coroner is almost entirely reliant on printed sources (statutes, legal texts, guides to officeholding, etc.), largely from a later date, this refrain has been picked up by most scholars when referencing the early modern coroner. For example, T. R. Forbes has similarly argued that between the Middle Ages and the nineteenth century there were few advances in forensic medicine, and that the coroner, an amateur official with no legal or medical qualifications, had infrequent recourse to autopsies or witnesses with medical expertise.[50] Likewise, Malcolm Gaskill contends that the fact that the coroner's office did not have recourse to state funds to pay for professional medical autopsies "retarded its development as an instrument of medico-legal investigation until the nineteenth century."[51]

These contentions rest almost entirely on two facts. First, until 1836 coroners were neither required to seek medical expertise when conducting their inquests, nor were they given the authority or funds to ensure that medical experts would attend. Second, the relative lack of expert medical testimony in the extant coroners' inquests leads many scholars to the conclusion that such testimony was infrequently sought and irregularly given. The lack of statutory mandate, however, does not negate the fact that some sort of medical expertise was frequently sought. Instead, the records of the early modern period show a steady growth in the recourse to medical experts that belies the contention that inquest decisions were the result of unscientific guesswork. Furthermore, as will be demonstrated below, the importance of forensic medicine for criminal investigation has not been conclusively proved.

The final common characterization of the early modern coroner in the existing literature is that the coroner was generally negligent, corrupt, or both. T. R. Forbes, for example, states that as the coroner was only able to receive payment in case of homicide, and even then only if the suspect had been seized and convicted, coroners were rarely interested in suicides, accidental deaths, and murders by unknown persons. As he writes, "This system naturally encouraged corruption and neglect: many homicides were not investigated at all, or at best perfunctorily."[52] This characterization fails on at least two accounts. First, even a cursory look at the voluminous records produced by coroners refutes the suggestion that all deaths except homicides with known perpetrators were neglected. The fact is that inquests into accidental deaths alone outnumber those relating to homicides by a factor of more than three to one. Second, such assessments show little understanding of the importance of local officeholding in early modern English society. Most local officeholders in early modern England were unpaid amateurs. Prestige, honor, and the communal obligation of restoring and maintaining the peace of the community could often be as important to these local officeholders as financial remuneration.[53] Thus, it is shortsighted to suggest that lack of pay for local officers precluded dedication to the duties and responsibilities of local office.

Similarly, it has been argued that coroners only held inquests in cases that involved an obviously violent death. Forbes argues that "an inquest into a sudden death was usually considered unnecessary unless death was clearly due to violence."[54] According to Havard, this obstruction both facilitated and invited "the concealment of murder."[55] Once again, the fact that the majority of inquests involved accidental death and death as a result of sudden illness demonstrates that early modern coroners were concerned not simply with violent homicide, but with any sudden, unexpected, or suspicious death. Certainly the manner in which they carried out their duties did not in and of itself invite or facilitate concealment of murder.

Gaskill's account of the coroner in the early modern period also indulges in the familiar tropes of corruption, inefficiency, and neglect. He contends that coroners "remained unsalaried amateurs living in the communities they served, and consequently worked with variable efficiency."[56]

Furthermore, according to Gaskill, coroners frequently avoided holding inquests "far from the beaten track," usually called them only when signs of death were manifestly violent, and accepted bribes both to falsify verdicts and to hold inquests in the first place. Even an official drive "to press coroners into more uniform scales of activity" in the 1570s, he argues, failed to achieve noticeable or sustained results.[57] It must be granted that coroners probably worked with variable efficiency, as did all local officeholders in the period, and that negligence and corruption undoubtedly occurred, but the levels of efficiency, corruption, and neglect have not been satisfactorily examined or demonstrated with anything approaching academic rigor.

Perhaps because of such negative conceptions of the early modern coroner, scholars have failed to see the potential role of the coroner in the process of state formation and the growth of governance. The present study will address this neglect, not only by challenging the received wisdom regarding forensic medicine, corruption, and negligence, but also by highlighting the importance of the office of the coroner for the creation and regulation of the English state's monopoly of legitimate violence.

If the original creation of the office of the coroner in the Middle Ages was an attempt to restrict interpersonal violence and nonjudicial forms of dispute resolution, the medieval English state's claim to a monopoly of violence remained just that, a claim. What any system that seeks to restrict interpersonal violence requires, and what the English state lacked in the medieval period, was effective oversight of the officer responsible for the detection and punishment of those who committed acts of illegitimate physical violence. The legal official and the system necessary to enforce such a claim were in place from the twelfth century; yet it was not until the early modern period that innovations and circumstances combined to create an effective state monopoly of violence in England. It was the coroner who was responsible for detecting illegitimate lethal violence and for developing the system that monitored the monopoly of violence.

The present study will demonstrate that the English state had established a successful monopoly of lethal violence by the end of the sixteenth century, if not earlier. This is not to say that interpersonal violence and nonjudicial forms of dispute resolution ceased to exist in the early modern period. Nor is it possible to claim that all lethal violence was detected and punished after the creation of effective oversight after the 1530s. However, it will be shown that from the mid-sixteenth century the officers and apparatus of oversight necessary to restrict to the government the right to define legitimate and illegitimate violence were in place.

By the seventeenth century the detection, conviction, and punishment of illegitimate lethal violence were firmly and irrevocably tied to the central government. Private vengeance and nonjudicial settlement in cases of lethal violence, quite common in some areas well into the early modern period, were slowly but surely replaced by a newly reinvigorated coroner system. Disputes over death that for centuries had been resolved outside of the institutions of government were abandoned, willingly or not, in favor of adjudication by coroner, assize, and the central courts. The adoption of these institutions as the favored means of dispute resolution in cases of lethal violence bound the English populace to the crown's definitions of legitimate and illegitimate violence. Key to this legitimation of the crown's monopoly of violence was the existence of competing economic interests in the outcome of coroners' inquests, whether as a result of the system of forfeiture in the sixteenth and seventeenth centuries, or as a result of the monetization of the office of the coroner in the mid-eighteenth century.

Narratives of state formation often focus on processes of centralization and bureaucratization and of the growth of the institutions of government. Although I will touch on all of these facets of state formation to some degree, it is not the purpose of the present study to provide an account of institutional expansion, but rather to explain how lethal violence was regulated in early modern England — a prerequisite for the creation of a modern state. With this in mind it is important to remember that, as Michael Braddick and Steve Hindle have shown, state growth was not necessarily directed solely from the center, but was instead often the result of intersecting interests of center and periphery, a negotiation between the crown and the localities. Certainly this was the case to some degree in reference to definitions of legitimate and illegitimate violence in early modern England. These definitions were negotiated in coroners' inquests and the courts throughout the period and as such must have reflected the priorities and interests of both individuals and the state. However, from the sixteenth century, the venue for these negotiations over legitimate and illegitimate violence was restricted to the formal judicial institutions of the central authorities, the coroners' court, the assize, and the central courts in Westminster. While these were sites of negotiation, it must be remembered that the power of individuals to assert their definition of justice was severely circumscribed. We should not let an interest in subaltern agency obscure the repressive nature of the English judicial system. Negotiation certainly occurred, but on terms set by the state, in the venues created by the state, and by officers appointed and monitored by the state.

It must also be remembered that centralization, when it occurred, was not irrevocable. The pattern of the regulation of violent death, for instance, was not straightforward, consistent, or necessarily centralizing. Between the 1530s and the mid-seventeenth century, the oversight of the coroner system, and thus the oversight of the monopoly of violence, did indeed become more centralized as the courts of Westminster took on a larger role in the surveillance of violent death. However, from the mid-seventeenth century, the locus of oversight shifted away from the central institutions of the state to the localities. From the 1750s, oversight again became more intensive, but the crucial venue for oversight remained the county courts. Thus, the story of England's monopolization of lethal violence is not so much a narrative of centralization as an account of how the locus and apparatus of detection and regulation shifted to address the needs and conditions of the time. Although the locus of oversight may have changed over the years between 1500 and 1800, these years did witness the successful monopolization of lethal violence by the English government. Whether England became a modern state in 1530 or 1688 or later, it is clear that over the course of the early modern period the English state at last acquired the most basic prerequisite of any modern state, the exclusive right to define legitimate and illegitimate violence and the power to enforce a monopoly of violence. It had the coroner and the various individuals and institutions dedicated to its oversight to thank for its ultimate success.

ONE

Restricting Private Warfare

"YOUR BROTHER AND HIS FELLOWSHIP stand in great jeopardy at Caister . . . Dawbeney and Berny are dead and others greatly hurt, and gunpowder and arrows are lacking, and the place sore broken with the guns of the other party, so that but they have hasty help they are like to lose both their lives and the place."[1] On September 12, 1469, Margaret Paston sent this urgent letter to her eldest son John, imploring him to leave the pleasures of London behind and make haste to Norfolk to aid his younger brother in the defense of the Paston family's property. According to Margaret, time was running out, the enemy was becoming emboldened, and the attacking duke of Norfolk "hath been more fervently set thereupon, and more cruel" since the arrival of reinforcements. In fact, the duke had "sent for all his tenants from every place" and planned "to make a great assault, for they have sent for guns from Lynn and other places by the seaside, so that with the great multitude of guns, with other shot and ordinance, there shall be no man that dare appear in the place."[2]

The attackers were not part of an invading foreign army, but rather the Pastons' neighbors—John Paston III had even served in the household of one of the Pastons' primary antagonists, John Mowbray, duke of Norfolk. The trouble had begun, as trouble often does, with a dispute over a will. John Paston I, Margaret's husband and the younger John's father, was a prominent lawyer, whose business in London brought him into the orbit of the wealthy Norfolk knight Sir John Fastolf. The two men became friends, and, whether by fair means or foul, when Fastolf died in 1459, Paston claimed to be the chief beneficiary of the late knight's will. Given the substantial amount of property involved, it is unsurprising that Fastolf's generous bequests to Paston did not go unchallenged. Sir William Yelverton, Thomas Howes, and other Fastolf heirs declared the will false and began a campaign, both legal and military, against the Paston family for the control of the disputed lands. Central to this contest was Caister Castle in Norfolk. To make good on their claim, the Pastons—first Margaret and then John III—occupied the castle and soon found themselves under siege by the duke of Norfolk, who had acquired a claim to Caister from William Yelverton. While the siege ended in victory for Norfolk in 1469, the contest over the property of John Fastolf would rage for another decade before it was finally settled in the Pastons' favor.[3]

This image of warring private citizens with their personal armies and seemingly unbridled violence is one that often encapsulates our modern perceptions about the pre-modern world, a world in which disputes between neighbors were settled with the sword and where might made right. While this image is certainly a distortion of the medieval reality, there was indeed a time when the regional autonomy of the English aristocracy was such that the king's peace was often broken by the unchecked power of overmighty subjects. Feuds were fought between local magnates and vengeance, influence, and authority claimed by armies of retainers.

If the English crown hoped to create and enforce a state monopoly of violence, however, the nobility, and the private armies that enforced their power, would have to be effectively controlled. From the middle of the fifteenth century, successive monarchs began the gradual process of restricting the private warfare of their subjects. This regulation of nonstate violence was primarily concerned with cowing the nobility, eliminating their personal armies, and replacing their regional authority with individuals and institutions loyal to the crown. This project was remarkably successful, and by the end of the sixteenth century the power of individual subjects to wage war on the state or each other was permanently contained. Although popular violence against the state or its officers continued to occur throughout the period, such violence never seriously challenged the state's monopoly of legitimate violence. What follows is the story of how the private warfare of the English elite and that of their more humble brethren was regulated, restricted, and eventually controlled by the crown in the years between the Wars of the Roses and the early seventeenth century.

Controlling Elite Violence

As combat raged at Bosworth Field on August 22, 1485, Thomas, Lord Stanley and his brother Sir William Stanley sat with their retainers on a hill overlooking the battlefield waiting to see which way the wind would blow. Below, Henry Tudor and King Richard III were engaged in the last violent struggle of the Wars of the Roses, a series of conflicts fought since 1455 between the Lancaster and York branches of the royal family over the succession to the English throne. In the end, the Stanleys threw their armed might behind Henry Tudor, turning the tide of the battle and leaving the dead King Richard to the mercy of Shakespearean slanders and Leicester car-parks. Many harsh lessons were learned on that day of Tudor triumph, but foremost in the victorious Henry Tudor's mind must have been the dangerous power of the nobility. The Stanley affinity, after all, had sealed the fate of two kings on that summer day in 1485. The violence and disorder that characterized these decades of internecine warfare engendered an understandable desire among those in power to restrict the power of the greater magnates to raise private armies and engage in warfare and rebellion. As a consequence of these fears of elite power, the English kings of the late fifteenth and early sixteenth centuries pursued a number of interconnected strategies to ensure that the crown was never again challenged by the ambitions of overmighty subjects.[4]

The process of restricting the ability of subjects to wage war against the crown or each other—that is to say, to intrude on the state's monopoly of legitimate violence—was long and varied, but nevertheless a few key themes emerge that demonstrate how the grip of the state tightened in the early modern period. From the late fourteenth century successive monarchs passed legislation that sought to restrict the practice of noble retaining, which had so greatly contributed to the instability of the crown during the Wars of the Roses. In an attempt to rein in the restive and overly independent peripheral areas of England, border councils were established or reestablished with the aim of bringing royal control to areas that had previously exercised too much autonomy. The creation of a more or less fixed court and the end of the peripatetic nature of medieval monarchy also helped to coalesce power in the royal center, as well as to drain the regional power blocks of regional magnates. Additionally, the rise in importance of the central law courts in Westminster and the growing power of the justice of the peace in the counties served to blunt the regional influence of the nobility. Finally, the creation of a royal army in place of an army of feudal levies severed the raison d'être of magnate power.

None of these strategies were immediately or entirely successful, and regional power bases continued to exist to a limited degree until almost the end of the sixteenth century. However, by the mid-sixteenth century, the ability of the nobility and gentry to wage private warfare, against neighbor or state, was so diminished as to pose little practical threat to the security of the crown. In future, the crown's monopoly on the ability to wage war would not be challenged by great feudal magnates with their levies of armed retainers, whose time was at an end, but by mass rebellions led by bodies claiming a different origin of sovereignty. By the seventeenth century, the struggle for power was no longer a contest between state and subject, but rather between differing conceptions of the state. The state's power to monopolize warfare had been secured, and the only thing left to contest was who held the reins of that power.

Regulating Retaining

The power of the medieval kings of England was theoretically boundless but practically circumscribed by the complications of geography and limited resources. The solution to these problems was to invest a considerable degree of power and autonomy in the hands of regional noble magnates who would exercise authority on behalf of, and in the name of, the king. As a result, regional affinities with substantial power arose, especially in the peripheral areas in the North and on the Welsh Marches.[5] With their armed retainers, these nobles possessed an unquestioned ability to engage in warfare either against their local rivals or, at times, against the crown itself. The Wars of the Roses demonstrated with cruel effect the dangers to the crown of the private armies of overmighty subjects, and by the mid-fifteenth century statutes were introduced in an attempt to curb nonroyal power and violence.

The first major attempt to pass legislation restricting the practice of retaining among the nobility occurred in 1390, during the reign of Richard II, but enforcement had been piecemeal and largely ineffective. This was followed by further legislation in 1429 under Henry VI and in 1468 under Edward IV. The 1468 statute was an attempt by the monarch to solidify promises made in Parliament on May 17 committing the king to maintain law and order in light of recent disturbances in Derbyshire. Initial attempts were made to enforce the new statute—the dukes of Suffolk and Norfolk were both charged with illegal retaining shortly after the 1468 act's passage—but the effort was not entirely successful.[6] Edward's statute made retaining illegal except in particular instances for "lawful service," such as in the case of estate and legal advisors or domestic servants. These loopholes, practical though they may seem given the intricacies of running a large household estate, ensured that the legislation had little effect given the difficulty of differentiating between domestic staff and armed retainers.[7]

In any case, Edward IV's reign was perhaps too fraught and the need to appease his own noble supporters too great to force through his legislative attempts to rein in nonroyal power. In 1485, however, Henry Tudor came to the throne as Henry VII, and with his marriage to Elizabeth of York, daughter of Edward IV and niece of Richard III, the bloody rivalry between Lancaster and York was finally put to a fitful rest. Henry too had learned the lessons of the Wars of the Roses, and one aspect of his consolidation of power in the years after 1485 was to pursue legislation designed to regulate retaining. In 1504, a statute was passed that outlawed the practice of retaining.[8] Like Edward IV before him, Henry could not afford to alienate the magnates, especially in the early part of his reign, when the power of the crown had not yet been reasserted. As such, it seems likely that while the 1504 statute outlawed retaining altogether, the real purpose of the legislation was to regulate the practice and allow Henry the ability to target the power base of those who might seek to oppose him, an understandable desire in the wake of his own shaky claim to the throne and the rebellions of the pretenders Lambert Simnel and Perkin Warbeck in 1487 and 1490, respectively.[9]

Historians have long debated Henry's commitment to the restriction of retaining—it is certainly true that the practice continued—but it is also clear that the 1504 statute was not simply an empty letter. The paucity of the records of the period makes calculating the number of individuals charged and convicted for illegal retaining all but impossible. Still, there were several cases in which prominent nobles were targeted for enforcement. For example, in 1507, George Neville, Lord Bergavenny was fined £5 for every retainer and forbidden to travel to Kent, Surrey, Sussex, or Hampshire without approval from the crown. Given the large number of retainers maintained by Bergavenny, the fine amounted to an astronomical £100,000. After Henry's death in 1509, the newly crowned Henry VIII canceled the fine, but the point had been made.[10] This was not the only instance in which Henry VII decided to assert his power by punishing an individual for illegal retaining. John de Vere, the thirteenth earl of Oxford, Henry's ally and advisor, was likewise said to have been fined under the statute of 1504. Oxford had treated the monarch to lavish entertainments at his estate in Essex. When Henry noted the number of servants and staff maintained by the earl, Oxford was duly fined. This display of royal power was surely intended to demonstrate that even friends of the king were to be punished when they attempted to rise too high.[11]

The process of restricting retaining under Henry VII and his predecessors was an ad hoc, targeted campaign of exemplary punishment rather than a concerted effort to eliminate the practice altogether. By substituting individual, high-profile instances of enforcement and fines for a more general policy of enforcement, the antiretaining campaign of the late medieval period was consistent with the operation of the criminal justice system more generally. In the case of the broader judicial system, exemplary punishment was necessary because the officers and resources available to the state were not sufficient to prosecute every criminal or criminal act. As a result, this lack of resources created the need for a system that balanced terror and mercy in such a way as to discourage crime with a modicum of expenditure.[12] While it certainly would have been easier to enforce the laws against retaining, given that the targets of the law were few in number, well known, and easily located, there were practical reasons for pursuing a similar strategy of targeted enforcement. First and foremost, although the Wars of the Roses dramatically highlighted the very real danger posed by noble retinues and overmighty subjects, the fact remained that the crown was still largely dependent on feudal levies for supplying soldiers for the royal army. A militarily powerful nobility was also necessary for the control of the restive peripheral areas of the country, namely, the Welsh and Scottish borders. Thus, until the crown could bring the peripheries under the direct control of the monarch and create a new system for recruiting soldiers for the royal army, the restriction of retaining was, by necessity, piecemeal. By targeting the worst offenders or those nobles whose loyalty to the crown was in question, late medieval kings sought to curtail the military power of their subjects to the extent possible without undermining their own ability to make war and rule their kingdom. At the same time, however, innovations in army recruitment and in governance were beginning to create the conditions in which the crown no longer needed a militarily powerful nobility, a turn of events that made the complete eradication of retaining feasible.

The legislation of Henry VII's reign did not completely eliminate retaining. And yet, the number of retainers employed by the nobility did decline over the course of his monarchy. With select, public instances of enforcement, Henry began the process of restricting retaining, and thus the ability of private individuals to engage in nonsanctioned warfare slowly declined in the first half of the sixteenth century. By the dawn of the seventeenth century, the private militaries of the elite had practically disappeared. Although the process was never straightforward, it is clear that noble retinues declined from bodies numbering hundreds and even thousands of armed and liveried men in the late fifteenth century to affinities of perhaps twenty or thirty unarmed servants, stewards, and bailiffs by the seventeenth century.

Perhaps of greatest import, the ability of the nobility to recruit and maintain the loyalty and services of their gentry neighbors declined markedly over the period. In the late Middle Ages it was normal for nobles to have in their retinues gentlemen of substantial standing and estate, who wore the livery of the noble in question and whose first loyalty was to the earl or duke rather than to the crown. Even in the late fifteenth and early sixteenth centuries, it was common for great nobles like the earl of Northumberland to have "knyghtes and squires . . . as menial household men."[13] Though examples of gentry in noble livery can be found well into the late sixteenth century, for all intents and purposes, the practice died out over the course of Elizabeth I's reign. The reasons for this are complex, but the decline in gentry service seems to have been a result of a combination of changes in education and officeholding. As Lawrence Stone notes, in the fifteenth and early sixteenth centuries, it was normal practice for the gentry to send their sons to live in the households of the greater nobility as a means of education and career advancement. However, from the mid-sixteenth century, increasing numbers of gentry children were sent to formal educational institutions such as Eton and Oxford or educated at home by private tutors.[14] By the late sixteenth century it was unusual for gentry sons to be educated in the households of the nobility, a shift that helped to rob the aristocracy of an important element of their traditional military power base and an important link in the medieval feudal hierarchy. At the same time that the gentry were being drawn into new educational venues, the growth of government apparati led to an explosion in the number of offices available to the gentry. One of the key attractions of noble service was access to office and to political and administrative power. With the growth in crown offices, however, a rival venue or market for the services of the gentry was created, allowing the gentry to gain money, power, and prestige without putting themselves under the thumb of their aristocratic neighbors. As a result, the power of the crown and the gentry increased at the expense of the power of the nobility as the importance of noble households as sites of education and prestige declined.

The gentry were not the only ones to slowly abandon the nobility. In the fifteenth century it was common for the nobility to employ large numbers of personal servants or bodyguards. The fifteenth-century duke of Clarence employed 299 men, for example, but by the early decades of the seventeenth century, even the largest households were more likely to employ around 30 personal servants.[15] As one early seventeenth-century commentator put it, "a fewe discreet civill men will doe you more honor than scores of caterpillers of theise foggy tymes."[16]

Beside the gentry, the traditional backbone of noble military power in feudal society had long been the tenantry. In addition to rent, before the mid-sixteenth century it was expected that a tenant was obliged to provide his landlord with military service, especially in times of war. However, the aristocracy's ability to rally and muster their tenants for armed service declined across the sixteenth century. This seems to have been primarily a result of a restructuring of royal military recruitment practices. This restructuring will be discussed more fully below, but it suffices to say that whereas Henry VIII had depended on feudal levies for his continental wars and the suppression of rebellions, by the dawn of James I's reign in 1603, the crown no longer required tenant levies to supply the royal army. As a result, service in war ceased to be seen as a primary duty of the tenantry, and thus the ability of the nobility to maintain or raise a private army diminished to such a degree that in 1600 the earl of Lincoln was reduced to attempts to bribe his tenants with a fee of one shilling a day for military service in his feud with Sir Edward Dymock.[17]

The decline in gentry and tenant service over the course of the late fifteenth and sixteenth centuries severely crippled the ability of the aristocracy to engage in private warfare. In and of itself, however, this shift was not sufficient to completely eradicate the private warfare of nonstate actors. In order to create a state monopoly of violence, other changes and reforms were necessary. A combination of the decline of noble retaining, greater state control of the peripheries, a reordering of the judicial system, and a general centralization of government were all necessary to restrict the private warfare of the English.

Controlling the Periphery

The power base that had helped Henry VII seize the throne in 1485 had been based in the South of England. The power of the Yorkist faction, conversely, had centered on the North. It followed logically that once on the throne Henry would seek to assert royal authority over the restive, peripheral areas—the Scottish borderlands in the North and the Welsh Marches in the West in particular. These regions had long been violent areas where the king's writ was weak and the power of regional magnates semi-sovereign. Noble families such as the Percys and the Dacres in the North and the marcher lords in the West, with their large estates and armed retainers, were both necessary for controlling the periphery and a potentially dangerous thorn in the side of monarchical authority, a fact illustrated repeatedly in the years before 1485. It was even commonly said with only a modicum of exaggeration that much of the North "knew no prince but a Percy" for much of the late medieval period. Traditionally, the loyalty of the border magnates had been obtained through the granting of financially and politically rewarding offices such as lieutenancies and wardenships. In the aftermath of the Wars of the Roses, Henry VII sought to change this longstanding policy in order to secure the peripheries.[18]

Henry's solution to the problem of the wild borderlands, in addition to his attempts to regulate the practice of retaining discussed above, was to invest ultimate power in such areas in regional councils whose members were appointed by the king and whose authority was derived directly from the crown. The Council of the North was established in 1472—with the future Richard III as its first Lord President—and reestablished in 1489 and 1536, in an attempt to extend royal administration and royal justice into the semi-independent northern counties. The Council of Wales and the Marches was also established in 1472 and, though initially designed to act as the council of the prince of Wales, quickly came to have a function similar to that of the Council of the North.[19] Henry VII's innovation was to manipulate the staffing of the councils and other border offices to undermine the power of the border magnates themselves. Power was diffused by giving high office to local gentry instead of the nobility. This practice both separated the gentry from their noble patrons and bound these men to the crown through royal patronage. When border offices were given to powerful nobles, these men were now selected from among the midlands or southern nobility rather than from among the marcher lords. In addition, the salaries granted to those who held office in the borderlands were reduced so as to restrict the ability of the border nobility to create large affinities that could be used against the crown.[20]

Like the crown's efforts to restrict retaining, the attempts to wrest control of the lawless peripheral areas from the hands of powerful nobles was only partially successful. In the North, the existence of an actual military frontier meant that some leeway had to be given to the marcher lords if England's border was to be secured. Considerable power remained concentrated in the hands of the nobility until the union of the Scottish and English crowns with the accession of James VI and I in 1603. With the union of the crowns, the raison d'être of the northern nobility ceased to exist and the power of these families gradually declined.[21]

Crown control of the Welsh Marches was more successful. In 1536, the Welsh Act of Union was passed in an attempt to bring the principality more fully into the orbit of English power. Prior to the passage of the Act of Union, Wales possessed its own laws and law courts that rendered justice in the Celtic language of the area. As this system proved difficult to control, the Act of Union replaced these native laws and courts with English law and English courts operating in English rather than Welsh. Without the existence of an actual political frontier, the reduction of the power of the marcher lords could be sought without threatening the defenses of the region. Wales was henceforth to be divided into new counties along the English model, another attempt to bring Wales into line with English practices of governance.[22]

The creation of the Council of the North and the Council of Wales and the Marches and the gradual reduction of the border magnates went a long way toward reducing the autonomous power of the nobility and coopting them into the machinery of government under the careful eye of the crown and its ministers. However, the peripheral areas of England were not entirely cowed and continued to be a source of anxiety and attention for the crown throughout the early modern period.

The Fixed Court and the Decline of Regional Power

The creation of regional councils was not the only method by which the nobility were tied more closely to the crown through service. The gradual creation of a fixed court in the sixteenth century also helped ensure that power was concentrated in one location, thus severing, at least in part, the local power bases of the nobility. The medieval English monarchy was famously ambulatory, moving slowly but almost continuously around the realm. The peripatetic nature of the court had its own logic. Given the limited power of the individual monarch and the problems of communication, a mobile court was thought necessary to control nobles and populace alike. Face-to-face contact with their subjects allowed English monarchs to dispense justice and patronage and to provide their far-flung subjects with a lasting sense of the power and majesty of the crown.[23]

The success of this policy of authority through physical presence was, however, undermined by the fact that royal visits to any given area were necessarily irregular and limited. From the reign of Henry VIII, the royal rambles began to subside and the court took on a more fixed character. With the court in one place, anyone who sought to benefit from the patronage of the crown could no longer hope to remain on their estates, but rather was forced to flock to Westminster in hopes of preferment. Separated by necessity from their power bases for long stretches of time, a large proportion of the nobility became increasingly tied to and dependent on the crown. At the same time, the feudal power of the absentee magnates began to erode, replaced by the power of the crown and its representatives.

Legal Change and the Dwindling of Noble Authority

The invention of a fixed royal court created a new, permanent locus of power in Westminster, which tempered the regional autonomy of the nobility. This centralization of political power was complemented by similar trends in the structure of the judicial system, which likewise blunted the local authority previously enjoyed by the aristocracy. This legal change had two primary features: the rise in importance of the central courts of law, especially the courts of equity; and the growing power of the justice of the peace. Combined, these shifts in the locus of legal authority helped to increase the power of the crown while limiting the power of the nobility by diffusing power among the officeholding gentry.

In the early fifteenth century, local magnates still held considerable judicial power in their vicinities. Through the instrument of manor courts, the nobility sought to exercise their lordship over their tenants, especially in matters relating to land and title.[24] Those subject to this system, however, often chafed under its yoke, especially given that such justice was often seen as partial and expensive. Throughout the period, as the population of England expanded and demands for land grew, manor courts were increasingly used as a means to generate revenue for the nobility, and legal fees, fines, and amercements all grew to the detriment of local litigants.[25] Faced with biased and expensive local legal venues, such litigants began to cast their eyes toward Westminster as a potential site for their legal business.

The central courts, such as Star Chamber, Chancery, and Common Pleas, had long existed, but before the late fifteenth century their popularity with litigants was questionable. In general, the courts of equity had operated with some effectiveness in the years prior to the reign of Henry VI, whose "incompetence and favoritism had crippled the judicial system" and destroyed confidence in the law.[26] Under the leadership of Edward IV and Richard III, the reputation and effectiveness of the courts of equity began to recover, and in the reigns of Henry VII and Henry VIII the popularity and power of the central courts skyrocketed. To understand the reasons for this growing popularity and its effect on noble power, it is useful to examine two of the most important central courts, Chancery and Star Chamber, in some detail.

The Court of Chancery was originally designed to authenticate royal decrees and issue orders granting land, appointing officeholders, and relating to treaties with foreign states.[27] The rise in importance of Chancery in the late fifteenth and early sixteenth centuries was the result of a number of factors. First, the court was blessed with a series of exceedingly competent and energetic administrators, including John Morton, Thomas Wolsey, and Thomas Wriothesely, who initiated a series of reforms that reinvigorated the court's procedures and organizational structure.[28] Second, Chancery began to attract litigants for the very reasons that litigants were seeking alternatives to the local and manor courts, namely, its "flexibility, speed and power."[29] Proceedings in Chancery began with a bill in English that laid out the grievances of the litigant, rather than with the exacting Latin formula required of the common law courts. Similarly, whereas other courts were restrained to reaching verdicts that accorded with the formal dictates of the common law, Chancery, as a court of equity, simply sought to reach a decision on the basis of equitable fairness and commonsense. This flexibility in decision-making was enforced by the full power of the crown, and as such Chancery's summons were more likely to be answered and its verdicts more likely to be obeyed and enforced than those of other courts. As a result, the volume of business that flowed into Chancery more than doubled between Henry VII's reign and the end of Henry VIII's.[30]

To be sure, much of the new business captured by the Court of Chancery in the late fifteenth and early sixteenth centuries was poached from common law courts such as the Court of Common Pleas or from borough and ecclesiastical courts rather than from the manor courts alone. However, it is clear that the trend of the period was toward a centralization of justice, whether to Chancery or Common Pleas, and a removal of judicial authority from local courts of all types that might more easily come under the sway of local elites. Other royal courts were vital to this process of centralization as well.

The Court of Star Chamber followed a trajectory similar to that of Chancery. Since the fourteenth century, the king's council had claimed a legal role that tended to focus on matters which required the personal judicial authority of the monarch. As such, Star Chamber was particularly concerned with instances in which the aristocracy used their power to subvert the law or government, or to wage private warfare against one another.[31] The reasons for Star Chamber's rise in power and influence mirrored that of Chancery. Given that the effective functioning of the court relied to some measure on the power of the crown, the existence of a series of active monarchs, especially Henry VII and Henry VIII, helped to cement its authority. As with Chancery, Star Chamber's flexible use of English bills as well as its subpoena powers and royally backed verdicts also ensured its popularity with litigants from at least the early sixteenth century.[32]

The rise in power and popularity of the central courts in the late fifteenth and early sixteenth centuries had a significant impact, not least on the power of the nobility. First and foremost, at least in terms of the control of elite violence, the increasing use of conciliar justice chipped away at the ability of the nobility to turn to violence as a means of projecting power and resolving disputes. For instance, upon hearing that Sir John Fortescue and Sir William Say planned to settle a disagreement by recourse to arms, Henry VII personally sent letters instructing the parties to cease their use of "unliefull assembles and conventicles of our people" to confront one another and ordering the would-be combatants to avoid a "rupture of our said peas, at your uttermost perell." With this threat made, Henry then summoned the men to Westminster, where the matter would be adjudicated by royal council.[33] Not even the greater nobles could escape the attention of the central courts, as when Lord Dacre of the North, one of England's most powerful and independent magnates, was summoned to appear before the royal council in Westminster in 1488 to answer charges of riot.[34] The implication was clear: violence was the monopoly of the crown, and its use in the pursuit of disputes between private citizens would not be tolerated by the monarch. In its place, royal justice rather than private armies was to settle such contests.

While it did not play a direct role in controlling elite violence, the rise of the Courts of Chancery and Common Pleas did figure significantly in the gradual diminution of noble power. By operating as a more attractive and more powerful venue for litigation, Chancery and Common Pleas usurped much of the business of the local and manor courts that were either controlled or influenced by the local magnates. As a result, the judicial power and income of the nobility were diminished and those of the crown buoyed. Overall, by substituting arbitration by local nobles with royal arbitration in centrally located courts, the judicial power of the elites was tempered. This centralization of the judicial process undermined the traditional power of the nobility while at the same time bolstering the authority of the crown, helping to rein in the excesses of overmighty subjects. The process of judicial centralization was gradual and incomplete, and it is important to remember that such reforms were often initiated with the support of local elites rather than simply against them. The control of violence and the limiting of the perversion of justice were aims that met with the approval of most inhabitants of late medieval and early modern England. Thus, the innovation of Henry VII and his successors was not the creation of a novel notion of justice, but the monopolization of the definition of legitimate and illegitimate violence and the removal of the power to define violence and justice from the nobility to the state.

The rise of the central courts was not the only legal innovation that began to strip away the judicial power of the magnates. Across the fifteenth and sixteenth centuries the power, number, and constitution of the justices of the peace all expanded, with important consequences for noble authority. First, the growing number of responsibilities placed in the hands of the justices meant that judicial functions previously held by the nobility were shifted onto centrally appointed officers beholden to the crown. Second, as the number of justices increased over the period, local judicial power was diffused among a wider array of individuals. As a result, the concentration of power in any one individual was effectively reduced. Finally, the growth in the number of justices required that a greater number of these offices were held by the gentry, which in turn lessened the potential for abuse by a narrow group of elite officeholders.[35]

At the same time that invigorated courts and officers began to strip away the traditional authority of the nobility, those same nobles began to become more vulnerable to prosecution. Men who had previously been protected from prosecution by their power and status now found themselves the targets of the judicial process. In 1498, the earl of Suffolk was charged with murder in the Court of King's Bench, and other great nobles, such as Lord Dacre in 1541 and Lord Stourton in 1557, were convicted and even executed for murder. Classed as common murderers, these magnates were fated to suffer the indignity of death by hanging rather than by beheading, the traditional privilege of the nobility. The indictment and conviction of such men for murder was entirely novel and again demonstrates the desire of the crown to rein in the power of the landed elites and subordinate them to the judicial system and the rule of law. Indeed, there was a growing sense that one of the chief responsibilities of the crown was to protect the common people from the powerful. One of Edward VI's privy councilors went so far as to inform the king that it was the duty of the monarch to

preserve the commons "from the Tyranny of the Nobility," for the king was
the "bridle in Power over his Nobility."[36]

A Royal Army and the End of Feudal Levies

As mentioned previously, medieval armies were largely composed of feudal
levies, armed retainers loyal to a particular aristocratic landowner. This
state of affairs made it difficult for the state to wage war while at the same
time restricting the warfare of its subjects. One method of monopolizing
this type of violence was to regulate and eventually outlaw the practice of
retaining. This policy, however, would have been difficult to maintain if the
crown had continued to rely on the retainers of powerful magnates to man
its armies. Consequently, over the course of the sixteenth and early seventeenth centuries, the crown attempted both to restrict the existence of private armies and to create a royal army that did not rely on feudal power.

The seeds of a royal or national army had long existed in the form of
the militia, a military body composed of amateur soldiers selected through
a parish quota system for each county. There were, however, limitations
placed on the militia that fatally undermined it as a source of royal military
power. The lack of a coherent administrative structure made the militia
difficult to muster, train, and equip effectively. As the militia was designed
as a force responsible for local defense, there were also restrictions placed
on its use outside of England. Thus, even Henry VII, who had learned the
lessons of the Wars of the Roses well and was concerned to rein in noble
power, was forced to rely on noble retinues to fill the ranks of his army in
times of international warfare. For instance, in 1489, when Henry sought
to engage in combat in Brittany, he leaned on the services of men like Lord
Brooke, who alone supplied a personal retinue of around 1,000 men.[37]
This continued to be the status quo in all foreign interventions well into the
reign of Henry VIII.

By the mid-sixteenth century, however, recruiting practices were
slowly beginning to change. An important precedent was set by Henry VIII
in 1544, when, for the first time, he used the militia as reinforcements during a continental campaign.[38] Sending the militia out of the country was

technically illegal, but the fact that no objections were made allowed subsequent monarchs to embrace the practice of using conscripts in similar ways, endowing the militia with a new and important military and political purpose. During the reign of Edward VI, the administration of the militia was improved by the creation of the office of the lord lieutenant, whose duty it was to oversee the mustering of the militia in his particular county. As it transpired, this was a crucial development in that it removed control of the militia from the hands of the nobility and placed it in the hands of a royally appointed official. Nobles continued to dominate the ranks of the lord lieutenancy, but the nobles selected were generally those from whom some loyalty to the monarch could be expected. Thus, while the militia was still led by the nobility, it was in their guise as royal officials rather than in their role as local magnates. This development helped to ensure that the militia became a more politically viable resource for the crown. The training of the militia also improved across the sixteenth century. Especially under Elizabeth, it became, if not professionalized, at least better trained and better armed than previously. The gradual professionalization of the militia was combined with the growing use of foreign mercenaries as a means of undermining the military power of the nobility. While mercenaries were a potentially expensive solution, and one that was much resented when used within England, they had the benefit of professional expertise as well as a lack of natural loyalties to any noble or faction.

The makeup of the English army remained a balance between noble retinues, militia conscripts, and foreign mercenaries for much of the sixteenth century. The recourse to the feudal levy was often deemed necessary in times of political crisis or rebellion, when troops were needed on the scene quickly. In such instances, it is unsurprising that the crown would turn to local magnates to supply men rapidly in a certain locality. Despite their continued use, however, the trend across the sixteenth century was one of declining reliance on noble retinues and increased commitment to the use of conscripts and mercenaries. One of the immediate causes for this was surely the lessons learned from the very rebellions that feudal levies were occasionally needed to quell. For, in many instances of Tudor rebellion, noble retinues were used both to support rebellion and to suppress it. The danger was well illustrated by the case of Sir John Thimbleby, who in 1536 at the outbreak of the Pilgrimage of Grace mustered his servants and tenants seemingly in support of the king and in opposition to the rebels. This show of support for the crown, however, was a mirage, and Thimbleby and his men instead joined the rebellion.[39] It was in these times of political crisis that a ready fighting force was most needed, but it was also in these instances that it became clear that an army which relied on noble retinues was as likely to be used to challenge the authority of the king as to defend it. As such, the rebellions of the Tudor period were important milestones and motivating factors in the process of military change and the decline of noble power.[40]

Controlling Ownership of Weapons

The rise of royal armies and the decline of noble retaining were not the only factors in the state's monopoly of warfare. Another way of mitigating the violence of private citizens was to restrict the ownership of weapons, especially firearms, to agents of the state. The logic behind such a move is intuitive. If a state wishes to prevent the possibility of popular rebellion, it is necessary to restrict access to the weaponry necessary to truly challenge its authority. Thus, even in modern America, where the right of gun ownership is widely held to be a founding principle of the nation, access to the military technology necessary to wage war effectively—missiles, bombs, helicopters, tanks—is still rigorously controlled. In the early modern period, regulating access to firearms and other military equipment was likewise a method of preventing the populace's ability to mount a real challenge to the authority of the state.

The first successful attempts to control access to military equipment began in the sixteenth century as part of the crown's campaign to limit the power and violence of the nobility. At the dawn of the sixteenth century, the crown had already begun to distinguish itself from the nobility in its ability to project power. By this date, the monarch was the only entity that possessed the siege artillery necessary to reduce castles and other fortified positions to submission. Over the course of the sixteenth century, this monopoly of artillery was supplemented by the decline in the building and maintenance of private castles, the very symbol of noble power in the medieval period. Since the twelfth century, individuals had been technically required to seek a "license to crenellate" before building private fortifications. The purpose of this licensing was to regulate the ability of the nobility to create and maintain local power bases, although, given the problems of enforcement, there is some doubt that this requirement had the desired effect. Nonetheless, by the end of the medieval period, castle building was certainly on the wane. The last new private castle in England was constructed at Thornbury in Gloucestershire by Edward Stafford, third duke of Buckingham, in 1510.[41] Thornbury Castle was never completed, for Buckingham was executed for treason in 1521, a charge of which he was likely guilty.[42] The potential threat posed by a man like Buckingham building for himself a regional stronghold from which to foment rebellion is perhaps the reason that the number of licenses to crenellate declined dramatically in the sixteenth century. The destructive power of gunpowder and artillery likely had a significant impact on the building of castles as well. Whatever the cause, private fortifications were rare by the end of the sixteenth century as more comfortable manor houses replaced castles as the seats of the aristocracy. Not only were new houses built with no consideration of their defensive ability, but older castles were renovated with new windows and other accouterments that placed fashion before military value.[43] As Lawrence Stone aptly put it, "moats and drawbridges, portcullises and arrow-slits became things of the past."[44]

The accumulation and stockpiling of weaponry by the aristocracy likewise faded over the course of the sixteenth and seventeenth centuries. Just as medieval monarchs of necessity relied on noble retinues to form a royal army, prior to the late sixteenth century, private stockpiles of arms were needed to supplement the crown's often insufficient supply of weaponry. Given this need, and the very real power that the possession of arms conferred, the nobility continued to accumulate large numbers of weapons until the end of the sixteenth century. As late as the 1570s, for example, the earl of Leicester had stockpiled a mass of armaments including 100 guns, 1,500 rounds of shot, large quantities of gunpowder, 450 small arms, and equipment for 200 horsemen and 500 foot soldiers.[45] With arms such as these, and a well-fortified estate at Kenilworth, Leicester was a potential threat to both the crown and his peers. It is little wonder then that steps were being taken to remedy the problem of private ownership of large stockpiles of weapons.[46]

Leicester may well have possessed the greatest private store of military equipment seen in England for half a century, but by the late sixteenth century stockpiles such as his were becoming more and more of a rarity. As with the decline of noble retaining, the decline in private military stores was, in part, the result of efforts to centralize control of the royal army. To reduce the reliance on private arms, the crown began to build its own massive stockpile. By the mid-sixteenth century, the royal armory could already claim 6,500 handguns and 20,000 pikes, with large subsequent purchases from continental gun makers in 1558 and 1561. Because military technology was rapidly changing, new, more advanced weaponry had to be constantly purchased or produced; for instance, in 1578 the 6,500 handguns had been replaced by 7,000 calivers, the most advanced firearm of its day. Such acquisitions helped to ensure that no private individual could hope to rival the firepower of the crown. Thus, when the Protestant Sir Thomas Wyatt rose in rebellion against the Catholic Queen Mary in 1554, the royal stockpile was distributed to loyal courtiers for use against the rebels.[47] To supplement the ever-growing royal armory, a system of county arms depots was also set up. Beginning in the mid-sixteenth century, regional arms depots were created to supply the county muster, a network of local militias answerable to crown appointed officials rather than feudal lords. By the end of Elizabeth's reign, the responsibility for financing and supplying these depots had been shifted onto county authorities.[48]

The crown did not limit itself to the acquisition of arms and the creation of regional depots. Active steps were also taken to restrict the ability of private individuals to stockpile weapons. As we have seen in the case of the third duke of Buckingham, the attempt to create a military stronghold was often viewed with deep suspicion and could even be used as evidence of treason. In a similar vein, the stockpiling of arms could also arose the suspicions of trepidatious monarchs. For instance, when Thomas Howard, fourth duke of Norfolk, was arrested in 1571 for his role in the Ridolfi Plot—a Catholic conspiracy to oust Elizabeth and place Mary Queen of Scots on the throne in her stead—an inventory of the duke's armaments was taken. It has been suggested that the great extent of Norfolk's stockpile so alarmed the crown that it made the decision to execute him necessary. Norfolk's fate must have proved a powerful example to other nobles who might otherwise seek to acquire private stores of weapons. Other attempts were made to restrict private caches of arms. Driven by fears of sectarian violence and rebellion, in 1625, for instance, the crown seized the arms of all Catholic peers.[49]

Though such measures were often piecemeal and reactionary, restrictions on arms and the increased difficulty and expense of producing weapons, and perhaps especially gunpowder, had a significant impact on the nobility's ability to use force against the crown or their neighbors. By the early decades of the seventeenth century, no private individual could hope to rival the arms of the crown. Inventories taken in the 1620s indicate that most noble stockpiles were small, poorly maintained, and obsolete. The 1625 inventory of the weaponry held by the marquis of Winchester, for example, demonstrates the declining holdings of the nobility. The marquis possessed only six guns, and of the 300 or so small arms in his holdings, most were bows, bills, and other weapons that were far from the cutting edge of contemporary military technology. The decline in private military power was notable enough, even to contemporaries, for Walter Raleigh to remark that once "the noblemen had in their armories to furnish some of them a thousand, some two thousand and some three thousand men, whereas now there are not many that can arm fifty."[50] The result of this reduction in noble military power was to further cement the crown's monopoly over the implements necessary to engage in warfare. The restriction of arms in the sixteenth and seventeenth centuries helped to ensure that the warfare of nonstate actors was a thing of the past.

The Northern Rebellion and the Twilight of Feudal Power

The true test of the state's restriction of private warfare in the sixteenth century came when the crown was faced with open rebellion, and the progress made by the monarchy in this regard is best illustrated by the conduct and outcome of these uprisings. The Tudor period witnessed a series of rebellions and popular revolts; the Pilgrimage of Grace in 1536, the 1549 Rebellions, and the Northern Rebellion of 1569 foremost among them. The causes of these revolts are varied, complex, and debated, but for our purposes it is most important to ask how the threat of popular and noble revolt was dealt with by the crown, and how the possibility of such rebellions was eventually quashed in the mid-sixteenth century.

Though it shared commonalities of cause, aims, and social makeup with a long line of medieval revolts, the Northern Rebellion would be both the last popular rebellion and the last revolt led by the nobility in English history. This end of a long medieval tradition of popular rebellion was the result of a number of important factors. Over the course of the early sixteenth century, the ability of the various social classes to work in unison to pressure the crown had been fatally compromised. From the Middle Ages through 1549, the middling order and the lower order often acted in concert in an attempt to use popular protest as a means of forcing the crown to hear grievances, negotiate settlements and remember its duties. The failure of this unified approach in the 1549 rebellions, however, combined with the rising economic and social status of the middling sort to sever the ties of common interest between yeomen and laboring classes. At the same time, the cooption of the middling sort into the machinery of the state as officeholders and local officials likewise undermined the unity of the commons and prevented further joint action against the crown. These new proto-class divisions helped to ensure that the medieval tradition of popular protest was a vestige of the past.[51]

Another factor in the decline of armed rebellion was the shift in relative military power between the nobility and the crown. As discussed above, the restriction of aristocratic retaining and the rise of a royal army fundamentally changed the power relationship between the monarch and the feudal magnates. This change in military might was also reflected in the course of Tudor rebellions. Responding to the Pilgrimage of Grace in 1536, Henry VIII was forced to rely on a combination of false promises of concessions to the rebels, foreign mercenaries, and feudal levies to suppress the uprising. Three decades later, during the Northern Rebellion, it was possible for Elizabeth to turn to a royal army rather than feudal retainers to quell the revolt. Not only was the crown free from its reliance on the nobility to supply soldiers to oppose the rebels, but those magnates who joined and led the rebellion had difficulty securing the allegiance of their tenants. As recent research has shown, although the 1569 revolt was led by the earls of Westmorland and Northumberland, the movement largely consisted of common people who had no ties of allegiance or fealty to the noble figureheads. Rather than a feudal rebellion made up of armed retainers, the Northern Rebellion was a popular protest driven by concerns over religious change. The failure of the earls to secure the participation of their tenants and of lesser elites, combined with the new power of the royal army, ensured the ultimate failure of the Northern Rebellion and helped to end the possibility of such revolts in the future.[52]

Finally, the brutality of the suppression of the Northern Rebellion made popular rebellions increasingly unfeasible. Prior to the late sixteenth century, the crown's response to popular uprisings was surprisingly lenient. The ringleaders were of course executed, but the repression was selective and spared the masses by replacing terror with mercy. Elizabeth's treatment of the rebels of 1569, however, was exceedingly brutal. Because the Northern Rebellion coincided with other threats to Elizabeth's crown — the Ridolfi Plot, the excommunication of the queen by the pope — it was felt that leniency was not an option. Even though the revolt had been almost entirely bloodless, Elizabeth ordered not only the execution of Northumberland (Westmorland had escaped to the continent), but also the summary execution of 700 ordinary participants under martial law. These reprisals permanently tempered the power of the northern nobility, as well as making clear to the commonality that rebellion would no longer be tolerated as a tactic. Thus, in the aftermath of 1569, the crown emerged stronger and more secure. The threat of popular revolt and of feudal rebellion had been so diminished as to cease to pose a real threat to the stability of the state in the future.[53]

To return to the events related at the beginning of this chapter, Margaret Paston's pleas for aid were for naught and, whether for lack of will or lack of resources, John Paston II was unable to prevent Caister Castle from falling to the duke of Norfolk. In a bitter letter to his older brother, John Paston III recounted how the castle had fallen, stating that "as for the surrender of Caister, John Chapman can tell you as well as myself that we were forced to it . . . we were sore lacking in victuals, gunpowder and men's hearts, and lack of certainty of rescue drove us to the treaty."[54]

On the face of things, it would seem that the duke of Norfolk had won a legal dispute over the distribution of a deceased man's property solely through virtue of superior numbers and arms. The world, however, was changing, and although the wealth and influence of a man such as the duke of Norfolk were not entirely diminished, might no longer made right. The violence employed by Norfolk had won the immediate contest over physical possession of Caister Castle, but there were other theaters of dispute in which the balance of power was not so heavily balanced in the duke's favor. With his fighting force exhausted, John Paston II turned his energies to the emerging venue for the mediation of disputes, the courts of law. The suit dragged on for over a decade before it was settled in Paston's favor, but in the end it was settled by a patent from the king rather than by merit of arms.[55]

That the law triumphed over force in this dispute over property is illustrative of the changing nature of private warfare and elite violence over the course of the early modern period. Whereas violence among the aristocracy and between the aristocracy and the crown had once been commonplace, from the middle of the sixteenth century private warfare of this type began to be restricted and controlled. The private armies of the nobility were regulated and eventually abolished, the militia and the mercenary replaced the feudal levy, and the force of arms made way for the force of law in the management of disputes. Beyond the exalted ranks of the aristocracy, the ability of private citizens to make war either against their neighbors or against the state was also restricted, and the ability to assemble or to bear arms was brought under government control.

Restricting the private warfare of nonstate actors was an important step on the road to the creation of a monopoly of violence and thus a modern state. Although the process was, of necessity, piecemeal and incomplete, by the end of the sixteenth century, the crown alone was the sole entity capable of making war within the boundaries of England. A true monopoly of violence, however, consists of more than the possession of the exclusive ability to make war and control the warfare of nonstate actors. To truly obtain such a monopoly, it is also necessary to restrict and restrain the interpersonal violence of the state's inhabitants and to possess an exclusive right to use judicial violence. For it is only when the state alone and unchallenged defines legitimate and illegitimate violence that the most fundamental basis of the modern state is achieved. It is to the process of this achievement that we now turn.

Coroners and Communities

THE STATE IS ALL TOO OFTEN conceived of in abstract and amorphous terms, devoid of humanity but invested with its own logic and cognition. But states themselves are not conscious beings. Instead they are collections of individuals—rulers, officers, and bureaucrats—whose very humanity and individuality are crucial to the effective operation of its institutions. To understand the operation of the bureaucratic state, it is thus necessary to understand the individuals and officers whose actions and decisions constitute governance. Therefore, if we are to properly understand how violence came to be monopolized by the English state in the early modern period, it is of vital importance that we first come to terms with the office through which the control of violence was maintained. Given the ad hoc nature of crown efforts to limit private warfare, no single type of officer was responsible for controlling such elite violence. The campaign to restrict interpersonal violence, however, had long been the singular focus of one judicial officer: the coroner. Without an adequate appreciation of the intricacies of the coronership, its elections, duties, and operations, it is thus impossible to fully grasp the mechanisms of state power as they related to the control of violence.

Duties and Responsibilities

In his charge to the grand jury of the Quarter Sessions of Leicester at Michaelmas in 1690, the earl of Stamford made clear the basic logic that necessitated the existence of the office of the coroner. As Stamford expounded, "The Law is so tender and careful for the loss of Man, that it requires an Inquisition be made after, that so the offence may be punished according to its nature."[1] Since the twelfth century, when the office of the coroner was first established, the primary duty of the coroner, in both the popular and official imagination, was to hold inquests on the bodies of those who had died violently or in suspicious circumstances in order to determine the cause of death. The responsibilities of the coroner, however, extended in many different directions beyond the more familiar realm of the inquest.

As with most officeholders in the pre-modern world, the duties and responsibilities of the coroner did not remain static, but rather shifted in emphasis in the centuries after the creation of the office in 1194. Traditionally, the medieval coroner has been depicted as a more general county officer than his early modern counterpart. Perhaps the most important study of the medieval coroner, R. F. Hunnisett's *The Medieval Coroner*, contends that the office of the coroner reached its peak in terms of power and influence in the criminal justice system in the second half of the thirteenth century and declined thereafter. As Hunnisett writes, "By 1250 the identity of the office of the coroner was firmly established. Usually filled by men of some eminence locally, for the next half-century it was second in importance to that of the sheriff alone in the hierarchy of county offices."[2] According to Hunnisett, during this thirteenth-century zenith the duties of the coroner were more varied and expansive than they had been since the creation of the office or were to be again. In addition to holding inquests on the bodies of the deceased, medieval coroners were responsible for holding inquests into "treasure trove" and "wreck of the sea," as well as proclaiming and recording sentences of outlawry, receiving abjurations of the realm, organizing local elections, and hearing complaints against other local officials.[3]

Medieval historians generally agree that from this high point, the office of the coroner declined in both power and status during the fourteenth and fifteenth centuries. After 1300, the ranks of the office were filled by "slightly less eminent men" than previously and the duties of the coroner became gradually more restricted.[4] The reasons for this apparent decline are varied, however, and there is some debate over its proximate cause. In his account of the rise of medico-legal practice, J. D. J. Havard argues that the medieval decline was the result, first and foremost, of the statute of 1259 restricting *lex murdrorum*—the tax or fine paid by local lords or

communities when a violent death occurred in their jurisdiction—to felo-
nious killing. This restriction of the *murdrorum* fine seriously decreased
the amount of revenue received by the coroner for holding inquests, which
in turn, according to Havard, led to a decline in the prestige of the office.[5]

Hunnisett, however, maintains that the restriction of the *murdrorum*
fine did not in reality result in a decline in the importance of inquests. Instead, he argues that the most important factors in the decline of the coroner in the later Middle Ages were "the cessation of the general eyre . . . and
the fact that it was not followed by the establishment of any regular check
upon the coroner."[6] The Eyre, the circuit court of a royally appointed justice, had the power to appoint coroners to record crown pleas, and as such
provided much of the medieval coroners' business as well as royal supervision of their activities. The result of the loss of this forum, in which the
coroner acted as a crucial link between local and central authorities, was
that a number of the duties of the medieval coroner were duplicated and
gradually usurped by two rising figures in the criminal justice system: the
escheator and the keeper (later justice) of the peace. The escheator began
to take responsibility for appraising and taking possession of *deodands,*
the lands and goods of felons, outlaws, and abjurors of the realm, and for
holding inquisitions into treasure trove and shipwreck, duties formerly
belonging exclusively to the coroner. The justices of the peace subsumed
the coroner's responsibility to receive sureties for keeping the peace and
holding inquisitions *de gestu et fama.*[7] Furthermore, the justices began to
receive indictments for homicide, although indictments made on the view
of a body remained in the coroner's exclusive purview.[8]

Thus, it seems that from being a general county officer of the criminal
justice system, the coroner became in the late medieval and early modern
period an officer primarily concerned with the conducting of inquests into
suspicious, sudden, or unusual deaths. However, although both historians
of the medieval coroner and early modern manuals suggest that from the
late Middle Ages the coroner's duties were restricted to the investigation
of suspicious death, there is good evidence that in practice the responsibilities of medieval and early modern coroners were more similar than at

first appears. This may seem to be a question of limited import given our focus on the restriction of violence, but historians have long pointed to the coroner's declining responsibilities and power as a means of dismissing its effectiveness as an agent of control in the early modern period. It is therefore crucial to firmly establish that the coroner remained a vital and central figure not only in the administration of criminal justice, but in the wider governance of the country as whole.

The first and most common duty of the coroner other than the investigation of untimely death was the declaration of outlawry. From the early Middle Ages, those declared outlaws were deemed to be both beyond the protection of the law (and thus liable to private justice or vengeance) and outside the bounds of society. Those who offered them aid could be charged with abetting.[9] In most cases, men—women were exempt because they "were not sworn to the law"—were outlawed for failing to appear in court when charged with a crime or served with a writ. To take one example among many, in Essex in 1578 John Reven, Hugh Howe, and Edward Bryant "were called according to the law and did not appear, and therefore by the judgement of William Vernon and John Latham, gentlemen, coroners, they are outlawed."[10] In such instances it was the coroner's responsibility to begin the process of outlawing the recalcitrant individual and pronounce the sentence that was then signed by the sheriff. Before an individual could be outlawed, a proclamation had to be made on five consecutive court days and once at the door of the parish church in the dwelling place of the potential outlaw. On the fifth court day if the individual did not appear "the Coroner shall give Judgment that he shall be out of the protection of our Lord the King and out of the aid of the Law," and the outlawry was then entered into the coroner's rolls.[11] In the early modern period the pronouncement of outlawry was perhaps the coroner's most ubiquitous function other than the investigation of death, one of the many responsibilities that the early modern coroner inherited from his medieval predecessor.

The coroner's original raison d'être was closely tied to collecting various forms of revenue due to the monarch, such as goods forfeited by felons in cases of homicide and suicide and the deodands that resulted from fatal accidents.[12] In addition to these more familiar types of revenue, medieval coroners and their early modern counterparts were responsible for holding inquests in cases of treasure trove and shipwreck. Treasure trove was defined as "when any gold or silver, in coin, plate or bullion, hath been of ancient times hidden, wheresoever it be found, where no person can prove any property, it doth belong to the King."[13] When such treasure was found, the finder, and any who had knowledge of the treasure, were required by law to inform the coroner of the county or liberty where the horde had been found. In the Middle Ages the punishment for concealment of treasure trove was death, but by the early modern period those charged with concealment could instead expect a fine or imprisonment.[14]

Once the coroner was summoned, an inquest would be initiated that sought to determine whether the gold or silver found constituted treasure trove or whether some individual had a legitimate claim to the property. Coroners' inquests relating to treasure trove were somewhat rare, and it seems they were not usually compiled in the same way as inquests relating to death. However, other sources give some sense of the prevalence of treasure trove throughout the early modern period. The coroners of the city of Chester held an inquest relating to treasure trove in 1568, for example.[15] Similarly, there were several instances in the seventeenth century when the crown sent special commissions to investigate cases of treasure trove found on the lands of the Duchy of Lancaster, commissions that likely included the special coroners appointed to hold inquest within duchy lands.[16]

Like treasure trove, some shipwrecks were also deemed property of the monarch. The duty for investigating such cases again fell to the coroner. Wreck of the sea "in legall understanding is applied to such goods as after a shipwreck at sea are by the sea cast upon the land, and therefore the jurisdiction thereof pertaineth not to the Lord Admirall, but to the Common Law."[17] The logic behind the law of shipwreck was similar to that which undergirded the law of treasure trove: namely, that any property which did not have an owner became the property of the monarch. As Edward Coke explained in 1642, in medieval times it was almost impossible to determine the proper owner of goods lost at sea, and consequently they fell to the crown. However, by the early modern period, with its massive expansion of seagoing trade, it became necessary to alter the law to reflect the new commercial reality. In the mid-seventeenth century, it was granted that those who abandoned their ships because of their imminent destruction by either weather or hostile ships could later reclaim their property if it was found wrecked. Furthermore, owners of ships or the goods they were carrying were given a year and a day from the discovery of the wreck to claim their property before it was forfeited to the crown.[18]

As with treasure trove, the coroner was the local official responsible for investigating wrecks of the sea.[19] Coroners retained these responsibilities throughout the early modern period, and still hold responsibility for treasure trove in the present day. The retention of these duties in the seventeenth and eighteenth centuries reflects the coroner's original role as a revenue officer responsible for collecting those duties and properties due to the crown. In the early modern period, however, many of the revenue-collecting duties of the coroner took a back seat to the investigation of death—as we will see, a duty that was also inextricable from the collection of forfeit property. And yet, the early modern coroner performed other functions that belie any simplistic characterization of the coroner as merely a revenue officer. The responsibility for treasure trove and shipwreck demonstrates the coroner's central role in the adjudication of questions of crown property. It also brings to light the coroner's continued ubiquity in the more general governance of the realm, and the important place of the office in the wider system of investigation and control.

In addition to retaining some of their medieval responsibilities for treasure trove, shipwreck, abjuration, and outlawry, early modern coroners often functioned in a more general capacity in the county government. At the Somerset Assize in July 1632, an order by the justices issued a writ of *venire facias* "to the county coroners for returning a jury to try the traverse upon an indictment against the inhabitants of Chew Magna for the decay of the north part of Stanton Bridge."[20] Furthermore, the same county coroners were instructed that if the jury did not appear, they were to return a writ of *decem tales* "so that the indictment may be tried at the next assizes."[21] A dispute over responsibility for bridge repair or maintenance was not at all unusual. However, the fact that the county coroners were charged

with summoning a jury to hear the case again shows the broad importance
of the coroner as an agent of the state.

Other instances of coroners acting in capacities unrelated to death
give further glimpses into the wider duties of early modern coroners. In
1613 Richard Grammer, a laborer from Kelvedon in Essex, was charged
with stealing a peck of wheat worth 3s 4d from Richard Pearce. Grammer was indicted at the Michaelmas Quarter Sessions, found guilty, and
branded on the left hand.[22] Grammer's crime and punishment were nothing out of the ordinary in the early seventeenth century. Interestingly,
however, the case was listed as "certified to the office of the coroner."[23]
Such explicit references to the coroner in cases of theft are unusual, and it
is difficult to ascertain how common the practice was. However, in the late
seventeenth century William Greenwood counted appeals and accusations
of theft among the coroner's duties and stated that "in the presence of the
Coroner shall all appeals of Robbery and Larceny be framed"[24] While it has
been supposed that these duties were usurped by the justice of the peace in
the late Middle Ages, it seems that hearing accusations and appeals of theft
continued to number among the coroner's responsibilities at least through
the seventeenth century.

Although their duties are not clearly enumerated in the officeholding
manuals of the day, early modern coroners seem to have had some responsibility for the organization of county elections. For instance, in 1689
Mr. Thorey and Mr. South, the county coroners for Essex, were ordered
to be paid £20 by the treasurer of the west division of the county "for the
great trouble and charge they have been at in dispersing convention letters, attending the election and proclaiming the King and Queen at severall
market townes in the County."[25] The primary responsibility for ensuring
proper election procedure in the early modern period belonged to the sheriff, with various "returning officers" and clerks acting as subordinates.[26]
Despite the fact that the identity of these returning officers is not normally
specified, the evidence suggests that coroners, as county officers who had
worked beneath and in concert with the sheriff since the Middle Ages, were
regularly and actively engaged as returning officers in the organization of
elections.

The coroner's electoral role is confirmed by a debate that took place in the House of Lords in 1683. The debate related to a contested election held in Essex in January 1683.[27] The intricacies of the lords' debate are immaterial, at least for our purposes, but the discussion does provide some insight into the coroner's place in election procedure. The main point of contention was "whether the poll was duly closed or no."[28] According to Lewis Prescott, one of the witnesses, the election was to be held on Thursday, January 10. At 10:30 in the morning the coroner read the "Prince's letter" or proclamation, as was standard procedure before an election.[29] With the proclamation read, the voters in attendance began to shout their support for the various candidates, with the cries for Mildmay and Honeywood—two of the three candidates—the most vociferous. Satisfied that the election had been settled by popular proclamation, the crowd brought two chairs to carry the seemingly victorious candidates as was the popular custom. At this point, however, the third candidate, John Wroth, arrived with approximately 200 supporters and "demanded a poll."[30] The poll was held until 3:30, at which point "the Coroner came and did not poll above a quarter of an hour" before adjourning the polling until eight o'clock Friday. Over the next few days the coroner opened and adjourned the polling as many as ten times until Tuesday morning, when "the Coroner came; and, after he had polled above Three Quarters of an Hour, the Coroner bid the Crier make Proclamation."[31] The crier's proclamation signaled the end of the voting period, a fact that incensed the supporters of Mildmay and Honeywood. The defeated parties claimed that upwards of 150 of their supporters had yet to vote when the coroner closed the polls for the last time, a fact which they contended gave the election to Mr. Wroth.

One witness claimed that he saw one of the coroners push supporters of Mildmay and Honeywood away from the poll, while others suggested that the election had been completely aboveboard. Whether or not the supporters of Wroth or those of Mildmay and Honeywood were in the right is unknown, but one other piece of testimony gives further clues to the coroner's electoral function. Robert Neale was appointed one of the two clerks for the election and with the two coroners supervised the polling and the creation of the poll book. Mildmay's supporters claimed that the coroners had carried off the poll books during the counting of the votes. Neale testified that the clerks and coroners had indeed carried away the books, but did so because Mildmay's men "were very outrageous; which was the reason they did not let them in at the Casting-up of the books; but set Watchmen to keep them breaking down the doors. He said South and Thorey, the two coroners, the other clerk, and he himself "were at the Casting-up of the books; and does not know that anyone was to demand entrance, to see the Books cast up."[32]

From these accounts, we can glean a fairly complete picture of the coroner's role in the election process. It was the coroner's responsibility to read the monarch's proclamation, an act that formally signaled the start of an election. Next, the coroner was responsible for appointing clerks to take down the votes and to administer the requisite oaths. During the voting phase of an election the coroner was also responsible for the opening, adjourning, and final closing of the poll. Finally, it was the coroner's task to help the clerks in the counting of the votes and "casting up the books." In some places and times many or all of these functions could be performed by the sheriff, who held ultimate responsibility for county elections. It is clear, however, that the coroner's role in elections was often central, he being the primary official tasked with starting, supervising and tallying the results of electoral contests. These functions, and their importance to the government of the realm, made the coroner's place in county government doubly important. Coroners were responsible not only for the crucial task of investigating death, but also for overseeing the political lifeblood of an increasingly participatory nation.

These wider duties should not come as a surprise despite the contentions of the declining significance of the office made by historians of the medieval coroner. Although the justice of the peace came to usurp some of the coroner's original functions, the records and guidebooks of the early modern period make it clear that coroners retained a greater proportion of their medieval responsibilities than has been previously allowed. The coroner may indeed have lost some of his functions as a general county officer, and from at least the 1550s became answerable to the justices of the peace, but to minimize the role of the coroner in areas beyond the investigation of death is shortsighted. The main responsibility of early modern coroners was certainly to hold inquest on the bodies of the deceased, but they continued in many ways to act in a more general capacity as county officers and conservators of the peace. This broad role in the governance of the counties highlights the vital place of the coroner in the wider system of state surveillance and control.

Jurisdictions

The posts occupied by early modern coroners can be divided into three primary types of jurisdiction: county, borough, and liberty. Each county was allotted a certain number of coroners at any one time, each of whom was responsible for holding inquests on any suspicious death that occurred within the borders of the county in question. According to Greenwood's officeholding manual, "The number of Coroners are not set by the Law; In some Counties there are four, in some Counties six, and in some fewer."[33] This lack of consistency and absence of laws mandating precise numbers makes it hard to ascertain exactly how many coroners were operating in any one county at a given point. In practice, however, Sussex, Cheshire, Wiltshire, and most other counties maintained two coroners at a time throughout the period. Sometimes the jurisdictions of county coroners were further subdivided into smaller geographical areas. In Sussex, for instance, there was one coroner for East Sussex and one coroner for West Sussex. Similarly, Wiltshire divided its coroners between northern and southern jurisdictions.

Incorporated boroughs were also often granted the right to appoint coroners to oversee inquests within their boundaries. Grants to boroughs were made on an individual basis and were reiterated or even altered over time. Chester, for instance, was first given the right to "choose from themselves coroners in the aforesaid city as often as shall be needful" by Edward I in 1300.[34] This right was restated in more detail in the reign of Henry VII, who granted to the mayor of Chester and his successors the right "that every year they may choose of the more discreet and honest citizens . . . two citizens to be coroners."[35] The new stipulations of the Henrician grant that the mayor appoint two citizens as coroner each year probably reflected both the growing size of the city and the increased concentration of power in the hands of an urban elite led by the mayor and aldermen. The number of coroners operating within these urban jurisdictions varied from city to city and changed as cities grew. Chester had two active coroners throughout the early modern period, while the town of Rye in Sussex maintained only one.[36]

Finally, large landholders could also be granted the right to appoint a coroner to investigate suspicious deaths within the bounds of their lands. For instance, until 1590 the earls of Huntington were granted the right to appoint a coroner to hold inquests on their lands—referred to as Hastings Rape—in Sussex.[37] It was not just individual landowners who were given the right to appoint coroners for their lands; other holders of royal patents also chose coroners to investigate deaths that occurred on their lands. The bishop of Chichester in Sussex was granted the right to appoint a coroner for diocesan estates in that county.[38] Similarly, many Oxford and Cambridge colleges—major landholders in the early modern period and our own—were also allowed to select coroners to operate on their properties. For example, in 1650, a Peter Collins was appointed as coroner of all of King's College's lands in Cambridgeshire, a rather extensive jurisdiction that gave Collins significant power over scholars and tenants alike.[39]

When one combines the various possible jurisdictions, it is evident that a fair number of coroners were operating in any one county at any given time. In Sussex, for example, up to 18 coroners were operating at any one time in the sixteenth century. These consisted of two county coroners (one each for West and East Sussex), one coroner for each of the Cinque Ports of Rye, Winchelsea, and Hastings, and 15 coroners for various other boroughs (e.g., Chichester and Arundel) and liberties such as Hastings Rape, Battle Liberty, and the Duchy of Lancaster.[40] The total number of coroners for Sussex for all jurisdictions in the reign of Elizabeth I was 75.[41] This number of officeholders indicates a fairly low turnover for coroners in the second half of the sixteenth century. Especially when compared with most other local offices, for which one year of service was the norm, coroners proved to be a remarkably stable official presence in the localities.[42]

In addition to the more familiar jurisdictional divisions of counties, boroughs, and liberties, a few other exceptional jurisdictions existed in the early modern period. First among these special jurisdictions was the crown coroner, or coroner of the verge. Dating to the Middle Ages, when English monarchs lived a more peripatetic lifestyle with no single, fixed seat of power, the verge was defined as an area of 12 miles surrounding the monarch's court, and one that moved with the monarch.[43] A special coroner was appointed for the verge whose jurisdiction was limited to this 12-mile area. County coroners were not "suffered to interpose to enquire of felonies within the verge," even if the court moved to a place normally under their jurisdiction.[44] Inquests undertaken by county coroners within the verge, or by crown coroners outside of the verge, were often rejected by the court, as examples provided by Greenwood attest.[45] In practice, however, county and verge coroners often did work in concert after receiving authorization from the court, and from the late sixteenth century, when the court became more or less fixed in Westminster, the coroner of the verge often also served as county coroner for Middlesex, as Richard Vale did in the late sixteenth century.[46] The coroner of the verge became less of an active officeholder and more of a courtesy appointment over the course of the early modern period, especially as the court became fixed and crown coroners came to hold the office in conjunction with that of county coroner, which solved the earlier jurisdictional problem between county and crown coroners.

Another particularly tricky jurisdictional quandary, especially in a period of global commercial expansion, was that of who was responsible for holding inquests and investigating suspicious or violent deaths at sea or aboard ships. The general rule of thumb for such deaths was that if land could be seen on two sides of a ship, then the responsibility to hold an inquest fell to the county coroner. However, if land could not be seen from the ship in question, then the death fell under the jurisdiction of the Admiralty. According to John Godolphin's 1661 treatise on Admiralty jurisdiction, "The Admiral should have no jurisdiction where a man may see from one side to the other: but the Coroner of the County shall inquire of

Felonies committed there."[47] This rule was designed so that deaths that occurred in rivers or while a ship was in port—places that were relatively easy for local officials to access—would be the responsibility of the relevant county coroner, while deaths on the open seas—where the timely availability of a coroner would be unlikely—were left to the only authority readily available, the Admiralty.

These rules were taken quite seriously. For instance, in 1677 a sailor fell from a ship while it lay at anchor at the quay in the Wirral and drowned. As the death of the unfortunate sailor was an accident and occurred within sight of land on both sides, the coroner for the county of Chester was summoned to hold an inquest on the body.[48] In 1693, William Watson, a sailor from Hull, was riding in a "small boat" "goeing on board their Majesties ship the Humber then rydeing at naker in the river Humber."[49] Before Watson could reach the ship, the boat in which he was riding overturned and the sailor was drowned. Although Watson had been a sailor on a naval vessel, because it was at anchor in the River Humber within sight of land on both sides, the responsibility for the inquest fell to either the Yorkshire or the Lincolnshire coroner. As it happened, John Neville, the Lincolnshire coroner, held the inquest at Barrow on the Lincolnshire side of the river.[50] These cases were unremarkable and there was no dispute over the coroner's jurisdiction in either case, but they do illustrate the furthest bounds of a coroner's remit.

In many ways the Tower of London was seen as a city unto itself in the pre-modern period. As such, the Tower had its own coroner responsible for holding inquests on those who died suspiciously within the grounds of the Tower. According to an eighteenth-century Tower official, the "Liberty of the Tower has jurisdiction over causes and offences arising there and is free from government of city and county officers including Coroner of the City, coroners of Middlesex." Instead, the steward of the Tower was to act as coroner within the Tower liberty.[51] Although records of these unusual inquests are rare, the journal of an eighteenth-century Lieutenant General of the Tower offers a window onto the operation of criminal investigations within the Tower grounds. Adam Williamson served as lieutenant general of the Tower of London between 1722 and 1747. Between 1730 and 1734,

five individuals were found dead within the jurisdiction of the Tower. Four
of the deceased were found drowned in the ditch surrounding the Tower,
two accidental deaths and two suicides, and one body was driven by the
tide into Traitors Gate.[52] Although these types of death were not unusual
for any jurisdiction, the fact that few people lived in the Tower made filling
out a jury somewhat difficult. The obvious solution, and the one hit upon
by Williamson, was to order the various soldiers and guards to serve as
jurymen. In one case Williamson states that "the coroners jury was composed of the Ordnance and if any were wanting I ordered our warders to
make up the jury, and in all cases of this sort that fell within my province I
ordered that the warders should always compose the Jury."[53] The image of
the now-familiar warders composing a coroner's jury is perhaps somewhat
amusing, but these cases illustrate nicely the fact that coroner's inquests, and
the juries that were so central to their undertaking, were intensely local
affairs whose composition and characteristics were sure to reflect the characteristics of the particular community or jurisdiction.

Contested Jurisdictions

Although the jurisdictions of the various types of coroner seem clear in
theory, in practice there were often disputes over jurisdiction that on occasion became quite contentious and even violent. One such jurisdictional
dispute from the beginning of our period was so acrimonious that it eventually resulted in a suit in Star Chamber. The case in question arose out of
an inquest held in 1553 into the death of a woman at Walton, Oxfordshire.[54]
Frances Taylor, wife of Roger Taylor, was found hanged in the house of
George Owen at Walton. When word spread of the woman's death, a large
crowd, including scholars from the university, gathered at Owen's house
in hopes of catching a glimpse of the corpse. Worried that the morbidly
curious multitude might damage their landlord's property, various tenants
of George Owen, including Henry Walker and Baldwen Nede, hastened to
the house in an attempt to prevent the mob from getting out of hand. Upon
arriving at the scene, Walker and Nede, according to their later testimony in
Star Chamber, proceeded to call the county coroners. The county officials

were summoned because, as Walker and Nede stated, Owen's house was part of the county of Oxford and thus not within the liberty of the city of Oxford. The city had no "libertie to have or chose coroners or use the jurisdiction of coroners" outside the bounds of the city."[55]

The crowd, mostly made up of people from the city, did not agree with Walker and Nede's assessment of the jurisdiction, and when the county coroner appeared on the scene a short time later he was greeted by a procession of 200 people, armed with swords and other weapons, who marched out of the city led by an alderman of the city and the mayor bearing his mace of office. Owen's tenants chastised the mayor for bearing his mace outside of the jurisdiction of the city and for disrupting a lawful inquest. The mayor and his men refused to leave, however, and instead "with force and violence resist the said coroner of the countie to do his office."[56] The mayor's men then seized the body and house and forcefully dismissed the county coroner, replacing him with the two coroners for the city of Oxford, Richard Atkinson and Edward Clynton, who quickly impaneled a jury of 14 men. The city coroners, however, were not to enjoy the upper hand in this contest over the body of Frances Taylor for long, for a short time after their forcible removal from the house of George Owen, Nede and Walker returned "wyth many other evill disposed and riottus persons . . . to the number of xxx [30] persons being servants and tenants unto one George Owen esquire in riattus and warrlyke manor."[57] Armed with "bowes, billes, swords, daggers, staves, handgunnes and other weapons," Owen's tenants interrupted the Oxford coroners' inquest, "hurled downe the table wheratt the said coroners satt," and threw the coroners down the stairs of the house and out the door. Finally, Owen's partisans, now 100 strong according to the mayor's complaint, removed Frances Taylor's body from the house and kept it elsewhere for two days and would not permit the city coroners to view the body or complete their inquest.[58]

Having lost face and possession of the body, the mayor, alderman, and others from the city again marched upon Walton bearing the mace of office and proceeded to make "open proclymacyon in yor highnesses names according to the statute of unlawfull assemblys . . . that any persons ther ryatusly assembeled should quietly departe home." Owen's partisans were not cowed by the reading of the statute against unlawful assembly and refused to depart. For 12 hours the hostile crowed "mocked and dispitfully scorned" the mayor's proclamation and, instead of dispersing, escalated the conflict by throwing "stones and old shoes at the maior, Alderman and Comenyltey" and seizing the mace of office from the sergeant. With the mace in their possession, members of the crowd carried it in mock procession before destroying it and carrying away the pieces.[59]

The mayor and alderman of Oxford responded to this challenge to their authority and dignity by launching a suit in Star Chamber, and commissioners were sent out with a list of interrogatories to put to the accused. While the final outcome of the suit is unclear, as is the fate of Frances Taylor's corpse, it is clear from the extant materials relating to the case that the outcome hinged on the dispute over jurisdiction. According to the mayor and alderman, among the "sundrie grants, privildeges and liberties" granted by the crown to the city of Oxford was "that the sayd Maior, Alderman and Comynalitie of the sayd Cetye of Oxford . . . shoud chouse too substancyall and honest men inhabiting within the sayd City . . . to be coroners within the sayd citie and franchise."[60] The mayor and alderman further claimed that Walton, where the body of Frances Taylor was found, was within the liberty of the city and thus fell under the jurisdiction of the two city coroners, Richard Atkinson and Edward Clynton. In response to the claims made by the mayor and alderman of Oxford in their Star Chamber complaint, the defendants made reference to a legal case in which the court had previously ruled that Walton was not within the liberty of the city and thus the city had no right to have its coroners perform an inquest there. Furthermore, they argued that the mayor was well aware of the precedent created by the case they cited and should have known that Walton was outside his or his coroners' jurisdiction.

While the image of the mayor of Oxford marching out of the city with full regalia at the head of an armed body of perhaps 200 men to confront a similarly sized and armed group of men over a question of jurisdiction in the death of an otherwise unremarkable individual may seem surreal, it is not entirely surprising that such a dispute would arise in the mid-sixteenth century. As a result of a combination of demographic pressures resulting from rapid population expansion and the fixing of monetary obligations to parish boundaries with the advent of the Elizabethan Poor Laws, the sixteenth century witnessed increased tension over jurisdictional boundaries.[61] While disputes over boundaries between parishes were perhaps more common, it was not unusual for the authorities of neighboring coronial jurisdictions to argue over who had a right to hold an inquest and thus who had the right to the potential forfeitures of deodands, suicides, or felons.

Although disputes over jurisdiction usually involved debates concerning the right to hold inquests or take possession of forfeit property, occasionally jurisdictional boundaries were invoked for personal or political purposes. On September 29, 1729, the weavers of Bristol, who had been under growing financial strain from at least 1727, rioted as they had done several times in the previous two years. As with earlier weavers' riots in the city, the target of the mob was an unpopular employer, in this case Stephen Freacham. When the crowd reached Freacham's house, however, they found him waiting and armed. Exactly what happened next is unclear, but what is certain is that Freacham fired on the mass of weavers, ultimately killing nine people.[62]

Opinion in the city and its suburbs raged over whether Freacham had acted in defense of his life and property or whether he should be held responsible for the dead weavers. Within Bristol's city walls, many of Freacham's fellow citizens not only believed that he acted within the rule of law, but also desired the prosecution of the rioters. According to Freacham, "my fellow tradesmen being somewhat sufferen in the loss of goods damaged or destroyed by the mobb are very vigorouse for taking em up." Perhaps recognizing the precariousness of his situation, however, Freacham was of the opinion that he should take matters into his own hands and "finish my own troubles rather than presente others."[63] Freacham's troubles, and the reason for his letter to Henry Fane in 1730, were with the coroner for the county of Gloucester.[64] The coroner clearly felt that Freacham was criminally responsible for the deaths of the nine weavers, and although the city of Bristol itself remained outside the coroner's jurisdiction, he planned, according to Freacham, "to endite the officers of the out parish for not takeing me up."[65] It seems that while the Gloucester coroner could not arrest

Freacham in Bristol, he intended to have him taken when and if he left the city. In order to spur local officials to take such actions, the coroner intended to indict the officers of the parish immediately outside the city walls for their previous failure to arrest Freacham. Fearing the intentions of the coroner, Freacham wrote to Fane and requested that the matter be moved "out of his power."[66] Although it is unclear whether Freacham succeeded in having the case moved out of the jurisdiction of the coroner of Gloucester, he was arrested and convicted, but ultimately pardoned.

As these two cases of contested jurisdiction from either side of the early modern period demonstrate, while the jurisdictions of coroners were set in theory, in practice they were challenged, debated, and disputed in the same way other political and official boundaries were disputed in the early modern period. Most often, the jurisdiction of coroners was challenged in order to assert the power or rights of a city, liberty, or county to hold inquests, determine guilt, and seize forfeit property. On occasion, however, such disputes were attempts to influence the course of justice or to enforce one definition of legitimate violence or legal responsibility at the expense of a competing, contrary definition. Hence jurisdiction, and the protection of it, were often about more than simple lines on the ground or monetary gain. Instead, they were fundamentally an attempt to assert the rights of local communities and to define for themselves what constituted legitimate violence and criminal responsibility. Through this contest of definition, communities sought to protect, regulate, and reintegrate their communities in the wake of the destabilizing force of untimely death. It fell to the local coroner to adjudicate these definitional disputes and reconcile them with the dictates of the state.

Disputes over jurisdiction did occur, but it was just as likely that a coroner would assist a fellow coroner from another jurisdiction as it was for local officials or communities to wrangle over proper jurisdiction. Because there were relatively few coroners operating in any given county, coroners often crossed jurisdictions or held positions in multiple jurisdictions concurrently. For instance, of the 35 inquests held in Bramber Rape in East Sussex between 1558 and 1603, as many as 17 were held by county coroners, as against 18 held by the Bramber Rape coroner.[67] Although the proportion of

inquests in Bramber carried out by someone other than the rape's coroner
was on the extreme end of the spectrum, evidence from other jurisdictions
demonstrates that crossing jurisdictions was nothing unusual, especially
if a coroner was ill or otherwise indisposed. In the extant Sussex records
there are two cases in which either William Playfere, coroner of the liberty
of Hastings Rape, operated in another coroner's jurisdiction, or another
coroner carried out an inquest in Hastings Rape. On both occasions, in
1590 and again in 1594, Magnus Fowle, the county coroner for East Sussex, carried out inquests in Hastings Rape. The inquest in October 1594
occurred between the last known inquest held by Playfere and the next inquest held by his successor as coroner of Hastings Rape (although Playfere
was still listed as coroner at the East Grinstead Assize of 18 July 1595). Perhaps then Playfere, although still officially coroner of Hastings Rape, was
no longer active, making it necessary for another coroner to hold inquests
in Playfere's jurisdiction.[68] Thus, while the economic and social consequences of a violent death might sometimes lead to jurisdictional disputes,
this need was often overridden by communal desires for speedy justice and
the state's concerns for order and control.

Election, Selection, and Appointment

The method by which coroners were appointed differed depending on
the type of jurisdiction involved. The coroners of liberties, for instance,
were appointed directly by the lord of the liberty or his steward. The position of coroner in this type of jurisdiction was an object of patronage to be
dispersed at the discretion of the patent holder for an unlimited duration.
Liberties were usually limited to one coroner, although the larger liberties that possessed lands in several counties might have a separate coroner
for their lands in each county. In practice, the coroners of such liberties
often functioned in multiple capacities, acting as bailiffs or stewards, for
instance.

The selection of liberty coroners is well illustrated by the case of
William Playfere, who acted as coroner for Hastings Rape between 1566
and 1603. Although he operated as coroner in East Sussex, Playfere lived for

most of his life, and all of his time in office, at Hawkhurst in Kent.[69] Despite the fact that Hawkhurst was situated in the West of Kent close to the border with Sussex (Hastings Rape being the easternmost division of Sussex), it was unusual for a coroner, or any local officeholder for that matter, to reside outside his area of jurisdiction. Not only did Playfere not reside in his jurisdiction of Hastings Rape, he had never resided there or anywhere else in Sussex, which makes his selection as coroner of Hastings Rape all the more interesting. Perhaps the selection of an outsider became necessary after the lord of the liberty had trouble replacing the previous coroner, Richard Sharp. Sharp had held his last inquest as coroner of Hastings Rape in September 1552, and another coroner was not appointed in that jurisdiction until Playfere in 1566. In the intervening 14 years there was no coroner for Hastings Rape, and inquests held in the area were undertaken by one of the two Sussex county coroners.[70] It is not clear why the post was not filled until 1566, but perhaps a lack of qualified or willing candidates necessitated looking outside of Hastings Rape and Sussex for a coroner.

It is also possible that Playfere's selection as coroner was the result of personal connections with the earl of Huntingdon, who was responsible for appointing the liberty's coroner. Between 1568 and 1591, and again in 1595, Playfere, in addition to serving as coroner, also acted as bailiff of Hastings Liberty for the earl of Huntingdon. Although it was not unheard of for coroners to serve as bailiffs, neither John Hebden, who preceded him as bailiff of Hastings Liberty, nor Robert Laycock, who succeeded him, served as coroners.[71] Thus, the offices of coroner and bailiff of Hastings Liberty were not inseparable. It seems, then, that Playfere must have been particularly favored by the earl of Huntingdon to have been appointed to both positions concurrently. Direct connections between the two men are unknown, but both had connections with evangelical Protestant circles, and it is possible that this worked in Playfere's favor.[72]

Coroners of cities and boroughs were occasionally selected through elections. In most cases, however, they were either appointed by the common council or the mayor, or remained part of the mayor's responsibilities ex officio. The mayors of the Cinque Ports boroughs of Rye, Hastings, and Winchelsea in Sussex, for instance, officially served as coroners for their

respective towns during their terms in office, though the practical work of
holding inquests was often performed by deputies acting on behalf of the
mayors.[73] For those boroughs in which the mayoralty and coronership remained separate offices, the selection of a coroner generally followed a few
common patterns. According to one contemporary guidebook, city coroners, like other urban officers, were to be chosen by the commonality or
burgesses unless "they have been chosen (time out of mind) by a certain select number, commonly called Common-Council or suchlike name, and not
in general by the Commonalty or Burgesses." If such a precedent existed,
"such ancient and usual elections are good and well warranted by their
Charters, and by Law also."[74] Most urban coroners were selected through
this type of restricted election, although, as the guidebook states, practices
differed from city to city based on precedent and charter. The restricted
nature of urban elections should come as no surprise given the growth of
oligarchical government in cities and towns across the sixteenth century.[75]

    As we have seen, most cities and boroughs had one or two coroners
at any one time as specified by their charters. Chester, as a city of significant size, had been granted the privilege of appointing two coroners in
the Middle Ages. Although two coroners operated at any given time, it is
clear that the governors of Chester tried when possible to stagger the election and retirement of each coroner so that two novice coroners were not
elected at the same time. Although this policy was never explicitly stated in
reference to coroners, a 1466 entry in the Chester Assembly Book makes it
clear that city officials did think about officeholding in this way. The entry
states that murengers—the local officials charged with the maintenance of
the city walls—are "to be henceforth chosen for two years, one retiring
each year and another taking his place."[76] Coroners often held office for
more than the two years stipulated for murengers, but it seems likely that
the appointment of coroners was supposed to occur in a similar manner.
The lists of coroners for the sixteenth and early seventeenth centuries are
incomplete, making it impossible to tell how often this staggering was accomplished in practice, but by the mid-seventeenth century the terms of
office suggest a deliberate strategy of sequential election. For instance, in
1663 John Poole and Richard Harrison were operating as Chester's two

coroners. When Poole stepped down as coroner at the end of 1663, John Hulton was chosen to replace him. At the end of 1664 Harrison in turn retired and was replaced by John Maddock. Hulton left office in 1673, to be replaced by Robert Caddick. When Maddock stepped down in his turn in 1676, William Harvey took his place as coroner.[77] This strategy did not always work; in 1679, for example, both coroners stepped down (whether as a result of poor health, death, or a simple lack of interest in maintaining the position is unclear) and two new coroners were appointed simultaneously. Despite the occasional failure, this staggering of appointments was a relatively effective method of providing on the job training for amateur officials new to the post.[78]

The government of Chester also took pains to ensure that the selection of coroners and other officials was accomplished quickly and with as little corruption as possible. In 1584 it was explicitly declared that "all offices [are] to be filled within a week of the decease of the previous holder, in order to make impossible the obtaining of letters of recommendation from influential persons."[79] The desirability of some offices was such as to cause candidates to seek out the imprimatur of important or powerful patrons, though others were more apt to try to shirk the responsibilities of urban citizenship. To prevent qualified citizens from declining the obligation to serve, those who avoided office were fined. In 1549 a complaint was made that "some wealthy citizens, who make full use of the privileges of their freedom, and are well able to bear the burdens of office, nevertheless decline the honor; penal fines are therefore laid down for refusing election."[80] Thus, it was important both that that the selection of officeholders should not be influenced by outside interests and that those eligible for office perform the duties of office when called upon to do so.

The regulation of urban officeholders such as coroners did not cease after selection. In order to ensure that proper protocol was followed, Cheshire officials relied on a number of methods of oversight. The simplest and most straightforward method of controlling the behavior of officers was through penal fines similar to the aforementioned fine for declining office. In addition, the governors of Chester employed auditors to review the accounts of outgoing sheriffs, coroners, and even mayors. In 1577, auditors

were appointed to review the accounts of various officers for the previous
two to three years. In 1579, "all Mayors, Sheriffs and others, who have held
office since the last mayoralty"—1575—were ordered to "present their accounts to a new body of auditors."[81] The final weapon in Chester's arsenal
of oversight was the threat of loss of franchise. Loss of the franchise was a
serious affair and as such was reserved for grave offenses, whether or not
they related to the performance of the office in question. Richard Wright,
coroner and sheriff of Chester, was punished with loss of the franchise in
1577 when he was accused of conniving in the elopement of the daughter
of an alderman. Wright refused to submit to judgment and was therefore
"disfranchised."[82] This incident neatly demonstrates how the actions and
behavior of officers, and indeed citizens in general, was policed and punished by the city authorities.

　　As opposed to most liberty or borough coroners, county coroners
were elected by the freeholders of the county in question. The process of
electing a coroner was fairly uniform from county to county and proceeded
in a standard manner. When the need to elect a new county coroner was
recognized, the sheriff or his undersheriff would "sue forth a writt for the
electinge and choseinge such able men within the said county for coroners as shal be fit to undergoe that office."[83] A writ of *coronatore eligendo*
was then issued by the Court of Chancery to the sheriff of the county in
question. The proper writ secured, the sheriff then proceeded to hold an
election by "the Freeholders or Suitors in open and full court."[84] Next, the
sheriff was to "return and certifie into the Chancery the election of every
such coroner and their names," and the county clerk was to administer the
oath of office.[85] In taking his oath of office the coroner swore as follows:
"[You] well and truly shall serve our Soveraign Lord the King in the Office
of a Coroner; and as one of his Majesties Coroners of the County of Y and
therein you shall truly and diligently do and accomplish all and every thing
and things appertaining to your Office, after the best of your cunning, wit
and power, both for the profit and good of the Inhabitants within the said
County, taking such fees as you ought to take by the Laws and Statutes of
this Kingdom and not otherwise, so help you God."[86]

As shown above, the responsibility for carrying out the election of coroners primarily fell to the sheriff and his deputies. The election process, however, was supervised by the justices of the assize courts. Often, it was an order from the assizes that spurred the election process in the first place. At the Taunton Assize in August 1651, for instance, Henry Rolle and Robert Nicholas, justices of the Upper Bench, ordered that an election of coroners be held because "it appeareth to this court that there is a great wante of coroners in this county."[87] In this case the "great wante of coroners" was likely a result of one Mr. Pitts stepping down as coroner at the same assize session after claiming to be "very unfit to execute that office."[88] Having initiated the election procedure, the assize justices continued to monitor the progress of the election. At the same Taunton assize they gave an order that the sheriff or undersheriff "give an account thereof att the next assizes and general gaol delivery to be holden for this county."[89]

Elections of coroners were held regularly and at fairly consistent rates throughout the early modern period. Inconsistent record survival makes it impossible to say exactly how many coronial elections occurred. However, by examining writs for the election of coroners, and the returns of these writs, in Chancery we can arrive at an approximation. Between 1560 and 1587 there were at least 53 elections of coroners.[90] Between 1603 and 1625 there were approximately 43 elections, and between 1625 and 1634 there were 34 elections.[91]

The number and frequency of elections seem to have remained fairly consistent across the period. If we look at the number of known elections of coroners in the late seventeenth and eighteenth centuries, we see similar numbers as in the late sixteenth and early seventeenth centuries. For instance, there were 26 elections between 1660 and 1685, 46 elections between 1686 and 1709, and 49 elections between 1710 and 1735.[92] Although there was some fluctuation in the number of elections across the period, it seems that they varied from a low of about one per year between 1660 and 1685 to a high of almost four per year between 1625 and 1634, with most periods seeing about two elections in any given year. Given the length of many coroners' tenures, this figure seems understandable.

These known elections were also spread fairly widely in geographical terms. For the period between 1660 and 1685, 20 different counties were known to have had at least one election. Between 1686 and 1709, 24 counties were represented in coronial elections, whereas and 23 counties held elections between 1710 and 1735, with most counties represented at least once in the records.[93] Given this spread, it seems that each county had, on average, one known election every 12 or 13 years. In reality, it is likely that each county had far more, but the available data suggest that every county was holding at least occasional elections of coroners and returning the results to Chancery. The numbers also imply that even if many of the relevant records do not survive, the elections of county coroners were held at a consistent rate across the early modern period.

The elections of coroners, like those of other officeholders of the period, were sometimes contested and occasionally disputed, or even overturned. Few early examples of contested or disputed elections exist, but there are tantalizing hints that they did occur from time to time. The details are hazy, but one such instance of a disputed election likely occurred in 1585 in Herefordshire. In a letter to Sir John Scudamore, Thomas Atkins states that there had been much "disorder tochyng the election of a coroner at Hereford."[94] Unfortunately, Atkins does not provide any further details about the dispute or its cause, and so we can only infer that the election of coroners, while not always as rowdy and fraught as parliamentary elections in the eighteenth century, were on occasion matters of dispute and thus unlikely to be mere formalities.

By the eighteenth century, it is clear that the elections of coroners were regularly contested, with rival candidates campaigning for votes and favor. Detailed examples of coronorial elections are rare, but those instances in which such elections are recorded suggest that by now contested elections were the rule rather than the exception. The elections of county coroners for Somerset in 1739 and 1741 provide one such example. In 1739 John Cannon, an excise officer and writing master from Glastonbury, records that on November 13 "Mr. William Nicholls, Wilcox and others at this time busyed at this time about the town getting votes for one Mr. Clothier of Ivelchester, who set himself up as a candidate for coroner as did others."[95]

The electioneering of Clothier and his supporters had offended some in Glastonbury who felt the campaign was both disorderly and exclusionary. Cannon states that "most of the freeholders in Glaston were disgusted by the managing of it [the campaign] . . . by reason they feasted and carouzed by themselves only, or as many as they selected, or that were obliged by debt or labour and so consequently complied soon."[96] Many of the residents of Glastonbury clearly considered this factionalism to be contrary to the proper conduct of elections and resolved to resist "their threats and flatterys."[97]

Unfortunately for those who, like John Cannon, felt that the Clothier faction had behaved without proper decorum, Clothier was duly elected coroner. Clothier, however, subsequently declined the office "on account of his being restored Gaoler of the prison at Ivelchester again," leaving a new vacancy.[98] Following Clothier's refusal of the office, a new round of electioneering began. On November 26 "one Dorrington, a school master of Yeovil, came to Glaston with one Charles Bucey" in an attempt to secure votes for the upcoming election for county coroner.[99] Dorrington's efforts were rewarded when he convinced "Mr. Stibbens, Mr. Nicholls and others to use their interest in getting votes for him as a candidate for coroner."[100] It seems that the same faction that had secured the election of Clothier was now putting its political muscle behind the Yeovil schoolmaster. Cannon himself was "importuned to be in their [the faction supporting Dorrington's candidacy] company at the George Inn, but declined them as I had done a day or two before for one White of Langport, another candidate."[101]

White and Dorrington were not the only candidates for the office of coroner to seek Cannon's vote and endorsement. On December 8, Edward Cooth of Shepton Malet went to the Rose and Crown Inn in Glastonbury and "sent for his friends requesting their vote and interest at the next election of a coroner, he offering himself a candidate for that place."[102] This time Cannon heeded the request to attend the candidate's fete. He offered Cooth his vote provided the would-be coroner could physically make it to the election, which was to be held at Ivelchester—a difficulty given the winter season and Cannon's lack of a horse. In response, Cooth "promised to find a horse and discharge mine and his friends' expenses at Ivelchester the election day."[103] In an attempt to further ensure that Cannon's vote was his, Cooth told Cannon that he had already received the "interest of Mr. Richard Slade, Mr. Cowper, the Councelors Davis and How, Mr. Newman, Mr. Proves, Mr. Thomas Cooth and many more great men too tedious to mention."[104]

The Dorrington faction, however, was not content to let Cooth and his supporters operate unchallenged, and soon after Cannon's conversation with Cooth, "Mr. William Nicholls, Clothier and others intruded themselves into our company and artfully endeavored to pump out and discover Mr. Cooth's strength, using crafty insinuations and flatteries to delude and draw him to relinquish his hopes, interests and further attempts as a candidate, persuading him to turn over his interest and votes for Mr. Dorrington."[105] The machinations of the Dorrington faction did not escape Cannon's notice, and he quickly separated Cooth from Dorrington's partisans. Cannon then reproved Cooth for behaving so imprudently and "admonished him to be aware of such sycophants and be more wary not to discover any more of his secrets in the affair in hand than what were absolutely necessary."[106] Having been informed of Nicholls's behavior, Cooth remained at the Rose and Crown all night, receiving the promises of 30 men or more.

Cooth was wise to heed the advice proffered by Cannon as the writing master had prior experience in the operation of an electoral campaign for the coronership. Sixteen years earlier, in 1723, Cannon had attended the wedding of his cousin's daughter at the groom's house in West Pennard. Following the wedding, and in an atmosphere of "jolly mirth and pleasant discourses," some of the wedding guests proposed that Cannon stand as candidate for one of the county's two positions of coroner, a post that had recently become vacant at the death of the incumbent, Joshua Beach of Somerton.[107] Cannon agreed to the proposition and spent two weeks canvassing. He focused much of his electoral strategy on securing the interest of a local notable, Thomas Uphill of Stone, who he hoped would in turn secure him the support of Gerrard Martin of East Pennard. Uphill agreed to give Cannon both his vote and his assistance in securing the votes of others, but he also advised that Cannon decline the office for fear that the post would have a corrupting effect. Cannon eventually did withdraw from the contest, not because he feared the malignant influence of the coronership, but rather because his kinsman John Hayme transferred his support from Cannon to another candidate, his brother George Hayme.[108]

The 1739 election was scheduled to be held on December 12. That morning John Cannon rode forth from Glastonbury with about 30 other men who had promised to vote for Cooth. There were four candidates for the office of coroner—Mr. Edward Cooth, Mr. Dorrington, Mr. White, and Mr. Norman—and the partisans of each man crowded into Ivelchester to cast their votes. According to Cannon, "there was a vast company and great struggle for them all."[109] There was some disagreement over who should be eligible to vote, with some gentlemen, Cannon included, claiming that only those who could prove they possessed a certain amount of property should be allowed to vote. The undersheriff in charge of the proceedings, however, did not require the voters to swear the customary oath that they had such lands, a fact that Cannon complained swung the election in Dorrington's favor. Instead, the Dorrington faction's "indirect and fraudulent designs" in packing the polls carried the day. The Yeovil schoolmaster was duly elected coroner with 428 votes and sworn in on January 15 at the Wells Quarter Sessions. Cooth had come in second with 370 votes, while White secured 295 votes and Norman 250.[110]

Although Cannon was disappointed in his attempt to secure the coronership for his preferred candidate, he would get a second chance to influence an election just two years later when Dorrington's fellow coroner George Hayme—one of the men who had run against Cannon when the coronership had been vacant in 1723—died in 1741. Cannon spent July 8–10 canvassing and sending letters on behalf of a Mr. Rowley's candidature for the office.[111] A little over a month later, on August 15, Cannon had a run-in with John Goodson, one of Rowley's rivals for the coronership. Goodson was, according to Cannon, "very drunk" and offended Cannon by offering what amounted to a great insult for the proud writing master. In Cannon's telling, Goodson "affronted me by saying I knew not how to write or anything else as well as he and told me the letters wrote by me in favour of Mr. Rowley was nonsense for which they were filed against me in derision.["112] Goodson continued his drunken tirade by wagering that with the help of a Mr. Parker then present he could secure 50 votes in Glastonbury alone. He boasted that "if he had not the election he would be damned and other such profane expressions very much offensive to the company and worse to his reputation or gaining interest for the intended post."[113]

Once again Cannon was to be disappointed when his preferred candidate was outmaneuvered and the candidate he held in contempt won the election. The election was held at Ivelchester, as usual, on November 25. There were three candidates for the coronership, Mr. Rowley of Mere, John Goodson of Blastonborough, and Mr. Shute of Milton Fauconbridge. Rowley was supported by such notables as Cannon, William Allwood, George Brooke, John West, Shadrach Handcock, and Joseph George, while Goodson had the interest of Cannon's brother and nephew as well as James Chaffey-Cowper, esquire, and Thomas Taunton. A "vast concourse of freeholders" had gathered to cast their votes, but, as was common in elections in the period, some last-minute wheeling and dealing took place to swing the election. After initial polling failed to indicate a clear winner, Rowley agreed to step aside and throw his support and votes behind Goodson for a consideration of twenty or thirty pounds. With Rowley's backing Goodson carried the day, defeating Shute by 402 votes.[114]

These remarkably detailed accounts tell us a number of things about the election of coroners in the eighteenth century and perhaps earlier. The Somerset elections of 1723, 1739, and 1741 show that by at least the eighteenth century, the elections of coroners were often contested between multiple parties. We know from Cannon's writings that all four of the eighteenth-century coroners' elections he witnessed had multiple candidates. In 1723, the election had at least three candidates before Cannon himself stepped down, while the first election in 1739 certainly had more than one candidate, given that Cannon informs us that Clothier set himself up as a candidate for the office "as did others." In the second 1739 election, it is evident that there were four candidates by the time of the election, and if the attempt by the Dorrington faction to get Cooth to cease campaigning and give his votes to Dorrington is any indication, there might well have been other candidates who dropped out of the race before the day of the election. Finally, the 1741 election had three candidates at the time of the election.

The number of electors who participated in the elections of coroners in Somerset is also of importance. Cannon records that there were a total of 1,343 votes cast at the 1739 election. This number is fairly consistent with the number of electors in contemporary parliamentary elections, if perhaps on the low end of the scale. The parliamentary election for Westmorland in 1701 involved 1,169 electors, while that of more populous Kent in 1713 involved 5,033 voters.[115] The number of parliamentary voters in Northumberland in 1722 numbered a mere 1,960.[116] These numbers suggest that by early to mid-eighteenth-century standards the Somerset coroner elections outlined by Cannon drew a substantial proportion of eligible voters to the polls. The election of coroners was clearly an important, contested county event that roused the interest of a wide swath of the political nation. Far from being a formality or a sinecure, by the eighteenth century the election of coroners was important enough and the office of sufficient power and prestige to involve multiple candidates and a large, combative electorate.

In addition to having multiple candidates and a significant electorate, the Somerset elections demonstrate that the candidates and their supporters actively engaged in campaigning. Dorrington traveled from Yeovil to Glastonbury (a distance of some 18 miles) in an attempt to secure votes, and White traveled from Langport to Glastonbury (a journey of about 12 miles) for the same purpose. The partisans of each candidate also attempted to persuade voters by holding fetes at local public houses, by providing the means of transportation necessary to get their voters to the polls, by reimbursing voters for the expenses they incurred in traveling, and by securing the support of influential individuals. Finally, there were accusations that some factions attempted to influence the election by registering voters who did not meet the necessary qualifications for the franchise or by paying rival candidates cash considerations to stand down. All of these aspects of the eighteenth-century Somerset elections — multiple candidates, a substantial electorate, electioneering practices, factionalism, and possible corruption — suggest that the election of coroners differed very little, if at all, from the election of members of Parliament. Both types of election were often competitive, contested, and disputed events, and although the coroner's role was more circumscribed and local than that of the MP, the means of selecting each officer was more or less the same.[117]

The will of the electorate alone was not enough to formally appoint a coroner, as the approval of central officials was also required. When the time came to elect a new coroner a writ of election was secured from the Court of Chancery, with the chosen man's name then submitted to that court. However, a writ of Chancery also had the power to overturn these elections, a power that was exercised on a fairly regular basis. Elections were most frequently overturned because the chosen individual was not of sufficient status to be eligible or because the proposed candidate held another position that disqualified or excused him. While some historians have argued that the status of those holding the position of coroner declined from the late Middle Ages, early modern coroners were still technically expected to be knights with significant landholdings.[118] While the requirement of knighthood was regularly ignored in the early modern period, occupation and landholding were not. Even in the late seventeenth century such qualifications were still taken seriously. In his 1681 treatise *The Annals of King James and Charles I* Thomas Frankland states that "where an insufficient coroner hath been chosen by a county, the whole county has been answerable to the King for the coroners fault."[119] Similarly, John Sadler's 1682 treatise declared that merchants who had been elected coroner were likewise to be removed from office.[120]

If these potential coroners were removed for their lack of status, other were removed or excused for holding positions that may have conflicted with the duties of a coroner. When Henry Clapcott was elected county coroner for Dorset in 1648, for example, he claimed that his position as attorney of the Common Pleas excused him from holding office as coroner. Although Clapcott was initially fined, the assize judges discharged these fees and declared that a new coroner was to be elected after Clapcott produced a "writ of privilege" that substantiated his claims.[121] Similarly, in 1739 Mr. Clothier—whose contentious election as coroner was described above—stepped down as coroner after he had been appointed jailer of the prison at Ivelchester.[122]

The most frequent cause of a coroner leaving office, however, was not disqualification, but rather death or inability to perform the office. Of those considered unfit to serve, some were removed from office at the order of the assize, as Benjamin Randoll was at the Taunton Assize in August 1650. Randoll was judged by the assize justices to be "a man soe infirme that hee is unfit to execute that office [coroner]," and was consequently issued a writ of ease, excusing him from service.[123] Other coroners took matters into their own hands and secured their dismissal when they became unable to act as coroner. In 1652, John Sweetinge, a coroner for Somerset, presented the assize with "a certificate under the hand of Doctor Marwood" stating that Sweetinge was "a man soe infirme that he is not able to undergoe the execution of that office without danger to his life."[124] The court agreed and so advised Sweetinge to apply to the Lord Commissioners of the Great Seale for a warrant *de coronatore anovendi et de alio eligendi* that would set aside Sweetinge's election.

Unlike many borough coroners, a county coroner did not have a fixed tenure in office, so the decision to step down was usually left to the coroners themselves. Even so, it seems that coroners were generally expected to serve for an extended period of time, with few remaining in office for only a year or two. In the reign of Elizabeth, for instance, the 12 known Sussex county coroners spent, on average, nearly seven and a half years in office.[125] In the late seventeenth and early eighteenth centuries Sussex county coroners served for even greater lengths of time. The coroners for East Sussex averaged an impressive 22 years in office between 1689 and 1784.[126]

Some borough and liberty coroners also remained in office for numerous years. For example, Chester coroners between 1519 and 1761 averaged about four years in office each.[127] Liberty coroners often held onto their posts even longer, with coroners of the liberty of Lewes Rape in Sussex averaging almost five years in office in the Elizabethan period. The coroners of Elizabethan Hastings Rape, also in Sussex, maintained an even more impressive average of 12 years apiece, although this was partly the result of two long-serving coroners.[128] The relative longevity of county, borough, and liberty coroners was unusual for local officeholders in the early modern period (other than justices of the peace) and must have been at least in part a product of the serious and complicated nature of the job. Given the difficulty of the position, the extended tenure in office must also have had a positive impact on the efficacy of the coroner system, as many coroners were men of long experience.

Although county coroners were elected officials, it was not uncommon for successive generations of the same family to hold the post. Richard Lane, who was a county coroner in Sussex between 1578 and 1597, was succeeded as coroner by his son Thomas Lane, who served from 1597 to 1600. Thomas Lane was not the only son of Richard to become a coroner. In addition to serving as county coroner, Richard Lane also held the position of coroner for the liberty of Bamber Rape, Sussex, between 1592 and 1595, at which point the office was given to William Lane.[129] This practice of hereditary elected office was not unusual and seems eminently practical. As formal training was nonexistent, it is not surprising that the electors would select a man with both a familiar surname and a likely familiarity with the position. Borough and liberty coroners were even more likely to have some family connection to the position. William Playfere, coroner of the liberty of Hastings Rape between 1566 and 1595, was succeeded in that post by his son Samuel, who operated as coroner until 1603.[130] In a similar vein both John Alcock and his son—also named John—served as coroners of the borough of Prescott in Lancashire in the mid-seventeenth century.[131] In Chester, the surnames of the city's coroners repeat themselves over and over throughout the early modern period, with multiple generations of Goldbournes, Oultons, Maddocks, Bathoes, Massies, and Bingleys appearing as coroners. Given the oligarchic nature of urban society in the early modern period, one would expect such a repetition of surnames because a small number of families dominated the eligible pool of potential officeholders. In liberties the occasional instance of hereditary officeholding also makes some degree of sense when one considers that a personal relationship with the lord of the liberty was likely necessary for those who aspired to hold office.

The influence of politics and faction on the makeup of the county judiciary has long been known, with changes in government, especially from the late seventeenth century, resulting in purges from the bench of local party stalwarts.[132] The relationship between the coroner and politics, however, is less well known and, unfortunately, much less clear. It seems likely that the election of coroners—especially after the advent of political parties in the late seventeenth century—was influenced to some degree by wider ideological debates and contests between factions. Evidence of such election disputes is, however, exceedingly rare and the degree to which the election of coroners was affected by wider political struggles is murky, but electoral party politics likely did on occasion impinge on the election of coroners. As we have seen above in the Somerset coroner elections of the eighteenth century, local factions did coalesce around particular candidates for the office. While the influence of local factions and interests is indisputable, it is not clear whether these local factions were in any way tied to national factions or parties, nor is it clear whether the candidates felt themselves to be representatives of a particular national interest group. Although such national connections remain shrouded, it seems likely that, at least in the eighteenth century, party politics must have had some impact on the elections of county coroners.

If the election of coroners was sometimes influenced by the wider political context, once elected, coroners seem to have been more immune to changes in government than other county officials. Unlike justices of the peace, coroners were not removed from office upon the death of the monarch. Coroners were elected by the freeholders of the county and as such their status as conservators of the peace did not end with the death of the monarch. Justices of the peace, on the other hand, were appointed by commissions or letters patent from the monarch, making them *justiciarios suos* whose position was tied to an individual monarch.[133] Similarly, there is no evidence of purges of coroners following changes in government or faction after the introduction of parties. Even during the Civil Wars most coroners seem to have largely survived the purges of officeholders that occurred when territory changed hands. For instance, on October 1, 1646, following the siege of royalist Chester and its capture by the forces of Parliament, an order was given to remove many of the officers who had held positions in the government of the city while it remained loyal to Charles I. It was decreed that the mayor, both sheriffs, all 24 aldermen and 40 common councilmen were to be removed from office due to their suspect loyalty.[134] This was a common fate for cities and other areas that changed hands during the Civil Wars. The city's two coroners, however, seem to have escaped this systematic replacement of royalist officeholders with parliamentary men. As these men were appointed by the royalist government of Chester, this oversight appears rather strange, but it seems that most coroners who held office during this turbulent period in English history remained in office throughout the war or retired and were replaced of their own volition. This suggests that the duties and responsibilities of the coroner were seen as either apolitical or important enough to transcend matters of politics.

Even if most coroners were immune to the frequent political purges during the Civil Wars, once the victory of Parliament had been secured, some coroners did face removal from office. For example, in 1652 John Hoody of Northever in Somerset was elected as one of the two county coroners. Despite his victory, he did not remain in office for long. When the assizes met at Taunton in March of the same year it was "nowe alleged in court that hee [Hoody] was formerly in armes against the Parliament." As a result of this accusation the court found him "not fitt to execute the said office." He was not allowed to be "sworne for the execution of that office" and a new election was ordered.[135] The removal of a coroner for political allegiance was rare and seems to have been limited to a few cases in the immediate aftermath of the Civil Wars. Coroners remained insulated from factionalism even after the rise of adversarial party politics in the late seventeenth and eighteenth centuries, when justices of the peace and other officers became the regular targets of political purges.

It is dangerous to draw firm conclusions from what is admittedly incomplete evidence. However, it is interesting to speculate as to why coroners seem to have been insulated from the purges that beset other county officeholders when the political winds shifted. The most likely explanation for this relative immunity is that the importance of the coroner's role in the regulation of violence transcended party or faction. The detection, investigation, and punishment of illegitimate violence was a universal concern, a vital project of all governments and regimes. As such, maintaining a competent, well-established officer dedicated to policing violence was crucial. Justices of the peace could be replaced because their duties and responsibilities shifted with the priorities of the government or the faction in power. The duties of the coroner were both an unchanging and a consistent concern of every faction or party. It is interesting to consider that while other officeholders might change frequently with changes in favor or government, coroners—due to their long tenure in office and their insulation from political purges—perhaps provided a level of continuity unusual in county officers. It must have been comforting for those whose friends or relatives had died in suspicious or violent circumstances to know that while justices of the peace and lord lieutenants came and went, the investigation of untimely death was to some degree beyond the reach of party politics.

Payment and Remuneration

Like most local or county officeholders in early modern England, coroners were unsalaried amateurs. However, despite the fact that coroners were unsalaried, from 1487 they did receive a payment of 13s 4d for all inquests that returned a verdict of murder or manslaughter.[136] For instance, a London coroner was "payd . . . 13s 4d as his fee" in 1730 when an inquest found the deceased had been murdered.[137] Later that same year the coroner was less fortunate when an inquest returned a verdict of accidental death. As a local official noted, "the coroner bringing it an accidental death he had no fee by Law due to him; he grumbled, but went without it."[138] In practice, payments received from cases that led to homicide verdicts were far from significant. Over the nearly 30 years William Playfere operated as coroner he was eligible to receive fees in only 14 cases (11 percent of his total cases) for a total of a little over £9 (which is less than the fine he received in 1577).[139]

The situation had not improved a century or more later when John Neville operated as coroner of Lincolnshire. In fact, if one accounts for inflation the remuneration received by Neville was far less than the already paltry sum obtained by Playfere in the sixteenth century. Neville was eligible to receive the statutory 13s 4d fee in only eight of his 42 cases (or 19 percent) in the late seventeenth and early eighteenth centuries, a proportion similar to that of Playfere. On the whole, Neville thus received a total of only £5 5s 8d in the course of his long tenure in office.[140]

It was not until 1752 that new legislation made coroners eligible to receive fees in cases other than those resulting in a verdict of murder or manslaughter.[141] Instead of basing remuneration on the type of case, under the new laws coroners were to be paid £1 per inquest and an additional 9d per mile traveled in the commission of the inquest. The altering of the payment method was intended to encourage coroners to hold inquests on all types of cases and not just those that might lead to a fee. Additionally, the new system was intended to ensure that coroners would not avoid holding inquests in remote locations by paying them more for inquests that required more travel. Although the frequency with which such out-of-the-way or non–fee-granting inquests were avoided has been overstated by most historians, it is clear that this was of some concern to contemporary officials. As we will see, the practice of paying by the mile after 1752 had little impact on the honesty or efficiency of coroners. Coroners across the early modern period were more likely to be characterized by dedication and competence than by corruption and inefficiency. The change in payment structure did, however, clearly affect the amount of income that could be accrued by those in office.

While William Playfere made only £9 in almost 30 years in office in the late sixteenth century, and John Neville made only a little over £5 in his years as coroner, many of those who operated after 1752 made considerably more in fees. John Clare, coroner in Wiltshire, made over £19 between December 1752 and May 1753, another £18 between May and September 1753, £24 between October 1753 and April 1754, and a massive £34 6s 8d between May and October 1754. Over the course of his career as coroner, between 1752 and 1772—a tenure in office roughly the same as Playfere's or Neville's—Clare received a total of £1,089 5s 2d in fees.[142] Even when one accounts for inflation and the fact that Clare held a greater number of inquests than either Playfere or Neville, it is evident that the legislation of 1752 and the payment of coroners per mile rather than simply for inquests leading to homicide indictments had a tremendous impact on the amount of money that could be made from the office of coroner. Before 1752, the amount of money made in fees was probably not much greater than the expenses incurred in traveling to inquests. After 1752, a diligent coroner could make enough in fees to significantly supplement his income. Before 1752, the office of coroner was primarily desirable as a symbol of status in local society. After 1752, the office was of value not just for what it said about the influence or power of the holder, but also because it provided a steady and significant income.

The lack of salary may have contributed to the real or perceived corruption of early modern coroners. There is evidence that coroners of the period occasionally accepted bribes in exchange for specific verdicts and sometimes demanded payment before they would undertake an inquest at all.[143] As late as 1728 Sir John Gonson, in his charge to the quarter sessions grand jury of the city and liberty of Westminster, stressed that the jury members must enquire as to whether or not coroners performed their duties and "whether they or any other judicial officers are guilty of bribery by taking gifts or rewards to pervert justice, or are guilty of extortion, by taking fees where none are due or before they are due, or greater fees than by law are due to them."[144] Some coroners certainly attempted to collect fees beyond what was due to them, as happened in London in the eighteenth century. On November 4, 1734, "a Man whose name was Noel from the West Indies [and thus possibly a slave] being lunatic drowned himself in Tower ditch."[145] The lieutenant general of the Tower of London summoned a coroner to examine the body. The subsequent inquest found that the death was a suicide and thus the coroner should not have been eligible to receive a fee. Despite this, "the Coroner insisted on a fee of 13s 4d [the statutory amount in cases of homicide] but a prosecution being intended against him on the Stat. I of H8 [I Henry 8, c. 7], he returned the money and promised to insist on his fee when the Person came by his death without Murder no more."[146] While this individual coroner certainly attempted to secure a fee to which he was not legally entitled, it is clear that such behavior did not go unchallenged by those who knew the law. In this case, the threat of litigation alone was enough to ensure the return of the ill-gotten fee, and also to chastise the coroner into promising not to take undue fees again.

The level of malfeasance should not be overstated. Such corruption certainly existed in early modern England, and although the concern with corruption among coroners was real, it was not limited to coroners. Corruption was a major problem—or at least it was perceived to be—in most areas of the legal and administrative systems, and it would remain so throughout the early modern period.[147]

T. R. Forbes, for example, states that because the coroner was only able to receive payment in case of homicide, and even then only if the suspect had been seized and convicted, coroners were rarely interested in suicides, accidental deaths, and murders by unknown persons. As he writes, "This system naturally encouraged corruption and neglect: many homicides were not investigated at all, or at best perfunctorily."[148] This characterization, however, fails on at least two accounts. First, even a cursory look at the voluminous records produced by coroners will demonstrate the inaccuracy of the suggestion that all deaths but homicides by known perpetrators were neglected. The fact is that inquests into accidental deaths alone outnumber those relating to homicides by a factor of more than five to one. Second, such assessments show little understanding of the importance of local officeholding in early modern English society. Most local officeholders in early modern England were unpaid amateurs. Prestige, honor, and the communal obligation of restoring and maintaining the peace of the community could often be as important to these local officeholders as financial remuneration.[149] Thus, it is shortsighted and not a little condescending to suggest that lack of pay for local officers precluded dedication to the duties and responsibilities of local office.

Any state that hopes to maintain and enforce its monopoly of violence requires an officer dedicated to the regulation of that violence. Furthermore, effective control of violence necessitates that this officer be competent, efficient, and stable. As we have seen, on balance the early modern English coroner more than met these standards. The contested nature of coronial elections demonstrates that in an age when many local offices were losing their prestige, the office of the coroner remained a coveted and sought-after position, a fact that speaks to the continued power of the office. Likewise, the wide range of functions still performed by the coroner illustrates the office's continued centrality in both the judicial system and the apparatus of government more generally. The low turnover and relative insulation from the vagaries of faction and party politics also meant that the office of the coroner was one of the more stable aspects of county justice. Finally, despite the lack of regular pay, there is little evidence of widespread corruption or lassitude. Instead, the records suggest that most coroners were committed and competent. All of these characteristics indicate that given proper investigative powers and robust oversight, the early modern coroner was well placed to act as the primary agent of the monopolization of violence.

Socio-economic Status

Coroners, like local officers of any stripe, did not operate in a social vacuum. Rather, officers of the state were also members of communities, both derived from, and intricately intertwined with, the societies in which they operated. Given the interconnectedness of local officeholders and local society, it is imperative that any attempt to come to terms with an office and its functions also address the social and cultural backgrounds of those individuals who held office. If the men who filled the ranks of office were individuals with social existences inseparable from their communities of origin, they also acted in a distinctly formal capacity as officers of the crown. Because coroners remained embedded in English society, an understanding of their role as cogs in the machinery of state must take the office's proper social context into account.

As we have seen, statutes and contemporary guidebooks dictated that coroners were originally to be chosen from among the knights of the shire. According to one manual, "of ancient times this Office was of such estimation, that none should have it but a Knight" with at least "a hundred shillings rent of Freehold" because officers were supposed "to give grace to the place, and not the place (only) to grace the Officer."[150] By the sixteenth century, however, this statute had been modified so that all men were eligible "who have sufficient within the County to be responsible for all that doth or ought to do by his said office."[151] In his *Institutes of the Laws of*

England, Edward Coke expanded on this vague notion of qualification, adding that there were five properties required of those elected as coroners. According to Coke, a coroner was to be *"Probus Homo," "Legalis Homo,"* "Of sufficient understanding and knowledge," "Of good ability and power to execute his office according to his knowledge," and "Diligent in executing his office."[152]

For contemporaries, the reasons for requiring status qualifications were readily apparent. According to Greenwood, the common law required "men of sufficient ability and livelihood because, "the Law presumes that they will do their duty, and not offend the Law for fear of punishment, whereunto their lands and goods be subject," so that "they might execute their office without bribery" and so that "they be able to answer to the King all such fines and duties as appertain to him."[153] In other words, the early modern coroner had to be a man of some means in order to prevent the possibility of bribery, to allow the officer to afford the expenses incurred for travel and accommodation, and to make sure that any fines which the county owed to the crown could be paid by the coroner, who would then seek reimbursement from the county.

A blinkered focus on the theoretical changes to the status qualifications of early modern coroners has led a number of historians to focus on the decline in the prestige of the office to the point that the potential commitment, capacity, and rectitude of coroners are summarily dismissed.[154] Though maddeningly vague to the historian, the official qualifications stipulated by common law for coroners were treated quite seriously by contemporaries. For instance, shortly after he was elected coroner for the county of Kent, William Herlizon was amerced for the sum of 40s for sending a false return to King's Bench. Herlizon could not afford to pay the fine and so was removed from office by a Chancery writ secured by the sheriff.[155] In short, the freeholders of Kent had legally elected Herlizon as one of the coroners for the county; however, when his lack of financial wherewithal meant that he could not afford the costs of the office, county officials wasted no time in removing him from office. In a world of amateur officeholding in which status was seen as the only insulation from corruption and influence, the fact that the qualifications of coroners were taken seriously suggests that the office was seen as too important to risk its degradation by unqualified men.

Quick as the authorities were to remove from office those who did not have the financial wherewithal to perform the required duties, the inexactitude of the qualifications did allow for considerable discretion in selecting officeholders. While the specific property qualifications of the medieval statutes were abandoned, the vague early modern qualifications allowed county electors and officials to select coroners from a range of backgrounds. Some men in the period attempted to avoid service as local or county officers. As a consequence, the flexibility in selection criteria allowed by the early modern regulations broadened the pool of potential officeholders while maintaining the standards for those chosen to serve.

Status, Literacy, and Education

Although a complete examination of the socio-economic background of the early modern coroner is impractical—both because of the number of coroners involved and because of the lack of surviving records pertaining to their personal as opposed to official lives—there are a few methods of gleaning some basic information about the general status of early modern coroners. It is important to note the status or occupation given to coroners in the inquest and deposition records. Most nonurban coroners were listed in the records as "gentlemen." Of the 39 men who acted as coroners in Sussex during William Playfere's tenure in office, 77 percent were either listed as gentleman or were mayors of Rye or Winchelsea, who held the office of coroner for their borough ex officio.[156] This was not simply a courtesy title, as a fair number of coroners were not referred to as such and instead were given either a superior title, such as esquire, or no title at all. The term "gentleman" was somewhat nebulous in the period, but broadly speaking an early modern gentleman was among the roughly 2 percent of the population who had landed wealth sufficient to allow a degree of leisure and consumption unavailable to the masses.[157] In practice, the wealth of a gentleman ranged from around £200 per annum to more than £10,000, to take the example of mid-seventeenth-century Kent, with landholdings

likely ranging from 50,000 to 20,000 acres.[158] Given that most coroners
were styled gentlemen in the records, it seems reasonable to conclude that
the average coroner was a local landowner of some substance who did not
follow a trade, but instead lived on the income of his land, likely in the form
of rents. While most coroners could not aspire to the ranks of the nobility,
it is clear that some, such as those styled "esquire," were in fact members
of a more elevated status group.[159] However, coroners were more likely to
be members of the lesser or parish gentry—higher in status than those who
filled the ranks of local office as constables or churchwardens, but of generally lower status than those who held county offices such as sheriff, sat on
the county bench, or acted as deputy lord lieutenants.

The second clue to the general status of early modern coroners to be
gleaned from the official records is the ubiquity of signatures. David Cressy
has argued convincingly that given the structure of early modern education, the ability to sign one's name is most likely evidence of literacy.[160]
According to Cressy's estimates, between 1580 and 1700 male signature
literacy ranged from 97 to 100 percent for members of the gentry and the
professions, from 51 to 73 percent for yeomen, from 53 to 72 percent for
craftsmen, from 21 to 27 percent for husbandmen, and from 15 to 22 percent
for laborers. Overall, roughly 20 percent of males were literate in the sixteenth century, a figure that rose to about 60 percent by the mid-eighteenth
century.[161] The records of coroners' inquests and depositions show that
practically every coroner who held office in the period was literate. I have
found no instances of a coroner signing a document with a mark rather than
a signature. Although the ability to sign is not a precise measure of either
education or status, it is clear that all early modern coroners were literate
and thus members of the upper twentieth to sixtieth percentile of the population in terms of educational achievement. This does not tell us much, but
it does suggest that at a bare minimum, coroners were of sufficient status to
warrant an investment in education.

The level of general educational attainment of the average coroner is
impossible to know, but the possessions of some individual coroners may
provide some insight into the reading habits of the men who held that office. Among the papers of John Neville, a prolific Lincolnshire coroner of

the late seventeenth century, is a list of items that seems to be an inventory of Neville's own possessions. If so, the inventory's contents allow a rare glimpse of the types of books an early modern coroner kept. Among the sundry entries relating to linens, bedclothes, and other common household items, the inventory lists a number of printed works including "Casors fables, an embassy from the Hollanders to China; Heraldry; Mathematical writings by R.S.; 2 pedigrees . . . a Few joyners books; 2 papper books; 2 gumwork landsckips . . . the Turkish History; 2 great bibles, bishop Sandersons sermons; the writings of fanshaw."[162] This list only relates to those books found in Neville's "long chest," and it is likely that a complete inventory of the coroner's possessions would reveal a larger collection of books. Still, we can surmise something of Neville's education and interests. The subjects of Neville's library are not at all surprising. Like most contemporaries of his social standing, he was interested in genealogy, history, foreign affairs, religion, and mathematics, the building blocks of the broad classical education typical of the county gentry.[163]

Training

That coroners were literate men from among the upper levels of local society is clear. How they were trained or acquired the knowledge necessary to perform their duties, however, is a murky subject. Like most local officials, coroners were amateurs, and as such there was no requirement or expectation that they possess any legal or medical knowledge or training. This lack of required training, however, does not mean that all coroners were without legal experience. As one might suspect, many coroners did have legal training of some sort, and a number were practicing attorneys as well as coroners. We know from a letter written on behalf of a Mr. Richard Holmes of Burpham, Norfolk, requesting his selection for the county bench that Holmes was both an active attorney who held "several of his grace of Norfolk's courts" and a coroner.[164] Whether his service as coroner disqualified him from the county judiciary was questioned—Holmes wanted to remain coroner in addition to becoming justice of the peace—but it was decided that "the office of coroner is no Disqualification to the Commission of the

Peace."[165] Holmes was far from unusual in combining legal training and service as coroner. It is difficult to know just how many coroners shared a similar background, but given the segment of society from which most coroners came, and the fact that as the coronership was an elected office — and one often held for many years — those standing for election were likely to have some affinity for the position, many coroners likely had more legal knowledge than was required by law.

For those with formal legal training and those without, it would have been necessary to acquire a more complete understanding of the duties of a coroner as well as the procedures and record keeping involved. The mere fact that the thousands of coroners' inquests and depositions written across the country and across the period have a uniform style and substance suggests that those who wrote the documents had some form of training and some knowledge of proper procedure and record keeping. Undoubtedly some of this was accomplished through the auspices of assize justices and King's Bench, the mandated final repository of all coroners' inquests. As we will see in a later chapter, both courts — and particularly King's Bench — frequently summoned or fined coroners for defects in their inquests. These proceedings against coroners were almost always dropped when the inquest was altered to the satisfaction of the court in question. To take but one example among many, in 1591 Magnus Fowle, one of the county coroners for Sussex, delivered an inquest to the Lent Assize. The inquest informed the court that in July 1590 two "saylers," John Treyfote and another whose name was unknown, had feloniously killed one Gawen Eloquens at Newhaven. Not long after submitting his inquest to the assize, Fowle was summoned to King's Bench to answer for defects in the same inquest. Fowle amended the inquest, adding the place of residence of the deceased and informing the court that the accused had not fled. With these additions interlined, the process against Fowle ceased.[166] Such a high degree of oversight of the form of legal documents must have encouraged coroners to follow proper procedure when drawing up their records and in this way provided a measure of uniform education for coroners throughout the realm.

There were, however, a number of other ways this informal training was accomplished in the early modern period. Many of those individuals who became coroners had some other prior experience with office-holding. David Dymock (also spelled Dymmoche) served as coroner of Chester between 1610 and 1616. Prior to his tenure as coroner, however, Dymock had served as a common councilor in 1574 and as sheriff in 1575.[167] He also was appointed to command and train a body of 100 soldiers provided by the city in 1590 and finally became an alderman in 1594, all before becoming coroner 16 years later.[168] Thus, by the time Dymock became coroner he had been entrusted with a variety of civic offices, including others with criminal justice functions, over a period of nearly 40 years. While he may have been new to the office of coroner, Dymock was hardly a man without experience of governance or the law. His background was not at all unusual, and in Chester and other places, both urban and rural, there seems to have been a ladder of office that at once reflected the varying levels of prestige accorded to each office and ensured that those who held the most vital or difficult offices had some general level of experience.

This hierarchy of prestige and experience was maintained in Chester through a system of fines that were imposed on those who attempted to hold offices out of order, thus skipping rungs on the ladder of office. In 1587 one man was fined for being chosen sheriff before he had served as "leevelooker," a municipal inspector of markets. Similarly, in 1648 it was stipulated that anyone who became alderman without serving as sheriff first was to be fined £40, a significant sum.[169] While the exact hierarchy of office-holding in Chester is never made explicit, the fees charged to various officers for the maintenance of the city walls gives some sense of the ladder of office. In 1644, the greatest fees were paid by justices of the peace, followed by sheriffs and aldermen, followed by sheriff peers, councilmen, and ordinary citizens.[170] While coroners are not mentioned in this list, combining the evidence of the maintenance fees with the biographical information on various officeholders reveals the coroner's fairly exalted place in the hierarchy of civic government. William Wilson, David Dymock, and the majority of those coroners for whom the relevant information is available became coroners late in their careers, after having served as councilors, sheriffs, aldermen, and serjeants. This suggests that the office of coroner was held in high esteem, or at least that the office's nature required that its holder be a man of great experience in public office.

Other coroners followed in the footsteps of their fathers or other relatives when they became coroners. The practice of multiple generations of the same family acting as coroners was quite common and must have meant that those coroners who served as part of a family tradition had some level of familiarity with the office, as well as a convenient source of practical advice near to hand. Samuel Playfere, coroner of Hastings Rape in Sussex, became coroner in 1595 after his father's retirement from the office. William Playfere had operated as coroner since 1566 and thus was likely to have been coroner for the greater portion of Samuel's life.[171] Although there is as yet no evidence of Samuel accompanying his father in the course of his duties, it is unlikely that William could serve as coroner for 30 years without imparting to his son some knowledge about the office, especially given that Samuel was to succeed him as coroner.

Once in office, many coroners clearly operated in tandem with another coroner from their jurisdiction. As we have seen, it was the policy of Chester to stagger the appointment of their two coroners so as to ensure that each new coroner had the benefit of working with, and learning from, a coroner who had already been in office for some time. This practice was clearly intended to provide an officeholding apprenticeship of sorts, a means of training amateur officials in the intricacies of a complex legal post.

Although there is no evidence that this policy of staggering officeholders was officially replicated for county coroners, in practice these coroners did occasionally work in tandem. Since each county had at least two coroners, and the likelihood of both coroners retiring from office at the same time was slim, it seems reasonable to assume that some newly elected coroners sought out the advice and instruction of their more experienced peers. This method of training was widespread in the early modern world and was not limited to the unofficial instruction of legal officers. Seventeenth-century soldiers, like legal officers, had little in the way of formal training, but were instead instructed through a combination of theoretical manuals and what Charles Carlton calls "practical apprenticeship."[172] This entailed interspersing raw recruits with grizzled veterans as a means of getting the novice soldiers up to speed. As the earl of Essex noted in the prelude to the expedition against Cadiz in 1596, "I do mingle the old soldiers and the new that one may help discipline the other."[173] In a society oriented around amateurs, such practical apprenticeships were crucial for training nonprofessionals to carry out a variety of offices and positions for which they had no experience or formal instruction.

Those coroners who did not have the luck to be able to learn the ropes from a more experienced colleague or from their fathers could instead turn to the multiplicity of guidebooks available in the period that informed amateur officeholders about the parameters of the office and its duties and responsibilities.[174] Officeholding manuals were fairly common from the beginning of the early modern period and exploded in popularity with the concomitant growth of printing, print culture, and literacy in the sixteenth and seventeenth centuries.[175] As early as 1514 John Rastell, who had served as coroner of Coventry from 1507–1509, published general guides to officeholding and the law that included descriptions of the duties of coroners. Rastell, who after serving in various legal capacities in Coventry had set himself up as a printer in London, also published the legal treatises of Anthony Fitzherbert—the former recorder of Coventry—which also included material on coroners and other officers.[176] To these early manuals were added such manuals as the legal treatises of Edward Coke in the early seventeenth century and the guides for county officeholders of Michael Dalton and Nicholas Collyn in the mid-seventeenth century, all of which appeared in numerous editions throughout the period.[177]

Perhaps the most comprehensive guide for the curious or inexperienced coroner was that produced by William Greenwood in 1659, *Bouleuterion or A Practical Demonstration of County Judicatures*.[178] Greenwood's manual, like many other officeholding guides, not only outlined the duties and responsibilities of the county, liberty, and borough coroner, but also provided examples of summons and writs that a coroner would be responsible for drafting and issuing in the course of his duties. The examples given in such manuals were often extensive and specific, designed to cover almost any topic that might arise in the course of a coroner's duties. Greenwood's list of sample writs ranges from such run-of-the-mill issues as "an Inquisition of Murder" and "An Appeal of Mayhem" to such esoteric topics as "An Inquisition for Man-slaughter, where one was Starved, and perished for want of sustenance" and "Inquisition where one is slain by misfortune by a Cart loaden with Hay."[179]

In addition to samples of writs, Greenwood provided a step-by-step outline of the procedure of an inquest from summons and jury selection to binding over witnesses and returning verdicts.[180] The required steps were laid out in straightforward language that must have been easy to follow for all those with even basic literacy. One can imagine coroners of the period reading out the steps word for word, copying model documents, and inserting the names of the deceased, jurors, witnesses, and suspects in the places indicated by italics in the manual. If a newly elected coroner followed Greenwood's guide in this manner he would read as follows: "When you come to the place of appointment call the Bailiff, Constable etc. to make a return of their Warrant. Then command one to make three Proclamations, calling the jury after this manner. 'You shall diligently enquire and true presentment make . . . how and in what manner *A.B.* lying dead came to his death.'"[181] If it was necessary to bind over a witness to ensure appearance in court, the recognizance was to be written thus: "The two and twentieth day of *May* in the year etc. *A.B.* of *C.* in the foresaid county acknowledges himself to owe and be indebted, etc. under condition etc. That if the said *A.B.* do personally appear before the Justices . . . at the next Assize to be holden at the Castle of *Y* for the said County and then and there deliver and set forth his knowledge touching the death of *E.F.* . . . then the present Recognizance to be void."[182] With a guidebook in hand, even a novice coroner would know exactly what to do, say, and write simply by following along in his manual and inserting the relevant names, places, and dates in the places indicated by the author.

The examples of Latin writs may well have been intended to provide those ignorant or uncertain of the language with a word-for-word formula for each type of writ a coroner might conceivably need to issue. If this is true, as seems likely, good knowledge of Latin would not have been a prerequisite of the office, meaning that a wider range of individuals could potentially operate effectively as coroners, despite having no formal training in the law. By the early seventeenth century, when such officeholding manuals became widely available, the training of coroners and other officials was in large part a matter of self-education through the use of such guides as Greenwood's *Bouleuterion*.

From the perspective of the state, the ready availability of guidebooks, templates, and other officeholding aids was crucially important. These materials helped to ensure a level of standardization and uniformity of practice and record keeping not available before the growth of print in the sixteenth century. Standard forms of conduct, investigation, procedure, and records in turn drastically improved the central authorities' ability to monitor the activities of local officeholders and ensure their proper functioning. As we will see, records were the lifeblood of the oversight of the coroner system, and the need for uniformity in record production greatly improved the ability of the courts in Westminster to assess and control the monopolization of violence. Because such standardization of training and practice was difficult before the print revolution, the effort to regulate violence only became possible in the early modern period.

Even those coroners who did not rely on the knowledge provided by guidebooks or more experienced coroners likely had other resources to draw on when performing their duties. It was common in the period for coroners to be accompanied by a clerk or recorder when carrying out an inquest. These local officials — and especially recorders, who were generally the chief legal advisors to urban administrations — were usually lawyers, often had a fairly sophisticated knowledge of the law and legal procedure, and could be relied upon to both draft legal documents and provide legal advice to novice coroners.[183] William Wilson, variously coroner and sheriff of Chester between 1652 and 1662, was at one point charged by the government of the city for not paying the recorder of the city the customary fee for his advice.[184] This important case illustrates the fact that coroners and other local officials could counteract their lack of official training or knowledge of the law by seeking out other local officials who possessed more legal expertise.[185]

Because of their comparatively long tenure, coroners were well placed to acquire the skills and knowledge necessary to effectively perform the tasks required of them. While constables and other local officials often rotated out of office on an annual basis, coroners usually held their positions for years and even decades at a time, a situation that must have given those elected or selected as coroners the time necessary to familiarize themselves with the intricacies of their office. Given the importance of the office and the complicated nature of its duties, the length of tenure of most coroners is unlikely to be a coincidence. Although it must have taken time and inclination to master the ins and outs of the position, early modern coroners, while not formally trained, did have the resources necessary to acquire something approaching professional expertise in matters relating to death and criminal investigation.

Popular Attitudes toward Coroners and the Coroner System

The bumbling amateur judicial official was a common comic trope in the early modern period. Night watchmen, constables, and lawyers are depicted as lazy, decrepit, incompetent, and corrupt, a veritable plague of Dogberrys. From Shakespeare to Hogarth to Gillray, lesser legal officials were subject to ridicule and revulsion in every conceivable form of popular culture and at every point from the dawn of the sixteenth century through the nineteenth. Such caricatures of petty officialdom, however, sometimes tell us more about comedic tastes and traditions than the reality of governmental competence, as many modern historians have been at pains to suggest.[186] It has become clear that cultural depictions of constables and others often misrepresented the dedication and competence such officers showed in practice. And yet, in a justice system that was largely staffed by amateurs and necessitated private involvement in the legal process, popular perceptions of and confidence in the system was vital to its proper functioning. If the outward image of constables and night watchmen was one of incompetence, what of popular perceptions of coroners and the coroner system?

If a crucial aspect of the monopolization of violence is popular acceptance of the state's right to define, adjudicate, and punish violence, then such acceptance must be won either by force or by the general belief that the system itself functions with efficiency and competence. In an era before opinion polls, it is difficult to surmise what the populace at large thought of the coroner system. However, an investigation of popular literature and print media reveals that, on the whole, coroners were viewed as competent and professional rather than bumbling and corrupt, a far cry from the depictions of other early modern officeholders.

The court records of the period indicate that corruption, or at least accusations of corruption, did exist. This is to be expected in light of the national character of the coroner system and the longue durée of this study. What is remarkable, however, is the relative paucity of such complaints. As will be detailed in Chapter 5, not only was the number of accusations against coroners low, but it was most likely to involve relatively minor improprieties. For example, it is rare indeed to find accusations that the coroner failed to hold an inquest or accepted a bribe to influence the verdict. When accusations of malfeasance do occur, they are most likely to involve the acceptance of payment for inquests that were not legally eligible for such remuneration—those relating to a natural or accidental death. In these instances, the illicit payment resulted from confusion over the law as often as from mendacious money grubbing. In addition, even small infractions and inaccuracies regularly brought fines from the central courts, a fact that surely provided a disincentive to potentially corrupt coroners.

It is, of course, possible that corruption and incompetence simply fell through the cracks of the legal system or that the records of such accusations failed to be recorded. If, however, surviving official documentation does not accord with the reality of public sentiment, then we should be able to hear the echoes of popular discontent reverberating in the voluminous print literature of the period. Depictions of officeholders in newspapers and literature abound, most of them comically negative or critical. Representations of coroners are likewise legion. An examination of seventeenth- and eighteenth-century British newspapers reveals that coroners are referenced on over 5,000 occasions between 1600 and 1750. Most of the references relate to deaths and their investigation—the every-day work of the coroner—or to the election of new coroners.[187] Yet in these thousands of reports of investigations, few if any question the coroner's actions or probity or the inquest process or verdict. In fact, it is much more likely for the coroner to be portrayed in a positive light, characterized by competence rather than corruption. To take but one example of many, on April 18, 1747, the newspaper *Old England or the Broadbottom Journal* reported on the death of John Franklin in Oxford. According to the paper, Franklin, a scout at Christ Church College, was found early on the morn-ing of April 4 in "the Quadrangles of the said College, in most deplorable Condition having several Marks of Violence upon his Body." The coro-ner was called and an inquest convened. After considering the evidence, and "maturely weighing the Matter," the jury brought a verdict of willful murder. The key characterization of the coroner process in this instance is maturity. The author of the report was unlikely to have been present at the inquest, so the attribution of maturity to the inquest process was probably a consequence of the author's general opinion of coroners and the coroner process. Without having witnessed the event, the writer simply assumed that the coroner had behaved professionally and the inquest was maturely handled. Such an assumption, and many others like it, suggests that the popular perception of the coroner process was one of competence. Lest we worry that the writer was simply hesitant to negatively editorialize, the author suggested that the cause of death was a result of the "barbarous Pas-time of some young Debauchees."[188]

References to coroners and inquests in early modern print literature follow patterns similar to those of newspapers. In general, such materials mention coroners either as part of the criminal investigatory process or in officeholding manuals. As with the newspaper accounts, the most common depiction of coroners in popular literature is simply as judicial officers performing their duties. Editorial commentary in reference to coroners is rare, and where it does exist is more likely to be positive than negative in character.[189] One might be tempted to suggest that these mundane, businesslike depictions tell us nothing about popular perceptions of the coroner system. However, the very lack of negative commentary illuminates much about attitudes toward coroners. Given the nasty, fractious, and deeply critical nature of seventeenth-and eighteenth-century print culture, the fact that coroners are almost universally depicted as officials performing routine tasks suggests that both writers and readers accepted the image of coroners as competent and trustworthy. A contemporary literature that regularly portrayed lawyers as grasping, constables as bumbling, and watchmen as incompetent portrayed coroners as none of these things, and instead provided an image of a bland and steady official. In both newspapers and print literature, coroners were never stock characters of comic derision, nor were they targets of popular outrage or animus. Printed accounts of coroners were usually dry and laconic because authors and audiences alike expected from coroners not corruption or incompetence but boring regularity. Thus, coroners were not objects of popular ridicule because such ridicule did not accord with popular perceptions. Even in the nineteenth century, when the public nature of the inquest was taken up as a cause célèbre by radical reformers, the target of criticism was not coronial corruption, but rather government suppression of the vaunted inquest process.[190] Many aspects of early modern justice and governance were subject to criticism and complaint, but the coroner system did not number among them. If the English state was to secure a monopoly of violence, this popular acceptance of the competence and efficacy of the coroner system was vital in ensuring a necessary level of compliance with the state-mandated process of investigation, adjudication, and punishment of violent death.

The impression of competence derived from the printed materials of the period suggests that the status and training of the early modern coroner helped to create a government official who inspired confidence rather than derision. This combination of elevated status, uniform training, standardized procedures, and public confidence was vital to both the coroner's ability to operate effectively and the state's ability to monitor the activities of its agents. Without these attributes, the coroner would be denied important local information and assistance, and without standardized records, the authorities would be blind to the actions of its officials. In the early modern period these crucial criteria coalesced in a way that made the control of violence a real possibility for the first time.

THREE

Proving the Case

ANY STUDY OF A STATE'S ATTEMPTS TO establish and enforce a monopoly of violence must address the fundamental question of whether or not the officeholder responsible for the detection of illegitimate violence generally operated effectively and efficiently, and whether or not corruption, negligence, and incompetence reigned supreme. The questions we must ask, then, are: Were coroners, as amateur officeholders, sufficiently trained and otherwise equipped to adequately and satisfactorily investigate and resolve cases of suspicious or violent death? And did coroners have the tools and techniques necessary to carry out their duties competently? To answer these questions we must turn to a discussion of early modern methods of criminal investigation and the value of forensic medicine for the detection of lethal violence.

Most treatments of investigation and detection in the pre-modern world focus unduly on the development of forensic medicine as a prerequisite to effective criminal justice. With some minor variations, the traditional historiography suggests that in the benighted age before the late eighteenth and early nineteenth centuries, when the errors of Galen still reigned supreme, medical experts, such as they were, were rarely sought for their expertise in criminal investigation or for their testimony at criminal trials. On the rare occasions when medical expertise was sought during investigation or trial, so the story goes, the lack of accurate medical knowledge and sophisticated techniques meant that such testimony and evidence were usually of little use for policing or criminal investigation. Given the limits of medical knowledge and the inaccuracy of forensic medicine, it is argued, effective policing and criminal investigation were impossible before the modern age.

The traditional medical modernization narrative outlined above has its roots not only in traditional Whig-liberal views of the past, but also in the cultural concerns, interests, and misunderstandings of the present day. The modern obsession with forensic medicine, made obvious by the panoply of medico-legal dramas available in contemporary literature, film, and especially television, has led to a distorted view of its importance. Recently, it has been suggested that this cultural interest in forensics has altered the way people perceive detection and criminal investigation, which in turn has had an impact on the expectations of jurors and the outcomes of trials. The so-called "CSI effect" hypothesizes that the popular and widespread consumption of fictional portrayals of crime labs and forensic investigators has led potential jurors to have "unrealistic expectations about the type of evidence typically available during trials, which, in turn, increases the likelihood that they will have a 'reasonable doubt' about a defendant's guilt."[1] In a similar manner, the modern perception of forensic science as infallible and therefore crucial for the effective operation of criminal justice has in turn altered our interpretation of the rise of forensic medicine, its importance in criminal investigation, and its impact on policing in the past. There seems to be a substantial industry devoted to books whose titles proclaim "the birth of modern forensics" or some variation thereof. By focusing on celebrated cases and celebrity trials that in many cases did rely on forensic evidence, new forensic techniques, and medical testimony, historians have missed the forest for the trees.

By examining coroners' inquests and the depositions taken by coroners it is possible to rectify the inaccurate view of early modern forensic medicine and the related misunderstanding of early modern criminal investigation and detection.[2] Doing so will demonstrate that when the focus is shifted from what medical experts knew or believed (based on their formal training and learned medical treatises) to what they actually did in the context of criminal proceedings, our view of their potential efficacy changes.[3] When the evidence is weighed, it becomes clear that in the early modern period the effective regulation of interpersonal violence did not rely on forensic medical techniques. Instead, then as now, a combination of local knowledge, communal engagement, and witness testimony was the key to effective detection and criminal investigation.

As will be demonstrated, relative forensic capability is not in fact a useful criterion for assessing the effectiveness of a criminal justice system. We cannot dismiss the capacity of the early modern state to control violence based on a backward-looking consideration of relative scientific sophistication. Because forensic ability is not an adequate tool for determining the success or failure of a legal system, and because forensic medicine is not a deus ex machina for effective criminal investigation, the competence, capability, and energy of the coroner become paramount for the working of the early modern criminal justice system. Thus, the monopoly of violence rests not on medical capacity, but on the abilities of local officials. When early modern detection and investigation are considered in this context, it becomes readily apparent that the English criminal justice system possessed the techniques and methods necessary to enforce a monopoly of violence on the ground level from at least the beginning of the sixteenth century. Central to the effective use of these traditional tools of law enforcement—witness testimony and communal knowledge—was the local officeholder, and no local official was more important for the maintenance of criminal justice and the regulation of interpersonal violence through these methods than the coroner.

Narratives of Policing and Forensic Medicine

Traditional accounts of the office of the coroner and the investigation of sudden or suspicious death in the early modern period, with few exceptions, suffer from a condescending view of the medical knowledge of the past as well as teleological view of scientific progress that negates the possibility of any accurate investigation of death before the advancements of forensic scientific and medical knowledge in the long nineteenth century. Typical of this line of thought, J. D. J. Havard argues that "throughout this period the investigation of sudden death was almost entirely unencumbered by the evidence of medical men, and the verdicts were arrived at by a process of guesswork."[4] This belief has led Havard to argue that the early modern coroner system both facilitated and invited "the concealment of murder."[5] Another oft-cited authority on the development of forensic and legal medicine, T. R. Forbes, has much the same opinion as that of Havard. According to Forbes, there were few advances in forensic medicine between the Middle Ages and 1836, and the coroner, as an amateur official with no legal or medical qualifications, had infrequent recourse to autopsies and expert medical witnesses.[6] Such insights have led David Paul to conclude that the early modern period, and indeed the period between the Middle Ages and 1829, represented the "nadir of the coroners' system in England."[7]

More recently, scholars of crime and legal medicine have been a bit more nuanced in their treatment of the coroners' system and the use of forensic medicine. However, while some recent works have disputed the level of sophistication of early modern medico-legal knowledge or argued that recourse to such knowledge in the criminal justice system was more routine at an earlier date than previously believed, most scholars assume that effective detection and accurate investigations into suspicious death were only possible after the regular adoption and use of modern forensic medical techniques.[8] For instance, in his treatment of homicide, Malcolm Gaskill contends that before the eighteenth-century investigations, inquest and trials relating to death or murder were primarily concerned with symbolic expressions of community opinion; in this reading, facts confirmed and conformed to previously held communal notions of right and wrong, guilt and innocence. In the late seventeenth and early eighteenth centuries, according to Gaskill, these symbolic and providential types of testimony gradually began to be ignored or discredited by legal officials and medical reports, and evidence was given more weight; facts now determined verdicts rather than confirming verdicts that had already been reached.[9] Although Gaskill concedes that this shift was gradual and uneven, he contends that "formal and semi-formal agencies" of prosecution and policing were slow to fill the void left by providence. Despite his nuanced account of changing mentalities, Gaskill still concludes, like Havard and Forbes before him, that because coroners remained untrained amateurs and "were only usually summoned when the signs of death were manifestly violent, the skillfully performed murder was easier to get away with than perhaps historians have realized. Even if coroners had investigated every suspicious death, primitive forensic techniques meant that cause of death was likely to remain a mystery anyway."[10]

While it is true that medical evidence was increasingly sought and used from at least the late seventeenth century, Gaskill's characterization of the pre-eighteenth-century period is flawed. First, Gaskill overstates the number of references to providence, magical methods of discovery, and bleedings of corpses in the period before 1700. An examination of close to 500 coroners' depositions has found very few instances of these methods being used or pursued, and thus it seems clear that cases which involved these phenomena were the exception rather than the rule.[11] Second, even if the pre-1700 period did witness the frequent resort to providence and magical methods of discovery of guilt, this rhetoric of providence does not preclude proactive investigation or the consideration of more objective "facts."

Recent studies have also shown that modern juries frequently use scientific evidence in the same way Gaskill argues that pre-1700 jurors used providence, bleeding of corpses, and so on. These studies demonstrate that jurors often accept or dismiss scientific or medical evidence based not on its validity, but rather on whether it helps to confirm and rationalize decisions about innocence and guilt that they already have. One such study has argued that "it is also possible that the portrayal of science as the ultimate crime-fighting tool actually encourages the pre-existing over belief in the value of the flawed scientific findings that jurors confront in actual trials. People are already motivated to find ways to legitimate or justify their desire to convict. Science provides one way to do so, causing people to see within scientific evidence the level of certainty that makes them comfortable with a guilty verdict. Here, it is the credibility of science that is crucial, because jurors seek a form of justification that is plausible and compelling to bolster their own desire for certainty."[12] It seems unlikely, therefore, that modern trials, court cases, and criminal investigations are in reality significantly more a matter of the "trial of fact" than their early modern counterparts. Rather than a shift from a reliance on providence to a reliance on science and facts, the early modern period was one in which a veneer of medical expertise was added to the effective traditional methods of policing long available to English coroners and jurors, an integration of scientific and communal forms of knowledge rather than a transition from traditional to modern.

Coroners' Depositions and Their Evidence

The analysis below is derived from the examination of roughly 500 depositions collected from the Northern Assize Circuit, Lincolnshire, and the palatinate of Lancashire between 1640 and 1750.[13] These depositions consist of the witness statements taken by coroners in the course of their inquests. On some occasions justices of the peace took depositions in cases of sudden death, either in conjunction with the coroner or independently. These depositions have been excluded from the present study. An initial overview of these depositions provides a sense of the type of evidence contained within early modern coroners' depositions, as well as illuminating the process of investigating death in early modern England.

The approximately 500 coroners' depositions correspond to 131 cases of sudden or suspicious death that were investigated by coroners in the fulfillment of their duties between 1640 and 1750. Thus, on average, each case contained 3.78 depositions.[14] In terms of gender, 64 percent of deponents were men and 36 percent were women. Of the roughly 40 percent of men whose occupations were given, 8 percent were listed as laborers18 percent as husbandmen, 9 percent as yeomen, 38 percent as tradesmen or artisans, 5 percent as servants, 8 percent as gentlemen, 5 percent as nonmedical professionals, and 9 percent as innkeepers.[15] Women employed to lay out the bodies of the deceased for burial were deposed on seven occasions, while 24 women were interviewed as expert witnesses in cases of suspected infanticide.[16] Perhaps surprisingly, constables were called to depose in only eight cases in the sample period. Given that the ages of deponents are rarely given — only in about 10 percent of cases — little can be gleaned about patterns of age. However, it does seem that the ages of deponents were more likely to be given when the deponent was a minor. If this was indeed the case, then we can have at least a rough estimate of the number of minors who gave depositions. Such an estimate reveals that only about 3 percent of all deponents were 20 years old or younger.[17]

What can we conclude for an examination of early modern coroners' depositions as a whole? It is clear that each inquest involved a relatively high amount of communal participation, given that, on average, about four people gave evidence at each coroner's inquest. It seems from the evidence at hand that the social composition of deponents largely conformed to contemporary ideas about hierarchies of status, age, and gender. The evidence of laborers was less likely to be sought than that of the more substantial inhabitants of the community. Similarly, women were far less likely than men to give evidence at coroners' inquests, unless the inquest related to a case of suspected infanticide. Finally, it seems that the evidence of minors was less often sought than that of adults of either sex.[18] Although evidence was sought from whoever had it, it is clear that traditional hierarchies based on status and gender, authority, and credibility had some influence on what evidence was thought worthy of recording.

The Limits of Forensic Medicine for Criminal Investigation

The general level of competence and increased demand for medical testimony in the seventeenth and eighteenth centuries, combined with modern preoccupations with the importance of forensics, might lead one to conclude that medical testimony, such as that outlined above, was crucial for effective policing in early modern England. In other words, the provision of medical evidence would make the satisfactory resolution of a coroner's inquest more likely. As intuitive as such a conclusion may seem, however, when one examines the coroners' depositions that involved medical testimony and compares them with those inquests which, for whatever reason, did not make use of medical evidence, it is clear that the actual impact of forensic medicine in the early modern period was negligible. It is important to reiterate that the unimportance of medical evidence in the early modern period was not necessarily a result of incompetent medical practitioners;

indeed, the medical knowledge and abilities of most doctors and surgeons throughout England were sufficient to properly handle the vast majority of cases of unexplained death encountered by coroners. Instead, the lack of impact of forensic medicine on the outcome of coroners' inquests in the period was a result of the fact that, just as in modern criminal investigation, a significant majority of cases were untimely solved or concluded by such nonforensic means as witness testimony.

On May 9, 1695, Edward Darbishire, one of the county coroners for the palatinate of Lancashire, was called to the house of John Hollinhurst in Tarleton to view the body of his wife, Margret, who had recently died in suspicious circumstances.[19] Since it transpired that there were no eyewitnesses to Margret's death, the case would seem to be a perfect example of the type of case that necessitated forensic medicine. Indeed, Darbishire, in his capacity as coroner, requested that Thomas Orme of Ormskirk, surgeon, "goe along with him to Tarleton to search the wounds of Margt the wife of John Hollinhurst." After searching the body of the deceased, Orme reported that he "did find two large wounds upon her head one whereof was upon the forepart of her head halfe an inch broade and halfe an inch deepe and did further finde on the left side of her neck three or four large black blew spots which together with the wounds aforesaid this inform[ant] believes was the occasion of the said Margt Hollinhurst death."[20]

From his deposition, it seems that Orme did a satisfactory job of examining the deceased. He noted the size, position, and severity of Margret's wounds and from his knowledge and experience of such wounds determined that they were the cause of her death. It all seems rather neat. However, there are a few qualifications that must be made regarding the medical evidence provided by Orme. Despite the seeming competence of his medical examination, Orme's testimony did not bring the coroner any closer to a verdict or a suspect. Orme had confirmed that Margret Hollinhurst had died from the wounds visible on her body, but he had not ventured to explain whether the wounds had been the result of an accident or deliberate malice, and if a deliberate act, who might have been responsible. It seems unlikely that, even with modern medical knowledge and techniques, such information could have been found through forensics alone. However, even if Orme's testimony had led to a clearer understanding of who or what had inflicted Margret's mortal injuries, his evidence would only have confirmed what everyone in the neighborhood already knew. For if we examine the other depositions and testimony gathered by the coroner in this case, it becomes clear that not only did many of Margret's neighbors in Tarleton know how Margret had died, they had solid evidence to prove it.

Darbishire had not simply gathered the testimony of Orme alone. In fact, he had recorded the depositions of six other individuals who had knowledge relevant to the case.[21] Nicholas Whittle of Leyland, the first witness whose statement was recorded by the coroner, had deposed that on May 4 at about nine o'clock in the evening Henry Dandy of Tarleton, wheelwright, came to his house and told him that "hee the said Henry Dandy was bewitched." Whittle inquired of Dandy "whoe had bewitched him woe answered Sodds wife (meaning the wife of John Hollinhurst of Tarleton aforesaid)." According to Whittle, Dandy then offered him half a crown "to goe along with him to kill the said Hollinhursts wife," a request that Whittle duly refused.[22] Four days later, on May 8, Dandy again met with Whittle in Tarleton, at which time he told Whittle, "thou know's I would have given the halfe a crowne to have gone with mee to kill Hollinhurst wife but now the needs not for the work is done."[23] Whittle's testimony was supported by similar evidence provided by Hugh Johnson and William Park, both of Tarleton. Like Whittle, they separately deposed that in the weeks before Margret Hollinhurst's death they had been told by Dandy that he had been bewitched by the said Margret. Each also claimed that Dandy had told them "hee must have blood of her before hee could prosper."[24] Together, these three witnesses established a credible suspect and motive.

The cause of Margret Hollinhurst's death became clearer with further depositions of local inhabitants. Robert Hunter of Bretherton informed the coroner that on May 9 Henry Dandy had visited him at his house in Bretherton to seek repayment of a debt owed to him by Hunter because he (Dandy) was going abroad. Hunter claimed not to have the money and, perhaps suspicious of his behavior, mentioned to Dandy that "hee heard they were gone to bury Hollinhurst wife whoe the neighbourhood reported hee the said Dandy had killed and the said Dandy answered it was too true and then went away."[25] In their statements, Ellen Gill, the daughter of Richard Gill of Ruftore, and Janet Blackhurst, Margret's granddaughter, each explained to the coroner how on May 8 they had found Margret bloody and dead on her own bed. As they suspected foul play, they did not disturb the body.[26] Finally, James Blooer, an innkeeper in Warrington, deposed that almost a month later, on June 1, Dandy had come to his house for a drink of ale. In the course of his drinking, Dandy had asked Blooer "whether if a man was troubled in his mind as hee then was hee this informant [Blooer] cold ease him or noe and asked further of this informant whether it was his fortune to bee hanged."[27] Fearing that Dandy had done something wrong, the innkeeper urged him to unburden his soul; "Thereupon Dandy laid his hand upon his heart and said hee had . . . killed a woeman that had bewitched him which was seaventy years old and upward." The curious innkeeper pressed Dandy for more details about how he had killed the woman, to which Dandy replied, "with a stone by giving her a stroke therewith upon her forehead and said further hee followed his blow and this informt further asked the said Dandy whether hee had killed her with the blow and hee said hee thought not for he heard her groane and thereupon the said Dandy said with his hand hee throttled her and this informt asked him the said Dandy wht hee did soe and hee then told further to this inform that his stepmother advised him to it but whether to kill her or get blood of her this inform knows not."[28] With the deposition of the Warrington innkeeper the coroner had unearthed the final gory details of Margret Hollinhurst's death (Fig. 2).

In his own testimony, Orme had stated that he was called to search the wounds of Margret Hollinhurst "woe was supposed to be murthered by one Henry Dandy."[29] Thus, it is clear that even before any medical examination had taken place, many people in Tarleton were sure that Margret had been murdered and that they knew the culprit. It seems evident that even if the medical evidence provided by Thomas Orme was removed, the testimony provided by a number of witnesses would have provided the coroner with a clear picture of how Margret Hollinhurst had met her untimely death and at whose hand. In fact, the witness evidence provided a good deal more

Figure 2. Places of residence of witnesses in the inquest of Margret Hollinhurst.

detail and information about the death than medical evidence, no matter how sophisticated, ever could. Through the gathering of local knowledge the coroner knew not only that Margret Hollinhurst had been murdered, but when, why, and by whom. By gathering the evidence of the community and even those with information further abroad, Darbishire was able to piece together a coherent explanation for the death of Margret Hollinhurst. On the evidence of three witnesses, the coroner had discovered that Henry Dandy had for weeks suspected Hollinhurst of bewitching him. Dandy's statement to two of the deponents that he must get the blood from Margret or else he would not prosper reveals the reasoning of the suspect and his motive for attacking the old woman. Perhaps he had been unwell of late or his business as a wheelwright had fallen on hard times. Whatever the reason, he seems to have believed that his problems were caused by Margret Hollinhurst and that the only solution was to assault or kill her, which he did, first with a stone and then by throttling her. The evidence that the killing was a premeditated act was substantiated by testimony that he had sought to ensure that Margret would be alone when he assaulted her. Finally, the coroner discovered from local witnesses that Dandy had fled Tarleton and admitted his guilt to an innkeeper in Warrington. Indeed, it seems that the consultation with a medical expert was more a matter of confirming what was already known and already deposed by members of the local community than it was a means of initially discovering the truth.

The majority of untimely deaths investigated by coroners in the early modern period were not homicides. Instead, most inquests were held on the bodies of those who had died as the result of an accident. Furthermore, of those inquests that were the result of homicide, very few were the result of premeditated murder. Because most homicides were not premeditated, but instead the result of arguments and temporarily inflamed passions, a large proportion of killings had witnesses, and the majority did not involve any attempt to hide or conceal the criminal act. For instance, in December 1692 Joseph Pim of Brigg in Lincolnshire was called to give his medical opinion regarding a wound found on the body of the recently deceased Francis Bealy. As he deposed to the coroner, John Nevile, on inspection of Bealy's body Pim found a wound in the deceased's right arm which he believed was caused "by the shot of a musquit."[30] Furthermore, Pim added that he believed the wound "to be mortall, and believes of the said wound he died and by no other means."[31]

Taken in isolation, it may seem that the medical evidence provided by Joseph Pim was the crucial piece of testimony delivered at the coroner's inquest. While we have no reason to doubt his medical testimony or its accuracy, it is clear that the evidence provided by Pim left a number of questions unanswered, namely, how did Bealy receive the gunshot wound and who was responsible for the unfortunate man's death? In essence, it remained to be seen whether Bealy's death was the result of an accident or murder. In order to answer these questions the coroner turned from medical evidence to the testimony of eyewitnesses. In fact, he had already interviewed two such witnesses before recording the testimony of Joseph Pim. Christopher Pim had previously deposed that on December 26 he went with the deceased, Francis Bealy, and John Harpam into the fields in Brigg to shoot some birds. In the course of their hunt Bealy, "being about to goe over a hedge a musquit which the deceased Francis Bealey had acci-denttely went of[f] and wounded the said Francis Bealey in his right arme of which wound the said Francis Bealy on the day after died."[32] Nevile then interviewed John Harpam, the second witness mentioned by Christopher Pim, who confirmed the details of Pim's earlier testimony.[33]

Again, it seems that the crucial evidence was provided not by the medical expert, but by eyewitnesses. Although the medical testimony given to the inquest by Joseph Pim matched that provided by the eyewitnesses, it only confirmed what was already known in the community. Furthermore, the medical testimony could not provide answers to the questions raised by the witnesses' evidence, namely, how had Bealy received his wound and was anyone else involved? In all likelihood, even a modern medical expert would have difficulty providing any more answers than Joseph Pim. Thus, as in most cases in the early modern period and today, witness testimony and not forensic medicine provided the crucial pieces of the puzzle and al-lowed for a satisfactory conclusion to John Nevile's inquest.

This general pattern of the primacy of witness testimony and lo-cal knowledge, and the relative unimportance of forensic medicine, was repeated again and again across the early modern period. Medical testi-mony was almost never sought in isolation, but rather in conjunction with witness testimony; I have found only one case that included medical tes-timony alone. Coroners' inquests that included medical evidence had on average roughly four separate nonmedical depositions.[34] In addition, fully 71 percent of inquests that involved medical evidence also included direct eyewitnesses to the act leading to death or confessions by the suspected killer.[35] Given that a large proportion of these inquests involved both medi-cal testimony and eyewitness testimony, it is interesting to ask whether the two types of evidence tended to agree in their verdict on the cause of death. In a substantial majority of inquests that included medical testi-mony, over 70 percent, the medical evidence did not contradict witness testimony, but rather confirmed what was already known by members of the community.[36]

The small percentage of cases in which medical testimony contradicted or failed to support witness testimony usually followed a similar pattern. This pattern consisted of deaths that occurred after a well-established violent event (an assault or an accident) but where there was disagreement over whether the immediate violence or a subsequent malady was the ultimate cause of death. These inquests, then, were the result of an unusual coincidence of violent injury and later illness. Traditional witnesses in these cases tended to assume that the death was caused by violence, whereas medical experts, often called long after the original violent event, were more likely to depose that the cause of death was unclear and could have been the result of a later, unrelated illness. The distinction was important, for if the deceased had died as a result of a violent act the charge would be murder; however, if a later illness was deemed responsible, the initial violence would be considered assault.

The fact that violence had occurred was rarely debated; rather, discussion centered on whether it had been the cause of a long, lingering illness that ended in death. Such a confluence of events—violent injury followed by a completely unrelated illness—would have been unlikely, and thus the disagreement between traditional and medical witnesses must have often been the result of caution on the part of medical experts who were unable to separate injury from illness. Infanticide cases also occasionally contained contradictory evidence, with midwives, as medical experts, often suggesting that the infant was fully formed, and thus born alive, while some witnesses claimed the child had been stillborn.[37]

Only a handful of inquests contained medical evidence that in any way contradicted witness testimony, and none of these inquests involved the discovery of "secret homicide"; they merely disagreed with witnesses as to the proximate cause of death. For instance, when Edward Nelthorpe died at Barton, Lincolnshire, in January of 1694, eyewitnesses testified at the coroner's inquest that the deceased had likely died as a result of a beating received at the hands of one John Gilby. Although Richard Beck, the "chyrurgeon" who examined the deceased's body, noted injuries consistent with the beating described by the eyewitnesses, he did not agree that the injuries were sufficient to cause death. Instead, after describing Nelthorpe's wounds at some length, he concluded that "said wound this informant believes was not mortal."[38] If it is true that medical testimony rarely contradicted and most often confirmed traditional witness testimony, it is also true that very few cases relied entirely on medical evidence to reach a verdict.

The evidence provided by depositions from the Northern Assize Circuit, palatinate of Lancashire, and Lincolnshire between 1640 and 1750 clearly shows that even those cases without medical evidence were usually resolved satisfactorily through witness testimony and, therefore, did not suffer due to a lack of medical evidence. The inquests that did not contain medical testimony had, on average, roughly four depositions per inquest, almost exactly the same proportion as those cases which did include medical evidence. Also similar was the percentage of cases that had the benefit of containing eyewitness testimony or a confession. Approximately 72 percent of both types of cases—those with and without medical testimony—had either a confession or the depositions of eyewitnesses.[39] Furthermore, it was rare in cases without medical evidence that the depositions provided by witness contradicted one another (only 6 percent of these cases contained any depositions that contradicted another, or an inquest verdict that contradicted the witness depositions).[40] The majority of the inquests—over 70 percent, both with and without the testimony of medical experts—had eyewitnesses or confessions, and only a very small minority went unsolved, without a clear verdict, suspect, or cause of death. If medical evidence did in fact provide a significant advantage in the quest for an accurate verdict, we would expect those inquests which lacked medical testimony to be listed as unsolved or unresolved at a higher rate than those with medical testimony. Although inquests occasionally state that a death was caused by "persons unknown" or by "causes unknown," these cases were rare and were no more likely in cases without medical testimony than in those with. One can therefore conclude that the involvement of professional medical testimony had little impact on the success or failure of the early modern English criminal justice system to adequately police instances of sudden or suspicious death.

In those inquests that resulted in a verdict of suicide, a determination had to be made as to whether the death was indeed a suicide and not the result of murder or an accident. In this instance it is perhaps useful to compare the strategies used by coroners in two different cases of suspected suicide. Mary Doltyn was in her house in Gleadles Moorside, Yorkshire, in March 1641 when her neighbor Marmaduke Feales burst into her house "cryine and skreaminge and desired her to goe into his house."[41] Afraid of what she might find, Doltyn waited for some other neighbors to come before she entered the Feales's house. When the assembled neighbors entered the house they found Anne Feales, the wife of Marmaduke Feales, lying dead on the floor. Marmaduke told Doltyn and the others that he had found his wife hanged and had cut her down before summoning help. Doltyn deposed that she "saw a rope there hanging" which Anne Feales had supposedly used to hang herself.[42]

Almost 30 years later, in 1670, Dorothie Dalby of Haxey, Lincolnshire, was informed that one of her neighbors, Robert Thompson, had not been seen for three days. Thompson's long absence was clearly cause for concern, for Dalby and some other neighbors decided to search the missing man's house to see if they could find any sign of him. When they entered the shop attached to Thompson's house, Dalby and the others found Thompson's dead body hanging from a "hempen cord, by the neck."[43]

On the surface both deaths seem to have been the result of suicide, but how could the coroner be sure enough of the cause of death to find a verdict of suicide in his inquest? In neither case were medical professionals called to examine the bodies or otherwise testify as to the possible cause of death. However, it is unlikely that the investigation of such deaths would have benefited from medical expertise. It seems likely that even modern medical forensics would have had difficulty in establishing whether the two individuals found hanged had committed suicide, or if foul play was involved. Thus, the coroners turned to the best evidence available (both then and now) for resolving their respective cases—witness testimony.

The investigation into the death of Robert Thompson in 1670 seems to have been fairly straightforward. After interviewing several witnesses to establish exactly when Thompson had last been seen, Robert Barnard, the coroner conducting the inquest, interviewed multiple witnesses as to Thompson's state of mind and general disposition. Robert Taylor deposed that Thompson was "severall times a lunatic man and did not carry himself onely as a madd man when he had gotten drinke but att other times also for severall years past . . . being sometimes raging and sometimes extreme sad and melancholy."[44] In a similar vein Thomas Taylor told the coroner's inquest that Thompson "was for severall yeares past, att such times as he had got drinke and att severall other times did behave himself as a Lunatick man and for the most part did carry himself as a lunatic."[45] Such testimony regarding the deceased's mental state was crucial in establishing that the death by hanging was indeed suicide.

Despite the similar circumstances surrounding the cause of death and the finding of the body, the death of Anne Feales was not quite as straight-forward as that of Robert Thompson. As in the case of Thompson, the coroner in Feales's case sought information from her neighbors and the local community to confirm whether her death was indeed a suicide. Instead of evidence about the melancholy and unstable state of the deceased, John Burdett, the coroner responsible for investigating the death, received multiple testimonies that pointed the blame for Anne's death squarely at her husband, Marmaduke Feales. Mary Doltyn deposed that three days before her death Anne had come to her (Doltyn's) house and asked for a refuge from her husband, who she feared "would kill her that night."[46] Doltyn also told the inquest that she herself had heard Marmaduke Feales "say often before that time, that he would eyther kyll or hange the said Anne his wife."[47] Anne Bradbury also testified that Anne Feales had told her that she feared her husband "would eyther kill or hang her," for Marmaduke had previously threatened her, "he haveing a knife in one hand and a rope in the other, and . . . he put the rope three times aboute her necke, and one tyme she fell downe as dead being strangled with that roape which he had put aboute her neck."[48] Other witnesses testified to having seen the marks that Marmaduke's frequent beatings had left upon Anne. Marmaduke had

even bragged to Anne Hartley that he had beaten his wife so severely that
"from the crowne of her head to the sole of the foote I have not lefte one free
spotte on her."[49] Thus, far from wanting to kill herself, Anne Feales was trying to save herself from her husband, for as she herself said, "life was sweet
and she would faine save yt." Instead, the evidence of friends and neighbors, the collected knowledge of the local community, whom very little in
the way of past history and behavior ever escaped, strongly suggested that
Marmaduke Feales had killed his wife. He had threatened to hang his wife
before, and had even attempted it on three previous occasions. For John
Burdett, it must have been clear that the death of Anne Feales was no suicide, but rather the awful deed of her violent and abusive husband.

If accidental death was the most common type of death investigated
by early modern coroners, it was also the most likely to have witnesses and
the least likely to be confused for another type of death. For instance, when
Edward Medley died at Wooton in 1691, medical evidence was given to the
coroner's inquest by John Richardson, who had examined Medley at his
widow's request. As it transpired, such evidence was hardly necessary given
that locals had seen Medley's own bay colt kick him in the head, giving him
a deep wound that bled "very ill at the forehead," and multiple witnesses
deposed that Medley had told them his horse had been responsible for the
wound that ultimately killed him.[50] Likewise, when in 1669 the bodies of
two young men, John Hutchinson and William Seaton, were found in a mill
pond of the Old Leat Mill in Garthorpe, the cause of death was hardly a
mystery necessitating sophisticated forensics. Four witnesses deposed that
they had seen Hutchinson and Seaton take off their clothes and go into the
mill pond, "pretending to wash themselves."[51] According to the witnesses,
Hutchinson "went into the deeps and took hold of William Seaton's hand,
whereupon the said William Seaton cryed out and said take hold of my
hand or we are both lost." One of the onlookers threw the bathers a halter
"in hopes thereby to save them, but the said John Hutchinson and William
Seaton was soe farr spent with the force and violence of the water that they
could not take hold of the halter but immediately was drowned."[52]

A similar pattern is repeated throughout the records of coroners' inquests and depositions: accidental deaths witnessed by a number of peo-

ple. In fact, most cases of untimely or suspicious death, be they accidents, homicides, or deaths through other causes, had direct eyewitnesses or witnesses with evidence provided by the deceased or their killer. In fact, over 70 percent of all cases examined for this study had eyewitness testimony or testimony given by the victim.[53] Thus, as most inquests involved deaths that were witnessed or deaths for which there was relatively little doubt as to the cause, medical evidence would have been potentially useful in only a small minority of cases. Even for the rare case in which forensic medicine was applicable at all, witness testimony most often supplied the crucial information.

The Coroner and the Centrality of Witness Testimony and Local Knowledge

In a close society that placed little value on personal privacy, very little must have gone unnoticed.[54] In early modern England rumor, gossip, and eyewitnesses served as a species of community policing and the cornerstones of criminal investigation, especially the investigation of untimely death. Although individual communities may have been suspicious of outsiders, as members of the county community, coroners were well placed to exploit local knowledge for the benefit of their investigations. This ability to collect and assess local information was vital given that early modern coroners relied on evidence provided by neighbors, friends, relatives, and other local residents. Given this reliance on communal knowledge, an exploration of the methods by which this local information was gathered and how it was used will illuminate the surprising effectiveness of traditional investigatory techniques for the detection of illegitimate violence.

When called to hold an inquest, an early modern coroner would, upon arriving at the location of the body, charge constables with summoning both jurors and witnesses and ensuring that they would appear. The inquest itself was sometimes held in the open, but often it was held in the home of a local inhabitant or in a nearby inn or alehouse. When the coroner's jury had been summoned and selected, the testimony of witnesses was heard. As Chapter 4 will demonstrate, in this period jurors, and perhaps especially coroners' jurors, were suppliers and seekers of evidence as well as assessors of evidence. In fact, in many cases coroners' jurors were also witnesses who both provided sworn testimony to the inquest and weighed the evidence provided by other witnesses. In Lincolnshire, for instance, Matthew Everatt served as a juror and a witness during the inquest on the death of Anne Staville in 1670.[55]

Although witnesses were often local residents, it was not unusual for them to travel some significant distance to give evidence at an inquest, or for the coroner to travel a significant distance to gather witness testimony. For example, in the case of Margret Hollinhurst outlined above, the coroner, Edward Darbishire, held his inquest in Tarleton, the town where Hollinhurst had died. Although three of the deponents were residents of Tarleton itself, others had traveled to the inquest, or were visited by the coroner in their place of residence. Robert Hunter came from Bretherton, about three miles away; Ellen Gill came from Ruftore (Rufford), about four or five miles away; while Nicholas Whittle came from Leyland and Thomas Orme, the surgeon, came from Ormskirk, each about ten miles from Tarleton. Finally, James Blooer, an innkeeper in distant Warrington, some 30 miles from Tarleton, provided a deposition.[56] The fact that the coroner tracked down witnesses from such disparate places, or that witnesses came forward to the inquest of their own volition from such distances, speaks to the dedication of some coroners and the circulation of information in early modern English society. The testimony of the innkeeper is especially telling, as it demonstrates that someone as far as 30 miles away from the place of the crime and inquest, who had happened to meet the accused murderer in an inn, was either found by the coroner or had heard the news of the death of Margret Hollinhurst and traveled to the site of the inquest.

It seems that many coroners were not content to simply record one or two depositions, but instead were willing to track down anyone and everyone who might have knowledge relating to a death, the deceased, or the suspect. When the body of William Barnesley was discovered at Rivelinge Lodge in Yorkshire in 1642, the coroner responsible for holding the inquest, John Burdett, was nothing if not diligent in collecting evidence. The inquest began at Stannington on April 29, when Burdett took the depositions of five individuals from the immediate vicinity: two from Rivelinge Lodge, two from Stannington, and one from Wadsley.[57] John Barnesley, son of the deceased, deposed that on April 23 he and his father were tending their sheep when their neighbor, Thomas Revell, demanded to know why William Barnesley was still grazing his sheep in copse wood in contradiction of a command given by a Mr. Bright. William answered that "there was non in yt, but as used to have beene in other yeares therefore I will neither take a sheepe forth nor putt none in."[58] At this point, according to John Barnesley, Revell took a birch rod that was sharpened at one end and stabbed William Barnesley in the left eye, causing blood to run "downe his clothes and some blood came forth at his mouth."[59] Five days later, on April 28, William Barnesley was dead.

On the same day that John Barnesley provided his testimony, George Hoyland deposed that he had seen William Barnesley and Thomas Revell together in the copse, and Eleanor Bilcliffe deposed that Thomas Revell had confided to her that he had had a quarrel with Barnesley over the grazing of sheep in the copse. Also giving evidence that day was Elizabeth Creswicke, who had examined Barnesley's wound on April 24 and confirmed that he had received a wound in his left eye about an inch deep.[60] Finally, William Barnesley's widow, Katherine Barnesley, deposed that her husband had told her of the quarrel and how he had been stabbed by Thomas Revell. She also shed more light on the potential source of Revell and Barnesley's quarrel. Katherine informed the inquest that about midsummer Revell had come to Barnesley and asked to purchase some wool belonging to Mr. Bright. Barnesley, however, was suspicious and said he would not sell Revell Bright's wool unless some of Bright's servants were present. Revell was clearly offended by this rebuff and told Barnesley "that he would doe him an ill turne for yt." It was Katherine's belief, therefore, that Revell "murthered the said William Barnesley of old malice."[61]

After these five depositions provided by members of the local community, the case must have seemed fairly straightforward. Witnesses had seen Revell and Barnesley quarrel and had seen Revell stab the deceased in the eye, Revell had even confessed as much to a neighbor. It also must have been clear that the wound Barnesley had received was serious, as it was recorded as being an inch deep and causing significant bleeding both from the wound itself and from the mouth. That Thomas Revell was responsible for Barnesley's subsequent demise must have been perfectly evident to both the coroner and the local inhabitants. The fact that the case was all but settled after the first five depositions, however, was clearly not reason enough for the coroner to suspend further investigations. Almost three weeks later, on May 19, John Burdett took seven additional witness statements at Wadley Bridge. This time the deponents came from further afield than the original five witnesses, places like Fulwood, Hallam, Dungworth, and Rickettfield. The seven new deponents mostly confirmed what the original witnesses had said, but also added new details about the deep-seated malice between Revell and Barnesley. The coroner learned that the previous summer Mr. Bright had employed Revell to manage his flock of sheep, see to their shearing, and sell the wool. Barnesley, who was then holding the wool for Mr. Bright, refused to give it to Revell unless some of Bright's servants were present to see the wool weighed, for Barnesley, according to one deponent, feared that Revell would take the best wool and leave the worst. Barnesley's refusal to deliver the wool led to an exchange of curses and, before the two men were separated, a threat from Revell that he would "beate out thy braines with a stone."[62]

Even though the case seemed clear after the first five depositions, the coroner sought more information regarding the background of the quarrel between the deceased and the accused, even though the later seven deponents provided little new information about the actual affray. It seems that the coroner tracked down everyone who knew anything about the case, or even simply knew someone who did, in order to fully understand the history of the relationship between the deceased and the suspect, their past disagreements and disputes. It may seem remarkable that so many people from within a five-mile radius had intimate knowledge of the relationship between Barnesley and Revell and their past encounters. The social knowledge possessed by the local community was both deep and of the highest importance for a local officeholder like a coroner. It was this knowledge, more than any other information, that helped solve criminal cases. In the close social world of early modern England there was scant privacy and much surveillance. As a result, there was very little that was not seen, heard, or remembered by someone. This local social knowledge was, and indeed remains, a key tool for criminal justice officials like the coroner.

The inhabitants of the community where a death occurred were often more than simply passive repositories of social knowledge. In many instances they took it upon themselves to gather evidence, both physical and oral. In this sense, local witnesses and the local inhabitants who sat on coroners' juries should perhaps be viewed as officeholders of a wider sort—active experts on local social, cultural, and geographic conditions who could be called on not only to passively judge fact and fiction, guilt and innocence, but also to proactively aid the process of criminal investigation.[63] For example, in 1617 the body of a man was found dead in the River Thames. Not content to simply hear witness testimony, the coroner's jurors in the case began their own investigation. It was known among the community that the deceased frequently fished at a certain location on the river. The amateur investigators visited the aforementioned place and found that part of the riverbank had been undercut by the current and had recently collapsed into the river. From this, the jurors surmised that the deceased must have been standing on the bank fishing when the ground beneath him gave way, plunging into the Thames. There was one problem with this hypothesis, however: the body of the deceased had not been found at the place where the bank had collapsed.

Living along the river as they did, the members of the community must have had some familiarity with and knowledge about water currents. Accordingly, the jurors devised a simple but effective experiment: they threw a stick into the water from the place where the riverbank had collapsed—the place they believed the deceased had fallen into the water—in order to test the effects of the current. As the investigators expected, the stick came to rest in the very place where the dead body had been found, confirming in their minds that the death was the result of a tragic accident.[64] The verdict in this case was thus the result of local social knowledge about the habits and routines of a member of the community, local geographic knowledge about the river currents of the area, as well as the initiative of the coroner's jury in seeking evidence and testing a hypothesis. Although the case is certainly remarkable, it is in no way unusual, and this type of amateur investigation and information gathering was often central for the policing and detection of crime and death in the early modern period.[65] In one extraordinary case, the family of the deceased even commissioned a portrait of the body of the deceased, wounds and all, to be used as evidence in subsequent litigation.[66]

In addition to the cooperation of the local community and the use of local knowledge and information networks, one of the key features of effective community policing is the creation and fostering of trusting relationships between criminal justice officials and the communities with which they interact.[67] The early modern coroner seems to have been especially well placed to have such a relationship. Coroners were members of the county or borough communities they served and as such were less likely to be seen as outsiders than some other officials. Unlike many local officials — such as constables and churchwardens — coroners held their posts for relatively long periods, often ten years or more. Additionally, unlike justices of the peace, who were also members of the county community holding office for longer terms, coroners were usually elected and as such would have had some level of popular support.[68] Coroners were also usually of a slightly lower social status than justices of the peace and thus closer in status to the people with whom they interacted. This, combined with the fact that coroners were amateur, nonuniformed officials, meant that there was little to differentiate them from the communities they encountered in the course of their duties.[69] While it is likely that distrust between coroners and communities did occur, it appears that coroners were better situated than most early modern officeholders to form long-standing, trusting relationships with those they encountered in their official capacity.

Coroners themselves also often employed creative methods to evaluate evidence. One such instance occurred in London in 1611, when an inquest was held on the body of a courtier who had reportedly been killed by another gentleman in a duel.[70] As both the deceased and the accused were prominent members of elite society, and as the deceased's influential relatives pushed for a thorough investigation, dozens of depositions were taken by the coroner responsible for the case. Faced with such an avalanche of evidence, the coroner resorted to some interesting techniques to sort and compare the available evidence. He began by making lists of questions to ask each of the deponents in order to create a standardized body of witness testimony.[71] Next, the coroner made a grid on a piece of paper. On the left-hand side of this paper he listed the specific questions he had asked each deponent. Across the top of the grid the coroner wrote the names of the key witnesses. The coroner then filled in the grid with the answers given to each question by each deponent, allowing him to quickly compare any answer a particular witness gave to that of another witness.[72] Finally, after taking the many depositions and comparing them by means of the grid, the coroner made lists of the evidence provided by the witnesses and what it suggested about the sequence of events that led to the death of Thomas Egerton.[73]

Although the vast majority of evidence collected and used by coroners and their juries took the form of witness testimony, on occasion physical evidence was presented to the inquest, usually in the form of clothing. For example, on June 23, 1750, the body of Robert Dent was found lying in a pit of water in Lancashire. Robert Parkinson, who assisted in removing the body of the deceased from the pit, deposed that "there appeared three wounds about his head which seem'd pretty large."[74] Along with the body, the knapsack of the deceased was also found in the pit. The contents of the bag must have seemed fairly mundane at first glance, the only item mentioned being a "strip'd shirt." In the course of the inquest, Andrew Grayham deposed that near the time of Dent's disappearance he and his master were traveling in the King's highway "not far from the pit where the deceas'd Robert Dent was lately found." According to Grayham, the travelers "observed a great quantity of Blood in the same highway."[75] As was often the case, the crucial evidence in this case was supplied by one of those repositories of local knowledge and information, an innkeeper. Richard Nuttall stated that shortly before Dent's disappearance, the deceased and another man, who claimed to be a glazier from Warrington, had come to his inn. The deceased and the glazier stayed all night at Nuttall's inn and left together the next day. According to Nuttall, before the two men left his inn the glazier lamented that he was in want of money. To this complaint Dent

replied that "he [the glazier] should not want any money so far as their Road
or way lay together, for that he the deceas'd had money enough." Having
supplied a possible motive for the death of Robert Dent, the innkeeper then
provided the piece of evidence that linked the glazier even more firmly to
Dent's death. At this point the coroner produced the seemingly innocuous
striped shirt that had been found in Dent's knapsack and enquired if Nuttall had seen it before. The innkeeper deposed that "the strip'd shirt now
produced . . . he verily believes was the same shirt which was worn by the
said glazier at this informants house."[76]

Although the records are unclear as to the final outcome of the Robert Dent's inquest, it was not at all unusual that a suspect would be identified by means of clothing. When the corpse of an infant was found in a
mug at Walton, Lancashire in 1730, Margaret Mollinieux was quickly ap-
prehended because witnesses testified that she had been pregnant and that
a piece of cloth that had covered the mug belonged to Mollinieux. A note
written by the coroner reads, "the Pettycoats of Margaret Mollineux being
seized in her house . . . it appears that part of the shiff that was found upon
the mug when taken upp is like the same with part of the petticoat and
Elizabeth Reilanes she has seen Margarte Mollineux wear that Petticoat."[77]
Similarly, William Buckley was eventually identified as the man who killed
Samuel Cook in 1722 after he was described by a witness as a "blackish
ruddy complexion'd man tall and in black clothes and a cap on his head
under his hatt." Although the witness did not know the suspect's name, his
description allowed the coroner to track him first to an inn, whose owner
recognized the man described as a Mr. Buckley who had recently lodged
with him.[78] It must be remembered that in the early modern period, before
clothing was mass-produced, an individual's garb would have been more
distinctive and distinguishable. At the same time the relatively high cost of
clothing meant that, for most people, changes of clothing would have been
infrequent. Thus, a person's clothing was more closely connected to the
individual in the minds of neighbors or witnesses than was the case after the
advent of modern consumer culture. As a result, in the early modern world
it was likely easier to identify someone by their clothing even at a distance
or when their back was turned.[79] Although physical evidence such as cloth-

ing could play an important part in identifying the dead or a suspect, such means of identification still relied on local knowledge to match the clothing with an individual, a fact which further emphasizes the centrality of communal knowledge and witness testimony for criminal investigation.

It has been argued that coroners were especially lax in the performance of their duties, taking long periods of time to begin inquests and avoiding those that were off the beaten track.[80] When one looks at the evidence from early modern coroners' depositions, however, it becomes clear that most coroners conscientiously discharged their duties in a timely manner, regardless of distance. Nearly two-thirds of depositions were taken by coroners within five days of the discovery of the dead body.[81] When one considers the amount of time it must have taken for the coroner to be summoned and travel to the place of death, the relatively short time between discovery and the interviewing of witnesses is rather remarkable. It must also be noted that the statistics do not reflect when the coroner began the inquest process, or when the coroner first interviewed a witness, but rather when the coroner formally deposed each witness. It is thus likely that an even higher proportion of inquests began within five days, and that many began even sooner.

When we examine the careers of individual coroners, the charge that they neglected to hold inquests when the place of death was too far away further loses its force. For instance, over the course of his tenure in office, William Playfere, coroner of the liberty of Hastings in Sussex, held 127 inquests in 33 separate towns and villages. Playfere seems to have been diligent in carrying out his duties even though many of these villages, such Ewhurst or Ticehurst, were tiny villages far from significant population centers. Furthermore, Playfere did not remain close to home, only holding inquests that were conveniently located near his residence; on the contrary, 88 percent of Playfere's inquests were held more than five miles from his home, and 58 percent over ten miles.[82] The distances traveled on a regular basis by Playfere were not at all unusual for early modern coroners, and those county coroners with large jurisdictions, like those of Yorkshire, often traveled even further to hold inquests. Undoubtedly some coroners were less conscientious than Playfere, but the idea that failure to hold

inquests in inconvenient locations was a characteristic of the office as a
whole is clearly untrue.

Some have suggested that because they only received payment in
cases of homicide, early modern coroners solely conducted inquests in
cases where the death was obviously or manifestly violent.[83] Even a cursory glance at the inquest records, however, shows that the vast majority of
inquests involved accidental deaths and suicides that often lacked obvious
signs of violence. One of the most common causes of death in cases of both
suicide and accidental death, and one that did not usually involve outward
signs of violence, was drowning. In order to ascertain the exact cause of
death for a person found drowned, coroners and their juries usually relied
on a couple of strategies: witness testimony as to the state of mind of the
deceased, and the examination of the body for bruises or wounds that may
have indicated a different cause of death or violence.[84] The establishment
of the mental state of the deceased was important in the resolution of the
death of Anne Staville in Lincolnshire in September 1670. According to
the evidence provided by Robert Raven, Staville had gone to the nearby
River Trent to fetch a pail of water. When she had not returned after "a longer time than she might have gone to the river and returned again," Raven
went to the river to search for her.[85] When he got to the river, Raven found
"some signs that she [Staville] had slipt into the river." Fearing the worst,
Raven found two men to take a boat and search the river for any sign of
Anne, who was found drowned shortly thereafter.

Despite the evidence provided by Robert Raven that suggested that
there were physical signs on the riverbank—evidence which pointed to an
accidental fall into the river and thus a verdict of accidental death—it was
clearly important for the coroner to establish that Anne Staville's death had
not been the result of suicide. This need to rule out suicide becomes clear
when one examines the other depositions provided in the case. The testimony of William Raven, Anne's master, and Anne Slingsley, Anne's fellow
servant, was sought in order to establish the mental state of the deceased.
Both Raven and Slingsley agreed that Staville "was no merrier since she
came to the house, then she was that day."[86] In other words, because Anne
Staville had been happy on the day of her death, it was unlikely that she had

taken her own life. The evidence of Anne's state of mind combined with the physical "signs that she had slipt into the river" was enough for the coroner's inquest held the day after Anne's death to conclude that the death was the result of a tragic accident and not suicide.[87]

In addition to establishing the mental state of the deceased, the coroner often relied on the evidence given by those who had laid out and prepared the body of the deceased for burial. The task of laying out the body of the recently deceased was most often (indeed, in the records surveyed here, always) the responsibility of women, who were usually paid for their services. In the process of stripping the body of the deceased and preparing it for burial, the women involved had ample opportunity to examine the body for marks, bruises, wounds, and other signs of violence. Because of this unique knowledge, the women who laid out the body were often deposed at the coroner's inquest when the circumstances of the death aroused suspicion. In Lincoln, such women were interviewed by coroners in seven separate inquests in the 1690s alone. Jane Sherwood, for example, was interviewed regarding the death of William Hall in 1692. Hall had languished close to death for a number of days, and there was a disagreement between other witnesses as to the cause of his death. Some believed Hall had died of natural causes, while others had deposed that injuries received by the hand of a Mr. Harding had been responsible for his death. Sherwood, who had been employed to "lay the deceased Will Hall in his winding sheet," was interviewed by the coroner due to her knowledge of the body of the deceased.[88] In her deposition Sherwood stated that she "could not by her inspection discover any wound or bruse upon the deceased's body but believes the deceased Will Hall dyed a naturall death."[89] This seems to have persuaded the coroner's jury, who found that William Hall "died a natural death and by no violent hand or any other means whatever."[90]

In a similar manner, when the body of John Stevens was found in a pool of water in Messingham in 1691, in addition to taking depositions from the individuals who found the body and the last people to see Stevens alive, the coroner interviewed Anne Suers and Anne Waterland. The two women had been employed to "stirp and wind up deceaseds body," and both deposed that in the course of their work they had "found neither wounds nor bruses upon the deceaseds body, but believe he came to his death by the fall into the water pools as above said and no other way."[91] It is evident that the coroner investigating the death and those who gave statements believed that it was important to establish that there had been no foul play, even when the death seemed from the first to have been an accident. This level of concern is important for the refutation of the claims that coroners were incompetent and lazy, only investigating cases that were clearly violent or clearly murder — or in other words, cases for which they would be paid. On the contrary, we see over and over diligence and attention to detail in coroners' inquests and depositions dealing with accident and natural deaths that belie the simplistic stereotype of sloth and inefficiency.

Although this type of amateur medical testimony is found less frequently in the records surveyed here than in testimony by medical professionals, it seems that such testimony was received and used in the same way. Rarely was such amateur medical evidence substantial enough to prove a case one way or another: instead, it seems that it was usually used to confirm what was already known from witness testimony. Such testimony, however, demonstrates again that professional medical expertise was not normally necessary to ensure effective investigation of suspicious death. Rather, witness testimony and local knowledge were, in the vast majority of cases, sufficient to conclude coroners' inquests. Thus, the focus of many modern scholars on scientific and medical knowledge and advancement when looking at criminal justice in the pre-modern period has led to a condescending, stereotyped view of the people of those times, and to a concomitant underestimation of their investigatory and problem-solving abilities. We do not expect, therefore, the ingenious but commonsense approaches used by early modern people in the investigation of crime, and instead assume that policing in the period must have been primitive and detection of crime unusual.

The Potential of Forensic Medicine in the Early Modern Period

The early modern reliance on witness testimony and other traditional investigatory techniques was a deliberate choice, a strategy borne out by long experience rather than a response to rudimentary scientific capacity. Even with modern forensics, the limitations of medical evidence and the small number of cases requiring its use mean that nonscientific evidence remains the backbone of criminal investigation. The early modern coroner's recourse to witness testimony was a conscious decision based on the effectiveness of the tool.

It is difficult to reach any definitive conclusion about the sophistication of early modern forensic medicine and its potential usefulness in criminal investigation. What is clear, however, is that over the course of the seventeenth century medical testimony was increasingly sought by coroners in their inquests. The records of the Northern Assize Circuit reveal that between 1640 and 1645 roughly 12 percent of inquests for which depositions survive included depositions given by medical experts.[92] Similarly, in Lincolnshire about 15 percent of inquests with extant depositions contained medical witnesses between 1669 and 1695.[93] By the eighteenth century, the proportion of coroners' inquests that made use of medical testimony increased substantially. Between 1690 and 1750, for example, over 30 percent of Lancashire inquests for which depositions survive involved expert medical testimony.[94]

While we can say that medical expertise was sought with growing regularity over the course of the seventeenth and eighteenth centuries, it is more difficult to evaluate the abilities or competence of medical experts in cases of suspicious death. In her article "Medical Knowledge and the Early Modern English Coroner's Inquest," Carol Loar has suggests that the medical knowledge and expertise brought to bear in the investigation of death may have been more sophisticated than has been previously assumed.[95] She argues that despite the fact that there were no statutory requirements in early modern England that inquests include autopsies or other medical evidence, coroners and their juries "regularly relied on medical knowledge and evidence when rendering their verdicts."[96] Not only was the medical evidence brought to bear in coroners' inquests more sophisticated and resort to it more routine than has been previously argued, but, according to Loar, such evidence was sought and used from at least the mid-sixteenth century.[97]

The evidence from the coroners' depositions of the palatinate of Lancashire, the Northern Assize Circuit, and Lincolnshire between 1640 and 1750 seems to bear out Loar's hypothesis. For instance, in 1722 James Low was "desired to view a wound upon the body of Mr. Crook deceased," who was then lying dead at Walton in Lancashire.[98] Upon examination of the body of Samuel Crook, Esquire, Low found "a large Punctured wound in the left side, with a Pretty wide orifice which entered betwixt the second and third of the short ribs." Low further deposed that he had "introduced a Prob[e] about five inches long" into the wound, which had allowed him to determine that the wound was "near half an inch wide" and entered "from below upwards towards the Posterior part of them [the ribs], and slanting upwards entered the Cavity of the Breast, a little above the midriff." Finally an examination of "the Angle of the wound and the holes made by it in the Deceas'ds coat and vest" allowed Low to conclude that the fatal wound had been made "by a hollow blade."[99]

From his examination of Samuel Crook's body James Low was able to inform the coroner that the deceased had died from a wound made by a hollow bladed sword and that the fatal blow had been delivered to the chest from slightly below while Crook was facing his killer. This information would have provided a fairly sophisticated picture of Crook's death. The medical evidence would have told the coroner that Crook's death was probably a homicide, that it was highly unlikely that such a wound had been made accidentally by such a weapon, and that the culprit was probably of elevated social standing, given the fact that hollow bladed swords were expensive. In fact, as the witness testimony in the case demonstrates, the picture that emerged from James Low's medical testimony was correct.

Like most homicide cases, the killing of Samuel Crook had a number of eyewitnesses. Joseph Etough of Houghton, Crook's 19-year-old servant, had been present at the death of his master, and his testimony was recorded before that of James Low.[100] Etough told the coroner that on Wednesday, December 9, he and his master had been riding along the high road near widow Thellow's house in Walton in le Dale between eight and nine o'clock in the morning when they met "two persons which this deponent took to be a Gentleman and his servant." As Crook and the unknown gentleman passed in the road, their legs collided, "whereupon the Gentleman said Something to his master [Crook] which this deponent took to be either an Oath or Curse." It seems that neither Crook nor the other gentleman was willing to give way when they met in the road, resulting in a collision and a curse. Such slights were apparently not to be forgiven, as both Crook and the gentleman "imediately dismounted and before they had drawn their swords met together and struggled." In the course of the fight the gentleman grasped Crook's sword in an attempt to take it from him, a move that Crook prevented by holding fast to the hilt. While the gentleman fought for Crook's sword, Crook "collar'd him and called him a Raskall, to which the Gentleman Replyed a Raskall dost thou say, and upon that they both Retired about three yrds from each other and drew their swords and began to Parry." The duel did not last long, for in "a very short time" the gentleman wounded Crook "into the left side with his sword." Crook immediately collapsed, dying half an hour later.[101]

The eyewitness testimony thus vindicated the picture provided by James Low's medical evidence. The killing had been a homicide, it had been perpetrated with a sword, and the killer had been of elevated social standing. Although the medical evidence only confirmed what was already known through eyewitness testimony, it is clear that Low's medical knowledge was sufficiently sophisticated to provide a fairly accurate picture of the crime on the basis of an examination of the body of the deceased alone. This level of medical sophistication was not the exclusive preserve of the eighteenth century. Indeed, a strikingly similar inquest and medical testimony from 1610 illustrate the relative continuity of forensic medical sophistication across the early modern period. When called to examine the body of John Egerton as part of a coroner's inquest being held at an inn in Highgate, London, in April 1610, Alexander Lillington deposed that he found "3 wounds given him [Egerton], one under the right arme going down ward towards the lung, an other on the foreparte of his right shoulder nere the kamnell bone going downward into the body and the third under the right shoulder blade behind going likewise downward into the body."[102] By means of an examination that must have been almost identical to that undertaken by James Low over 100 years later, Lillington also determined that the angle of the wounds suggested that the fatal blows "were given him being downe and not on his feet."[103] This piece of information—which in the context of a duel would have been crucial in establishing whether the killing was murder or manslaughter—was corroborated by earlier witness testimony.

In 1629 Francis Michell, one of the coroners for Essex, sought the opinion of two barber surgeons regarding the death of Henry Watford. The surgeons, Robert Joby and William Prossor, gave similar statements at the coroner's inquest. Both deposed that upon examining the body of the deceased they had found a bruise on the left arm "as broad as a shilling piece," an ulcer "about halfe an inch broad and not above a qrtr of an inch deepe" on the thigh of the deceased, and "some little red stripes by the stroake of a rod."[104] Although the surgeons were able to tell the coroner the type of implement used to make the wounds they found on Watford's body, they nevertheless deposed that the same wounds were not mortal, and thus the death was not a case of homicide. The conclusion reached by the two medical men was the same as that which had been reached by the community at large. While John Hornsby had witnessed Clement Sorrell's wife—Watford's mistress—"strike the said Henry Watford upon the shoulders and upon the backe 3 or fower stroakes with a switch or wand about halfe an ynch aboute," it was generally agreed from the evidence of those neighbors who had witnessed the beating, seen the wounds, or talked with Watford after the beating that neither "the said bruse or byle or the said whipping was the occasion of the said Watfords death But that hee dyed by the visitation of god."[105] Once again, the testimony provided by medical experts seems to have been accurate and relatively sophisticated. However, for all its sophistication, once again, the depositions of medical professionals simply confirmed what the local community and neighbors of the deceased already knew.

It thus is evident from the surviving medical testimony given during the course of coroners' inquests that from at least the early seventeenth century, the level of forensic medical knowledge was sophisticated enough to adequately address the vast majority of cases encountered by an early modern coroner. Early modern forensic medicine was obviously still a long way from modern techniques involving DNA or even fingerprint analysis. However, in a world where secret, premeditated homicide was the exception and where most violent deaths were spur-of-the-moment events involving blunt instruments, clear wounds, and many witnesses, the techniques employed by early modern surgeons were usually sufficient to determine the cause of death. It is true that James Low's and Alexander Lillington's medical examinations failed to identify the killer or to determine who had drawn their sword first, but this information would be difficult if not impossible to obtain even with the benefit of modern forensic medicine. Then as now, this type of information could only be provided through witness testimony.

Toward Professionalized and Medicalized Detection?

Given that the frequency of medical testimony in coroners' inquests increased across the seventeenth and eighteenth centuries and that such testimony was rarely vital to the satisfactory conclusion of investigations into suspicious death, an important question remains: why was medical testimony increasingly sought if it regularly failed to contribute much of value to the resolution of coroners' inquests? The answer must lie, as in the case of modern trials, in the perception of the efficacy of forensic medicine rather than the practice. Like the modern CSI effect, it is likely that the growing belief that truth and fact could and should be best discovered through science blinded early modern people to its shortcomings.

Barbara Shapiro has argued that the early modern period witnessed a shift in conceptions of fact from an idea based on legal concepts to an idea based on natural philosophy and science. This shift also constituted a change from conceptions of fact as a probability established through witnessing or empirical observation to a conception of fact as certainty or objective truth based on the laws of nature. According to Shapiro, this shift in mentalities occurred sometime in the late seventeenth or early eighteenth century.[106] This chronology fits fairly well with trends in the use of medical evidence in criminal cases. As we have noted, forensic medicine was used with growing frequency in coroners' inquests from the late seventeenth century. The process by which these conceptions of truth and fact filtered down to the level of coroners' inquests is not entirely clear, but a tentative outline can be given. It has been shown that socio-economic elites were the first to seek the medical opinions of surgeons and physicians in the course of inquests.[107] This is unsurprising, as these early adopters had the resources necessary to pay for medical examinations, had long sought and trusted the expert opinions of medical men, and were more likely to have embraced Enlightenment concepts of truth and fact. Furthermore, inquests held on the deaths of such social and economic elites were more likely to be printed and sensationalized in popular literature, and thus accounts of forensic medicine and its potential efficacy may have reached and influenced a wider, more popular audience.[108] Popular accounts of medical investigations into the deaths of elites and the simple fact that medical experts such as surgeons and physicians were becoming more populous throughout the country combined to make the recourse to medical experts both increasingly possible and attractive.[109] As concepts of what best constituted fact changed in the late seventeenth and early eighteenth centuries, it is possible that judges, coroners, and other legal officials increasingly turned to medicine as a means of discovering legal truth, despite the continued reliance, in practice, on witness testimony. It is reasonable, then, to suppose that the increasing use of forensic medicine in coroners' inquests in the early modern period is more closely tied to cultural perceptions of science, truth, and fact than to the actual efficacy of forensic medicine.

Although even as late as 1750 coroners remained amateur officeholders with little or no medical training and forensic medicine was still not vital to the successful investigation of suspicious death, it could still be argued that the investigation of death was becoming professionalized and medicalized. We have seen that as the period progressed, expert medical testimony was increasingly sought by coroners. It should be stressed, however, that the increasing resort to medical evidence was not a result of any growth in the importance of forensic medicine in practice, but rather the perception that scientific and medical evidence should be sought as a means of discovering truth and fact in criminal cases. It is clear that professional medicine played an increasingly large role in the criminal justice system from the late seventeenth century; however, it is not clear whether or not the more regular resort to medical evidence significantly improved policing and detection in early modern England.

When we compare the evidence garnered from the examination of early modern coroners' inquests with that provided by twentieth-century studies of crime and forensics, it becomes even more evident that it is untenable to evaluate the effectiveness of the early modern English criminal justice system, and more specifically the coroner system, by a simple analysis of the relative sophistication of forensic science or the frequency of its use. Despite the popular perception of the infallibility of forensic science and its importance in modern criminal investigation, modern studies have demonstrated the many inadequacies of forensics and the continued importance of traditional forms of evidence and traditional investigation techniques. B. Parker's pioneering 1963 study "The Status of Forensic Science in the Administration of Criminal Justice" found that only 1 percent of criminal cases used any sort of scientific evidence.[110] In a similar vein, a 1975 Rand Corporation study concluded that the most determinative factor in predicting whether a given crime would be solved was not forensic evidence but the information provided by the victims of crimes to the first responders. The same study also calculated that fingerprints, one of the primary symbols of modern forensics, led to the identification of the offender in only 1 percent of cases.[111] Another study has argued that one of the key factors in arrests leading to successful convictions was the testimony of two or more witnesses.[112] More recently, a study of the use of forensics in the American criminal justice system funded by the U.S. Department of Justice found that 70 percent of the resources of American forensic labs are used for routine drug and alcohol identification, and that crime labs had over 500,000 backlogged requests at the end of 2002.[113] Even when examining cases of suspected homicide, the same study concluded that "homicides among non-strangers and cases with witness reports were significantly more likely to result in arrests. Forensic evidence was not significant."[114] Overall, the study found that only about 2 percent of all cases in the sample "had forensic evidence that linked a suspect to the crime scene and/or victim."[115]

In addition to the aforementioned studies, which cast serious doubt on the centrality of forensic science for modern policing, a number of recent works question the perceived infallibility of modern forensics — even its twin bedrocks, fingerprints and DNA. Simon Cole, for instance, has analyzed all known cases of fingerprint misattribution in the United States and concluded that the actual error rate of fingerprint identification is significantly higher than experts had previously believed.[116] Jonathan Koehler has similarly suggested that error rates for DNA matches are higher than is usually thought — one out of hundreds or thousands rather than the one in a million or billion many people believe.[117] Furthermore, Koehler concludes that DNA evidence should be used to determine whether the "suspect is the source of the genetic evidence" rather than whether the suspect is guilty of the crime.[118] Such errors and doubts about forensic evidence have led to calls for reviews of such evidence and its use in criminal cases. In the last few years, the U.S. Department of Justice has initiated a nationwide review of all criminal cases before the year 2000 handled by the FBI Laboratory's hair and fiber unit — more than 21,000 cases, not including those handled by state and local forensic examiners trained in the same methods by the FBI — prompted by the belief that many of the cases may have been tainted by "exaggerated testimony or false forensic evidence."[119] Similarly, the state of Mississippi has recently received numerous petitions asking for reviews of autopsies handled by a disgraced forensic pathologist who performed roughly 80 percent of all autopsies undertaken in Mississippi between 1989 and his dismissal in 2008, nearly 1,700 a year. Several convictions based on forensic evidence provided by the pathologist have already been overturned on appeal. In response to the criticisms, Mississippi's former state medical examiner commented that the problems were not unique to Mississippi "and are able to persist because scientific testimony is too often viewed with uncritical reverence."[120]

These modern statistics provide an interesting point of comparison with those available for early modern England. What emerges from such a comparison is that both modern and early modern criminal investigations relied heavily on witness testimony rather than forensic evidence to resolve criminal cases. Given the centrality of witnesses in the process of criminal

justice, it is important to note that the proportion of early modern coroners'
inquests that had at least one witness (72 percent) is similar to the proportion for modern homicide cases (76 percent).[121] Therefore, if we concede,
as the evidence for early modern England and modern America suggests,
that the availability of witness testimony is the central factor in the resolution of criminal cases, it seems that there is little difference between the
potential effectiveness of modern and early modern justice systems when
dealing with known cases. In fact, in a number of regards, the early modern
English justice system may have been more effective than its modern counterpart in the investigation of violent death. Modern studies have shown a
steady rise in the rate of "stranger homicide" in the twentieth century due
to a rise in gun-related violence and violence related to street gangs and
narcotics—crime types that are notoriously difficult to solve.[122] In contrast
with the growing proportion of stranger homicide in the modern period,
homicide in early modern England was much more likely to be a crime of
the moment between people who knew each other and were known to the
local community, making detection easier. Another modern study has also
stressed that the evidence provided by victims of crime to first responders
is often a crucial factor in finding the culprit.[123] Given that early modern
victims of homicide may have been more likely to linger for hours or days
before death—due to the state of medical abilities and the lower number of
gun-related fatalities—it may be that a higher proportion of early modern
victims survived long enough to give evidence.[124]

It therefore seems clear that any major difference between the relative effectiveness of modern and early modern policing has little to do with
the advancement of forensic science or forensic medicine. To be sure, the
growing sophistication of medical science across the early modern and
modern periods has had many beneficial consequences, but in terms of
the operation of the criminal justice system, the benefits have perhaps been
overstated. As we have seen, medical advancements had only a limited impact on the identification and apprehension of criminals and the efficient
operation of the criminal justice system. This is not to say that forensic
medicine was never or is never useful in helping to solve cases or detect
crimes—certainly it was and is at times—but rather that any contention

that early modern policing was ineffective or any comparison of the relative effectiveness of policing (between eras or countries) based solely on forensic medicine, its sophistication, or the frequency of its use is fundamentally flawed.

My goal is not to dispute the basic chronology of the development of modern medicine in general or forensic medicine in particular, nor is it to discount the importance of those developments. Instead, the present study questions the importance of the early modern scientific and medical revolutions for criminal justice and the policing of lethal violence. An examination of early modern coroners' inquests and depositions has shown that rudimentary forensic medicine does not preclude effective policing. Witness testimony was far and away the most important resource available to the early modern criminal justice system, and such testimony retains its place of importance to this day. In contrast, the importance of forensic science for early modern criminal justice was more cultural than actual, more perception then reality. It is reasonably certain, however, that such advancements in medicine did help to keep alive victims of accident and malice who would surely have died in an earlier period. It was in the treatment of victims rather than the detection of criminals that the scientific and medical revolutions of the early modern period proved their worth.

The examination of coroners' inquests and depositions reveals that rudimentary or underdeveloped forensic techniques were not a bar to the creation of an effective monopoly of violence. Not only is it true that forensic medicine was sufficiently developed by the end of the sixteenth century to adequately address the vast majority of suspicious or violent deaths encountered by the coroner, but it is also clear that the relative sophistication of sixteenth- and seventeenth-century forensic medicine was immaterial to the effective detection of interpersonal violence. Because most criminal investigations throughout time have relied on witness testimony and local knowledge rather than more scientific methods for explaining and prosecuting lethal violence, the medical knowledge of early modern coroners is of little consequence for discussions of the monopolization of violence. Early modern coroners, like their counterparts in modern criminal investigation, made regular and inventive use of the most important tools of criminal investigation, the knowledge and testimony of local communities. Because the effective use of these techniques is the crux of criminal investigation, it can be argued that from the beginning of the early modern period, and perhaps even earlier, the techniques and methods of detection were in place to take the first step in the restriction and regulation of nonstate, illegitimate violence.

FOUR

One Concept of Justice

THE JURY SYSTEM HAS LONG BEEN presented as a bulwark against the vicissitudes of state power. By allowing common citizens to participate in the definition of justice, the jury system provides a useful check on the state's ability to administer justice in its own interest. In terms of the monopoly of violence, the jury might perhaps be seen as a venue for contestation of the state's definition of legitimate and illegitimate violence, a cornerstone of the monopoly of violence. If the English state was to create an effective monopoly of violence, it would have to ensure that the jury system did not undermine its ability to exclusively define legitimate and illegitimate violence. Thus, the jury could not be allowed to systematically or unilaterally define justice through jury nullification or similar tactics.

The history of the early modern jury is a well-worn topic, and rightfully so, given that the jury was a key venue for the interaction between state and society in the period. Cynthia Herrup and others have suggested that the early modern justice system was characterized by discretion at every level. The need for local participation in the legal process, so the story goes, made it necessary for the crown to cede much of the power of judicial decision-making to local people, local interests, and local conceptions of justice. As a result, the justice system as a whole, and perhaps particularly the jury, became of necessity a site of negotiation, where central and communal notions of justice were forced to compromise in order for the system to function. While it is certainly true that the early modern English justice system required popular participation to function, a reexamination of the jury system that explores the geographical origins and personal relationships of jurors reveals that deliberate steps were taken by the authorities in jury selection to temper local agency in the judicial process. Such a reexamination demonstrates that the early modern jury was not a site for ne-gotiation between two concepts of justice, but rather a venue designed to extract local knowledge and information without sacrificing the process or definition of justice to the whims of local communities.

In an age before professional policing and administration, it was nec-essary to secure local knowledge by incorporating local individuals into the justice system as jurors. However, the need for information did not mean that the state ceded its monopoly of justice to the dictates of local society. Instead, by carefully selecting those who sat on each type of jury on the ba-sis of status, geography, and relationship to victim or defendant, the early modern legal system went to considerable lengths to appropriately balance the scales of justice between the twin needs of impartiality and information, control and participation. The early modern jury was not so much a venue for the articulation of communal conceptions of justice as it was a state-controlled tool for extracting information and implementing central and elite judicial priorities.

This type of jury was vitally important for the provision of justice in general, but especially for the monopolization of violence. If coroners' juries and trial juries were composed only of men whose interests aligned with the government, it would prove difficult to secure information about violence in far-flung areas of the country. Conversely, if such information was secured through the participation of local jurors alone, it would be impossible to ensure that they would not subvert the law to serve justice as they or their community saw it. Local participation was necessary to sup-ply information, but the independence of a local jury was also a potential threat to the monopolization of violence. To secure and protect a monopoly of violence, the English state needed to ensure that all lethal violence was detected, prosecuted, and punished. This need often ran counter to the desires of local individuals and local communities who might accept other, nonstate forms of dispute resolution, such as feud or wergild, or might ex-cuse some types of violence — accidents, suicides, duels, revenge killings — altogether. The use of extrajudicial forms of dispute resolution undermined the authority of state institutions and the dictates of state-promulgated laws. Excusing types of violence deemed illegitimate by the state but legitimate by local custom likewise undermined the state's right to define justice. Local redefinition of legitimate and illegitimate violence also undermined efforts to protect population resources and to make those resources legible to the state. The successful monopolization of violence, therefore, depended on the creation of a jury that ensured local participation while leaving the power to define illegitimate violence in sole possession of the state and its agents.

Our exploration of the function of early modern juries will begin at the bottom with coroners' juries, the clearest and most overlooked example of the use of geographical composition for the purposes of information gathering, before moving to different types of petty juries and ending with a discussion of the grand jury. I will demonstrate that at each level a balance was sought between the needs of impartiality and information, with the exact balance reflecting the jurisdiction, geographical scope, and purpose of each type of jury. Although the constitution of each type of tribunal differed, all sought a membership that would address the particular needs of the specific jury in question.

Through the examination of the full range of early modern criminal juries as tools of state power, it becomes clear that the coroner's jury, directed and often dominated by the coroner, was a crucial aspect of the apparatus of the state's monopoly of violence. Without local information and local knowledge, the state's definition of legitimate and illegitimate violence could not be enforced. Hence, the coroner's jury and the balance of its composition were a key aspect of the central authority's growing power over violence and death. When viewed in relation to the contemporary jury system as a whole, it becomes clear that the restriction of lethal violence and the regulation of death was part and parcel of a wider system of state control that sought to effectively restrict crime and violence in a world without widespread professional judicial officials or policing. Thus, the jury system in general and the coroner's jury in particular can be appropriately viewed as a mechanism of state power in an amateur world, rather than a site of negotiation between state and society.

Theories of Jury Function

While the historical literature explores a wide range of issues relating to the early modern jury, historians of the early modern period tend to view the jury in similar ways.[1] Following Cynthia Herrup, historians tend to see the widespread participation in the judicial process as evidence that the jury represented a communal definition of justice in opposition to the representatives of the state such as justices and judges. Thus, the jury, and indeed the criminal justice system as a whole, is often seen as a site of negotiation between the interests of crown and community, a venue in which local individuals possessed real agency and the power to influence the course of justice.[2]

While it would be foolish to deny the role of the community in the judicial process, the current focus on negotiation and agency unduly masks the repressive and exploitative nature of early modern criminal justice. This is not to say that the common people of the period had no ability to act on their own accord. Social historians have done a great service in illuminating the myriad ways in which everyday individuals sought to determine their own destinies. Uncovering the hidden transcripts of resistance and the strategies employed by the seemingly powerless to navigate an unequal world has provided an important corrective to histories of the elite. And yet, the early modern world *was* a world of vast inequalities of power, a world in which the lives and actions of a large swath of the population were regularly subjected to the whims of the powerful and the dictates of the state. Regular men and women certainly had an active part to play in the power dynamics of early modern England, but these relationships were mediated on terms set by elites and in institutions created and governed by elites.

The early modern jury was not intended to be a site of negotiation between government and populace, but instead was part the machinery of state control. In an era with limited formal judicial structures, the need for local knowledge and local information necessitated the use of local men on juries of all types. By selecting jurors on the basis of both economic status and geographical origins, the crown and its agents sought a means of securing the local information about crime, offenders, and society necessary to maintain control without sacrificing completely the state's interests in the impartial application of its laws. Thus, the goal of the jury system was not primarily the accommodation of two competing conceptions of justice—local and state—but rather an attempt by the state to use jury composition as a means of obtaining needed local knowledge and information without diluting the needs of centrally dictated justice.

Perhaps because of the focus on petty or trial juries and on socioeconomic status, historians of the English judicial system tend to dismiss the possibility that the early modern jury possessed self-informing functions. Instead, the accepted narrative is that while the medieval jury had some responsibility to self-inform by seeking and collecting their own evidence, by the sixteenth century this function had been replaced by the appearance of witness testimony.[3] With increasing numbers of nonjuror witnesses testifying at trial, jurors were no longer suppliers of evidence, but weighers of facts presented by others.[4] It is undoubtedly true that early modern jurors were charged with considering evidence in novel ways with greater regularity than their medieval counterparts. However, it is not at all clear that their new role in considering facts and hearing testimony in any way eroded their function as suppliers of local information and knowledge. In fact, judicial discretion would have been impossible without local information, given that it required knowledge about the defendant's reputation, criminal history, status, and credit in his or her community. Some of this information was supplied by witnesses, but knowledge of defendants, prosecutors, and their local circumstances was also supplied by those jurors who sat in judgment of their neighbors. If we move beyond a narrow focus on socio-economic status and trial juries to consider jurors and the jury system more holistically, it is apparent that the early modern judicial system used the composition of juries as a method for balancing the dual needs of impartiality and discretion. Rather than privileging one over the other, early modern juries were thus both suppliers and triers of evidence, both neighbor and judge.

The Coroner's Jury

In the traditional preamble to their inquest concerning the death of James Harrison of Nether Burnham, Lincolnshire, in June 1669, the jurors succinctly outline the intended purpose and responsibility of the early modern coroner's jury: "wee whose names are subscribed being impannelled, sworne and charged by Robt Bernard gen. one of his majesty's coroners in the said county, to inquire how and in what manner James Harrison, late of Nether Burnham aforesaid husbandman, whose body is found lying dead, came unto his death, upon view of the body of the said James Harrison and the testimony of witnesses . . . ."[5] Although it is more likely that the inquest—of which this preamble was a part—was written by the coroner or a clerk, the document to which the jurors affixed their signatures or their marks represented the final product of the work described in the preamble and the ideal to which a coroner's jury aspired. According to the law, the jury's role was to inquire into the cause of death of those who died in violent or suspicious circumstances, to collect evidence and hear witnesses, and finally to present a verdict to the coroner. The law of the period further specified that coroners' juries were to be selected from "persons of the four next adjacent villages" and to number at least 12.[6] In practice the number of jurors varied from the minimum of 12 to twice that number. In the reign of Elizabeth, West Sussex averaged 15 jurors per inquest, while East Sussex averaged 14.[7] This average remained relatively stable throughout the early modern period; in late seventeenth-century Lincolnshire, for instance, the average number of jurors per inquest was about 15. No specific qualifications were mandated by law for coroners' jurors except that they could not be felons or outlaws and that they were to be the "discretest, ablest and best" of those summoned for service.[8]

In order to ensure that the required number of qualified jurors reported to the site of the inquest, coroners sent orders to local officials such as bailiffs, constables, or serjeants commanding them to summon the requisite number of local men. In 1621 at Ludlow, Shropshire, for example, the town's coroner sent a written charge to the local serjeants requesting that they "geve express warning to xxiiii sufficient inhabitants within this towne to be and personally appeare before me Richard Fisher gent., coroner to our soveraigne lord the king for this towne and libtes [liberties] of Ludlow by fowre of the clock in the afternone of this present daye and then to vewe the body of one Hunffrey ap Rule."[9] Having arrived, the jurors would be apprised of their duties and responsibilities as jurors. A Shropshire jury was told in 1739 that "[y]ou shall diligently enquire and a true presentment make of all such things as shall be given you in charge or shall come to your knowledge concerning the several deaths of William Loyd and Sarah his wife and a true verdict give thereof to his majesties coroner of this town according to your evidence so help you god."[10] This statement has the sound of an oath, and although it is unclear whether the jurors were supposed to recite this oath or whether it was merely a charge read to them by the coroner or a clerk, it was of the utmost importance that the jurors were made aware of the gravity of their responsibilities. Lest one conclude from this charge that the role of the early modern coroner's jury was passive, an earlier statement made by another Shropshire jury more explicitly highlighted their active role in the inquest process. In reporting their findings to the coroner, they declared that "this jury having carefully and diligently tried all matters and after the finding out of the truth and informacion of theire own knowledge are persuaded to find . . ."[11]

The Socio-economic Makeup of the Coroner's Jury

The law stipulated that the jurors charged with this active pursuit of truth were to be selected from among the "best" and more substantial men of local society, generally small landholders and local tradesmen of some importance in the community (although usually they were of a lower standing than the coroners themselves). A sample of coroners' jurors from Lincolnshire in the seventeenth century paints a similar picture.[12] Of the 199 jurors whose status is known, roughly 16 percent were listed as gentlemen, 82 percent were styled yeomen, and 2 percent tradesmen of various sorts. The only other convenient measure of jury status besides the listed occupations is the examination of signatures. As mentioned in Chapter 2,

the examination of signatures is at best a rough guide to educational attainment and thus an even rougher guide to individual status. Even so,
taking a closer look at the signature patterns on coroners' inquests may
yet provide some notion of the general status or educational level of coroners' jurors. Taking the inquests for Lincolnshire as a sample, we see
that slightly over 76 percent of jurors endorsed the final inquest with a
signature, while slightly over 23 percent endorsed the document with a
mark.[13] Given that in early modern educational practice reading was generally taught before writing, we can thus be relatively certain that about
three-quarters of Lincolnshire coroners' jurors were literate by the mid-
seventeenth century.[14] We can say less about the quarter of the jurors who
did not possess the ability to sign their own names. They may well have
had some literacy, perhaps leaving school after learning to read but before
learning to write. When compared to the literacy rate for the country as a
whole — around 30 percent by the mid-seventeenth century — the fact that
around 75 percent of coroners' jurors could read and write suggests that,
on the whole, coroners' jurors came from among the more educated segment of local society.[15] Clearly, then, most jurors were literate, suggesting
a status of middling or above, even if a substantial minority remained illit-
erate. The pattern of signatures, however, did not remain static across the
30-odd years of the Lincolnshire records. Whereas in the earliest inquests
the proportion of signatures to marks was fairly even, by the end of the
1690s the vast majority signed their names — only 17 jurors used marks
after 1696.[16]

Although only a small proportion of coroners' jurors were listed as
gentlemen, it is significant that almost every coroner's jury recorded in the
Lincolnshire records between 1669 and 1701 contained at least one gentleman.[17] The fact that there was almost never more than one gentleman
on an inquest jury suggests that this was not a mere accident of demography.[18] As the natural and traditional leaders of local society, it seems that
a single gentleman was sought out by coroners to serve on each inquest
jury. Whether the representative gentleman was sought as the foreman or
leader of the jury or to lend authority and credibility to the proceedings is
unclear — probably a bit of both — but it is evident that the participation of

local gentlemen was seen as beneficial, and perhaps even necessary, for the undertaking of a coroner's inquest.

A much smaller and patchier set of coroners' inquests from the borough of Ludlow in Shropshire in the late sixteenth and early seventeenth centuries presents a glimpse of jury status and occupation in an urban setting, in contrast to the more rural picture provided by the Lincolnshire records. In Ludlow a similar proportion of jurors were listed as gentlemen: 16 percent in Lincolnshire and 18 percent in Ludlow. However, whereas the vast majority of Lincolnshire jurors were listed as yeomen (82 percent), the largest status group among the Ludlow jurors (nearly 64 percent) was made up of tradesmen or artisans of various types including tailors, saddlers, butchers, weavers, and stay makers. A mere 9 percent of Ludlow jurors were listed as yeomen, with another 5 percent listed as laborers.[19]

The differences between the status and occupation of the jurors of Lincolnshire and Ludlow are not surprising given the differences between the jurisdictions. Lincolnshire was a large and largely rural county, and as such it is not surprising that more jurors were yeomen than tradesmen. Ludlow, as a borough, maintained a small but vital cadre of artisans, and since the jury pool was restricted to residents of the borough, it makes sense that that Ludlow coroners would rely on tradesmen rather than yeomen for their juries. As these examples illustrate, since jurors would be unable or unwilling to travel great distances to sit on juries, coroners were more likely to recruit jurors from areas close to the place of inquest, resulting in a fairly limited pool of potential jurors. Because coroners' juries were likely to be local affairs, the composition of such juries reflected the occupational makeup of the local community, with urban juries containing more tradesmen and fewer yeomen and rural juries containing more yeomen and fewer artisans. While the specific occupational structure of coroners' juries therefore differed from place to place, the general status level of jurors remained broadly the same regardless of location. A substantial majority of coroners' jurors could be classified as belonging to what contemporaries termed "the middling sort."[20] While members of the upper orders, such as gentlemen, regularly participated and members of the lower orders such as laborers were occasionally listed as jurors, in early modern England service on a coroners' jury was primarily a local, middling affair.

The socio-economic status of jurors, and indeed all officeholders, was seen by contemporaries as directly related to the impartial, disinterested application of the law. Wealth, status, and the power they brought were thought to be a useful insulator against the temptations of bribery. If the poor were allowed to hold office, they might be tempted to ignore the law in exchange for payment. Those with more economic independence, on the other hand, could be expected to put the interests of the law above their own gain. This way of thinking went hand and hand with more general conceptions of the connection between socio-economic status and credibility, morality, and honesty. In reality, of course, no such direct connection between social power and moral compass existed, and elite official corruption often seems to have been the rule rather than the exception. However, in creating the rules for jury selection, the salient point is not that status actually equated with honesty, but that those who crafted legal policies believed that status and impartiality were indeed synonymous. Morality aside, the restriction of jury service to local elites helped ensure that those members of the public who aided in the enforcement of the law would share an interest in law and order more similar to that of the political elites than to the interests and opinions of that section of the populace that felt the weight of the law.

The Limits of the Jury Pool

Many of the jurors found in the inquest records appear to have served on more than one jury over the course of their lives, with identical surnames also appearing with noticeable regularity. This is not surprising, given that early modern jury pools were fairly small and relatively restricted. Small jury pools and repeated service did provide early modern coroners' inquests with some distinct benefits. Foremost among these advantages was undoubtedly the high likelihood that some members of any given jury would have had prior experience with the procedure and operation of a coroner's inquest. Thus, while the coroner was always on hand to inform the jury of proper protocol, surely much of the jury instruction was supplied by the jurors themselves, with veteran jurors guiding the novices.

In addition to those who served on multiple juries, it was not uncommon for individuals with some tie to the case — a relative or friend of the deceased, or a witness to the death — to act as a juror during the inquest. For instance, in Sussex in 1522, Anthony Baynard, Alexander Bourne, and John Parker discovered the body of a 12-year-old servant girl named Lucy in a pit full of water in "le Cheker" inn in Battle. The two coroners of the liberty of Battle, John Wylegose and Robert Chalcrofte, were duly summoned and convened an inquest. Among the jurors selected by Wylegose and Chalcrofte to serve on the inquest were Baynard, Bourne, and Parker.[21] The practice of witnesses serving as jurors continued throughout the early modern period. In 1670 a coroner's jury investigating the drowning death of Anne Staville contained two men with ties to the case. Matthew Everatt not only served on the jury, but also provided a witness statement concerning the deceased's state of mind on the day she died. Another juror, Richard Slingsley, was likely a relative of Anne Slingsley, who also provided information to the inquest.[22]

Four years after the death of Lucy, in 1526, Stephen Roote and John Stapely, coroners for the archbishop of Canterbury in Sussex, convened two separate inquests at Groombridge. The first found that Margery Avys had feloniously hanged herself in the kitchen of the house she shared with her husband Robert. For the second inquest, related to a suspected murder, the same jury was again impaneled by Roote and Stapely, with the notable exception that one of the original jurors was replaced for the second inquest by Robert Avys, the husband of the subject of the first inquest.[23]

One might be tempted to dismiss these practices as holdovers from the self-informing juries of the medieval period and to disappear as the period progressed and advances in communication and transportation made such irregularities unnecessary or impossible. However, even in the late seventeenth and eighteenth centuries, coroners' juries continued to contain people with direct knowledge of, or interests in, the subject of the inquest. Take, for instance, the inquest on the body of Robert Nescoll at Winteringham, Lincolnshire, in 1691. Nescoll was an old man, "aged seventy years and upward," according to the inquest.[24] Weak and likely poor, Nescoll

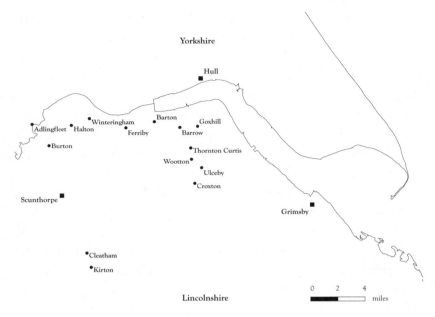

Figure 3. Towns of early modern Lincolnshire.

was traveling from Ferriby to his brother's home in Aldingfleet. Given that it was the constable of Ferriby who conveyed him to Winteringham, the next stop on the way to Aldingfleet, it is likely that he was being moved to his brother's because his current parish of residence no longer wanted to pay for his care. William Roberts, the constable of Winteringham, then moved Nescoll to the next town, Halton. The constable of Halton, William Bainton, in turn brought the old man to Burton, where he was placed in the charge of Christopher Palgrave and John Hall, constables of Burton. Realizing that Nescoll had no money to pay for his lodging in Burton or the rest of his journey, Palgrave and Hall brought him back to the constable of Halton and demanded money to cover their expenses. The Halton authorities followed suit and sent the weary old man back to Winteringham with requests for reimbursement. Already ill, and confronted with bad weather the entire trip, Nescoll succumbed to the rigors of this pointless and seemingly endless traveling and died in Winteringham (Fig. 3).[25]

As sad as the death of Nescoll may seem, and as revealing of the short-comings of the early modern poor relief system as it may be, the subsequent inquest is interesting mostly for one aspect of how the inquest jury was composed. The constables who had ushered Nescoll between the various towns were called to give depositions at the inquest, as normal procedure would require. However, one of these constables was not only a deponent but also a member of the jury. Christopher Palgrave, who deposed that he and John Hall had conveyed Nescoll from Burton back to Halton because he lacked the money to pay for his travels, was duly impaneled as a member of the jury that inquired into Nescoll's death.[26] This is interesting not only because Palgrave was a witness, but also because Palgrave's actions in sending a weary old man back on the road in bad weather could be seen as contributing to Nescoll's death, if not legally then perhaps morally. The fact that such a man was sought out for jury service leads one to question whether the purpose of early modern coroners' juries was simply to weigh evidence impartially.

The practice of service on multiple juries and the service of inter-ested parties was likely the result of a number of factors related to the make-up of English society and the purpose of early modern juries. Given that jury pools were small, travel difficult, and many eligible men avoided, or at least tried to avoid, jury service, coroners were likely to seek out those men who had previously been willing to serve on an inquest jury. At the same time, because failure to appear for jury service was fairly common, even with the threat of fines or the inducement of pay, jurors were likely to be a self-selecting group of men who felt that the obligation to serve was impor-tant. As such, expediency was likely a major factor in selecting a coroner's jury. In 1744 a Shropshire coroner, perhaps for the sake of convenience, went so far as to make the owner of the "White Lion where the body of Richard Bayranel lay dead" a member of the jury.[27] As the inquest was be-ing held in his establishment—a common occurrence in a period with few public buildings or even other private buildings large enough to host such an event—John Chipp, the proprietor of the White Lion, was a perfect ju-ror: of middling status, readily available, and unlikely to be absent.

Early modern English juries were not designed to be impartial judges of fact, but rather were intended to be active repositories and suppliers of communal knowledge and local information. Some historians have questioned whether self-informing juries ever actually existed. The evidence of coroners' juries demonstrates that at least some early modern juries were undoubtedly expected to function as both providers and weighers of facts.[28] Not only is this evident from the makeup of coroners' juries—which did not *exclude* but instead actively *sought* relatives, witnesses, and friends of the deceased to serve as jurors—but the importance of a self-informing jury was also intrinsic to the laws governing the selection of coroners' jurors. As previously noted, coroners were instructed to summon potential jurors from the immediate vicinity of the death. In addition, unlike trial jurors, coroners' jurors could not be challenged or disputed. As William Greenwood states in his guide to officeholding, unlike other juries "in these Inquests lie no exceptions or challenges to the persons of the Jurors."[29] The reason for this prohibition on jury challenges seems to be that the normal objection of bias made against trial jurors did not apply to coroners' jurors because they were *supposed* to have knowledge of the people and events involved.

Because English juries—or at least coroners' juries—were viewed as self–informing to some degree by contemporaries, it is unsurprising that coroners intentionally sought out men to serve on juries who may in hindsight be viewed as partial or otherwise tainted. Individuals who had served on many juries, sometimes even on the same day, were thus seen as assets rather than detriments to the inquest process, bringing their knowledge gained through experience to bear and perhaps guiding first-time jurors through the responsibilities of the office. Similarly, witnesses, friends, and relatives of the deceased were not seen as hopelessly compromised, but were instead valued for their ability to provide much need local insight and context. It was the juror's role to bring what knowledge he had to the attention of the coroner and his fellow jurors, not simply to weigh the evidence provided by others. As criminal proceedings of the period so often relied on the character, reputation, and trustworthiness of accuser and accused to decide cases based largely on oral testimony rather than physical evidence, a detailed local knowledge was essential rather than detrimental to the operation of early modern juries. Coroners' juries were thus information gatherers and suppliers rather than the interpreters of evidence familiar in our own period.

The Geography of Early Modern Coroners' Juries

While early modern juries may not have met modern standards of impartiality, steps were taken to ensure some level of objective decision-making and to involve the wider county community in legal decision-making. The records of Lincolnshire provide an interesting venue for examining how the dual purposes of the early modern legal system were accomplished. As mentioned above, most coroners' juries contained members from the place of death or the home of the deceased. Every inquest in Lincolnshire between 1669 and 1701, however, also contained jurors from at least one other town or parish. In fact, the vast majority of inquest juries were made up of men from three or four towns or parishes other than the place of inquest. Of the 38 inquests for which the place of residence of the jurors is known, each had jurors from an average of four distinct localities, with a minimum of two and a maximum of five different places of residence.[30] The distribution of jurors between towns tended to be as even as possible for any one inquest. For example, when John Neville, coroner for Lincolnshire, convened an inquest on the body of Edward Medly at Wootton in 1691, he summoned 16 jurors, four from Wootton itself, four from Thornton Curtis, four from Ulceby, and four from Croxton.[31] This method of dividing the number of jurors as evenly as possible between three or four different towns was repeated again and again throughout the period.

The process by which this division of the jury was achieved is aptly described in the records of an inquest taken by Nicholas Cunliffe, coroner for Lancashire, in 1697. Cunliffe had been called to hold an inquest on the body of Thomas Duckworth, who had been found dead at the village of Dillworth in June 1697.[32] Upon arrival at Dillworth on June 9, Cunliffe summoned a jury from the surrounding towns and villages, charging the constables of each with bringing a certain number of potential jurors. William Roads, likely the constable of Thornby, was charged with bringing four jurors to the site of the inquest. Edward King, constable of Dutton, was responsible for bringing two jurors from his jurisdiction, including the "primus juror," or foreman. The constable of Axton, surname Ratliffe (first name unknown), was to bring four jurors from Axton. Two further jurors were to be summoned from Ashton and two from Dillworth itself. In addition to securing the Dillworth contingent of the jury, constable Jeremy Page was responsible for bringing the five witnesses to the inquest. All were charged, and the witnesses bound over, by the coroner to appear at the house of "Widdow Horrobry" in Whalley two days later, on June 11, "by 10 of ye clock in the morning to give evidence."[33] The manner in which coroners ordered the gathering of jurors makes the intentionality of the division of jurors between towns or villages clear.

Not only were jurors usually, and intentionally, evenly divided between a number of towns, there also seem to have been regular patterns of jury service based on the location of the inquest. For example, inquests taken at Barton in the 1690s usually contained jurors from Barrow, Ferriby, and Harstow in addition to jurors from Barton itself. Similarly, inquests taken at Barrow in the same period always had jurors from Barton and Goxhill. Inquests from Kirton always had jurors from Cleatham, and inquests in Cleatham always had jurors from Kirton, and this pattern repeated itself again and again. One reason was surely the proximity of the jurors' places of residence to the site of the inquest. An examination of the residences of the various coroners' jurors in Lincolnshire shows that they were likely to come from places within a five- to ten-mile radius of the inquest site. If proximity alone were the only consideration, however, it would not have been practical to draw jurors from an average of four different locations, as coroners in the period repeatedly did. Instead, jurors would all have been summoned from the location of the inquest, with perhaps one other location if the numbers necessary could not be supplied from the place of the inquest alone. In reality, however, coroners in Lincolnshire never convened an inquest consisting of jurors from a single place, and only on rare occasions was a jury composed of men from only two places. This suggests

162 One Concept of Justice

that there was more for the coroner to consider when summoning jurors than simply proximity and efficiency. Coroners, it seems, went out of their way to impanel juries composed of men from a number of locations, perhaps as a means of involving the local community in the legal process or as a means of ensuring that the verdict reached by the jury would be viewed as legitimate by both local and county society.

The records for Gedling in Nottinghamshire seem to confirm the pattern noted for Lincolnshire. On average, the constables of Gedling sent four men to serve on each coroner's jury between 1672 and 1710, the same average number of jurors per town noted in the Lincolnshire records.[34] The Gedling jurors traveled to Radcliffe (about 3 miles away), Sneinton (2.5 miles away), and Burton Joyce (2.5 miles away) twice; to Colwick (1.5 miles away) three times; to Nottingham (4 miles away) on four occasions; and to Arnold (3 miles away), Stoke Bardolph (about 2 miles away), and Carlton (half a mile away) once each.[35] As we can see, the jurors of Gedling generally stayed within a five-mile radius of their homes, a reasonable maximum distance when one takes into account that the men had to be summoned, travel to the place of inquest, serve on the jury, and travel back home, perhaps for several days in a row. An early seventeenth-century Shropshire jury, for instance, was informed by the coroner after a day spent concluding an inquest that they were "to meete agayne at the newe howse upon Saturday the 27th day of this instant Aprill at three of the clocke in the afternoon to seale the indenture."[36] One would hardly expect such a jury to travel more than five or ten miles on multiple occasions over the course of a week, a month, or possibly more (Fig. 4).

The distances that jurors traveled to the site of the inquest also illustrate one goal of an early modern coroner's jury: to obtain jurors who had local knowledge without sacrificing the power of the state to local opinion. By including, and even seeking out, witnesses, friends, neighbors, or relatives of the deceased to serve on coroners' juries and seeking jurors from two or three other towns within a five- to ten-mile radius, early modern coroners managed to impanel juries that brought to bear direct knowledge of the death or the deceased and ensured local participation in the legal process. At the same time, composing juries in this geographically diverse

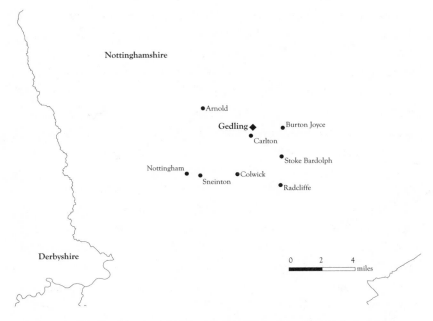

Figure 4. Gedling and its environs in seventeenth-century Nottinghamshire

manner also restricted the influence of local communities to define justice as they saw fit. The calculated nature of jury selection suggests that the authorities actively sought to temper the influence of local participation by spreading the jury between those who could provide local legal knowledge and those who, because they lacked ties to the specific community in question, were less vulnerable to local pressure.

Jury Payment

In an attempt to ensure participation on coroners' juries and to compensate jurors who traveled significant distances, local authorities often paid a small sum to each man who answered the call to jury service. When a body was found, the coroner would instruct the local constables to bring a certain number of eligible men from their jurisdictions to the site of the inquest to serve on the jury. In addition to securing the men necessary for the inquest, each constable was responsible for paying each juror a fee for his appearance, for which the constable would be reimbursed at the end of his term in office. The constables' records for Gedling show that payments were made to coroners' jurors on 19 separate occasions between 1672 and 1711—a total of £6 2s 11d. At an average of 6s 6d per jury, this sum represented a not insignificant outlay for the constable and ultimately the parish. If we look at the payments to juries where the number of jurors from Gedling is known, we can estimate that roughly 1s 6d was paid to each coroner's juror.[37] This outlay was intended to make up for the lost wages or other income of the jurors, as well as food or lodging if that became necessary.

Donald Woodward has estimated that the average daily wage of a craftsman in the 1690s was about 1s.[38] If we consider that the Gedling jurors were most likely to come from the middling ranks of society, it would be reasonable to conclude that the daily income of most coroners' jurors was close to that sum. Thus, the payment of, on average, 1s 6d to each Gedling juror probably represented slightly more than the jurors could expect to make on a daily basis. It seems, then, that the payment made to jurors for their service was not simply designed to make up for lost wages, but also to provide some reward for past service or incentive for future service.

While constables paid potential jurors a small sum to appear and serve on inquest juries, coroners had the power to fine those men who failed to appear for jury service. In order to ensure compliance with jury summons, the fine levied on absent jurors could be fairly severe. A Mr. Northorp, for instance, was fined 10s by John Neville, coroner for Lincolnshire, when he failed to appear for jury service as summoned in 1692.[39] Similarly, a juror was fined at Ludlow in Shropshire in 1744 for failing to appear as ordered. Although the amount of the fine was not stipulated in this case, Greenwood suggested that those who failed to appear for jury service should be fined 40s, a considerable amount even in the mid-eighteenth century.[40] Although fines for failure to appear are somewhat uncommon, they were enforced on occasion, suggesting that while a significant number of people may have tried to avoid jury service, a small but significant proportion faced stiff penalties.[41] Participating in such local facets of the criminal justice system as coroners' juries was important both for officials and for the health and peace of the community. As in many other areas of early modern society, this vital participation was encouraged by carrot and stick, payment and fines.

Jury – Coroner Interaction

While the duties and makeup of the early modern coroner's jury are clear, the manner in which coroners and jurors interacted in the course of an inquest is more opaque. Though descriptions of inquests in action are rare, enough evidence exists to allow a tentative analysis of the relationship between coroners and their jurors.

Coroners and jurors usually worked in concert. On occasion, however, the interactions between the representative of justice and the representatives of the community were fraught or contentious. Generally speaking, these disputes hinged on divergent interpretations of justice—rather than simple corruption—which led the coroner and jury to disagree about the proper verdict in a particular case. The case of a killing at York in the sixteenth century provides one such example. The records do not provide the name of the deceased, but the dispute over the verdict is clear. Evidence was given at the inquest that a man named Robinson was responsible for the killing. Despite the evidence presented at the inquest, the jury declined to find a verdict of murder in the case. The coroner, John Dixon, "refused to receve the same verdicte and caused them to make an other verdicte," whereupon Robinson was arraigned and tried at the next assize.[42] In this case, as in others, the opinion of the coroner was paramount. The coroner's jury evidently felt that the information provided at the inquest was not sufficient to suggest a verdict against Robinson and presented the coroner with a verdict that reflected this opinion. Despite the jury's interpretation, the coroner threw out their verdict and demanded that they make another verdict that more closely accorded with his reading of the evidence. In this the coroner prevailed, as the jury did indeed come to a new verdict that matched the coroners' instructions and was duly certified.

This is just one example of the limits placed on negotiation and agency in the early modern justice system. Historians have argued that failing to reach a verdict and finding against the evidence were strategies that used the participatory nature of the system to enforce the law according to local notions of equity and justice. Time and time again, however, juries that reached verdicts which conflicted with the interpretations of judges and other officials found themselves overruled, fined, or even prosecuted in higher courts. Juries were responsible for delivering verdicts, but their independence was largely circumscribed by the presence of state officials who set and enforced the boundaries of acceptable verdicts.

Not all coroners' juries were so easily cowed, and coroners did not always prevail in clashes with their juries over the proper interpretation of the evidence at hand. Take, for example, the dispute over the inquest into the death of William Marshall in Somerset in 1637. Marshall was a sheriff's bailiff with a reputation in the county for violent and heavy-handed behavior. He had been accused of extortion, breaking and entering, and using threatening words—telling one terrified woman that he would "rip up her guts"—in the course of carrying out his duties.[43] At the Somerset Assize of July 1635, a dispute between Marshall and a Robert Brodribb was referred to Sir Henry Berkeley and Thomas Lyte, two justices of the peace in Somerset.[44] Two years later, Marshall was sent to arrest Edward Cooke on a civil process. Finding Cooke locked in his house, Marshall and his deputies attempted to break in to effect the arrest. In the course of the break-in, Cooke shot Marshall, leading to the latter's death. Valentine Powell, coroner of Somerset, impaneled a jury to inquire into the circumstances of the bailiff's demise. The jury refused to return a verdict—likely because of Marshall's reputation for brutality and his unlawful attempt to break into Cooke's home. As a result of their failure to return a verdict, the jurymen were bound over by the coroner to appear at the Chard Assize in March 1637, where they were fined 40s each, except James Dryall who was fined the princely sum of £5.[45] Ultimately, the case was removed to King's Bench, where in 1639 the court found that Marshall's attempt to break into Cooke's house was illegal and therefore Cooke's actions amounted to manslaughter rather than murder.[46] The intransigence of the inquest jury was thus vindicated and their version of justice upheld. It is not clear whether Valentine Powell bound over the jury because he felt Marshall's death should have been found to be a murder or simply because the jury failed to return a verdict of any sort, but it was not unheard of for coroner and jury to disagree over the proper definition of justice.[47]

It is difficult to know exactly how common such disputes over inquest verdicts were or whether they were usually resolved in favor of the coroner or his jury. Thus, it is also hard to say with any certainty how much influence the coroner had over verdicts or how much autonomy was given to coroners' juries.[48] On balance, however, it seems that the coroner's instructions were usually followed. A coroner had the power to throw out his jury's verdict and demand that they make another, a power that was used with some regularity. Juries had their weapons, too, as we have seen. If coroner and jury disagreed, the jury could simply refuse to submit any verdict at all. In these cases the juries risked a fine, but the stalemate was then usually resolved by one of the central courts, providing the jury a venue for its convictions and complaints to be heard. The recourse to the central courts was a viable strategy in disputes between coroner and jury, but it is important to remember that such a strategy still placed the ultimate decision-making power in the hands of a government tribunal staffed by centrally appointed officers.

Accusations of bribery confirm the supposition that coroners had significant influence over the outcome of inquests. William Cooke, for example, accepted over £4 from friends of William Burton to find that Burton had died by misfortune rather than suicide as the evidence suggested.[49] Although such cases of bribery are rare, when they do occur the party whose influence is sought is almost always the coroner rather than the jury. That those seeking to pervert justice would focus their attempts at bribery on the coroner instead of the jury suggests that the coroner had, or was at least seen to have, greater power to alter an inquest verdict.

The vagaries of the judicial records mean that the direct interactions between coroner and community are necessarily weighted toward encounters characterized by dispute or suit. As a result of this imbalance, it is important to tread carefully when making conclusions about the nature of the relationship between any officeholder and the populace at large. As ever, confrontation and collaboration were both part of a criminal justice system that relied on popular participation. And while the judicial records paint a picture of warring factions, the reality is that the interactions between coroner and community were more often constructive than contentious. Jurors, witnesses, and even towns were fined for negligence, corruption, or simple intransigence. Coroners, too, were accused by communities of failing to perform their duties, whether due to corruption, incompetence, or sloth. Instances of accusations against either community or coroner are comparatively rare: confrontation was the exception and cooperation the rule.

The reality of cooperation, however, should not be taken as evidence that the coroner's jury was a venue for negotiation between popular and official notions of justice and legitimate violence. The rules of the game were made by the state, and it was through the coroner that these rules were enforced. The primary function of the coroner's jury was to collect the information necessary to regulate illegitimate violence and prevent private vengeance. To do this it was necessary to incorporate the participation of local men without compromising the state's definition of justice. As we have seen, this was done by balancing the composition of the coroner's jury according to the criteria of geographical origins and social status. In this way, information could be gathered without conceding the definition of legitimate violence to the populace.

Evidence of this can be gleaned from the patterns of central court litigation involving coroners and their juries. While it is true that both coroners and coroners' juries were regularly sued in the central courts, a phenomenon that will be explored more fully in Chapter 6, each group was usually charged with a different violation. Coroners' jurors who refused to reach verdicts, or who delivered verdicts that were contrary to the evidence or differed from the conclusions reached by the coroner, were regularly sued in Star Chamber or summoned to appear at King's Bench. That they occasionally prevailed does not negate the fact that their initial independence resulted in legal action by the central courts. Coroners who clashed with their juries or overruled their verdicts, on the other hand, were rarely prosecuted by the central authorities. Instead, coroners were generally subject to litigation only in cases where their behavior subverted the interests of the crown: when they colluded with jurors, heirs, or creditors to reach verdicts that were disadvantageous to the state, or when they attempted to keep or disperse forfeit goods that should have gone to the crown. Therefore, it is reasonable to conclude that because of the influence and power of the coroner over his jurors, and because of the emphasis of central oversight on any actions of jurors and coroners that subverted the interests of the state, the function of the coroner's jury was primarily to enforce the state's definition of justice and restrict what it considered illegitimate violence.

The coroner's jury was thus an instrument used by the state for the regulation of violence and the enforcement of its definition of justice. However, the coroner's jury was also part of the machinery of state control more generally, one aspect of a system of power that included a wide variety of juries with a range of jurisdictions and functions. In order to fully understand the coroner's jury's place in the legal system as a whole and its role in the regulation of crime, it is important to examine its purpose, composition, and function in comparison with other types of early modern juries. In so doing, it becomes evident that rather than an anomaly, the coroner's jury's balancing of the needs of information and control was a common feature of the entire early modern jury system, a system that was less a site of negotiation than an expression of state power and a tool of governance.

The Coroner and the Trial Courts

When a verdict was reached by the coroner's jury, those inquests that related to indictable offenses, such as homicide or suicide, were referred to the assize courts or their urban equivalents for trial. Previous accounts have tended to assume that coroners' role in the justice process stopped when they handed over their inquest records to the trial courts. However, trial records indicate that nothing could be further from the truth. To begin with, as trials for homicide were usually the result of indictments based on the coroner's inquest, a trial could not commence without the coroner and his evidence. Indeed, those with knowledge of the criminal justice system were at pains to stress the critical role played by the coroner and the coroner's inquest. No commentator was more knowledgeable than Edward Umfreville,

author of *Lex Coronatoria,* the most thorough guide to the office and himself a coroner for Middlesex in the late eighteenth century. Concerned to
impart to his readers the seriousness of the office's responsibilities, Umfreville informed the prospective coroner that "what most strongly calls for
this care is the great credit given to the coroner's inquisitions, depositions,
&c. in the superior courts." Citing Chief Justice Fleming in the case of
Vicars v. King, Umfreville notes that in cases "when a coroner's inquisition finds a fact to be only manslaughter, and the same fact at the sessions
is found to be murder, in this case the verdict before the coroner is rather
to be credited, because the coroner examines the evidence on both sides,
but on an indictment at the sessions they only examine the witnesses for
the king."[50]

  To illustrate in practice the coroner's centrality even in this initial
stage of the trial procedure, we can look to the example of a homicide case
that was not quite tried at the Old Bailey, London's central criminal court.
In 1679, "Four young Gentlemen Scholars of Westminster School" were
arrested and accused of killing a bailiff who had attempted to make an arrest
near the school.[51] The young scholars claimed that the jurisdictional war-
ren of London provided the students freedom from arrest on the grounds
of their school, and accordingly their actions in resisting arrest were entirely justified. Whether their claim would have held up in court will never
be known, for when it came time for their case to come to trial the coroner
charged with investigating the killing asked for a postponement, "declaring
that the Kings Evidence was not ready."[52] The coroner informed the court
that approximately "seven more Scholars" were present when the killing
took place and proposed that the trial be "put off till the next Sessions"
in order to give him time to locate and depose all of the witnesses to the
unfortunate bailiff's death. The court agreed and the trial was delayed.[53]
The scholars disappear from the historical record after this postponement,
but the lesson to be taken from this case is readily apparent. It was the
coroner who was responsible for gathering, organizing, and submitting the
evidence on behalf of the crown. Thus, without the coroner there was not
only no investigation or arrest, but also no trial.

The coroner's role in the post-inquest, pre-trial phase of the justice system seems to have been well known to contemporaries. When James Anderton and John Farrell were killed in 1698, the five individuals suspected of the crime sent a note to Robert White, coroner of Westminster, informing that officer that they would "[s]urrender them selves at the House in the Old Bailey the first day of the present Sessions" and "there by desired the said Coroner to prepare for the Tryall accordingly." Thus spurred to action, White sent messages to the various witnesses he had previously deposed, giving them notice that they would soon need to appear in court.[54]

That the coroner was the central figure in the process of bringing a trial for homicide or suicide is clear, but even after the trial itself commenced, the coroner remained a crucial part of the trial apparatus. This role has gone largely unnoticed by historians as a result of the nature of early modern trial records. Most such records are rather laconic affairs, bland summaries rather than detailed transcripts of speech and action. As a result, the role of the various legal officers in trial procedure is often obscured; the records certainly occlude the important part the coroner played in the conduct of trials involving violent death. By looking at some unusually detailed trial records, the true place of the coroner in the later stages of the justice system is finally revealed.

The coroner's most common role at trial was as a supplier of evidence. This aspect of the coroner's role could take a number of forms: as a supplier of written depositions that could be used both as evidence in and of themselves and for comparing to other witness testimony; as a supplier of oral testimony; and as a supplier of physical evidence. An extraordinarily detailed case from the Old Bailey in 1692 provides an unusual glimpse of the coroner at trial. Unlike most early modern trial accounts, we have an exact transcript of the 1692 trial of Henry Harrison for the murder of Dr. Andrew Clenche, from indictment to plea to jury selection and examination of witnesses. The level of detail allows us to follow both the words and the deeds of the accused and witnesses, as well as the court officers. As a result, the full range of the coroner's responsibilities at trial becomes evident.

According to Mr. Darnell, "Councel for the King and Queen against the Prisoner at the Barr," the quarrel between Harrison and Dr. Clenche began over the repayment of a loan Clenche had given to a friend of Harrison's, a Mrs. Vanwicke. Mrs. Vanwicke, a widow, had provided a mortgage on her house as collateral for the loan, and when she proved unable to pay, Dr. Clenche had her evicted. Incensed about the treatment of his friend, Harrison confronted Dr. Clenche, "abused him with very scurrilous Language," declaring that "Dr. Clenche was a Rogue and a Villain, and deserved to have his Throat cut." He was only prevented from making good on his threat when a bystander intervened and kept Harrison from drawing his sword.[55]

The circumstances of the actual murder, as presented by the prosecuting attorney, were hardly as mundane as the initial argument over money. According to the prosecution, Harrison launched a rather elaborate scheme to murder Dr. Clenche. On the night in question, Harrison and an accomplice hired a coach and directed the coachman to the house of Dr. Clenche in Brownlow Street in Holborn. When they arrived, the conspirators instructed the coachman to fetch Clenche and tell him that "two Gentlemen in a Coach at the End of the Street desired him [Clenche] to go with him to a Patient that was very Sick." The gentlemen then instructed the coachman to drive with haste to a series of destinations, ending up at a market, where they requested the coachman to buy a couple of "fowls." The driver bought the chickens as instructed, but when he returned to his coach, the two gentlemen were gone and the "Doctor left in the Coach murther'd with a Hankerchief tied fast about his neck."[56]

As the murder had taken place within the confines of the coach and the coachman did not know the identity of the two gentlemen, the murder of Dr. Clenche might have remained a mystery, if not for the fact that at least two witnesses came forward who claimed to have seen Henry Harrison in the coach with Dr. Clenche, while others testified to his ownership of the handkerchief found around the deceased's neck. This evidence, combined with testimony detailing Harrison's previous threats, was enough to indict him for the murder of Dr. Clenche. When the day of the trial arrived, however, one of the witnesses who had placed Harrison in the coach on the night of Clenche's death was found to be missing. According to the prosecution, this key witness's absence was no accident. The witness had been "[s]pirited away and cannot be heard of, although he hath been described in the Gazette, and a diligent search and inquiry has been made after him." Even with a crucial witness's absence, all was not lost, for all the evidence used by the prosecution in the trial had been gathered by the coroner, Mr. John Brown, in the execution of his inquest on the body of Dr. Clenche. The coroner had not only interviewed the missing boy, but had the witness's testimony in writing. The boy's examination under oath before the coroner was therefore submitted as evidence.[57]

The coroner's role in this case did not end with the submission of this written evidence. Later in the trial, Brown was called as a witness and asked to read the testimony given to him by one Andrew Boswell and to swear that the testimony was given under oath. In early modern English trials, oral testimony was generally privileged above written testimony.[58] In a case such as this, when the witness was not available to give his testimony orally, the coroner was called to provide oral testimony based on written evidence of previous oral testimony. As such, the coroner's oral testimony legitimized the written account of an absent witness's oral account. In this way, the coroner could function as both gatherer of evidence and supplier of oral testimony about that evidence at trial, a role not previously noted by historians.

In addition to acting as witnesses, coroners often were charged with holding and presenting any physical evidence at trial. This was certainly the case in the trial of Henry Harrison. A Mrs. Jackson was called to testify as to the ownership of the handkerchief found around Dr. Clenche's neck. She stated that several days earlier Harrison had lodged at her father's house. In the course of his stay, the witness claimed she had seen the fateful handkerchief in Harrison's possession. After providing this testimony, the handkerchief was "produced in Court by the Coroner" so that Mrs. Jackson could identify the murder weapon as the same handkerchief she had seen in Harrison's possession. Later, when the coachman who had conveyed the accused and found the body was questioned, the handkerchief was again produced by John Brown, the coroner.[59]

It is not surprising that the coroner, as the primary official charged with collecting evidence and gathering witness testimony in cases of violent death, would perform roles related to the handling of evidence during the trial phase as well. Coroners were active at trial in other ways as well. Looking at the Henry Harrison trial, we once again see the full range of roles that a coroner could adopt. For instance, a Mrs. Sheriff told the court she had heard Harrison say to Mrs. Vanwicke of Dr. Clenche that he "deserves to have his Throat Cut; well, Madam . . . be contented I'll manage him as never any Man was managed." Upon hearing this rather damning piece of testimony, Harrison interjected to ask the witness, "What had you for your Swearing?" The witness apparently did not acknowledge the defendant's question, for the coroner himself demanded, "Witness, he asketh you if you had anything for Swearing against him." To which the witness replied that she had received no payment for her testimony.[60]

Lest we think this interjection of the coroner into the proceedings of the trial was unique, a second instance of the same behavior occurred in the Harrison trial. When a Mr. Carden, drawer or barman at the King's Head Tavern, was later called as a witness, the coroner once again interjected. On this occasion, however, he did not simply repeat a question asked to the witness, but instead asked his own question. After Carden was sworn in, Harrison asked him what time he had seen the coach arrive at the King's Head, if he saw anyone with the coach, and what they were wearing. Carden responded that the coach had arrived at eleven o'clock at night and that he saw a man in a "Hanging-Coat" standing by the side of the coach. At this point, the coroner interjected to ask Carden "[w]hat time of night you shut your Doors, especially on Monday Nights [being the night of the murder]," and if they had been shut when the coach arrived.[61]

Unlike the previous instance, the coroner's question to Carden reveals an independent attempt on the part of the coroner to secure evidence about the night of the murder not asked by the prosecution or the defendant. That the coroner's mind would operate in this manner is not surprising given that part of his responsibility during the inquest would be to ask questions of witnesses and suspects alike. What is perhaps surprising, though, is that the coroner would take such an active role in the trial itself on behalf of the prosecution. Traditionally the coroner has been viewed as an officer responsible for gathering the evidence used to secure an indictment or for supplying evidence to be used at trial. It is clear, however, that during the trial itself the coroner remained a vital member of the prosecution team, providing physical evidence, oral and written testimony, and even helping to question witnesses.

While the trial of Henry Harrison is unusually detailed, coroners in many other cases behaved in ways similar to the coroner in that case: as witnesses, as suppliers of evidence, and as interrogators. In a 1693 Old Bailey trial, the coroner, a Mr. White, was the first witness called. The evidence he provided was the written inquest deposition of a witness who had died in the period between the inquest and the trial. As in the Harrison case, the coroner was called not only to provide written evidence of a deposition, but to read the deposition out loud in court.[62] In 1722, an iron poker that had been collected by the coroner at inquest and was said to be the weapon used in the killing of Mary Ingram in a domestic dispute was produced by the coroner as evidence in court.[63] Ten years later, a different coroner again played the role of interrogator. Corbet Vezey was accused of locking his wife Mary in the garret of their house and leaving her there to starve. A witness testified in court that on a previous occasion he had come to Mary Vezey's aid after she had jumped from the roof of her house into the street. Following this testimony, the coroner interjected to ask the witness if Mary had explained "why she got upon the House." The witness replied that Mary had stated that "she did it thro' Necessity, as thinking it better to make an end of her Life in that manner, than to starve to Death."[64] Like the Harrison trial, that of Corbet Vezey is closer to a direct transcript of trial proceedings than the usual summaries of trials in the Old Bailey records. Thus, it seems likely that the expanded role played by the coroner illustrated here was more the rule than the exception. Incomplete trial records may have obscured this role to some extent, but it is clear that coroners performed a wide variety of crucial roles at the trial stage.

The ways in which the evidence provided by coroners was used, whether in the written form of the inquest records or in the form of oral testimony, further demonstrate the importance of the coroner and inquest to every aspect of the judicial process. The most common way inquest evidence was used at trial was to compare witness testimony given in court with that given previously at the coroner's inquest. This tactic was used by prosecution and defense alike, as demonstrated in the trial of Jane Griffin for the murder of her servant, Elizabeth Osborn, in 1720. Two witnesses, a Mr. Lund and a Mr. Tannet, testified that on the day of Osborn's death they had been dining at the Three Pigeons, an inn owned by Jane Griffin's husband, when the proprietor summoned them to the parlor to assist an injured woman. When the witnesses arrived in the parlor, they found Osborn "lying on her back on the ground," seemingly murdered. When they asked how Osborn had come to her present state, they were told by Mr. Griffin that "the Bitch had murder'd herself." The witnesses then examined Osborn's wounds and eventually succeeded in reviving her, if only temporarily. The witnesses first asked if the dying woman recognized them, later seen as key evidence that Osborn was aware enough to provide accurate testimony. After establishing that Osborn was capable of knowing the truth, they then asked whether she had stabbed herself as Mr. Griffin claimed. Osborn insisted that she was not responsible for her own injuries, at which point she was asked who was responsible for her wound. Osborn replied that it had been her "Mistress," Jane Griffin. When asked the same question a second time, Osborn once more stated that her "Mistress" had stabbed her.[65]

The testimony given by the two witnesses who heard Elizabeth Osborn's testimony immediately prior to her death was certainly damning evidence for the accused. In her defense, Jane Griffin sought to discredit this evidence by claiming that there were inconsistencies between the testimony given at the coroner's inquest and that provided at trial. She claimed that "when Mr. Lund and Mr. Tannet gave their Evidence before the Coroner's Inquest, that they then deposed that the Deceased, when ask'd by Mr. Lund who did it, said only Miss—not Mistress, which they now swear." This apparent discrepancy in testimony was crucial for Griffin's defense. If the deceased had said a "Miss" had killed her, that might not necessarily refer to Griffin specifically. However, if the deceased had truly said "Mistress," there could be no doubt that she was referring to her employer.[66]

As defenses go, Jane Griffin's attempt to undermine the testimony of Mr. Lund and Mr. Tannet was rather weak and ultimately to no avail. The strategy of highlighting inconsistencies between evidence given at inquest and that given at trial does, however, reveal some interesting information about the place of coroners' evidence in the trial system. While unsuccessful in this instance, the tactic was common enough to suggest that it was generally agreed that such evidence and testimony should be consistent in order to be convincing. Furthermore, it is remarkable that the defendant was able to mount such a defense at all. In order to claim that the evidence given at trial contradicted that given previously at the inquest, Jane Griffin must either have been present at the inquest or had access to the inquest records before or during her trial. While Griffin may well have been present at the inquest, other examples of widespread knowledge of inquest testimony at trial suggest that defendants and prosecutors alike had some access to the written inquest records. The fact that both prosecution and defense could and did regularly employ such a tactic suggests that the coroner's inquest, and the evidence it gathered, was not merely a preliminary step in the justice process to be superseded by the criminal trial, but instead a vital stage of information gathering and criminal investigation.

Those who failed to provide evidence at the coroner's inquest could also have the validity of the testimony questioned in court. Returning once more to the trial of Henry Harrison for the murder of Dr. Clench, we can see this tactic in action. One of the key witnesses for the crown was a young woman named Elianor Ashbolt, who swore in court that she had both seen the defendant in the coach on the night in question and heard him speak. This combination of sight and sound helped her to identify Harrison as the man at the scene of the crime. Ashbolt's testimony did not, however, go unchallenged. Later in the trial, she was forced to explain why she had not testified at the coroner's inquest if she possessed such important corroborating evidence. The implication was clear: evidence presented at trial but not at the inquest was deemed suspicious and potentially untrustworthy. Hence, before the weight of Ashbolt's testimony could be properly gauged, her failure to present her evidence at the coroner's inquest had to be adequately explained.[67] Whether judge or jury found her explanation—that her mother had not wanted her to get involved in such an unseemly matter—convincing is not readily apparent, but the mere requirement that such an explanation be given in court illustrates an important evidentiary requirement: that evidence given at trial should, as much as possible, align with that given at the coroner's inquest.

The verdict reached at the coroner's inquest was also given considerable weight in court, and juries were advised not to find against the inquest verdict without just cause. The clerk of arraigns instructed a jury at the trial of Sarah Malcolm for the murder of Ann Price in 1733 that Malcolm "stands charged on the Coroner's Inquisition for the said Murder" and that if they found her guilty of the felony, they were to inquire as to whether Malcolm had any property to be forfeited. "But," the clerk continued, "if you quit her on the Coroner's Inquest, you must find how Ann Price came to her death."[68] As the clerk explained, the task of the trial jury was not simply to find the defendant guilty or not guilty of murder. Because the coroner's inquest had already reached a verdict of murder, if the trial jury decided to find contrary to the inquest, they would also be charged with providing a new explanation for Ann Price's untimely demise.

In these and numerous other cases, it becomes clear that homicide and other trials involving death were unique. In these cases, the fact that someone had died could not be disputed. As the coroner and his inquest jury had already reached one verdict as to the cause of death, and because of the weight given to the inquest verdict, juries who reached a decision at odds with the inquest were required to offer their own explanation of the cause of death. Violent death was too serious an offense to allow a simple guilty or not guilty verdict. Thus, if the individual charged by the coroner's inquest was found not to be responsible, the matter could not rest until a new suspect or a new cause of death was provided. Death would not be allowed to go unexplained. It was the coroner's responsibility to ensure that every death was detected, explained, and adjudicated.

The verdict reached by the coroner and his jury could sometimes even be determinative. For instance, in 1715 Thomas Baker was indicted at the Old Bailey and charged with the murder of Henry Tyrrel. In his defense, Baker informed the court that "the Prosecution against him had

been carry'd on with great Violence and Malice." As evidence of the mali-
cious nature of the charges against him, Baker turned to the verdict of the
coroner's inquest, which had acquitted him. Baker was ready to call witnesses to prove his innocence, but given the evidence of the inquest verdict, "the Court judg'd it unneccesary."[69] In a similar manner, in 1693 a
jury that found the defendant not guilty of murder was required to provide
a different cause of death in order to "satisfy the coroner's inquest."[70] In
another case a man accused of murder was discharged even though he had
confessed his guilt to the coroner's inquest. The coroner had determined
that, although he had caused the death, it had been the result of "misfortune," and so the accused was released.[71] As the coroner's inquest had not
reached a verdict of homicide, there was no need for the trial to proceed
further. In a charge given to a jury in 1786, the court instructed the jurors
that as the coroner's inquest had charged the defendant with manslaughter
and not murder, the jury could "go no further than what the Coroner's
inquest had made it." Thus, the jury could only find the defendant guilty
or not guilty on the charge of manslaughter, and could not charge the defendant with murder, once again illustrating the power and influence of the
coroner's inquest even at the trial stage.[72]

What these examples illustrate is that the coroner's role in the justice
system was not limited to the pre-trial stages of investigation. While the
coroner's most important function may have been the initial examination of
physical evidence and the collection of witness testimony, the trial records
of the period indicate that the coroner's work was not done after the indictment. Coroners remained vital judicial officials throughout the trial phase,
providing evidence, supplying testimony, and helping to examine witnesses
and defendants. As such, it is clear that the coroner's role in the regulation of lethal violence was crucial and essential through all phases of the
judicial process. The coroner, the coroner's jury, and their inquests were
thus the sine qua non of the monopolization of violence in early modern
England. Together, they gathered and assessed the local information that
would be used at trial and ensured that it was used properly and effectively
at that later stage. This effort, however, would be for naught if trial juries
effectively challenged the state's monopoly of violence by substituting local

conceptions of justice at the expense of state definitions. As we shall see, such a substitution of definitions of justice was not the norm in the early modern period, because all juries were part of the apparatus of state power that began with the coroner and his jury.

The Petty Jury

Because coroners' juries were usually impaneled to render judgment on one individual case, it was possible, and even advantageous, to tip the balance of impartiality and local knowledge further toward the accumulation of knowledge when selecting jurors. Conversely, petty or trial juries were expected to hear multiple cases, either at quarter sessions or the biannual assizes. As such, it was not usually possible to ensure that each case had jury members with particular knowledge of the individual or his crime. Thus, at least on the surface, it would seem that the balance of trial juries was weighted toward impartiality rather than knowledge or discretion. In reality, however, measures were often taken to ensure that, like coroners' juries, trial juries functioned both as suppliers of facts as well as impartial applicators of state laws.

Quarter sessions and assize jurors were selected from among the freeholders of the county in question. Constables of hundreds—the administrative divisions of a county—were charged with informing the freeholders of their jurisdictions that attendance was required at the next meeting of the quarter sessions or the assize and ensuring that they appeared. Previous studies of the composition of early modern petty juries reveal that such jurors were generally "drawn from bottom ranks of the parochial elite," a middling sort comprised of yeomen and tradesmen.[73] In both selection procedure and status, trial jurors were similar to coroners' jurors, and many individuals served on both types of jury at some point in their lives.

The elevated status of trial jurors relative to the population at large was intended to ensure the impartiality of the jury. In a world in which social status and economic credit were regularly equated with honor and moral rectitude, the importance of status for jurymen was self-evident.[74] Not only were the socio-economic elites viewed as more honest and disinterested, but by virtue of their wealth, they were seen as being less susceptible to bribery or the corrupting influence of powerful interests. Edward Coke, for instance, sought to purge the jury of mean or insufficient men as part of a wider campaign against corruption in the 1620s. For Coke and other reformers, men of insufficient wealth or estate were dangerous because they were more easily corrupted or influenced.[75] The frequent complaints about the lack of qualified men serving on juries and the exclusion of potential jurors of inferior status demonstrate the importance of the status of trial jurors for perceptions of competence and indifference.[76]

Competence and impartiality, however, were not the only attributes important for early modern juries. As with coroners' juries, it was crucial for the proper functioning of the justice system that petty juries were able to supply and knowledgeably weigh information about their local and county communities. Many counties possessed hundredal or "present-ment juries," which were responsible for detecting crime and disorder in their hundreds and for presenting the resulting criminal cases to the quarter sessions and assize.[77] This type of petty jury was explicitly self-informing and as such, the geographical background of its members and the informa-tion they provided concerning their local communities were crucial to its proper functioning, as well as to the proper functioning of the quarter ses-sion and assize systems as a whole.

Contemporary legal writers agreed that trial juries should be com-posed as much as possible of men with local knowledge of the place in question. In 1621, while speaking in support of a House of Commons bill "for avoiding insufficient jurors," Edward Coke argued that jurors should not only be "sufficient . . . in estate and understanding," they should also be men from "most near the place" of the person on trial.[78] Matthew Hale, in his *History of the Common Law,* similarly stressed the importance of the geographical origins of jurors. In his section outlining the procedures of jury selection, Hale states that in addition to being men of "estate" and "quality," trial jurors "are to be of the Neighbourhood of the Fact to be inquired . . . and two of them at least of the Hundred."[79] It has been sug-gested that the dictates of Coke and Hale did not accord with reality, but it is evident from the court records of the period that a serious effort was

made to ensure that men with local knowledge served on trial juries whenever possible.

Evidence for the importance of petty juries as suppliers of facts is
plentiful if one reads between the lines of contemporary documents. For
instance, in the mid-seventeenth century an order was issued from the
Essex Quarter Sessions that sought a remedy for what it claimed was the
"defective" nature of the presentments made by the county's petty juries.
According to the order, the presentments made by the "petty Juries for
the severall Hundreds" were inadequate because the members of these
juries did not have the requisite level of knowledge about the crimes and
infractions that occurred in the county. The justices sitting at Quarter Sessions reasoned that "Constables and Churchwardens were the most fitt to
serve upon those Juries, beinge the best accquainted with the greivances,
annoyances and distempers in this County." Hence, it was ordered that
"the Bayliffs of every hundred doe for the future impagnell the Constables
and Churchwardens of every parish, village and hamblett to serve as petty
Juries, whereby all misdemeanors, nusances and breaches of the peace may
bee duely presented and punished."[80]

Whether such juries were more effective in prosecuting crime than
juries without local knowledge is immaterial. The reasoning behind such
an attempt to reorganize jury composition, however, is clear enough. The
Quarter Sessions justices felt that the existing juries were not effective in
combating crime and disorder in Essex. The reason for the insufficiency of
the jurors was not because they were men of low status or little understanding of the law, a common contemporary complaint that has perhaps obscured other concerns about the function of the early modern jury. Instead,
the justices considered the juries to be insufficient because they were failing
to present the full range of crimes and breaches of the peace that existed.
Again, this failure to present was not thought to be a result of the status or
impartiality of the jurors, but rather a reflection of their incomplete knowledge of the offenses being committed in the county. Thus, constables and
churchwardens, men with greater knowledge of local affairs and local concerns due to their positions in local government, were ordered to serve on
future juries in place of regular freeholders.

The implication is clear: petty juries, especially in their role as presentment juries, were supposed to possess detailed knowledge of crime and disorder in their local areas. Fear that the petty juries lacked this local knowledge was a serious enough concern for the Essex justices to attempt a full-scale reorganization of the county's juries, a tactic replicated in Kent and possibly other counties in the period.[81] Therefore, any claim that early modern juries were not, at least in part, self-informing must take into account the fact that the early modern authorities clearly considered this to be a crucial function of the jury system. Indeed, one Essex jury made the need for geographic diversity in jury composition explicit. The jury had been asked to explain why it had failed to make presentments for offenses or disorders in certain parishes within their jurisdiction. In response, the jurors replied that they could not supply information about offenses in some parishes "by reason there is none of the jury [from those parishes]."[82] Thus, the jurymen themselves recognized that without local knowledge supplied by jurymen, they were helpless to enforce the law in those areas.

The Essex authorities were not alone in their attempts to engineer petty juries so as to increase the odds that local knowledge was brought to bear on as many cases as possible. In 1655, the Somerset sheriff Robert Hunt wrote in his memorandum book that the bailiffs of the hundreds were given "strikt warrants to returne all the freeholders in the several hundreds" for service as petty jurors at assize and quarter sessions. Furthermore, Hunt ordered his bailiffs to divide the potential jurors from each hundred in two and "take halfe of every hundred to serve the first assizes and thother halfe to serve the second assizes."[83]

At first glance, this practice of dividing the jurors of each hundred into two groups seems odd. Surely it would have been easier for both bailiffs and jurors to have the freeholders of half the hundreds serve at one assize and the remaining hundreds' freeholders serve at the second. However, when one considers the importance of the self-informing jury, the purpose of dividing the hundreds themselves becomes apparent. It seems likely that the sheriff was dividing the jury pool in such a way as to ensure that there were representatives of each of the county's hundreds present as jurors at both of the county's assizes, creating a jury whose members brought as wide a range of local knowledge as was possible.

Organizing the jury pool in this way was important given the manner in which trial juries operated. A single trial jury often heard and rendered its judgment on several different criminal cases in succession.[84] As a result, it would be impossible to select a single jury whose members would all have knowledge of the persons or places involved in several different cases. Therefore, if a self-informing jury was still an important ideal, it was necessary to engineer the county's jury pool so that representatives of as many hundreds as possible would sit on each jury. Every juror may not have had personal knowledge of aspects of each case, but using this method of jury selection would substantially increase the odds that each jury would have at least a member or two who *was* familiar with the person, place, or circumstances involved in each case the jury considered. Thus, it seems evident that early modern judicial officials considered it important for the proper functioning of a trial jury that the broadest possible geographical swath of the county community was represented at the assize. This broad representation in turn was intended to ensure, as much as possible, that local knowledge of crimes, individuals, and circumstances was considered by the courts, without conceding the authority to define justice or legality to the interests of any one community. In this way, the need for both local knowledge and state control could be addressed and balanced by dividing each jury between elite representatives of a wide range of hundreds.

Patterns of presentment and prosecution can also supply clues to the function of the petty jury as suppliers of information. Studies of Terling in Essex and other places have shown that those individuals most likely to be presented by a jury or prosecuted in court were outsiders and recidivists.[85] Take, for example, quarter sessions and assize prosecution for selling ale without a license, a common and growing concern in the late sixteenth and seventeenth centuries. As Keith Wrightson demonstrates, of the 28 cases of selling ale without a license involving Terling residents between 1525 and 1700, fully half were directed at individuals new to the village, while only a handful of prosecutions targeted established residents. The Terling authorities also made a concerted effort to rein in the activities of repeat offenders such as John Aldridge and Thomas Holman.[86]

It is unsurprising that people without local ties and individuals whose repeated offenses tried the patience of the community should be the special targets of local prosecution efforts. Intuitive though they may be, these prosecution patterns imply something larger about the makeup and function of early modern juries. For it to be possible for local communities to focus their judicial energies on outsiders and repeat offenders, it would have been necessary for the juries responsible for the presentment and prosecution of local offenders to have fairly precise local knowledge. That is to say, petty jurors could only focus their prosecutorial attention on outsiders if they knew who belonged to the community and who did not. Similarly, if the needs of local justice demanded that many or most first-time offenders be spared the rigors of prosecution and recidivists be given a full measure of justice, the jurors who presented and tried such cases needed knowledge of the criminal pasts of the men and women who came before them. For the discretionary aspects of the English judicial system to work on a local level, it is clear that local knowledge was needed. This knowledge could be supplied by witnesses, but often, especially in the case of presentments, it came from the jurors themselves.

Indeed, contemporary commentators recognized that the information supplied by jurors was a crucial part of the system. Contrary to the arguments of modern historians, Matthew Hale, for instance, made clear the importance of the self-informing jury. In his rules for trials by jury he informed the reader that "the Trial is not here simply by Witnesses, but by Jury; nay, it may so fall out that the Jury upon their own Knowledge may know a Thing to be false that a Witness swore to be true, or may know a Witness to be incompetent or incredible, tho' nothing be objected against him."[87] In this passage Hale demonstrates that although the jury is not the sole supplier of facts—a role shared with witnesses—it is also not simply a receiver of information. Instead, the role of the jury is to use their own knowledge of people and events in conjunction with facts supplied by others and instructions from the judges to come to an equitable verdict.

Like the officials responsible for composing juries, Hale recognized that for justice to prevail, a balance between knowledge and impartiality was required.

Now that we have seen the importance of local knowledge for the early modern justice system and the importance of a geographically diverse jury to provide this information, a further reason for the perceived necessity of property qualifications for jurors becomes apparent. As Peter Lawson and J. S. Cockburn have argued, by virtue of their standing in local and county society, petty jurors were more likely to share the interests and values of the crown and its judicial agents—justices and judges—than those of the common people.[88] Because the justice system, as the main apparatus of state control, required the participation of local individuals to operate effectively, the use of economic qualifications can reasonably be seen as a means of ensuring that those selected to help administer justice held similar values and possessed similar interests as those in power. The purpose of selecting jurors of high social status was thus not simply to provide impartiality, but also to combat the potential partiality of local men judging their neighbors by selecting those locals who "would prove more receptive to instructions from the bench."[89] The regular judicial interference with jury verdicts in the guise of orders, instructions, and other inducements is further evidence that, at least in the minds of those in power, the jury primarily functioned as a supplier of local information rather than a representative deliberative body or a site of negotiation between crown and community.[90] The need for local participation may have necessitated some level of accommodation with local opinion, but by combining local representation with property and status qualifications, the state sought to temper the effects of communal interest and reinforce its own conceptions of justice and order.

Mixed Juries

Of all the types of legal cases considered by the early modern judicial system, trials involving immigrants or foreign residents were among the most difficult in which to balance the needs of impartiality and discretion. The potential pitfalls were legion. On the one hand, it was clear that foreign defendants needed some sort of insulation from the vagaries of a potentially xenophobic English jury who understood little of the defendant's life and circumstances. On the other hand, a true jury of an immigrant's peers, one consisting entirely of aliens, might be just as partial as an all-English jury, though in the defendant's favor. In terms of discretion, the problems were similar. An English jury may have had a better understanding of English law, or at least popular notions of justice, but no knowledge of the immigrant experience. Conversely, an alien jury would have some sense of the general life and background of an immigrant, but little understanding of English law and justice. Faced with such a seemingly untenable situation, the English legal system sought the most practical means of balancing the concerns of impartiality and discretion: it split those juries which judged cases involving foreigners in two, to create "mixed" or "party" juries consisting of equal numbers of English and foreign jurors.

The practice of allowing foreign residents the right to request a trial *de medietate linguae* (the legal term for a trial by mixed jury) had its origins in the Middle Ages, when the Jewish community of London was granted the privilege.[91] By the early modern period, the right to a mixed jury had been extended to all foreign residents—with the exception of Gypsies, Scots, the Irish, and the Welsh—and did in fact provide a remarkable level of protection for aliens accused of crimes.[92] This was accomplished by dividing the jury so that while one half might be overly judicious and the other half overly lenient, combined they would serve the needs of a fair trial.

For instance, in 1727 one Bernard Massip (or so his name was rendered in English) was charged at the Old Bailey for "stealing a Cloth Coat, Waistcoat, Shirt, Stock and Handkerchief to the value of 34 shillings" from Crispin Tomlinson. Before the trial could begin, however, the records indicate that "the Prisoner being an Italian, and not understanding English, he desired (by the Mouth of a Gentleman in Court) that he might have the Privilege which is granted by the merciful Laws of England, in such Cases, i.e. When a Foreigner not having the Advantage of our Speech, stands upon his delivery before any Court of Judicature, he may have the Liberty of a Jury chosen for that purpose, consisting of six English Men and six

Foreigners, which Request was granted him."[93] Once Massip's request for a mixed jury had been accepted by the court, 12 jurors were sworn, six Englishmen and six foreigners of unknown provenance. While there were property or wealth qualifications for the six English jurors, the foreign jurors were not subject to the same standards of status.[94]

In part this probably reflected the difficulty judicial officials faced when seeking foreign jurors. Finding six qualified, male foreign residents to serve on a jury, especially outside of London, must have proved a complicated task. However, it is also likely that status qualifications were not deemed necessary because of the intended purpose of the trial *de medietate linguae*. The foreign contingent of a mixed jury was not present to act as impartial surveyors of facts or evidence. Instead, their express purpose was to counterbalance the potential harshness or injustice of an all-English jury. As such, their socio-economic status was immaterial. Property qualifications for jurors were enacted to assure that those charged with passing judgment would be men of substance and character, men whose verdict could not be swayed by influence or bribe. The foreign half of a mixed jury, however, did not need to meet such a property qualification for the very reason that they were sought precisely because they were likely inclined to view the defendant favorably from the beginning. To further ensure that the foreign contingent of the jury would bring to bear knowledge of the immigrant experience that might mitigate the xenophobia of the English jury, whenever possible foreigners from the same country or city as the defendant were sought to serve on mixed juries.

Such a conclusion is bolstered by the way jury challenges were regulated in trials *de medietate linguae*. The jurors who comprised the English half of the tribunal could be challenged like any other jurors in a standard trial.[95] The foreign jurors, however, could not be challenged, and both prosecution and accused were required to accept the first six foreign jurors called.[96] This may seem an obscure, innocuous piece of procedural minutia, but the inability to challenge any foreign juror speaks volumes about the purpose of such trials. As with the lack of property qualification, the absence of the juror challenge in these cases was a result of the fact that the foreign portion of the mixed jury was present primarily because their

personal knowledge and experience as fellow foreigners would temper any
injustice done by the English jurymen. In normal trials, the purpose of
challenging a juror was to prevent a biased individual from unduly favoring
or unduly sympathizing with the defendant. The absence of the challenge
for the foreign half of the mixed jury thus indicates that a bias in favor of the
defendant was in some instances deemed unimportant, and was even actively sought. By dividing the jury between English and foreign jurors, the
early modern judicial system was performing the same function performed
by juries of all types—the balancing of the needs of discretion and local
knowledge with those of impartiality.

 The parallels between the composition of coroners', petty, and mixed
juries are striking in other ways. As we have seen, those responsible for con-
vening coroners' juries and petty juries went to great lengths to ensure that
they possessed a degree of geographical diversity that balanced the needs
of knowledge and impartiality. The geographical composition of mixed juries shows that trials *de medietate linguae* sought a similar balance. If the
sole purpose of the mixed jury was to provide impartial justice, any non-
English foreigner would suffice, regardless of whether they came from the
same country as the defendant. When one examines the geographical background of mixed jurors, however, a different picture emerges. Throughout
the Middle Ages and most of the early modern period, it was deemed important to at least attempt to fill the foreign half of a mixed jury with individuals of similar national origins as the defendant. Marianne Constable has
argued that from the sixteenth century, legal treatises began to define the
law governing mixed juries in a manner that focused on the protection of
those who could not speak English rather than on the protection of specific
foreign communities. Therefore, according to Constable, the foreign half
of a mixed jury no longer needed to be composed of individuals of the same
nationality as the defendant. While Constable is correct in her assessment
of the legal literature, the trial records themselves indicate that mixed juries
with the same national origin as the defendant continued to be common,
perhaps even the norm, well into the eighteenth century.[97]

 Take the case of George Nicholson, a Dane indicted for killing Richard Emmerson in an impromptu duel in London in 1686.[98] As a foreigner,

Nicholson requested a trial *de medietate linguae,* as was his right. The trial
was to take place in London, a city teeming with French Huguenot refugees
in the wake of the revocation of the Edict of Nantes in 1685, and with Dutch
merchants and refugees who first came to England during the Eighty Years'
War in the sixteenth and early seventeenth centuries.[99] Nicholson, however,
was from Denmark, a country that did not have a large expatriate community in England in the late seventeenth century. In such a case it obviously
would have been easier for the London authorities to round up jurors of
French or Dutch descent. And yet, when Nicholson came to trial his case
was heard by a jury of at least six Englishmen and at least six Danes.[100]
Given the size of the Danish community in London, it is exceedingly likely
that they personally knew Nicholson.

The lengths to which the judicial system went to secure a half-Danish
jury in Nicholson's case were repeated throughout the early modern period
as a whole. Between 1674 and 1750, 20 percent of mixed juries had the
same national origins as the defendant, a number that is likely far below the
actual rate given that most trial records do not mention the place of origin
of the jurors beyond the fact that they were "foreigners" or "aliens." In fact,
the vast majority of cases for which information regarding place of origin
is supplied list the foreign contingent of the mixed jury as being from the
same country as the defendant.[101] As with other aspects of the trial *de medietate linguae,* the attempt to secure jurors from the same place of origin as
the defendant suggests that their purpose was more than a simple counterbalance to the potentially biased English jurors. Instead, it is evident that
such a practice was deemed desirable because, ideally speaking, the foreign
members of the jury would also bring a particular set of knowledge to the
trial: knowledge of the background and experience of the defendant.

By the early years of the eighteenth century, most legal manuals were
beginning to declare that "it is not necessary . . . that the foreigners [on a
jury] should be all of the same Country that the Foreigner is of, who is to
have the Trial."[102] This may have been part of a more general shift from a
jury system balanced between impartiality and the need for local knowledge to one that favored impartiality alone. However, it seems clear that
well into the eighteenth century, in many cases an effort was made to match

the place of origin of the defendant and that of the foreign jurors.[103] Thus, even when it was no longer legally necessary to seek out foreign jurors of a particular nationality, many judicial officials continued to do so, a fact that speaks to the deep-rooted belief in the importance of both impartiality and knowledge in the judicial process.

The Grand Jury

As its name implies, the grand jury was the most elite type of jury in terms of both its power and the status of its members. Whereas the middling sort and parish elites served on coroners' and petty juries, those who served on grand juries tended to come from a higher socio-economic group. Evidence from seventeenth-century Cheshire and Sussex reveals that, on the whole, grand jurors were chosen from the lower ranks of the county gentry.[104] In its capacity as a judicial body—the administrative function of the grand jury is not relevant for our purposes—the grand jury performed two important functions. The grand jury was responsible for hearing bills of indictment at quarter sessions or assizes and deciding whether the bill was true, and could thus be sent to trial, or false, in which instance the case was dismissed. The grand jury additionally functioned as a county-wide presentment jury, indicting individuals or various corporate bodies for a wide range of crimes and infractions.

Given the dual nature of the grand jury's responsibilities, it is obvious that such a deliberative body would, by design, need to create a balance between supplying local knowledge and information on the one hand, and impartiality on the other. That is to say, as a presentment jury, knowledge of local affairs would have been a necessity if crime and disorder were to be effectively regulated. Conversely, when hearing bills of indictment, a certain degree of impartiality was necessary in order to fairly judge the merits of a given case. This division of functions is made explicit in Henry Fielding's charge to a Westminster grand jury in 1749. When considering an indictment, Fielding told the grand jury, "a perfect knowledge of the Law in these Matters is not necessary," for the "Business of a Grand Jury is only to attend the Evidence for the King; and if on that Evidence there shall appear probable Cause for the Accusation, they are to find the bill true."[105] However, in their role as a presentment jury, the grand jury was, according to Fielding, responsible for "presenting all Offences which shall come to your knowledge."[106]

It is clear from the records of the assizes that the acquisition of this knowledge was not simply a passive reception of information procured by others. Indeed, the grand jurors often took an active role in supplying and confirming local knowledge about crime and disorder. In 1634 in Cornwall, for instance, when a dispute arose over the repair of Tregeare Lane, two justices of the peace and "six of the grand jurors living nearest" to the road in question traveled to "view Tregeare Lane and to either settle the dispute about its repair or to certify the next assize, whereupon the indictment shall be tried."[107] Similarly, at the Taunton Assize in Somerset in 1647, justices were ordered to investigate "murders and riots" in Pilton and Bridgewater "about which the grand jury has complained."[108] In these instances, the local information supplied by members of the grand jury caused an investigation to be launched.

If it is clear that the early modern grand jury was required to balance the needs of impartiality and local knowledge, the question remains: how was this balance created in practice? As with the other varieties of jury discussed previously, this crucial balance was ensured by the manner in which grand jurors were selected. As with petty juries, sheriffs and their subordinate officers were charged by the centrally appointed assize judges with impaneling men from every hundred in a particular county. In Cheshire, each grand jury was normally composed of men from three or four different hundreds. According to John Morrill, men from three or four specific hundreds may have been chosen intentionally because there was "reason to believe that there were serious unreported misdemeanours and administrative defaults in those areas which required particular attention."[109] Grand juries in Sussex were similarly composed of men of diverse geographical backgrounds.[110]

This contention is further supported by three key pieces of evidence. First, judges often sought jurors who were not originally impaneled by the sheriff, even when there were plenty of qualified candidates who had been impaneled.[111] One logical reason for such a policy is that the judge in question believed that the unimpaneled juror brought important knowledge to bear that was not represented by the other potential jurors. This special knowledge was likely to relate to the circumstances of a specific geographical area or a specific offense. Second, as Morrill has shown for Cheshire, there was an impressively even distribution of grand juror service between the county's various hundreds. With two exceptions, each Cheshire hundred provided between 40 and 60 grand jurymen in the years between 1625 and 1659.[112] Finally, the geographical backgrounds of grand jurymen differed according to the location of the sessions, with men from surrounding hundreds being preferred. For example, when the sessions were held at Chester, the grand jurors were evenly drawn from nearby Wirral, Edisbury, and Broxton. As Morrill notes, this practice cannot have been a matter of convenience, as jurors were impaneled from all hundreds and had to appear at sessions even if they were not selected to serve.[113] Instead, it is clear that the selection of grand jurors followed the same pattern explicitly stated in the selection of coroners' juries. That is to say, jurors were selected from three or four hundreds nearest to the site of concern in order to supply jurors who had knowledge of the local area, local crimes, and local persons while still ensuring that some level of impartiality was maintained by spreading the jurors across several administrative areas.

When one examines trial and grand jurors in isolation from the rest of the judicial system, it is tempting to conclude that by the early modern period the English jury had been divorced from its previous role as a supplier of local knowledge and information. Because these juries were composed of men of relatively elite social standing with little apparent connection to the defendants they tried, it may seem that the disinterested application of the law was the jury's sole function. However, by examining both the status *and* the geographical backgrounds of a wider range of juries, it becomes clear that local knowledge and information remained a vital part of the jury system. This is not to say that every jury had members with the same place of origin as every case or every defendant. Rather, it is clear that at every level of the justice system—from coroner's jury to presentment jury, and from trial jury to grand jury—a balance was sought between local knowledge and state authority that reflected the function of each tribunal. Thus, each type of jury balanced these dual needs in a unique manner according to its purpose and its jurisdiction.

The balance created in the early modern period can perhaps best be viewed as part of a continuum that stretched from the Middle Ages into the nineteenth century. In the medieval period, with the formal apparatus of state power severely lacking, the need for local knowledge and information was such that the jury was composed in a manner weighted toward the supply of local knowledge. Without the more numerous legal officials and judicial bodies of a later period, medieval justice of necessity relied heavily on the participation of locals to supply information about crime and criminals. As a result, the medieval jury was more of a communal body than a strictly governmental institution, a body whose members' chief duty was to bring relevant information to bear on the cases they heard. The need for local participation in turn forced the state to concede more power in applying and enforcing the law to local definitions of justice. With the growth of the formal structures of state power—the growing number and power of justices of the peace, the stricter centralized regulation of the coroner, and the expanding authority of assize and quarter sessions as instruments of rule—from the sixteenth century, the early modern jury reflected a balance between information and authority that began to tilt toward the state's interest in the enforcement of order. The need for local knowledge was still important enough to require juries to be composed of a blend of local representatives and economic and social elites whose views and interests were close to those of the crown. By the nineteenth century, the formal structures of state power were robust enough to shift the balance even further away from the needs of information and toward those of impartiality and state control of the judicial process. With the growth of the state, those men selected to serve on juries were no longer chosen for their knowledge of community and commonality, but rather as individuals who would be likely to apply the law in a manner that accorded with the interests of governance.

The early modern period can thus be viewed as part of a transition from a judicial system in which communal participation was valued above

impartiality to a system weighted in favor of impartiality over participation. This was a long process that followed the contours of the growth of
the state. The balancing of jury composition in the early modern period
mirrored the emergence of a modern state that sought to increase its control over its constituent parts. Rather than a venue for negotiation and accommodation between center and locality, the English jury should rightly
be viewed as part of the apparatus of state building and state control. In
early modern England, state control required the incorporation of local
men into the machinery of justice in a way that addressed the limits of state
power without ceding the powers of justice to local conceptions of equity
or justice. Whatever the aim of jury selection in the medieval period and
whatever it would become in the nineteenth and twentieth centuries, the
strategy behind jury selection in the early modern period can perhaps best
be seen as a method of obtaining crucial local knowledge and information
without sacrificing judicial control or the state's definition of order and
justice to peripheral interests. The perceived tension in the early modern
period between discretion and local knowledge on the one hand and central authority on the other was thus not the result of a dysfunctional justice
system or a legal order at war with itself. Instead, the competition between
discretion and state power was part of the very design of the English jury
system, a system that actively sought to ensure that the accused in each
trial was judged as knowledgeably as possible. By weighing the needs of
information and authority at every level of the jury system, necessary local information and local participation were acquired without sacrificing
the state's exclusive definitions of justice and of legitimate and illegitimate
violence to communal notions of justice.

The early modern English jury system was not a check on the state's
ability to monopolize violence, but instead a crucial apparatus of state
power and an important tool for the regulation of violence. The romantic
notion of the Anglo-American jury system as a body of independent citizens serving as a bulwark against the repression of the state is clearly false
in the early modern period. For the majority of men and women in early
modern England, there was no such thing as a jury of their peers. Instead,
juries were elite institutions of government control, whose members shared

geography with defendants, but interests in the effective maintenance of order with the state. Early modern juries were composed in such a way as to dilute the possibility of communal interests overriding the dictates of the law. By insisting on juries composed of elites, the state sought to insulate the jury from making common cause with defendants or communities. By mandating juries composed of members from multiple localities, the state could seek information without leaving the final decision solely in the hands of men whose loyalty to their neighbors might trump loyalty to the law. Participation could be secured, with negotiation over who defined justice and who decided how and when that justice was applied. In the case of violence, the state was thus able to secure information about deaths in every coroner of the country while retaining its sole right to decide what violence was investigated, prosecuted, and punished.

Economic Interest and the
Oversight of Violence

BY THE EARLY DECADES OF THE sixteenth century, England had in place two of the prerequisites for an effective monopoly of interpersonal violence: an officer dedicated to the regulation of violent death and the techniques of investigation necessary to detect it. However, if the English state hoped to enforce its exclusive definition of legitimate and illegitimate violence, it had to ensure that its laws regulating violent death were rationally and consistently enforced.[1] While most criminal justice systems allow some room for discretion at various stages of the judicial process, some aspects of any legal system are supposed to be beyond the discretion of victims, communities, juries, or local officials. Foremost among these exceptions in this period was the investigation of death.

If lethal violence in all its forms—accident, suicide, homicide—was to be effectively regulated and the state's monopoly of violence maintained, it was necessary to provide oversight of the coroner system charged with the investigation of untimely death. It had been long established that all suspicious deaths were to be investigated by coroners, and heavy fines were imposed on communities and coroners who failed in this duty toward the deceased. However, in a society dependent on amateur officeholders with few institutions specifically dedicated to the oversight of local officers, how was effective surveillance accomplished or even attempted? How did the crown and its central agents ensure that the investigations performed by local officeholders were regular, accurate, and consistent? How and when did early modern states create and maintain the monopoly of violence that was so crucial for the emergence of modern, centralized nations?

This chapter will demonstrate how the investigation and investigators of death were monitored by the central authorities in early modern

England. An examination of the records relating to coroners and the investigation of death in the Court of Star Chamber and the Court of King's Bench indicates that by the mid-sixteenth century, a situation had arisen in which competing and overlapping individual financial interests created a system of surveillance that monitored the investigation of death by means of self-interested central court litigation. By creating a system of forfeiture overseen by a centrally appointed and controlled officer (the almoner) and a central venue to adjudicate the system (the Courts of Star Chamber and King's Bench), the English state was able to harness the various economic interests of almoner, heir, creditor, and coroner as a means of regulating both violent death and the coroner system that was designed to investigate it. As such, it will be shown that from the middle of the sixteenth century, the English state had obtained an effective monopoly of legitimate violence for the first time in its history, and that this monopoly was born out of the multifaceted pecuniary interest in the outcome of coroners' inquests.

The first early modern attempt to regulate the coroner system through legislation dates to 1487, when a new statute was passed that required coroners to hold inquests on all suspicious deaths reported in their jurisdictions.[2] This statute was followed by further legislation under Henry VIII in 1509 and 1510 that established the procedure by which coroners would record their verdicts and certify their inquests at King's Bench. The Henrician statutes also stipulated that coroners were to receive a payment of 13s 4d for every homicide verdict.[3] In a further attempt to create a more efficient system and regulate the activities of coroners, a series of statutes were enacted under Mary I between 1554 and 1555. These statutes stipulated that coroners were henceforth responsible for interviewing witnesses and mandated fines for neglect of duty.[4] Furthermore, the Marian statutes provided the guidelines for supervising coroners and punishing them for corruption or neglect of duty throughout the early modern period. The sixteenth-century legislation, however, did little to put in place a practical apparatus for enforcement of these regulations, and it is thus to the apparatus of surveillance and enforcement that we must now turn.

Oversight by Justices of the Peace

Since the Middle Ages, the assize courts and the justices of the peace provided regular, if often informal, supervision of coroners. From at least the
fourteenth century, coroners were required to attend the quarter sessions
overseen by the county commission as well as the assize courts at which
their inquests were first registered before being certified in King's Bench.[5]
As the justice of the peace rose in importance in the late Middle Ages,
coroners increasingly came under their oversight. In 1380 justices of the
peace were officially empowered to hear indictments regarding accusations
against coroners for negligence and corruption and to punish them accordingly, formally acknowledging a practice that had existed since the middle
of the century.[6]

As a result of these medieval innovations, which were reiterated and
reinforced by statutes in the sixteenth century, the early modern coroner
was in the first instance under the supervision of the justices of the peace.[7]
Although much of this supervision was informal, and thus has little archival
resonance, some examples of how justices of the peace monitored coroners
and their work demonstrates the close working relationship that could exist
between these two county officials. The oversight was often subtle in form,
but its significance should not be overlooked as a result. In April 1693,
Nicholas Cunliff, one of the coroners for the Palatinate of Lancaster, learned
that a Charles Marsden of Gisborne in Yorkshire had died after falling from
a horse in Lancashire. The day after Marsden's death, without notifying the
proper authorities and before the coroner could hold the required inquest,
the corpse of the deceased was carried away to Gisborne. In response, the
coroner drafted a letter to the Lancashire Assize notifying that court of the
improper and illegal removal of Marsden's body. In addition to Cunliff's
signature, the letter carried that of Thomas Stanley, justice of the peace.[8]
The dual signatures may not seem significant, but the presence of the justice's signature on a letter from a coroner to the assize suggests that Cunliff consulted with Stanley, and perhaps even sought his approval, before
informing the assize justices of the illegal removal of a corpse. This letter

demonstrates both that the two county officials often worked in tandem, and that justices often supervised the actions of coroners.[9]

Indeed, much of the interaction between coroner and justice of the peace was not a matter of punitive supervision, but simply an instance of two county officials working together toward a common goal. For example, the inquest into the death of George Dixon in Pontefract, Yorkshire, in 1641 resulted in the examination and deposition of four witnesses, all residents of Pontefract. Three of the witnesses were examined by the coroner of Pontefract, Thomas Awstwicke. One of the depositions, however, was taken by Thomas Wilkinson, justice of the peace. All four depositions were submitted to the assize together, which shows that there must have been coordination and consultation between coroner and justice.[10] Although most depositions relating to death were taken by coroners, justices did pitch in on occasion, as in London in 1611, when multiple justices assisted the coroner in carrying out examinations relating to a particularly intricate case in which the death resulted from a duel.[11]

Both coroners and justices had the power to bind witnesses to appear in court and to commit suspects to jail; however, the fact that justices often took recognizances and committed suspects to jail as a result of inquests taken by coroners further demonstrates both the synchronicity between local officeholders and the oversight of coroners provided by justices. For example, in 1580 coroner John Homfrey held an inquest on the body of Charles Pavye, who had died from wounds received in a brawl.[12] As a result of the inquest, five individuals were bound over to appear at the next assize. Three of the recognizances were taken by the coroner at the inquest, while two others were taken by the earl of Northumberland in his capacity as justice of the peace.[13] Even these routine, seemingly mundane interactions demonstrate the potential oversight provided by justices of the peace. The very fact that justices were present at inquests, holding depositions, and binding suspects or witnesses over to appear in court shows that the work of coroners was closely observed by superior officials who, for the most part, worked cooperatively with coroners in the pursuit of justice but who also monitored, reported, and punished those coroners whose conduct was less than satisfactory.[14]

Those coroners who were accused of corruption or negligence could be, and occasionally were, fined at the assize.[15] In 1615, Cuthbert Leighe was accused of feloniously killing William Melsham at Thakenham, Sussex. Although Leighe was eventually convicted of manslaughter at the East Grinstead Assize later that year, the coroner, John Tainton, was amerced the sum of £5 for "nott perfect examinations touching the death of Melsham."[16] In a similar manner, William Playfere, coroner of Hastings Rape, Sussex, was fined at the Horsham Assize of 1577, where he was amerced £10. The reason for the fine is not stated, though we do know that he had been excused from attending the East Grinstead Assize on February 25, and thus the fine could have been from an unexcused absence from the assize. In any case, the magnitude of the fine (£10 was a considerable sum in 1577) suggests that the infraction was considered serious.[17] Although the amercement of coroners at the assize was not uncommon, it seems to have occurred with less frequency than summons to the central courts, a subject that will be addressed more fully below. Between them, justices of the peace and the assizes provided the first level of oversight of the coroner system and the investigation of suspicious death from the late medieval through the early modern periods. By working in conjunction with coroners to investigate death, to ensure the appearance of witnesses, and to apprehend suspects, justices also monitored and supervised coroners and their actions. If those actions failed to meet the standards of the justices, fines could be expected to be levied at the assize.

As the interactions between justices and coroners were often informal, it is hard to say for sure just how effective the surveillance provided by the county commission was. Amercements at the assize, likely initiated by county justices, were unusual but not unknown, and usually a matter of the individual discretion of particular county justices. Assize orders relating to coroners were also uncommon in the period before about 1650. Only ten assize orders for the Western Circuit related to coroners between 1629 and 1648, and none of these involved accusations against a coroner. Most were simply orders for coroners to perform specific tasks rather than actions taken against them for corruption or neglect.[18] As such, this form of oversight likely operated with variable efficiency, and thus a more regular, centrally enforced system of supervision was necessary to ensure the effective, efficient operation of the coroner system. The venue for this central system of oversight was the central courts in London.

Oversight by the Almoner and the Central Courts

If justices of the peace provided the first, local, level of surveillance of the early modern coroner system, from the sixteenth century the central figure in oversight on a national level was the royal almoner. Originally almoners were members of most medieval aristocratic households, where they were responsible for collecting and distributing alms on behalf of the noble family. The office of the royal almoner, first mentioned in 1103, performed similar functions for the royal household, if on a larger, national scale.[19] In addition to his role as a preacher at court and director of the monarch's charitable bequests, however, the royal almoner was responsible for redistributing the property forfeited to the crown by felons and as the result of accidents.[20] The laws establishing the right of the crown, and specific franchise holders such as the lords of liberties and incorporated boroughs, to seize both the property of felons and outlaws, and goods involved in fatal accidents, originated in the thirteenth century and remained in place throughout the early modern period despite challenges in the 1650s. Every case that came before a coroner, as the official responsible for investigating such instances of culpable death, included the possibility of forfeit property, creating an indelible link between coroner, forfeiture, and almoner.[21]

In the early modern period, the almoner primarily made use of two of the central courts to secure forfeit goods: the Court of King's Bench and the Court of Star Chamber. In the early sixteenth century, the almoner seems to have been most active in the Court of King's Bench, but from the 1530s, when the almoner first won his right to sue in Star Chamber, both courts were used with relative frequency.[22] The rise of Star Chamber was part of the Henrician law reforms of the early sixteenth century, which shifted much business from the common law courts such as King's Bench to the conciliar courts and courts of equity. As a result, the amount of litigation pursued by the almoner increased dramatically from the 1530s, an increase that resulted in a growth of litigation in both Star Chamber and King's Bench.[23]

The forfeiture system and the office of the almoner have largely been ignored by historians of state formation and historians of criminal justice alike. Some recent historians of suicide have examined the almoner in some detail, but their focus on suicide has perhaps led them to dismiss the role of the almoner in state building. Rab Houston, for instance, has argued that rather than being simply punitive, forfeiture for suicide "was also a means of enforcing trust and community among survivors through the mechanism of lordship."[24] Following Otto von Gierke, Houston sees this lordship as not simply a hierarchical expression of power, but also a force "that helped maintain social cohesion and even promote community, driven by ideas of public duty, secular obligation and religious charity."[25] Thus, for Houston, the almoner, and the central courts through which he sometimes operated, was simply another manifestation of attempts to establish and maintain "negotiated communities" through the exercise of good lordship.[26]

Houston, however, is primarily concerned with the almoner's role in cases of suicide rather than his place in a system of oversight or state control. When we turn our attention to those Star Chamber and King's Bench cases that involved coroners or their records, however, it becomes clear that in conjunction with the central courts and private informers and litigators, the almoner played a key role in the surveillance of coroners and coroners' investigations into suspicious death. This centralization of the oversight of lethal violence was not an accident, but rather the result of a series of conscious decisions made to strengthen state surveillance of death. The creation of a system of forfeiture that punished illegitimate violence through the seizure of property was the first step in regulating culpable death. This system was given greater central control by placing the responsibility to monitor it in the hands of a crown official, the almoner. Allowing the almoner to sue in Star Chamber was likewise a conscious decision made by the crown to give more powers of enforcement to the almoner and put some teeth into the forfeiture system. Finally, the state actively encouraged the use of the central courts — courts more closely controlled by the central authorities — as the key venue for the resolution of forfeiture litigation. As a result of these actions, the growing appeal of the central courts as venues for litigation for almoners, royal patent holders, and private individuals helped place the instruments of oversight more firmly in the hands of the state, which in turn helped to provide a robust system of supervision that was largely separate from any attempt to create cohesive communities.

Star Chamber and the Oversight of Death

Until it was abolished in 1641, the Court of Star Chamber played a central role in the oversight of the coroner system. Given the court's age-old remit, this focus on the coroner and the restriction of violence should come as no surprise. As we have already seen in Chapter 1, two of the most important original functions of Star Chamber were the regulation of riot and the punishment of perversions of justice such as perjury, subornation, conspiracy, and false jury verdicts.[27] From the reign of Henry VII, Star Chamber also functioned as an instrument for keeping the king's peace by "suppressing violence and keeping down men too great to be dealt with by the ordinary courts."[28] Star Chamber's flexibility in hearing cases, its relative efficiency, and its considerable power to enforce its decisions made it a popular choice for both official and private litigants in the early modern period.

Due to this historic role in the regulation of illegitimate violence, Star Chamber had been a venue for such litigation since the Middle Ages. Litigation relating to the coroner and the coroner system, however, began to expand greatly in the 1530s. In part, this expansion of litigation was an aspect of a more general expansion of business in the conciliar courts, as their efficient and effective nature made them increasingly popular alternatives to the common law courts, an expansion expressly championed by the crown. However, another key driver of the growth of forfeiture litigation was the newfound ability of the royal almoner to sue in Star Chamber. The exact context of this newly granted power is not entirely clear, but it is certain that it was a decision made by the crown. Given the position and duties of the almoner and the specific function and jurisdiction of Star Chamber, the decision to allow the almoner access to this conciliar court seems intuitive. Star Chamber had its roots as a court in the judicial function of the king's council. As such, Star Chamber was merely the monarch's council sitting as a court, a function that seems to have become effectively separate from its advisory function by at least the early sixteenth century. As the almoner was a member of the king's household, and Star Chamber a court made up of the king's council sitting as judges, it logically follows that such a court would be seen as an effective tool for the judicial activities of a member of the household. In addition, Star Chamber and the royal almoner were both in large part concerned with regulating and punishing illegitimate violence. As a result of this common purpose, Star Chamber must have been seen as a natural venue for litigation initiated by the almoner and involving forfeiture and the coroner system. The granting of this new power also had potentially beneficial consequences for both crown and almoner, consequences that surely influenced both the almoner's desire to gain access to Star Chamber and the crown's decision to grant it. From the perspective of the almoner, the ability to sue in Star Chamber provided a venue for litigation that had greater powers of enforcement than most contemporary courts. Shifting forfeiture litigation to Star Chamber also benefited the crown both by giving teeth to the forfeiture system that helped regulate lethal violence, and by allowing for greater central control of the entire process. From the 1530s, then, the convergence of interest and function between Star Chamber and royal almoner led to a significant expansion of litigation relating to violent death, litigation which, as we will see, ushered in a new era of oversight and a new level of central control over nonstate violence.

Star Chamber's surveillance of nonstate violence was accomplished not simply by the crown-appointed royal almoner, but also through the informal apparatus of litigation initiated, informed, and contested by private citizens and royal patent holders. In most cases of suspicious death investigated by a coroner, there was the potential for property to be found forfeit. In cases of suicide, the goods of the deceased were officially forfeit to the crown. So too were the goods of those convicted of murder, as was any object found to be the proximate cause of death in cases of misadventure or accident.[29] All of this forfeit property was theoretically to be given to the crown as punishment for crime and payment for the loss of subjects.

In reality, most forfeit property was granted to the royal almoner, with a substantial portion granted to royal patentees who were given the right to claim forfeit property on their estates or within their liberties.[30] These royal grants gave a number of officers and local magnates a direct economic interest in the outcome of coroners' inquests. The interests of theses grantees, however, did not go unchallenged by the heirs to felons or the owners of deodands (goods of felons and those goods forfeited because they were found to be the proximate cause of death), who also had something to gain, or lose, by the outcome of inquests.[31] By pursuing litigation related to death, challenging litigation brought by the almoner, and providing local information and insight into cases concerning death, people in the localities also proved to be a crucial facet of the oversight of coroners in the early modern period. This confluence of self-interest between almoner, patent holders, and heirs—and the resolution of these competing interests in the central courts—meant that a high proportion of the early modern coroner's work underwent regular and intense scrutiny. The scrutiny provided by the watchful eyes of competing, self-interested litigants in turn helped regulate death and the officers responsible for its investigation. By contesting verdicts, examining coroners' records, and suing in court, early modern litigants provided a level of amateur surveillance of the coroner system. In this way, the coopting of private individuals and crown officers filled the regulatory gap created by the relative absence of official instruments and institutions of government oversight. In order to see how this informal system of supervision worked in practice, a thorough examination of the records of Star Chamber and King's Bench is critical.

In the Elizabethan period, 427 pieces of Star Chamber litigation involving the almoner survive. Of this total, 368 cases, or 86 percent, concerned disputes related to suicide. The remaining 14 percent mostly consisted of litigation over the property of those who died as a result of accidental death, with a few additional instances of disputes relating to homicides.[32] These proportions remained relatively stable throughout the reigns of Elizabeth I and her successor. Over the course of James I's reign between 1603 and 1625, I have found 173 Star Chamber cases involving disputes over the investigation, verdict, or property of suspicious deaths.[33]

A significant majority—78 percent—of these cases related to suicides. This is hardly surprising, given that suicide cases had the greatest potential to yield significant forfeit property. Accidental deaths made up about 19 percent of such Star Chamber litigation, while homicide made up just under 2 percent of the total.[34] Accidental deaths were the most common type of culpable death in the early modern world. Such deaths, however, were also the most likely to lack forfeit property, as accidental deaths resulting from such events as drowning were unlikely to produce a deodand. Homicides always had the potential for forfeiture, but as the least frequent type of violent death, they appear with less frequency in central court litigation.

In terms of the geographical spread of those Star Chamber cases that were initiated by the almoner, some interesting patterns emerge. If we examine the records relating to the almoner in the reign of James I, for instance, we find that the almoner pursued litigation relating to coroners' inquests in 32 of the 39 counties in England and two Welsh counties.[35] It is true, as may be expected given the population and governmental pull of London, that the county with the highest number of Star Chamber cases relating to the almoner in this period was Middlesex. However, while Middlesex had the highest number of relevant case, it still only represented 13 percent of the total cases. Furthermore, if we exclude Middlesex, the Home Counties are fairly underrepresented. In fact, the western counties of Cornwall, Devon, Dorset, and Somerset represent a higher percentage of the total cases involving the almoner (15 percent) than Surrey, Kent, Essex, Hampshire, Hertfordshire, Buckinghamshire, Bedfordshire, and Sussex combined (14 percent).[36] This suggests that the oversight of the coroner system provided by Star Chamber litigation was widespread and encompassed the whole of the country, rather than simply those areas close to the capital, where surveillance would be easy and litigation convenient.

Perhaps the most direct way the Court of Star Chamber oversaw the activities of individual coroners was through litigation, usually initiated by the almoner, but also brought by central legal officials such as the attorney general or private individuals. This type of litigation usually sought subpoenas against an individual coroner for some defect in his conduct while carrying out an inquest. These defects usually involved one or more of the following: packing a jury with partial or biased members, suppressing evidence, undervaluing forfeited goods, failing to reach a verdict, or failing to certify the verdict at the next assize. In almost every case, those initiating litigation were primarily concerned with the behavior, actions, or records of the coroner because they were thought to have prevented the proper redistribution of forfeited goods, at least from the perspective of the complainants.

This concern about how the behavior of coroners, and thus the outcome of inquests, might effect the distribution of forfeited goods is apparent in a suit initiated against Richard Robinson in 1620.[37] As coroner for Cumberland, Robinson was charged with investigating the death of Michael Baker, who had been found drowned. According to the almoner's complaint, the common opinion of the county was that Baker had killed himself, and much evidence was presented at the coroner's inquest to that effect. Since, however, a verdict of suicide would mean that Baker's goods and possessions would all be forfeit, and thus his widow would be put in a difficult circumstance, the widow and one of Baker's friends bribed Robinson to ensure the jury delivered a verdict of accidental death. The coroner was said to have "slighted and neglected the enquiry and taking of much material and plane evidence" and to have in "sundry ways also diswaded hindered interrupted discountenanced and disradarded all such evidence as was given in or to bee given in therin on yor majesties behalf." As a result of the coroner's underhanded efforts, "the said jury was drawne moved and induced" to find a false verdict of accidental death.[38]

The difference between the redistribution of goods in a case of suicide and a case of accidental death was often very different, if not always straightforward—a reality that often led to disputes over the outcome of inquests and questions over the coroner's conduct. For instance, in 1621 a London man named Edward Geesingbury died not long after he had been involved in an accident with a coach and horses.[39] Richard Stone, coroner for the City of London, undertook an investigation into the matter, which concluded that Geesingbury's death had been the result of suicide and not the accident with the coach. The almoner, however, had information that contradicted the verdict given by the coroner and his jury. According to the almoner's complaint, evidence was given by "gentlemen" of standing and "credit" that Geesingbury had died as a result of wounds he received when a coach crushed his leg.[40] The almoner accused the coroner of conspiring with the owner of the coach that had injured Geesingbury, William Duckett, to pack the jury with men partial to Duckett's cause. The jury, he alleged, in turn ignored the evidence supporting an accidental death. From Duckett's standpoint, it was of the utmost importance that the coroner's inquest should return a verdict of suicide rather than accidental death, for if the cause of death was determined to be the injuries caused by Duckett's coach and horses, those items would be forfeited to the crown as the deodand. The almoner also claimed that Stone knew that Geesingbury was a poor man, and that as such his heirs would have little to lose if his death was declared a suicide and his goods forfeit. In response to these allegations, Humphrey Stringer, one of the jurors, replied that they had found the death to be the result of suicide due to the testimony of a surgeon who had declared that the wound Geesingbury received by the coach was not mortal. Furthermore, the surgeon testified that after the accident with the coach, the deceased had risen from his sickbed and stamped his leg on the ground until the marrow came out, suggesting that the death had been caused not by the coach, but by Geesingbury's suicidal actions.[41]

Whether the coroner and his jury or the almoner was right about the cause of death is immaterial. What is important to note is that a variety of individuals had a direct economic stake in the whether Geesingbury's death was ruled suicide or accidental death. William Duckett, as the owner of the coach and horses involved in the accident, stood to lose his goods, and perhaps his means of making a living, if the death was ruled an accident. Geesingbury's heirs stood to lose whatever goods and property might pass to them from the deceased if the verdict was suicide. Finally, the almoner clearly thought that the value of the coach and horses was greater than that of whatever property Geesingbury might forfeit as a suicide, and thus hoped for the death to be considered an accident. Because of the multiplicity of opposing economic interests, the contestation of an inquest such as this makes it clear that a coroner's behavior was subject to fairly intense scrutiny. Whether or not Stone actually conspired to corrupt the inquest, it is

evident that such attempts or accusations would not go unnoticed when the
redistribution of property regularly hinged on the outcome of inquests.

In addition to being sued for attempting to pack juries and corrupt
the verdicts they delivered, coroners and their juries were also regularly
charged with failing to deliver or certify verdicts. The most common accusation of this type was that the coroner or the jury had refused to deliver
a verdict in order that goods or property which should have been forfeited
to the crown would remain in the possession of the original owner or his
or her heirs. One such case occurred in Elizabethan Staffordshire, when a
coroner and a William Prynce were accused of delaying the delivery of a
verdict to prevent some of Prynce's property from being declared a deodand.[42] The trouble began when a wagon laden with timber and drawn
by six oxen and two horses struck and killed an unknown person. As the
wagon and livestock were the proximate cause of the person's death, they
(or their value) should have been turned over to the crown as a deodand.
Understandably concerned over the potential loss of property valued at
£20, Prynce recruited the coroner responsible for the inquest to help him
convince the jury not to "geave up any verdict at all, or to stay the taking of
the verdyt for some longe tyme, or if the verdit should be taken not to certifie the inquisition whereby it might or should appeare how and by what
means the said partie came by his death."[43]

As often happened, failure to deliver or certify a verdict in this case
did not hide the irregular activities of the coroner and jury from the agents of
the crown. The almoner demanded on more than one occasion that Prynce
hand over the goods or their value. When Prynce refused, the almoner initiated proceedings against him in Star Chamber.[44] This wholly unremarkable case serves to illustrate the point that oversight extended not only to
potentially corrupt or inaccurate verdicts of coroners subject to oversight,
but also to failure to reach a verdict. Thus, any notion that coroners and
communities regularly conspired to defeat the crown by simply neglecting
to complete or register inquests is misplaced. The level of surveillance of
suspicious death was such that even the deliberate suppression of records
and the willful destruction of a paper trail did not preclude regular court
action against the negligent or corrupt.

Although coroners were sometimes the focus of Star Chamber litigation, the vast majority of cases did not involve any accusation against the
conduct of the coroner. In fact, only 10 percent of Star Chamber cases surveyed here contained such accusations. Additionally, a significant number
of those cases that did accuse the coroner of some sort of defect of conduct
involved claims that the coroner had failed to certify the verdict rather than
any more obvious form of corruption or malfeasance.[45] However, though
most cases did not involve direct accusations against the coroner, or even
any mention of the coroner, all Star Chamber litigation that disputed the
outcome of coroners' inquests helped perform an important measure of
oversight by scrutinizing and debating the work done by coroners and the
records they produced. As Paul Griffiths has shown, the records created by
early modern government and policing were "active archives" rather than
passive or rarely consulted documents consigned to molder away in dark
coroners. Such records were regularly consulted and debated, a process
that helped to monitor, police, and control both the activities of those mentioned in the records and those officials who created them in the course of
their duties.[46]

The scrutiny of coroners and their actions created by these overlapping interests could be intense, as the records of the period indicated.
For example, in 1610 the body of a man was found drowned in a pond
in Essex. Some members of the local community feared that the coroner
would discover that the death had been the result of suicide and conspired
to deceive the coroner into thinking that their neighbor had been killed as
the result of an accident or by an unknown person. In order to achieve this
deception, several locals "did remove the said corps from the place where
it was drowned before the said coroner and the jury could come a view the
same."[47] Not only did these local residents remove the body from the place
of death, they also, according to the complaint, carried the body away on
a ladder so that the position of the body at death could not be determined
and so that the motion of carrying the body on the ladder would cause
sufficient bruising to suggest a violent end. Not satisfied that the evidence
for homicide was strong enough, the residents made "six or seaven holes
cuts or wounds about the face or head of tha said corpse of purpose for to

make it seeme to the said jury that the said Francis Marshall had been hurt wounded and murthered by some other man."[48] When the coroner, John Nashe, arrived and began the inquest, the people behind the attempted deception sought to sway the coroner's jury by having a biased jury returned, and by suppressing testimony and witnesses prejudicial to their goal. One witness who had previously given evidence that Marshall had been disconsolate before his death was induced to change her story, while testimony that Marshall had made previous suicide attempts was also suppressed. Despite the rampant tampering, Nashe instructed the jury to find a verdict of suicide. When the jury ignored his instructions and returned a verdict of murder by a person unknown, Nashe refused to accept it. At an impasse, the inquest was adjourned until the next month, at which point further evidence was produced that suggested the death was indeed the result of suicide. Again, however, the jury returned a verdict of death by murder. Again the coroner refused to accept the verdict. After a second adjournment of 20 days, the process repeated itself, with the jury returning the same verdict and the coroner still refusing to accept it.

The case remained unresolved until the almoner received information that a corrupt and recalcitrant jury had attempted to cheat him out of his portion of the goods that would have been forfeited if Marshall's death had been ruled a suicide, as the evidence and the coroner suggested. Because the almoner had an economic interest in seeing that this case was properly concluded, he initiated litigation against those who had sought to pervert the course of justice. While the motives of the almoner may have been economic and the conduct of the coroner beyond reproach, the litigation that ensued did serve to provide oversight of the coroner system and ensure that such attempts to corrupt the investigation of death did not go unchallenged. Thus, because the almoner had a financial stake in the outcome of the inquest, the attempts of a community to corrupt the coroner system for their own benefit were noticed and prosecuted.

Other, less overtly corrupt cases also provided an important measure of surveillance simply by consulting and making use of the records produced by coroners. In cases such as that following the death of Steven Crane, the use of coroners' records by litigants helped ensure their accuracy even when the coroner himself was not the subject of the suit. Shortly after his death, Raphe Scrivener, coroner for the county of Suffolk, convened an inquest to determine the cause of Crane's death.[49] In so doing, it was determined that Crane had drowned himself, and thus his goods and property were forfeit. The verdict in the case seems to have been uncontroversial and Crane's widow initially agreed to a composition (an agreement with creditors to pay less than is owed in return for immediate payment), so that the value of the forfeit goods would go to the crown as specified by law. When Crane's widow remarried a James Richardson, however, the new couple refused to give up the disputed goods or their cash value as settled by the composition, and instead leased out lands that should have belonged to the crown. The almoner may not have realized that the goods and property forfeited after Crane's suicide had not been delivered to him if he had not reviewed the records of the inquest taken by Scrivener and "remaining upon record in the crown office."[50] It was the detailed record-keeping system that alerted the busy almoner to a problem resulting from an inquest miles away. With the evidence of the inquest's result in hand, the almoner initiated litigation against Mrs. Richardson for the recovery of the late Steven Crane's goods. Although the coroner in this case was not accused of any sort of corruption, negligence, or other deficiency, simply by reviewing the records Scrivener created as coroner, the almoner provided a useful review of the coroner's behavior and records. Scrivener's behavior had been aboveboard, but the fact that the Richardsons' actions were not provided a useful check not only on those individuals who might fail to turn over forfeited property, but also on the records produced by coroners. Economic incentive ensured the regular review of coroners' inquests, behavior, and records by a central, crown-appointed authority.

It is important to reiterate that almoners were not the only ones to initiate litigation relating to cases of suicide, accident, and homicide in the Court of Star Chamber. The forfeiture system provided an incentive for private individuals, as well as state officials, to sue over inaccuracies or corruptions in the inquest process. Individuals and almoners both provided oversight of the coroner system as a byproduct of their pursuit of litigation, and especially in their pursuit of financial interest and pecuniary gain. In doing so, they joined the tidal wave of litigants entering the judicial system in the early modern period. According to Christopher Brooks, the very period in which the almoner began to sue for forfeit property in Star Chamber also witnessed a spectacular rise in popular recourse to the central common law courts, conciliar courts, and courts of equity. Although the sheer mass of central court records and frequent gaps in the available materials make any firm conclusion difficult, it is generally agreed that business at the central courts increased exponentially between about 1550 and 1640, with peak growth occurring during the reign of Elizabeth I.[51] The same period witnessed a stagnation or even a decline in suits initiated at county or manorial courts.[52] The theses proposed for this growth and centralization of litigation are contentious and legion, but the most convincing hypothesis suggests that increases in population, prices, and economic activity, combined with the failures of local courts and the declining costs of the central courts, created the conditions both for more litigation and for the growing appeal of the Westminster courts as a venue.[53] Given that growing popularity—especially for issues related to property, comprising up about 80 percent of the business of the Jacobean Star Chamber—it is of little surprise that private individuals initiated litigation over forfeit property of the dead in considerable numbers under the later Tudors and early Stuarts.[54]

One such suit involving a private complainant arose following the death of William Wygmore in London. Star Chamber litigation was initiated in this case not by the almoner, but by Wygmore's brother and other men who had provided evidence at the coroner's jury. The complainants averred that after Wygmore's death, the coroner for the City of London held an inquest as dictated by law. According to the complaint, however, the inquest over which the coroner, William Squire, presided was anything but aboveboard. Wygmore's brother and the other signees of the complaint claimed that Wygmore had been murdered by a Thomas Hopton, who had long held a grudge against the deceased and had threatened him before, once going so far as to wound him. The complainants stated that they had witnessed the murder itself and had provided details and testimony in depositions given before the coroner and jury that sat in view of the body.

The evidence for Hopton's guilt seemed overwhelming, but the coroner's attempts to influence the inquest undermined the cause of justice. By giving copies of the evidence to the accused and concealing "divers of the most effectual depositions frome the jurors," Williams hoped to spare Hopton the rigors of the law.[55] Not only was the coroner accused of suppressing some depositions, but he was also accused of admitting as evidence depositions "Hopton procured and produced against your highness who were not present att the murder committed."[56] Hopton himself was accused of bribing the coroner and his jury "not to fynde any murder." The complainants thus requested the court to subpoena Hopton, Squire, and the entire coroner's jury.[57]

What becomes evident from cases such as these is that oversight of the coroner system was not simply the purview of the crown authorities themselves, but also the responsibility of private individuals. The central courts, and Star Chamber in particular, were thus *sites* of oversight rather than merely apparati of oversight alone. In these legal arenas, an informal system of oversight was created in which competing and overlapping financial interests were at stake. As most cases under the coroner's purview involved property or money of some kind, there were almost always multiple parties—be they individuals or agents of the crown such as the almoner—with a direct economic interest in the outcome of inquests. Because the verdict of a coroner's inquest would have a direct impact on the redistribution of a deodand, its proceedings were closely scrutinized by heirs, almoners, and others with an interest in forfeited goods. Irregularities, inaccuracies, or accusations of corruption were regularly seized upon by those who had something to lose or something to gain from the outcome of a coroner's work. This very concern over the procedure and outcome of coroners' inquests created an atmosphere of oversight that stretched from the site of death to the central courts and that encompassed individuals, local communities, and crown authorities. The creation of economic incentives helped to align private interests and state interests in the proper functioning of the coroner system and the regulation of lethal violence. Private interests were encouraged by these measures to participate in the judicial oversight process and to provide a corrective for corruption that was otherwise unavailable in the relatively decentralized early modern state, which as yet lacked the resources to monitor the system through state means alone. Providing various parties with competing interests a vested stake in an honest inquest process helped to reduce corruption by both officeholders and private citizens alike. Thus, forfeiture litigation encouraged a justice system that was relatively free from corruption and thus efficacious for the monopolization of violence.

King's Bench and the Oversight of Death

In addition to Star Chamber, coroners, inquests, and almoners were involved in a large amount of litigation in the Court of King's Bench. This common law court held primary responsibility for the formal oversight of the records produced by coroners. All coroners' inquests were required by law to be sent to the Court of King's Bench, usually from the assize courts to which coroners first delivered their inquests.[58] Thus, King's Bench played a significant role in the oversight of the coroner system as both a repository of inquests and, like Star Chamber, as a site of litigation over forfeited property and the outcome of inquests. Given the voluminous records produced by King's Bench, it may prove useful to focus our attention on the records of one well-documented county. According to R. F. Hunnisett's compilation of Sussex coroners' inquests, there exist 1,423 inquests for that county between 1558 and 1750. Of these inquests, about 19 percent resulted in some form of litigation at King's Bench. About 36 percent of this litigation related to cases of suicide, while 49 percent dealt with cases of accidental death and 16 percent with homicide. Twenty-seven percent of the cases that led to litigation and 5 percent of all inquests involved processes against a coroner.[59]

If we break the numbers down into smaller units based on regnal years, a trajectory of inquest litigation can be seen. The years between 1485 and 1558 witnessed 243 inquests held in Sussex, of which 66, or 27 percent, resulted in some form of litigation at King's Bench. Of those inquests that resulted in litigation, 30 percent involved cases of suicide, while 30 percent dealt with accidental death and 32 percent with homicide. Coroners were specifically charged with defects in 30 percent of the cases that led to litigation and 10 percent of all inquests that resulted in actions against a coroner. A closer look at the numbers reveals a substantial growth in the proportion of inquests leading to litigation from the 1530s, peaking in the reign of Mary I, a period that also saw a significant growth in the numbers of coroners summoned to King's Bench for defects.[60]

Between 1558 and 1603, 582 inquests are known to have been held in Sussex. Of these surviving inquests, 112 resulted in some sort of central court litigation, or about two and a half cases per annum. In terms of a proportion of the total number of inquests, roughly 19 percent of all inquests resulted in litigation, mostly in King's Bench (109 of 112 cases). Approximately 43 percent of these litigated cases involved suicide, while 47 percent involved accidental death and 10 percent involved homicide. The reign of James I saw broadly similar trends. Between 1603 and 1625 there were 268 known inquests held in Sussex, about 23 percent of which resulted in litigation. Twenty-six percent of these cases related to suicide, whereas about 60 percent related to accidental death and 14 percent to homicide. The proportion of inquests that resulted in litigation is truly remarkable. The fact that between one in five and one in six cases of suspicious death produced central court litigation suggests both how closely tied to state institutions the adjudication of interpersonal violence had become, and the great potential such litigation possessed as a mechanism for monitoring the coroner system.

Further evidence of the effects of litigation on the oversight of the coroner is demonstrated by the frequency with which those officers were called to appear personally before the central courts. Coroners were specifically charged to appear at King's Bench in 24 percent of cases, usually to answer for defects in the inquest records in the Elizabethan period.[61] In the early decades of the seventeenth century, subpoenas were directed at coroners in 28 percent of those cases that involved litigation.[62] These defects ranged from failure to supply information about the place of death, the name of the victim, or the date of the inquest to failure to note the location of forfeit property. Such regular, close focus on the minutiae of coroners' records meant that few instances of inaccuracy or corruption escaped the gaze of the courts.

The inquest and King's Bench materials relating to the reigns of Elizabeth and James I show that from about the middle of the sixteenth century, the number of inquests that resulted in litigation increased in terms of both number per year and the proportion of the total number of inquests, as did the frequency with which coroners were targets of litigation. This suggests that the level of oversight that developed between 1558 and 1625 was remarkable in its intensity and pervasiveness. An individual coroner operating in this period could be relatively sure that any defects in his inquests would be caught and that as many as a quarter of his inquests would be scrutinized as the result of central court litigation. This is not to say that the number of defects present in inquests actually increased across the period, but rather that as time progressed, even minor discrepancies and inaccuracies in coroners' records were flagged by the central authorities.

To take the example of one individual coroner, we can return to the remarkable records of William Playfere during his tenure as coroner of Hastings Rape in Sussex. Playfere was summoned by King's Bench on seven separate occasions to answer for defects in his inquests over his 28 years in office.[63] Generally, the defect in question was a lack of information regarding the whereabouts of forfeited goods. When information regarding these goods was added, the proceedings against Playfere usually stopped. For instance, in July 1572 Playfere held an inquest over the body of 11-year-old John Allen of Catsfield. He discovered that John had died after falling from a "blind graye horse," valued at 3s 4d, into a pond, where he subsequently drowned. The coroner had not, however, noted the fate of the horse, which as the proximate cause of John Allen's death was the property the crown. Playfere was later summoned to King's Bench to answer for defects in the inquest. When information about the custody of the horse was interlined, the process against him stopped.[64] This seems to have been the case for most Sussex coroners summoned before King's Bench to answer for defects: what the central authorities were most often concerned with was the whereabouts of forfeited goods.

Coroners, however, were occasionally summoned to King's Bench for other defects in their inquests. In 1585, for example, a Sussex coroner was summoned for failing to provide the hour when a murder occurred. Similarly, in 1634 a different coroner was summoned for failing to record the victim's place of residence. The processes against both coroners were stopped when they amended their inquests to provide the missing information.[65] Although the litigation against these coroners ceased, the message must have remained clear: even tiny errors in the discharge of their duties would result in coroners being summoned to King's Bench. Those who failed to heed this warning were outlawed or fined. Given such an atmosphere of surveillance, it was surely in coroners' best interests to perform their duties conscientiously and accurately in the knowledge that the economic interests of the almoner and his agents would help to ensure that defects were noticed and coroners called to account.

Coroners were not the only ones subject to intense central interest in inquest procedures and records. Private individuals were also frequently called to answer for forfeited property. Sometimes these were individuals who refused to give up forfeit property, but on other occasions they were individuals charged by the coroner with holding such property until a resolution was made. Another group of people regularly targeted by King's Bench litigation were royal patent holders and lords of liberties. Forty-three percent of cases in the reign of Elizabeth and 30 percent in the reign of James I involved litigation aimed at lords of liberties—those individuals or institutions who had been granted the right to property found forfeit on their lands—or their agents. Sussex had a numerous liberties whose patents, among other things, allowed their owners to take possession of goods forfeited as the result of felonies or accidents that occurred in their jurisdictions, a right that the lords of liberties were often keen to assert. The involvement of patent holders provided yet another layer of competing interest in the outcome of coroners' inquests, and as such another level of informal oversight.

In a letter to his estate steward Richard Morris in 1629, Thomas Wentworth, first earl of Strafford, made clear his intention to keep any forfeit property that fell within his jurisdiction: "As for the deodand at

Eastwicke which you mention in your letter . . . I would have you let the Coroner know that I have camaunded you not to deliver the goods, but that I will justifie the keeping of them by my charter."[66] As the charter was locked in Wentworth's study with his other "evidence," the steward was unable to access the patent until the earl himself returned. Until that time, Wentworth instructed Morris that "[i]n the mean time I will keep my possession and I pray you doe soe take the goods and remove them if cause require to Woodhouse; for I am sumthing confident my charter will carry itt and tell both the Coroner and Amner [Almoner] that they shall not meddle with them."[67] The letter suggests that although Wentworth was at pains to exercise his rights as lord of the liberty, he was not entirely sure whether the forfeit goods in question actually fell under his charter, simply believing the charter for the liberty of Harwood was similar to that for his property at Richmond.[68] Despite this lack of certainty and his implication that the coroner or almoner might contest his claim to the forfeit property, it was clearly important to Wentworth to keep the deodand in his possession, whether for monetary gain or simply to assert his rights and power as a landowner.

The lords of liberties and their agents thus represented yet another party with direct economic interests in the accurate outcome of coroners' inquests and the proper distribution of forfeit property. Although litigation that targeted lords of liberties and their agents often ceased when letters patent were shown proving the liberties' right to forfeit goods, the fact that litigation was initiated at all is significant. Lords of liberties and their agents were sometimes outlawed for their failure to turn over property, and frequently arrangements were made with the almoner to settle the fate of forfeit goods. These contests between patent holders, almoners, heirs, and central courts shows that the rights to deodands and the goods of felons were frequently contested, providing yet another level of scrutiny of the duties and records of the coroner. Such a variety of competing economic interests surely helped to provide an intense level of surveillance of the coroner system.

The almoner was often the key figure in initiating forfeiture litigation in King's Bench. The almoner's role in King's Bench litigation and his use of that court to recover forfeit property or force compositions has not received much attention in the historical literature thus far.[69] As we have seen, the almoner made frequent use of Star Chamber as a venue for litigation. The Court of King's Bench, however, was at least as important in this regard. King's Bench provided the initial review of inquest records and as a result, a greater volume of litigation was initiated in that court. Star Chamber was thus, at least in terms of overall numbers, the secondary venue for litigation relating to death and forfeiture, handling mostly those cases that proved especially intractable. The two courts thus worked in tandem, with King's Bench handling most cases of defective records and missing property, and Star Chamber handling accusations of corruption and other difficult cases that necessitated the strong powers of enforcement. Thus, Star Chamber was the court of last resort and King's Bench the court of first resort.

In large measure, the role of King's Bench in the oversight of the coroner system was to review inquests, challenge those that were obviously deficient, and order officials to appear in court and surrender forfeited goods.[70] The involvement of the almoner or his deputy in these routine supervisions has been understated and unexplored. For example, although coroners were frequently summoned to appear at King's Bench to answer for defects in inquisitions, the defects in question, with few exceptions, were related to the value or whereabouts of forfeit property. Such processes against coroners often stopped when the inquest was amended and the almoner or his deputy acknowledged satisfaction with the alterations.[71] Similarly, when individuals or officers were called to King's Bench to answer for the whereabouts of forfeit property, it was common for processes against these individuals to cease when the almoner or his deputy acknowledged either that a composition had been paid or that letters patent had been produced which allowed the individual to receive the forfeit goods.[72]

As with Star Chamber, the role of King's Bench in the oversight of forfeiture, the coroner system, and suspicious death was not solely a matter of direct surveillance' it also served as a venue in which almoners, individuals, and lords of liberties could engage in litigation concerning the proper redistribution of forfeit property. By creating a venue for competing and overlapping economic interests to vie over forfeitures, the central courts provided a crucial link in the policing of suspicious death. Because the litigants who made use of the central courts—and officers of the courts themselves—used, consulted, disputed, and challenged the records made by coroners, when such litigation increased after 1530, oversight of the coroner system became more intense and thus more effective. A variety of competing interests thus had a direct economic incentive to contest and dispute the legitimacy of inquest procedures and verdicts. By providing a system of competing interests, and a centralized state institution in which to resolve these contests, the English state ensured that the actions and records of coroners would be subject to the careful attention of an array of economically interested parties.

The Efficacy of the System of Oversight Considered

In his recent work on suicide in England, Rab Houston presents a radically different portrait of the almoner as the benevolent restorer of communal harmony in the wake of the disrupting event of suicide. As evidence for this contention Houston relies on two main arguments. First, according to Houston, the almoner's role in acquiring forfeit property was charitable rather than self-interested. Indeed, the almoner's remit was specifically to take that property forfeited by felons and in accidents and put it to charitable uses. As Houston shows, on occasion we can even trace where such forfeited property went as charitable gifts.[73] The second aspect of Houston's attempted rehabilitation of the almoner is his contention that rather than seeking the property of the deceased suicide or its full value, the almoner often sought a cash composition (usually between 5 and 10 percent of the property's value).[74] The twin features of charity and composition, for Houston, demonstrate that the almoner's role was not that of a self-interested agent of state centralization but rather that of a cleric expiating sin and reconciling communities by means of a mutually agreed upon charitable redistribution of property.

While Houston is surely right to emphasize both charity and composition in his treatment of the almoner system, his rosy view of that system is belied by the contentious reality of litigation between almoners and local

individuals. First of all, even if the motives of all almoners were truly charitable—and we will probably never know how much, if any, of the forfeit
property individual almoners diverted into their own hands—charity and
self-interest are not mutually exclusive. The distribution of charity, especially on such a large scale, is both an opportunity to fund pet projects and
interests and a means of distributing patronage, reinforcing power and status.[75] Just because the ultimate use of forfeited goods was charitable, it does
not follow that the almoner had no self-interest in rigorously and ruthlessly
pursuing the goods of felons, as is borne out by the records of litigation.

Houston contends that the charitable redistribution of forfeit property by the almoner or other franchisees was primarily a means of expiating
communal sin and thus reconciling communities with God and with their
neighbors, a manifestation of good lordship. Even if we concede that this
was a possible benefit of the almoner system in cases of suicide, it ignores
the numerous cases of accidental death, which also fell within the almoner's
purview and which likewise frequently involved litigation. As we have seen,
cases of accidental death made up a significant minority of Star Chamber
cases (19 percent in the reign of James I) and a majority of litigation relating
to Sussex initiated in King's Bench (47 percent and 62 percent in the reigns
of Elizabeth I and James I, respectively).[76] Without including these cases in
our discussion of the almoner's role, it is impossible to accurately conclude
what the almoner really did in early modern England.

Because suicide was considered by contemporaries to be both a
crime and a sin, and because sin was often seen in communal terms, it is
reasonable to think that by giving a portion of a suicide's goods to charity, almoners helped communities purge themselves of sin and thus avoid
God's wrath.[77] It is more difficult, however, to see how this function of
expiating communal sin could be translated to cases of accidental death.
The vast majority of accidental deaths in the early modern period did not
involve any crime or sin, and hence there would have been no need for the
almoner to seize property involved in accidents that would have any benefit
for the local community. For instance, in 1574 Joan Cogger, age three, fell
while climbing the pole of her father's cart, landing on some rocks. Young
Joan died shortly afterward, and the coroner's inquest found that she had

died as a result of the fall from the cart. The cart was appraised at 2s 6d
and this amount was paid to the coroner as deodand.[78] In a similar manner, Margaret Lavander, age one and a half, died in her father's home by
falling into a tub containing "worte." The wort (an infusion of fermented
malt used in making beer) was hot and scalded the child badly. She died
two hours later. The tub was appraised by the coroner's jurors at 2d, which
sum was declared forfeit.[79] Neither of the cases specifically mention a composition; however, even if the sums paid were compositions agreed upon
by heirs and almoner, it must have seemed doubly unfair for those families
who experienced the loss of a child or a member of the family to also give
up goods or some portion of their value as a result of the death. Instances
such as these, in which the property declared forfeit as the result of an accidental death belonged to the deceased or the deceased's family, were not
at all uncommon. It is hard to see how seizing such property, or even a portion of it, could be seen by the deceased's heirs or the community as anything but an onerous and grasping imposition by the almoner, and hardly a
means of reconciling communities to each other or to God.

The other piece of evidence for the benign nature of the almoner
system, the use of compositions, is also less straightforward than it may
at first appear. It is clear that almoners often sought compositions rather
than the full value of forfeit goods or the goods themselves. It is difficult
to say for sure, however, how often compositions were arranged between
heirs and almoner as they are rarely mentioned in either Star Chamber or
King's Bench records. Even when compositions are recorded, the value of
the composition compared to that of the potentially forfeit goods is usually
absent. Even if we concede that almoners usually sought compositions, and
sought them because they wished to reach an equitable arrangement with
the heirs of the deceased, a number of questions still remain.

If almoners truly sought an equitable outcome, why did individuals
frequently refuse to pay even a composition and risk outlawry as a result?
Why did heirs and other beneficiaries seek to corrupt inquests and hide
forfeited goods? Why did almoners or their agents dispute small amounts
of money or initiate litigation over divergent valuations of goods? The
truth is, there is scant evidence that the resort to compositions had any-

thing to do with the practice of good lordship rather than a simple rational calculation on the part of grantees, creditors, and heirs that it would often be cheaper, faster, and easier to settle for a portion of the value of forfeit property in cash than to bring the dispute to court—a rationale similar to that in modern out-of-court settlements. Such an extralegal arrangement certainly does not preclude the presence of the bad feeling and disharmony that could sow the seeds of discord in a community and thus undermine the communal harmony that good lordship was supposed to create. The agreement to a composition also did not mean that all creditors or claimants were satisfied with the distribution of property, but rather that the grantee was satisfied with his or her share. Thus, the fact that the actions of almoners and other grantees were occasionally dressed up in a paternalistic rhetoric of good lordship and communal peace does little but disguise self-interested acquisitiveness, dispute, resistance, and the contestation of coroners' inquests.[80]

Along similar lines, Steve Hindle has argued that because suicides were often female and poor, the amount of property forfeited to the crown was likely to be insignificant. Thus, "the fact that the almoner sued fairly often suggests that the laws of homicide and suicide were of political and symbolic, rather than purely fiscal significance to the crown."[81] Such claims ignore the perspective of the heirs of suicides and other felons, for whom seemingly small amounts of money or property did not seem so insignificant. This perspective in turn led to the corruption and refusals to pay that necessitated litigation in the first place. Furthermore, even if most suicides were poor—and many were not—any discussion of the almoner's role in oversight that neglects cases of misadventure or accident is incomplete. Although not all cases of misadventure involved high-value goods, many, especially the all too frequent accidents involving horses, carts, and other livestock, often resulted in the forfeiture of a deodand of significant value. Even those inquests with no or little forfeit property were subject to significant scrutiny, along with the coroner who held them.

Because there was always the potential that a death might lead to substantial forfeit property, the records of every suspicious death had to be checked by someone in order to determine whether there was the potential for forfeit property and thus financial gain. Much of this work is likely to have been done by local deputies on the scene or through the examination of the inquests returned to King's Bench. Indeed, there are many examples of coroners being summoned to appear in King's Bench to amend their inquests by adding information about the value and location of deodands. In many of these cases, the newly amended materials simply informed the court and the almoner that the deceased had no property or that the property was insignificant. Although inquests on the bodies of the poor did not lead to financial gain or litigation, the mere fact that someone had to determine that the deceased was in fact poor or without property, and thus no deodand worth note would be forthcoming, meant that coroners and their inquest records were routinely mined for information. This scrutiny of coroners' records even in cases of the deceased poor helped to monitor and regulate coroners' activities and behavior.

The question remains, if litigation brought by almoners was indeed paternalistic, political, and symbolic rather than financial, as has been suggested, why was almost every instance of litigation interested in the distribution of forfeit property rather than in corruption or inaccuracy alone? Why is it that even those cases that are ostensibly concerned with issues of corruption and negligence are in reality concerned with property as well? For instance, when the coroner and his jury were accused of corruption for finding that Francis Tredway had drowned accidentally, the issue at hand was not solely to regulate and oversee those charged with investigating death, but rather whether or not property was forfeit.[82] If the verdict of the inquest was upheld, the death would be ruled an accident and the property of the deceased would pass to his heirs, in this case Tredway's widow. However, if the almoner was correct and the death was actually a suicide hidden by the corrupt machinations of the coroner and jury, then the deceased's property was forfeit and the almoner enriched. Thus, the important aspect of the coroner and jury's supposed corruption was not only that they had found the death to be accidental when the evidence suggested it was in fact suicide, but that the inaccurate verdict cheated the crown of property that should have been forfeit.[83]

One possible reason for the seemingly contentious nature of the almoner system is that only those rare cases that were disputed or intractable resulted in litigation, and thus most cases were resolved peacefully with mutually agreed compositions. If one looks at the records of Sussex, however, this argument loses its weight. When one compares the total number of coroners' inquests held in Sussex with the number of inquests that resulted in litigation, it becomes evident that the almoner's idea of an equitable settlement was frequently at odds with that of the heirs and family members of the deceased. Between 1558 and 1603, 112 of the 582 total inquests, or 19 percent, resulted in central court litigation. This proportion rose to about 23 percent of inquests between 1603 and 1625.[84] Thus, a high proportion of inquests led to litigation rather than to a speedy and equitable composition. This does not mean, however, that 80 percent of inquests led to uncontested or uncontentious compositions. Many, perhaps the majority, of those cases that did not result in litigation involved the deaths of individuals who possessed no goods or property, or related to accidental deaths in which no goods were declared forfeit as deodand. If we consider that many cases of untimely or suspicious death did not involve forfeit property, the proportion of cases that resulted in central court litigation is remarkable. The high rate of litigation per inquest in turn demonstrates that conceptions of what was a fair distribution of the deceased's property differed radically. If the almoner saw his role as an agent of communal reconciliation through equitable distribution of forfeited property as charity, the records of Star Chamber and King's Bench demonstrate that local communities and individuals frequently saw the almoner as a self-interested and grasping officer of the crown.

Even if almoners were unique among early modern officeholders in not seeking financial gain from their official positions, it is important to note that they, like many high officials, normally operated through deputies who engaged in litigation on their behalf.[85] It is certainly possible that as clerics, court preachers, and trustees of the monarch's charities, many almoners may well have taken their role in distributing forfeited goods in an equitable and charitable manner seriously. It is dangerous, however, to assume that high ecclesiastical position was synonymous with either a charitable mentality or a lack of interest in the perks of office. Whatever the moral character of the almoner, much of the actual work of securing forfeit goods was done by deputy almoners, who were generally lawyers rather than clerics. William Johnson, who acted as deputy almoner in the second decade of the seventeenth century, was just one of many lawyers who held the office in the early modern period.[86] In the records of King's Bench, the vast majority of references in forfeiture disputes mention the involvement of the deputy almoner rather than the almoner himself.[87] Of course, the fact that most forfeiture litigation was undertaken by lawyers rather than clerics does not exclude the possibility of equitable or charitable agreements being reached between the office of the almoner and the heirs of felons or the owners of deodands. However, any idea that the almoner was more likely to reach such agreements due to his faith or his position in the ecclesiastical hierarchy must be seriously questioned.

Central to the argument that forfeiture was a force for community cohesion rather than contention is the idea that the seizure of property allowed almoners or other franchisees to create order in local communities by ensuring the fair distribution of the forfeit goods.[88] This equitable redistribution entailed parceling out the forfeit property to creditors and heirs in a judicious manner by a seemingly disinterested party. Such a viewpoint is problematic on a number of points. This conception of forfeiture assumes that communities were grateful that an almoner or a franchisee, almost certainly an outsider, determined the distribution of forfeit property in return for an often substantial composition fee. This view is undermined by the large proportion of inquests in which the redistribution property was contested, the inquests were corrupted, and goods were hidden or undervalued. In some periods, over 20 percent of all inquests led to some form of litigation over forfeit property, a figure that belies the tidy picture of communal harmony previously posited by historians. If the purpose of the forfeiture system was not financial gain but communal peace and stability through the exercise of good lordship, it remains unclear why litigation over forfeit property between royal patent holders and royal almoners was so common. Roughly 8 percent of all Sussex inquests in Elizabeth's reign and 7 percent in the reign of James I led to processes being initiated against franchisees or their bailiffs.[89] Rather than being examples of debates over proper lordship or who would be allowed to reinforce communal harmony, the frequency with which the rights of rival franchisees contested the distribution of forfeit property suggests that financial concerns were primary.

Even those who stress the benign nature of the almoner do not view the efficacy of the almoner system in an entirely positive light. It has been argued that among the shortcomings of the system was the relatively small amount of litigation initiated by the almoner in Star Chamber. For some, the 132 Star Chamber almoner prosecutions for suicide in the reign of James I and 368 under Elizabeth pale in comparison to the almost 10,000 suicides reported to King's Bench between 1485 and 1659.[90] One can argue over whether the proportion of suicides that resulted in Star Chamber litigation was significant (and I certainly think that it was), but even if the relative insignificance of such litigation is correct, such analyses ignore a number of important factors that must be addressed if one wishes to evaluate the almoner's or central courts' role in the oversight of the coroner system as a whole. The contention that few suicide cases led to Star Chamber litigation ignores the substantial volume of litigation undertaken in King's Bench on the almoner's behalf. For instance, 104 cases of suicide in Sussex led to some sort of King's Bench litigation between 1509 and 1625.[91] Thus, the proportion of suicide cases that resulted in litigation in one county represented 1 percent of all suicides registered at King's Bench for the longer period 1485–1659. If one extrapolates this figure to include all English counties and combines it with the amount of Star Chamber litigation, it is likely that the number and percentage of suicide cases involving central court action were much more significant than has been allowed.

Discussions of the volume of litigation involving the almoner likewise largely ignore the almoner's role in cases of homicide and misadventure. Although these types of cases were far less common than suicide in the records of Star Chamber, they represent a majority of the cases involving litigation in King's Bench. Therefore, any attempt to elucidate the almoner's or the central courts' role in the oversight of coroners and of suspicious death must include an examination of homicide and especially misadventure, types of death that occupied a substantial portion of both the coroner's and the almoner's attention.

Some might wonder how the forfeiture system could effectively operate in an era of limited formal government structures. It has been suggested that formal agents of the almoner were rather thin on the ground given that deputy almoners were usually limited to one per county, and as a result amateurs and ad hoc local agents were often relied upon to provide information about deaths to the almoner.[92] It is unclear, however, why this state of affairs would seriously undermine the office of the almoner as part of a system of oversight. It is clear from the records that almoners' agents were often present at disputed inquests, and even took part in the inquests themselves. In 1593 Hamnet Warberton, coroner for the county of Cheshire, was called to view the body of Randall Lawton. After considering the evidence, the jury summoned by Warberton found that Lawton "was drowned by mischance against his will and not otherwise." Given that the death was ruled an accident, William Lawton, the brother of the deceased, took possession of "all the saide Randall Lawtons goodes chattlles and debts and desposeth the same as he thinketh good."[93]

And there the case might have rested if not for the fact that officers of the almoner had been present at the inquest itself. The agents relayed their objections and suspicions about the verdict to the almoner, who in turn initiated legislation against the coroner, William Lawton, and others thought to be involved in cheating the crown of its right to the goods of Randall Lawton. According to the almoner's complaint, Warberton, in his capacity as coroner, summoned "a number of dyvers honest and substantial persons by his precept of dyvers of the next towns adjoining to come appeare before him to be of the jury."[94] Summoning potential coroner's jurors in this manner was standard procedure; however, Warberton's selection of jurors from this pool was anything but. The almoner states that before selecting the jury, the coroner had "muche seacret conference" with William Lawton and Hugh Rowley, one of William Lawton's servants. After consulting with the brother of the deceased, Warberton "chose out of the said number of persons that were called for that service of your majestie such as were many of them indebted to the said Randall in lardge somes of money and some other that were and had been greatly beholden to the said Randall and other some which were servants of the said William Lawton."[95] Having selected jurors of dubious impartiality, the coroner dismissed those who were thought to be most impartial.

This suspicious selection process did not go unchallenged. Some of the almoner's officers "being then and there present" requested that the coroner allow some of those more impartial men in the jury pool to be allowed to serve on the jury. The coroner refused this request and instead in his charge to the packed jury stated that "in the tyme of popery the goodes of felons of themselves were distributed by the Almoner to poore people in hospitals and such like, but in thies dayes he did fynde by his books the Almoner had nothing to doe with the said goodes chattles and debts of felons de se but that the same was to passed by Administracon to the next of the kindred as in other cases maie happen by natural deathe of any partie."[96] After the coroner had given this inaccurate and prejudicial charge to the jury, the almoner's officers again interceded in the inquest and asked the coroner to give "some reasonable daye and tyme to geve a verdict" because the officers had found four witnesses, not then present, that they wanted to bring to the inquest to give evidence, suggesting that Randall Lawton's death was a suicide rather than an accident. The coroner agreed not to take a verdict before the almoner's officers' witnesses could be heard, but instead reconvened the inquest in secret at the house of William Lawton. Once reconvened, the jury returned a verdict of accidental death, giving Lawton possession of the deceased's goods and depriving the crown of the same.[97]

The level of surveillance in this case is extraordinary. Not only was the almoner informed about the process of the inquest and its verdict, but he also had multiple officers on the ground, present at the time of the inquest itself. These agents did not simply report back to the almoner, but actively challenged the decisions made by the coroner as he made them, even going so far as to seek out witnesses. This meant that the almoner's agents were not simply alerted that an inquest had taken place in the past; they heard that a death had occurred, discovered that it may have been a suicide, traveled to the site of the death in time to gather witnesses, attended the inquest as it took place, and then reported their suspicions regarding the impartiality of the verdict to the almoner so that appropriate legal action could be taken. It is evident that on many, perhaps most, occasions the almoner was well informed of the proceedings of relevant inquests by agents who were on the scene during the inquest or shortly thereafter.

To take one further example among many, when Thomas Chennell was found drowned in a Surrey pond in 1591, the coroner's jury quickly agreed that, based on his behavior prior to his death, Chennell had died by his own hand. Although there was general agreement as to the cause of Chennell's demise, when it came time to determine the value of the suicide's goods to be forfeited to the crown, cooperation broke down. According to the records, "the said Coroner thereupon in the presence of the Jurie tooke an inventorie of all the said Chennells goods and they were valued by the said Jurie to thre[e] score pounds . . . yet some others of the said jurie would not assent thereunto."[98] After this dispute over the valuation of the deceased's goods, the almoner's officers began to investigate the situation and interview witnesses and members of the coroner's jury. In the course of their investigations, the almoner's agents obtained confessions from members of the coroner's jury that they had intentionally undervalued the forfeit goods by £20 or 30 in order to keep the remaining property for their own use. Their deception having been discovered by the almoner's agents, three recalcitrant jurors then refused to return a verdict at all, hoping to "delay or protract the geaven upp of their said verdict until the goods may be wasted and consumed."[99] These renegade members of the jury were afterwards persuaded to join the ten other jurors and deliver a verdict. Instead of doing so, however, the three jurors next paid William Godhelpe, a poor neighbor, to flee the county, after which the jurors spread rumors that Godhelpe "was author of the said Channels death." This manufactured evidence was used as an excuse to further delay the completion of inquest, ultimately leading to the almoner's suit against the coroner and the three jurors in Star Chamber.[100]

Once again, it is clear from the records that the almoner had agents on the scene during the inquest process. These agents were far from being merely casual observers, instead seeking evidence, questioning witnesses and jurors, and reporting their findings back to the almoner—who eventually used their evidence to initiate litigation. Although most Star Chamber cases do not mention almoners' agents specifically, a significant number do, and it seems reasonable to suppose that many more cases did have almoners' agents present at the scene even if they were not mentioned specifically in the text of the complaints.

Almoners' agents took an active role in the surveillance of death. This surveillance would only be effective, however, if enough agents existed to monitor the many inquests that occurred throughout the country. A close look at the volume of coroners' inquests provides evidence that a single deputy almoner could have overseen the relevant cases that occurred in his county. Hence the presence of almoners' officers at inquests may have been routine rather than exceptional. For instance, R. F. Hunnisett's compilation of Sussex coroners' inquests shows that 582 inquests were held between 1558 and 1603. The almoner was primarily concerned with cases of suicide and accidental death, which accounted for 323 inquests, or approximately seven per year.[101] Similarly, James Sharpe and J. R. Dickinson have calculated that between 1601 and 1650 there were a total of 1,084 inquests held in Cheshire, 696 of which were suspected suicides or accidental deaths, or about 13.9 inquests per year.[102] Given the relatively modest number of inquests held—at most a little over one per month—in an average year one deputy almoner would have had little trouble overseeing the number of cases that might be of potential interest to the almoner.

Even if the deputy almoners were overtaxed by their duties and as a result the almoner was forced to rely on informal or ad hoc local agents, this would not have precluded effective oversight. In the early modern period, much administrative business was handled in an informal, ad hoc manner by commissioners or agents who were not a formal part of the crown bureaucracy. The important matter to consider when judging the merits of a system of oversight is the level of intelligence and information supplied, not the formal or informal status of the supplier. When it comes to the system of surveillance provided by the almoner, the level and detail of the knowledge provided by local agents were relatively sophisticated and nuanced. For example, in 1619 one almoner claimed to have evidence that a man he

suspected of committing suicide—but had instead been found by the inquest to have died by accident—had complained of having trouble sleep-
ing shortly before his death.[103] Another supplied evidence in his complaint
that a man who was thought to have died a natural death had given himself
a wound on the left side of his neck, one inch long and one inch deep.[104]
Forfeited goods that had not been turned over to the almoner are listed in
many cases in extraordinary detail, down to all debts owed to the deceased,
and even cloth and apparel.[105] Almoners even cited the personal histories
of people who may have committed suicide, in one case stating that it was
known that the deceased had tried to kill himself on numerous occasions
before.[106] The specific details given by almoners as evidence, which often
differ from those available in the inquest records, demonstrate that whatever the source of the local information, the almoner was well informed.

Almoners also made greater use of a variety of sources of information than has previously been allowed. It is thought that almoners rarely
consulted the coroners' records available in King's Bench and thus were
doomed to rely on and react to information supplied by agents or informants in the localities.[107] Although almoners often used information supplied by agents, their reliance on it was tempered by frequent reference and
recourse to the official documents created by the inquest process. In the
dispute over the cause of death of Randall Lawton cited above, for instance,
the almoner did not simply rely on his local agents for information, but also
consulted the inquest records available to him, noting that the verdict in
the case claimed that Randall Lawton had died as a result of an accident as
"by the inquisition will appeare."[108] A plethora of other cases further demonstrates the regular practice of consulting records, as in the suit over the
late Steven Crane's property discussed previously. In this case, the almoner
specifically references the inquest taken by Raphe Scrivener "remaining on
record in the crowne office."[109] Other cases simply mention the name of
the coroner who carried out the inquest, and his verdict.[110] This may seem
mundane, but it does imply that almoners were aware of inquest records
and consulted them as a matter of course. Further evidence of this type of
consultation comes from the fact that many Star Chamber cases even con-

tain copies of the coroner's inquest itself, or copies of inventories made by coroners or sheriffs.[111]

Even cases that censured the coroner for failing to certify an inquest imply that the almoner or his agents did consult records and noticed when they were inaccurate or missing. When Francis Leggat, coroner for Norfolk, was accused of not certifying an inquest "by reason whereof your majestie doth not know by any matter of Recorde howe the said person came to their death, nor yet what goods chattells and debts the said Henry Shay . . . was possessed of," the complaint lodged by the almoner was that he had no records to consult, a complaint one would not make if consulting records was not a regular part of the almoner's procedure.[112] All of the evidence suggests that consulting records and comparing them with information supplied by local agents or informants was a standard part of the almoner's repertoire and crucial for a proper understanding of the almoner's and central courts' role in oversight of the coroner system. This use of inquest records by almoner and central courts alike provided another important check on the regulation of violence by subjecting every action of the coroner to routine and ruthless scrutiny.

This robust system of oversight might have been undermined if cases escaped the notice of central authorities or took years before they reached the Court of Star Chamber.[113] If one takes the death of John Harrison as an example, the remarkable aspect of many cases is not that they took so long to reach the courts (six years in this instance), but that such cases were noticed at all. When Harrison hanged himself in 1599, it seems to have been an obvious suicide. Fearing the disgrace of suicide or the forfeiture of Harrison's property, some of Harrison's friends and neighbors removed the body from the place of death, took it to the parsonage house, and buried it "the nexte day following without any inquisition taken concerning the sayde death or a viewe of the body by the coroner as the law requires."[114] As a result of these actions, there was no investigation of the death, no inquest, and as a result no inquest records. If there had not been a robust system of information gathering and a significant amount of surveillance of suspicious death, a death like Harrison's would likely have gone unnoticed.

However, even six years later, the almoner was able to compile enough evidence from his agents on the ground to suggest that a suicide had taken place in faraway Yorkshire, that the death had been covered up, and that goods and property should have been forfeited to the crown.

In a similar case in which a coroner was accused of failing to certify a verdict, the almoner used information he had obtained that "the said coroner hath not certified any inquisition more than one this fowre or five years now last past, that yor majesties said almoner can fynde in the saide records" as evidence of the coroner's negligence and corruption. This information must have been the result of a combination of local knowledge and recourse to the records of King's Bench. Such knowledge demonstrates that almoners did not simply rely on written inquest records to find defects or corruption, but rather a combination of court records and local information provided by agents and informants to pinpoint instances of negligence or corruption.[115] Because the almoner was able to gather such information despite distances of space and time, litigation was initiated, a crime was detected, and oversight of the coroner system was effectively provided.

One may conclude therefore that from the early sixteenth century the oversight of coroners and their inquests was relatively widespread, rigorous, and effective. Because local individuals, royal patent holders, and crown officers had a venue in which to initiate litigation regarding the proper outcome of coroners' inquests—and thus the proper distribution of forfeited goods—there were few opportunities for corruption or incompetence in the investigation of suspicious death. Every instance in which the records produced by coroners were used, consulted, or disputed in central court litigation, whether brought by individuals or by crown officials and whether such litigation involved accusations against the coroner or not, became a moment of oversight and surveillance. By using coroners' records to either challenge or support the outcome of an inquest and the subsequent redistribution of property, central court litigants provided an important check on those officers held responsible for the investigation of death in early modern England.

Personal proclivity and a sense of the importance of the office may have induced most coroners to carry out their duties with integrity and efficiency. The supervision of justices of the peace surely persuaded others to take their responsibilities seriously. But in the context of a centralizing and bureaucratizing English state, early modern coroners were also subject to the regulatory wrath of the central courts, which were quick to prosecute and fine even the most mundane errors and omissions. The central courts were both instruments of regulation and venues of surveillance. A wide range of officers and individuals had a direct and tangible economic stake in the outcome of coroners' inquests. The difference between a verdict of suicide, homicide, or accidental death could be, and indeed often was, the difference between ruin and windfall. With so much at stake, almoner, heirs, creditors, patent holders, and state all had reason to monitor the proceedings of coroners' inquests, to challenge the outcome, and to pursue litigation against coroners or each other. This multifaceted and competing set of economic interests in coroners and their inquests ensured that every death in early modern England was closely watched, its investigation monitored, and its outcome debated, because with every untimely death someone stood to gain and someone to lose. While the economically interested parties contended over the spoils of death, the state gained an important instrument in the monopolization of violence. By creating a system of forfeiture, a central officer to oversee it, and a centrally controlled venue to adjudicate forfeiture disputes, the crown was able to use economic interests in the outcome of coroners' inquests as a way to effectively monitor violent death. From the early sixteenth century, therefore, a monopoly of lethal violence was created, regulated, and enforced.

SIX

The Changing Nature of Control

DESPITE THE WISHES OF BOTH historians and their subjects, history rarely unfolds in a straightforward, progressive manner. The gains and developments of one era are often followed by losses, setbacks, and decline. Those who view the early modern period as an era of untrammeled centralization and bureaucratization must bow to the reality that historical change is rarely that simple. The period between 1530 and 1640 did indeed witness a growing centralization of oversight of the coroner system, and with it the first effective state monopoly of lethal violence in England. This restriction of violence through centralized surveillance, however, did not remain static throughout the seventeenth and eighteenth centuries. Instead, political and economic realities intervened to disrupt the system of oversight and potentially threaten the monopoly of violence first created in the sixteenth century.

The robust central oversight of the coroner system achieved by means of forfeiture litigation contested in the central courts and spearheaded by the royal almoner from the 1530s began to erode by the middle of the seventeenth century. Star Chamber, as we have seen, was one of the chief venues for forfeiture litigation and one of the foremost instruments used by the almoner to challenge forfeiture decisions, thereby regulating suspicious death and its investigative officers. This vital instrument for the control of violence, however, was abolished in 1641 in the chaotic political and legal climate of the period of the Civil Wars, as part of the campaign against royal centralization and the prerogative power of the monarchy.[1] The office of the almoner, likewise a symbol of the arbitrary royal government and episcopal church structure hated by many who sided with Parliament, was also targeted. The office remained vacant between 1640 and 1660, meaning that both the principal agent of forfeiture litigation and one of the principal venues for such action were nonexistent in the middle decades of the seventeenth century.[2] Although royal almoners were again appointed after the restoration of the monarchy in 1660, and still made occasional use of the remaining central courts in the late seventeenth century, the amount of forfeiture litigation in the central courts did not again reach the levels seen in the late sixteenth and early seventeenth centuries. The proportion of coroners' inquests that resulted in litigation in King's Bench also fell from the middle of the seventeenth century. With the precipitous decline of forfeiture litigation in the central courts, a vital aspect of the surveillance regime was undermined.

This chapter will explore the roots of the erosion of central oversight of the coroner system and the concomitant decline of forfeiture litigation, but it is not simply a story of decline, nor of a return to the past. The second half of the seventeenth century was undoubtedly a time of crisis for state and citizen alike. The chaos and uncertainty of the era were no doubt at least partially responsible for shifting the gaze of the state away from the regulation of violence and toward other, more pressing political and military agendas. And yet, while the effects of such political and legal instability on the regular oversight of the legal system were indeed destabilizing, it will also be shown that even in an age of crisis the coroner system and the regulation of violence continued to operate. Inured to a system of justice, coroners and communities continued to hold their inquests, and culpability for violent death continued to be determined. The eyes of the central government may not have been fixed on the coroner system as strongly as before, but criminal death was still punished and the monopoly of violence maintained. More than a century of effective and rigorously enforced central oversight accustomed individuals and communities to government institutions and officers as *the* mechanisms for the adjudication of interpersonal violence. As a result, even when some aspects of central oversight eroded, the people as a whole remained bound to the coroner system as the best and only means of resolving issues relating to lethal violence. The exclusive right to define and punish illegitimate violence had been so firmly established in the years between 1530 and 1640 that there was no thought or possibility of returning to previous, extrajudicial forms of dispute resolution.

Feud, vendetta, and blood money were gone forever, relics of the past. The nature of central oversight was shifting across the late seventeenth century, but there was no question that the adjudication of violence was now a matter for the state.

The Civil Wars and the Abolition of Star Chamber

The general course and events of the English Civil Wars are not at issue here. The history of the quarrel between crown and Parliament in the mid-seventeenth century is well trodden and treacherous territory. It is, however, important to briefly discuss the effects of the midcentury convulsions on the judicial bodies responsible for the regulation of violence and the oversight of the coroner system. The conflict between Charles I and Parliament was in large measure a dispute over the rights of the House of Commons and the prerogative of the king. The Court of Star Chamber, as a prerogative court, was, along with other prerogative institutions such as the Council of the North, the Council of Wales, and the duchy of Lancaster, targeted for reform by Parliament as a means of limiting the discretionary powers of the king. In March 1641, a bill was introduced in the House of Commons that sought to regulate Star Chamber. In May, after two months of consideration and debate, the final form of the bill sought not simply to regulate Star Chamber but to abolish it entirely.[3] The bill was passed by both houses of Parliament by July 2, 1641, and upon receiving the signature of the king three days later, the Court of Star Chamber ceased to operate, effectively dismantling one of the primary mechanisms for the control of interpersonal violence.

The reasons for the decision to abolish Star Chamber are varied and complex, but can best be seen as a combination of the precarious political context of the early 1640s and the use—or perhaps abuse—of the court's powers by the king in the 1630s. Faced with growing opposition, Charles I had turned to the discretionary power of Star Chamber in an attempt to intimidate, silence, and control his political opponents. Fines and other, more severe punishments were meted out to such outspoken critics of the crown as John Lilburne, William Prynne, and Henry Burton. Prynne and Burton,

along with John Bastwick, another controversial Puritan writer, were arrested and charged with seditious libel in 1637 for publishing works critical
of church hierarchy in general and the policies of Archbishop William Laud
in particular. All three men were imprisoned, convicted, and sentenced to
fines, loss of degrees and benefices, pillory, ear cropping, and indeterminate
prison sentences. For Prynne, this was his second experience of the harsh
justice meted out by Star Chamber, as he had been similarly convicted and
punished in 1632 for his tract *Histriomastix: a Scourge of Stage-players,* a
condemnation of what Prynne felt to be the loose morals of contemporary
court culture.[4] Lilburne had similarly been brought before Star Chamber
in 1637 for printing and selling unlicensed works such as Prynne's *News
from Ipswich,* which attacked the growing power of the episcopate under
Laud.[5] Lilburne had refused to acknowledge the authority of the court and
been sentenced to be whipped, pilloried, and fined. This rough treatment,
which Lilburne outlined in his 1638 account *A Worke of the Beast,* and the
similar treatment by Star Chamber of other outspoken critics of the crown
helped to ensure that the prerogative courts came to be seen as both tool
and emblem of arbitrary government and tyrannical kingship.[6]

The use of Star Chamber in this way seemed to represent in micro-
cosm the arbitrary use of royal power and the dangers of an unlimited royal
prerogative. The parliamentary debate over the abolition of Star Chamber
revolved around whether, as the earl of Manchester argued in the House
of Lords, the prerogative court was a vital tool for the king in his role as
administrator of the laws of England and the ultimate judge of his subjects.
Most lords agreed with the earl of Essex, who countered the benevolent
paternalism of Manchester's position by instead citing the Star Chamber's
past and potential use as a tool of royal tyranny and arbitrary rule. In the
end, those who were of a mind with Essex carried the day and the bill abol-
ishing Star Chamber was duly passed.[7]

If not for the immediate political context of 1640–1641, events may
have been different, with Star Chamber reformed rather than eliminated.
The atmosphere that prevailed in the early months of 1641, however,
was tense to say the least. In April Charles's involvement in the so-called
First Army Plot had been exposed by the parliamentarian John Pym.[8]

It emerged that Charles had conspired with disaffected leaders of the army then stationed in York in an attempt to have the latter march on London in an attempt to control, cajole, or suppress a rebellious Parliament. The plan was abandoned due to lack of support among the soldiers, but when the conspiracy was made known, it caused widespread alarm, especially since it was claimed that Charles and his French queen had also attempted to secure French troops to assist in the occupation of London. With the duplicitous actions of the crown clear to all, the need to rein in the arbitrary powers of the monarch became all the more pressing.[9]

The king, however, was not the only one under pressure in these years. Parliament was also under duress and as a result went perhaps further in its actions against Star Chamber than it otherwise would have. London, by this period, was a hotbed of radical activity, and Parliament was being pushed, perhaps beyond its original intentions to demonstrate its reforming bona fides. Earlier attempts at serious reform, such as the Bishops Exclusion Bill, which sought to expel the bishops from their traditional place in the House of Lords, had failed as recently as mid-May 1641, barely a week prior to the introduction of the bill to abolish Star Chamber. A second reform bill, known as the Root and Branch Bill, was introduced later that May and called for the abolition of the episcopal system in England and "all its dependencies, roots and branches." also It too seemed, by the end of May, 1641, destined to fail.[10] The impatience of the radicals for further reform, combined with the seemingly capricious prior use of Star Chamber, was enough to induce Parliament to act.

The Act for the Abolition of the Court of Star Chamber (17 Charles 1, c. 10) was only one act in a series of reforming statutes passed in 1641, including the Triennial Act, which stipulated that Parliament should henceforth be summoned at least every three years, and various acts prohibiting novel forms of taxation.[11] Thus, the abolition of Star Chamber should properly be seen as part of a wider attack on arbitrary government and the prerogative of the crown. These reforms undoubtedly reduced the power of the monarch to act unilaterally. However, one unforeseen consequence was the disruption of the system of forfeiture that had been so important in the creation and maintenance of a monopoly of violence.

The Absence of the Almoner

With Star Chamber abolished in 1641, a vital aspect of the system of oversight was gone and a venue for the forfeiture litigation that spurred such oversight displaced. The tumultuous decades of Civil Wars and Interregnum, however, also had a profound impact on the royal almoner, the crown officer whose role in the forfeiture system was so crucial. As we have seen, it was the almoner who was responsible for initiating much of the litigation relating to violent death in the years between 1530 and 1640. It was also the almoner's agents who provided the best link between center and localities and the most direct information regarding violence, death, and forfeiture in the provinces of England. However, the office of the almoner was another casualty of the Civil Wars, and the position remained vacant for 20 years between 1640 and 1660.[12]

As with so many aspects of the legal system in this period, the reasons for the absence of a royal almoner are not entirely clear. The last royal almoner before the Civil Wars was Walter Curle, bishop of Winchester and a close ally of Archbishop Laud. As late as April 1640, a warrant was made to the Treasurer of the Chamber to pay Bishop Curle, in his role as royal almoner, the sum of £133 6s 8d "to be distributed in alms upon Maudy Thursday," as tradition dictated.[13] Whether the office itself was abolished or Curle was forced from the position is unclear — Curle retained his bishopric until his death in 1647 — but there is no evidence of another almoner being appointed until 1660, and no evidence of an almoner performing the office during the period of Civil Wars and Interregnum.[14]

Although it is difficult to say whether the absence of the almoner between 1640 and 1660 was the result of conscious policy or simply the chaos of the period, the possible reasons for the long vacancy are clear enough. The almoner was in theory a member of the royal household who was appointed by the monarch and whose responsibilities included the distribution of alms and charity on behalf of the king and his family. As an officer of the royal household rather than an officer of state, it seems logical to expect that the almoner was abolished along with the rest of the crown's household staff after the abolition of the monarchy. With no royal household, there was no need for a royal almoner to dispense alms on the monarch's behalf. The royal almoner was also a cleric, usually a bishop, and as such was a representative of episcopal church governance. Representing both royal prerogative and Laudian religious structure, it is no wonder that the office of almoner lay dormant during the Interregnum. However, given that the almoner was also responsible for the receipt of felony forfeitures, a power that transcended the royal household and episcopacy alike, it is somewhat surprising that no new office was created to deal with issues of forfeiture.

With the restoration of the monarchy in 1660, a new royal almoner was. Brian Duppa, bishop of Salisbury, a supporter of Laud before the Interregnum and one of four pre–Civil Wars bishops still alive at the Restoration, was appointed by the newly crowned Charles II as royal almoner in July 1660 and made bishop of Winchester in August.[15] The appointment of a new almoner, alas, did not signal a return to the system of forfeiture litigation that had existed before the disruptions of the Civil Wars. After 1660, the almoner was forced to operate without the use of the recently abolished Star Chamber, a favorite venue for the almoner's litigation. After 1660 the almoner did, on occasion, bring suits in King's Bench, but it is clear that the activity of this royal official never came close to approaching the levels of activity of the almoner in the years between 1530 and 1640.[16] Again, the reasons for the decline in activity of the royal almoner after the Interregnum are not clear. Perhaps without Star Chamber, the almoner's primary tool for initiating, pursuing, and enforcing forfeiture litigation in the years before 1640, securing felony forfeitures became more difficult and expensive, especially given the rising costs of legal action in the central courts. Whatever the cause, the almoner ceased to be a major player in forfeiture litigation after 1640.

The effects of the 20-year absence of the almoner are difficult to measure precisely, but when we consider the number of forfeiture cases initiated by the almoner in the late sixteenth and early seventeenth centuries, the potential consequences for the forfeiture system become apparent. The almoner was responsible for initiating forfeiture litigation in approximately 600 cases in Star Chamber between 1558 and 1625.[17] Although patent holders and the heirs and creditors of felons and the deceased also regularly initiated litigation, neither group matched the level of legal activity of the almoner. The almoner also often used his influence to goad King's Bench to summon coroners and other individuals to Westminster to answer for forfeit goods and defects in inquisitions. Given the crucial role played by the almoner in both initiating litigation and ensuring its resolution, the absence of the almoner between 1640 and 1660 must certainly have had momentous consequences for the system of oversight.

Without the litigation initiated by the almoner, and without the pressure the almoner put on the central courts to act, many cases surely avoided the scrutiny of the central authorities altogether. This lack of central impetus, combined with the rising costs of litigation in the courts of Westminster discussed more fully below, had lasting effects on the manner in which the coroner system was monitored. Even the remaining central courts, King's Bench in particular, ceased to be the primary or necessary venue for forfeiture litigation and thus also ceased to be the most crucial site for oversight of lethal violence. The result was a shifting of the some of the responsibility for oversight from the central courts and central crown officials to the regional organs of criminal justice, justices of the peace, quarter sessions, and assize.

King's Bench and the Decline of Litigation

Star Chamber was not the only centralized venue for forfeiture litigation, nor was it the only court whose business was disrupted over the course of the seventeenth century. Although it was never abolished as were the prerogative courts, the Court of King's Bench, which shared the responsibility for oversight of the coroner system with Star Chamber, experienced a decline in forfeiture litigation from the mid-seventeenth century. The remarkable intensity of oversight witnessed in the Elizabethan and Jacobean periods began to decrease slowly over the next two decades. Between 1626 and 1649, 143 inquests survive from Sussex. Of these, 16 percent, or about one per year, resulted in King's Bench litigation, a far smaller proportion than had led to legal action in the late sixteenth and early seventeenth centuries. The types of cases dealt with by King's Bench also changed in the years after 1626. The proportion of cases relating to accidental death rose to about 74 percent, while those relating to suicide and homicide decreased to 17 and 8.5 percent, respectively. The percentage of litigation that targeted coroners directly also declined to about 17 percent of cases.[18]

After the Interregnum, during which no Sussex inquests resulted in King's Bench litigation, the declining intensity of oversight continued. The period between 1660 and 1682 saw 187 inquests held in Sussex, of which just under 4 percent resulted in litigation, only one case resulting in litigation every three years. During these years no coroners were summoned to King's Bench as a result of their inquests.[19] Similarly, only 4 percent of inquests resulted in litigation between 1688 and 1750, and none of these involved coroners directly.[20] This data suggests that from about the middle of the seventeenth century, the level of oversight of coroners' duties and records provided by King's Bench litigation declined precipitously. This erosion of forfeiture litigation in general, and that targeting coroners specifically, cannot, however, be explained by the abolition of Star Chamber alone, given the continued functioning of King's Bench. Likewise, the 20-year absence of the almoner, while it surely contributed to the decline in oversight, cannot fully explain the long-term decline in forfeiture litigation from 1640 to 1750. To accurately assess the system of centralized oversight, we must also explore the changing financial realities of legal action and the effects of yet another seventeenth-century political upheaval.

The absence of the almoner in the middle decades of the seventeenth century and the abolition of Star Chamber certainly affected the ability of the central authorities to regulate lethal violence. However, King's Bench, a vital cog in the machinery of surveillance, continued to operate throughout the early modern period, and perhaps the system of central oversight would not have been so deeply affected by the absence of the almoner and the abolition of Star Chamber if not for other factors that led to an overall decline in the volume of litigation in the central courts. It was the combination of the disappearance of Star Chamber, the disruption of the office of the almoner, and economic changes that ultimately resulted in the breakdown of centralized oversight and the decline in forfeiture litigation in King's Bench.

In Chapter 5 we discussed the existence of a general increase in central court litigation from the mid-sixteenth century.[21] This massive rise in the volume of litigation was, at least in part, a result of the declining real costs of such litigation. That is to say, as the cost of pursuing legal action in the courts of Westminster fell over the course of the sixteenth century, they were increasingly seen as viable and attractive venues for dispute resolution. As the central courts became more appealing venues, they attracted more and more business from outside London. Thus, business that had previously been the preserve of local courts and informal means of resolution was increasingly located in the central courts.[22]

The high-water mark of the central court litigation boom, however, was only a temporary phenomenon, with the levels of litigation declining markedly from the mid-seventeenth century.[23] As with the rise in litigation in the sixteenth century, the decline in the use of the central courts in the seventeenth century seems to have been in large part a result of the decline of provincial business in the courts of Westminster as a consequence of the changing costs of legal action.[24] Several factors combined to make the real cost of litigation more expensive. First, attorneys' fees rose dramatically from the 1620s. Second, from the mid-seventeenth century, new charges were introduced for such procedural motions as inquests for damages, trials, and judgments. Finally, in 1694 Parliament passed a statute that introduced a stamp duty, making applications for bail, entries of affidavits, and other legal actions subject to a tax. In some places the stamp duty's effects were immediately apparent. In Shrewsbury, for example, the borough courts saw their lowest level of business in the whole of the seventeenth century in the first month after the stamp duty went into effect.[25] The combination of these growing costs meant that by the end of the seventeenth century the costs of litigation in the central courts were between five and ten times higher than local alternatives.[26]

The case should not be overstated, however, and it is important to note that the rising costs in the seventeenth and eighteenth centuries affected courts throughout England. Thus, the decline in litigation was not simply the result of provincial business shifting from central to local courts. Local and borough courts also witnessed falling levels of litigation across the seventeenth and eighteenth centuries as a result of rising costs and novel fees and state-imposed taxation. Rather than a shift from one court to another, from center to periphery, litigation in all courts, the courts of Westminster and the provincial courts alike, experienced a profound decline in litigation caused by rising legal costs.[27]

Debating Decentralization

That central court forfeiture litigation declined steeply from the mid-seventeenth century seems clear. However, while the context of the decline has been outlined above, the specific reasons are more complicated and have been the subject of some debate among historians of suicide. Michael MacDonald and Terence Murphy have argued that the decline in forfeiture litigation can, in large part, be directly tied to the abolition of Star Chamber in 1641.[28] They contend that in the absence of Star Chamber, the responsibility for supervising the coroner and forfeiture systems "reverted solely to King's Bench, a much more cumbersome and less effective tribunal."[29] Without effective central oversight, jurors began to resort to a variety of gambits for avoiding forfeiture, leading to a decline in both the number of suicides with property reported and the overall value of reported forfeit goods. In addition, MacDonald and Murphy see a concomitant rise in *non compos mentis* verdicts as further evidence of attempts by juries to avoid forfeiture.[30] After attempts to reinforce the law of forfeiture in the 1650s largely failed, legislation enacted in 1693 dealt a severe blow to King's Bench's ability "to enforce the law of suicide."[31] A result of the "cult of private property" that emerged in the wake of the Glorious Revolution, the 1693 statute, among other things, allowed the holders of royal patents to claim and seize the property of suicides in their liberties before an inquisition was held and made the officials of the court liable to fines if they infringed on the rights of patent holders.[32] This legislation combined with the absence of Star Chamber was, for MacDonald and Murphy, the proximate cause of the decline in forfeiture litigation in the central courts.

In contrast to MacDonald and Murphy, Rab Houston has argued that neither the abolition of Star Chamber nor the legislation of 1693 had so dramatic an impact. Instead, Houston suggests that the decline in forfeiture litigation was a result of "changing ideas of discretionary outside intervention in many aspects of life" and the invention of "new mechanisms . . . to deal with the central issues of debt and credit."[33] Foremost among these innovations was the development of the action for *assumpsit*, which allowed creditors to sue for debts relating to the informal or verbal contracts that were common in the period. This, combined with a move by the great lords from the localities to the court, necessitated an alteration in the operation of lordship that in turn shifted the locus of lordship onto parish administrative bodies such as the vestry.[34] Finally, according to Houston, after 1650 law "became less acceptable as a way of doing things," leading to a general decline in litigation.[35]

The effects of the decline in central court litigation are also disputed. MacDonald and Murphy contend that in addition to the rise in *non compos mentis* verdicts in cases of suicide, the factors that led to the decline in forfeiture litigation resulted in a growing failure on the part of coroners to return their inquests to King's Bench. Thus, the decline of central court forfeiture litigation undermined the ability of the crown to oversee the coroner system effectively in the late seventeenth and eighteenth centuries.[36] Houston, on the other hand, does not believe that the shift in venue of forfeiture disputes and their decline in the central courts had much of an effect on the detection or reporting of suicide.

Again, however, the historiographical focus on suicide, a small and declining fraction of those deaths for which the coroner was responsible, rather than on the coroner system itself creates a misleading picture of the process of decline. From a holistic perspective of the oversight provided by central court litigation of the coroner system, it is evident that while the abolition of Star Chamber must have had a significant initial impact, the disruption caused by its absence did not fundamentally alter the operation of the coroner system. Some of the burden for monitoring lethal violence had been shifted from the central courts to regional officials—justices of the peace and assize judges in the main—but despite the chaos of the Civil Wars, the coroner system continued to operate much as before. As we will see, individuals and communities still turned to the coroner alone to investigate and adjudicate instances of violent death. The nature of central oversight had changed, becoming more localized, but the monopoly of violence remained.

The importance of the abolition of Star Chamber for the oversight of the coroner system should not, however, be exaggerated. MacDonald and Murphy's claim that King's Bench was too "cumbersome" and ineffective to handle those forfeiture cases previously dealt with by Star Chamber is undermined by the fact that King's Bench had been the venue for a greater proportion of forfeiture business than Star Chamber throughout the early modern period; thus, any increase in caseload caused by the abolition of Star Chamber would not have greatly affected its ability to operate effectively. Instead, the decline in the proportion of inquests that led to litigation in King's Bench must be attributed to factors other than the abolition of Star Chamber. The absence of a royal almoner between 1640 and 1660 and the relative inactivity of the office after the Restoration were instead tied to changing attitudes toward private property, a shift in the venue of forfeiture disputes toward the localities, and the legislation of 1693, which effectively cut the central courts out of the picture.

Central court litigation was certainly in decline from the middle of the seventeenth century. While inquest returns dropped at various rates in various counties, a more important measure of the level of oversight provided by King's Bench is the proportion of inquests that resulted in litigation, a figure which declined precipitously from the middle of the seventeenth century. Contemporaries certainly thought that inquest returns were declining by the late seventeenth century. One King's Bench officer declared that coroners had "discontinued returning their Inquisitions into the Court of King's Bench and of course all Proceedings upon such Inquisitions were discontinued," a fact that he tied directly to the statute of 1693.[37]

Thus, although it is perhaps accurate to suggest that one reason for the decline of forfeiture litigation in the central courts was a move to more local jurisdictions for the resolution of such disputes, it seems clear that such a trend must have been influenced by the 1693 statute. These statutes in turn were the culmination of changing attitudes toward private property. The 1693 statute made it easier and cheaper for royal patent holders and individual heirs to contest and resolve forfeiture disputes in local courts or through informal adjudication, making the central courts less crucial as venues.

At the same time that local and informal venues were becoming more appealing, it seems that demographic and economic contraction or stagnation may have made the relative cost of using the central courts higher than it had been since the early sixteenth century, making litigation in the central courts less appealing in the late seventeenth century.[38] Such a move away from central courts to local institutions as the primary locus of forfeiture disputes must also have entailed a shift away from a system centered on a court and a crown-appointed central official with a national jurisdiction—and thus away from national oversight. Centralized surveillance was replaced by a system that relied more upon the individual discretion of officials and courts with county jurisdictions. This is not to say that local officials and courts had not previously played an important role in monitoring the coroner system, but rather to suggest that while the period between 1530 and 1640 possessed both local and national systems of oversight, after 1640 the supervision provided by the central courts as venues for litigation declined and the burden of oversight came increasingly to rest on the backs of local officials.

Forfeitures may still have been contested in the late seventeenth and eighteenth centuries, but it is evident that such contestation as did exist in this period was not part of a national system of oversight and proceeded in an informal, local way that did not allow for the same type of routine oversight of the coroner and his duties. By shifting the locus of forfeiture litigation and dispute from the central courts to a more local arena, it is clear that the supervision of the coroner system became a more piecemeal, localized affair that rested primarily on the shoulders of justices of the peace. This shift in the burden of oversight was part of a wider trend that saw the power, duties, and responsibilities of the county justices grow dramatically from at least the mid-seventeenth century.[39]

While it is true that the central authorities retained interest in the activities of coroners after the middle of the seventeenth century, it is also true that the level of surveillance provided from the center was considerably lower than that of the late sixteenth and early seventeenth centuries. As we have seen from the records of King's Bench, not only did the absolute number of inquests returned to that court decline, but so too did the proportion of inquests that resulted in legal action. No longer were coroners, royal patent holders, or the heirs of the deceased regularly summoned to King's Bench to answer for defects or the whereabouts of forfeit property. Without this routine litigation and without the contestation over forfeitures in Star Chamber, coroners and their records were no longer scrutinized as often or as effectively. Without the crown—in the guise of the almoner—as an interested party in the redistribution of forfeit property, there was little incentive to settle disputes over forfeiture in the central courts. As disputes changed venue and became more local and informal, the central authorities' role in the oversight of the coroner system also changed. The sophisticated, regular, effective system of oversight created by central court litigation was replaced by a system that was perhaps more efficient and responsive to local needs, but lacked the same level of centralization and regularity. While it is possible that the heirs of those who died as a result of suicide, homicide, and accident may have been in a better position to recover their property after the mid-seventeenth century, it is also possible that the oversight of the coroner system was less routine and certain than before.

The Coroner System after Decentralization

As we have seen, a number of factors—political, economic, and legal—combined in the second half of the seventeenth century both to shift the locus of oversight of the coroner system from the central courts to local officials and judicial bodies, and to erode the level of forfeiture litigation that was so crucial to the regulation of violence. Given these shifts in surveillance and litigation, one might expect that England would revert to the state of affairs that existed prior to the regulatory revolution of the mid-sixteenth century, with violence and death regularly ignored, undetected, or unpunished. This, however, was not the case. The records of the central courts may indeed imply a decline in regulation of violence; however, the records of more local jurisdictions demonstrate that even without the

full gaze of the state, the coroner system continued to function. This continued functioning is a testament to the real success of the robust system
of oversight of the previous century. The investigation, adjudication, and
punishment of lethal violence had been firmly removed from the hands of
nonstate actors and placed in those of an official responsible to the state. By
the mid-seventeenth century, this institutional transition was irreversible.
As a result, the shift in responsibility for oversight from central courts to
centrally appointed regional officials did not entail an erosion of the effectiveness of the coroner system.

The first test of the coroner system's ability to function with limited direction from the central courts came in the years of the Civil Wars.
With death, destruction, and displacement rife in the years of war, it is
no surprise that many county courts were disrupted or ceased to function
altogether. As we have seen, business at the central courts dropped dramatically, in part due to costs, but also by the mid-1640s as a result of the
dislocating effects of war and the creation of a rival royalist central court
system at Oxford. On top of this, in 1643 assize judges were forbidden to
travel on their circuits, and in many counties quarter sessions did not meet
for years. In Warwickshire, for instance, there were no quarter sessions for
three years in the 1640s.[40] But remarkably, this general disruption of legal
institutions did not affect the operation of the coroner system. The investigation of violent death was too important to be abandoned even in times of
chaos, a fact aptly illustrated by a close look at the operations of Cheshire
coroners during the Civil Wars.

Like most counties in England, allegiance in Cheshire at the outbreak
of civil war was split between crown and Parliament, although many sought
to keep the county neutral.[41] Chester began the war as a royalist enclave,
but other towns, such as Nantwich, Stockport, and Knutsford, sided with
Parliament, and fighting in Cheshire commenced with the First Battle of
Middlewich in March 1643. Chester, the home to the palatinate's courts,
was itself besieged by parliamentary forces from 1645 to 1646, with Charles I
commanding the defenses. By the time the city was taken by Parliament in
1646, much of Chester was in ruins. But it seems the people of Chester
had not yet suffered enough, and as so often happened in the early modern

world, plague followed the fighting in 1647 and 1648, further depleting an already vulnerable people.[42]

The effects of such turmoil on the operation of the criminal justice system seem, at first glance, to have been profound. Unlike most counties, where coroners' inquests were submitted by coroners at the biannual assizes before being sent to King's Bench, Cheshire's coroners' inquests were recorded in the palatinate's Crown Minute Books when they were submitted at assizes. The Crown Minute Books contain the records of coroners' inquests submitted twice a year consistently from the late sixteenth century. However, no coroners' inquests are recorded for almost five years between 1644 and 1649.[43]

Those years were a trying time for the country in general, and Cheshire in particular.[44] With chaos reigning, it is easy to understand the reasons behind the failure to hold court in these years and the consequent dearth of coroners' records. Although the court did not meet and no coroners' inquests were recorded, the coroners of Cheshire nevertheless remained active, investigating deaths, recording verdicts, and assigning culpability. This is evident from the unusual records entered into the Crown Minute Books in 1649. In that year the palatinate courts began to operate once more and the recording of coroners' inquests commenced anew. However, whereas before the Civil Wars each session of the assize generally saw between ten and 20 inquests recorded, at the first sessions of 1649, an astounding 87 inquests were submitted.[45] The reason for this large number of inquests is not that 87 people had died in violent circumstances in the previous six months, but that the inquests taken in the years when the courts were not operating were all finally submitted at once in 1649. Despite the date of the court session, all of the inquests recorded in 1649 were in fact held by coroners in 1645, 1646, 1647, and 1648, indicating that coroners continued to operate even at the height of the Civil Wars.[46] Remarkably, it seems that, on average, approximately 22 inquests were held each year, a number on a par with the average number of inquests held under normal conditions in the decades prior to the Civil Wars.[47]

The continued operation of the coroner system even in times of political crisis was not limited to the era of the Civil Wars. With the fall from power of Richard Cromwell in May 1659 and the restoration of the monarchy in 1660, the operation of the central government was again disrupted, if on a more limited scale than during the previous two decades. The disruption experienced by the Cheshire courts was much briefer in 1660 than in the 1640s; however, the Cheshire Assize did fail to meet for the fall sessions of 1659. Once again, rather than discarding their inquest records for the missed session, the coroners of Cheshire simply returned them at the first assize of 1660 along with any new inquests. The records of the Crown Minute Books indicate that rather than the normal 15 to 30 inquests for a normal session, Cheshire coroners returned 79 inquests at the assize of 1660, making up for the brief disruption.[48]

What, then, does the evidence of the Crown Minute Books tell us about the regulation of lethal violence in the mid-seventeenth century? The evidence shows that even in a time of chaos and uncertainty, when courts operated irregularly or not at all, when travel was dangerous and when oversight by the central authorities was greatly diminished, the coroner system continued to function as usual. In the years between 1644 and 1649, when the assizes seem not to have functioned, instead of ignoring their responsibility to hold inquests or discarding the inquest records for lack of their usual repository, coroners held inquests over the bodies of the deceased, recorded their verdicts, and saved the records for a time when the courts would resume their business. What this dedication suggests is that coroners, and the communities they served, had become inured to the system. The regulation of violence had succeeded to such a degree that when the oversight of that system by both central and local courts and officials was largely removed by war, the system did not grind to a halt. Instead, imbued with its own momentum the coroner system continued to function even during a period of intense crisis, demonstrating that 110 years of close, rigorous surveillance by the central authorities between 1530 and 1640 had permanently secured the state's monopoly of violence, a monopoly that went unchallenged even when the fate of the state itself was in question.

That the coroner system continued to function at the height of the Civil Wars is not the only evidence that the monopoly of violence was maintained even as responsibility for monitoring lethal violence shifted from the central courts to local judicial bodies. As we have seen, the volume of inquests returned to King's Bench from Sussex declined precipitously from the mid-seventeenth century. On the surface, this information could be taken as evidence of a decline in the efficiency or effectiveness of England's coroners, a seemingly logical conclusion given the reduced scale of central oversight. And yet the records suggest that, as happened during the disruption of the Civil Wars, coroners continued to perform inquests at similar rates despite the lack of surveillance. In this scenario, the paucity of coroners' inquests in King's Bench for the period between roughly 1640 and 1750 was not the result of a breakdown in the coroner system, but rather a consequence of the failure on the part of local courts to send their records to King's Bench as required and the absence of demands from the central courts to receive such documents.

Two key pieces of evidence suggest that the drop-off in inquests in the King's Bench records resulted from a failure to register such documents with the central courts rather than from a decline in the capacity of the coroner system to perform its most basic function. The first piece of evidence comes, once again, from the records of the Crown Minute Books of Cheshire. Because the Crown Minute Books contain coroners' inquests when they were submitted to the assizes and before those documents were sent to King's Bench, the Cheshire records may provide a more complete picture of the full range of inquests being held in a county in the late seventeenth and early eighteenth centuries. That is to say, as the inquests were recorded at the time of trial, the Minute Books contain inquests that may have been lost in transit to King's Bench or were never sent to Westminster at all. If the effectiveness of the coroner system did in fact decline, we would expect to see a sharp drop in the number of inquests recorded in the Crown Minute Books, similar to that witnessed for the records of Sussex derived from King's Bench. Instead, what we see is a relatively stable number of inquests from 1600 to 1700. For instance, between 1600 and 1650 the Crown Minute Books record 1,084 total inquests, while the period from 1650 to 1750 saw 1,360 inquests recorded.[49] These figures suggest that even without monitoring by the central authorities, coroners continued to operate similarly before and after 1650.

The second telling piece of evidence for the continued functioning of the monopoly of violence comes from the mid-eighteenth century. As was mentioned in Chapter 2 and will be discussed in greater detail in Chapter 8, in 1752 a statute was passed that changed the method by which coroners were remunerated for their endeavors on behalf of the state. Prior to that year, coroners had only been paid a nominal fee in cases of homicide. After 1752, coroners were to be paid a set fee for every inquest and a further sum for each mile traveled in route to the site of the inquest. Given this new system of payment, coroners were required to submit bills that detailed each inquest undertaken and the distances traveled for each. This seeming duplication of records allows us to examine any differences between the number of inquests claimed by coroners in their bills and the number of inquests recorded by the assize courts. When one compares the records of coroners' bills with the inquest records held by King's Bench, an interesting picture emerges. The number of inquests returned to King's Bench remains relatively stable both before and after 1752.[50] The coroners' bills, however, tell a different story. While the number of inquests returned to King's Bench remained consistently low across the mid-eighteenth century, the number of inquests recorded in coroners' bills after 1752 was much greater than the corresponding number of inquests. This suggests that instead of a decline in the activity of coroners, inquests were merely being underrecorded by the assize courts. Because the number of inquests recorded by the assize remained consistent before and after 1752, the records of the coroners' bills do not show that fewer inquests were being held prior to 1752. Instead, the coroners' bills merely allow us to see records of inquests that, while still undertaken, did not appear in the records before 1752. That is, coroners were holding a consistent number of inquests across the period, but only those that resulted in indictments were being recorded. Before the late seventeenth century, all inquests were recorded by the assize and placed in King's Bench. After this period, only specific inquests were so recorded. Thus, the decline in recorded inquests does not reflect an actual decline in inquests, but rather a change in record-keeping practice.

Take, for example, the records of East Sussex. In the ten years that followed the introduction of the new system of payment, the county coroners for East Sussex submitted bills detailing 108 cases of violent death.[51] In the same ten-year period, the same East Sussex county coroners returned only three inquests to King's Bench.[52] While the vagaries of document survival may be responsible for some of this disparity, it is clear that the drastic difference between the number of inquests indicated in the coroners' bills and the number of inquests returned to King's Bench is primarily a result of the failure to return the inquests to the central authorities after the bills and inquests had been submitted at quarter sessions and assize. The failure to return these documents could only be allowed if the central authorities no longer possessed the ability or inclination to fully supervise the coroner system as before.

What this evidence seems to indicate is that while coroners continued to hold similar numbers of inquests across the seventeenth and eighteenth centuries, most of these inquest records were not returned to King's Bench. Instead, it appears that though inquests regarding homicide continued to be sent to King's Bench, inquests relating to suicide, natural death, and especially accidental death were not so returned. A similar state of affairs prevailed in Cheshire, where an overall drop in the number of inquests recorded—from 1,360 in the period 1650–1700 to a paltry 619 in 1700–1750—seems to have been largely a result of a failure to record many instances of accidental death. Thus, in the period 1650–1700, 813 accidental deaths were recorded, as compared to only 387 in 1700–1750.[53]

The reason for such a shift in recording practices is not entirely clear, but it is likely a result of the declining activity of the almoner. Homicide was still seen as a serious crime, a challenge to both law and order and the state's monopoly of violence. Accidental death, however, was not so obviously a threat to order; thus, the records relating to such deaths were less likely to be demanded by central authorities, especially without the active involvement of the almoner, who in an earlier period was primarily responsible for pursuing the crown's interests in such cases. Therefore, it is reasonable to assume that with the almoner's power and activity diminished, the impetus to accurately record all instances of accidental death diminished as well. However, despite this lack of central concern with some types of inquest records, it is evident from the records of coroners' bills that the coroner system continued to function much as it had in the sixteenth and early seventeenth centuries, investigating and recording instances of homicide, suicide, accidental and natural deaths alike, even if the supervision provided by the central authorities was mostly concerned with homicide alone. It is not that death and violence ceased to be regulated after 1640, but that the records were no longer being sent to the central courts with the same regularity. Coroners still operated, but under a more distracted and local gaze.

The overarching narrative of the supervision of the coroner system—and thus also the oversight of suspicious death—in England between 1500 and 1750 is a story of centralization followed by decentralization.[54] Prior to the 1530s, the primary responsibility for monitoring coroners and their duties fell to local officeholders, primarily justices of the peace, and local courts. After the 1530s this localized system of oversight was supplemented by a reinvigorated centralized system of surveillance with a national jurisdiction. Driven in large part by the actions of the royal almoners and their pursuit of forfeit property, this new system was not the consequence of conscious efforts by the Tudors for centralization and state formation, as has been suggested by some historians. Rather, this new system of supervision through the central courts was an unintended consequence of a more general, demographically and economically driven rise in litigation in the central courts that pushed the primary locus of oversight out of the provinces and to the center.

Between 1530 and the mid-seventeenth century, the central courts— especially Star Chamber and King's Bench—were relatively cheap and effective venues for the contestation of forfeit property by almoners and franchisees, creditors and heirs. Through these frequent disputes over the proper redistribution of forfeit property, the work and records of coroners throughout England were regularly and effectively scrutinized, challenged, and disputed. The economic incentives that accompanied the granting of forfeiture to the almoner, combined with the competing economic interests of other franchisees, creditors, and heirs, made the supervision of the coroner system through self-interested litigation possible. When almoners won the right to sue in Star Chamber in the 1530s and recourse to the central

courts became more affordable in the mid-sixteenth century, the convergence of economic incentive and affordable, effective venues created the
conditions for heightened central litigation over forfeit property. Because
a large proportion of coroners' inquests had the potential to involve the
forfeiture of property, it was in the direct interest of almoner, franchisee,
and heir alike to keep a careful eye on the inquests undertaken and certified
by coroners. Thus, the fact that so many people had competing and overlapping economic interests in the outcome of coroners' inquests, combined
with the new availability of the central courts as an affordable and effective
venue for forfeiture litigation, created an atmosphere in which the actions
and records of coroners were constantly monitored and shortcomings and
corruption were detected and punished.

From the middle of the seventeenth century, this system of surveillance through both local officials and the central courts began to break
down. Star Chamber was abolished and litigation in the remaining central courts became increasingly expensive. This rise in costs, combined
with legislation designed to protect private property, caused the locus of
forfeiture disputes, and thus oversight of the coroner system, to shift back
to the localities. As a result, the primary burden of the oversight of suspicious death again fell on the justices of the peace and the assize and county
courts. This is not to say that the oversight of the coroner system became
more lax after the mid-seventeenth century. Indeed, a system focused on
the localities may have been more responsive to local needs. The shift away
from a system that contained both a local element of supervision as well as
a centralized component led by a crown-appointed official with a national
jurisdiction toward a system that placed increased reliance on local officials
with at most a countywide jurisdiction, however, certainly entailed that
greater weight be put on the individual discretion of justices whose efficacy
and competence was variable and contingent. It is reasonable to suggest,
then, that the period between 1530 and the late seventeenth century witnessed a more robust, routine, and effective oversight of the coroner system
and of suspicious death than the periods immediately before or after.

This narrative belies any neat conception of the early modern period
as a time that witnessed concerted or progressive centralization. Instead,

the history of the oversight of the coroner system suggests that at times centralization was the result of long-held practices or the vagaries of demography and economics. Furthermore, this picture suggests that state formation in early modern England was never simply a straightforward march toward centralization; rather, it proceeded in fits and starts, with both gains and losses. The period between 1530 and the mid-seventeenth century can thus be seen as a regulatory moment instead of part of a simple upward trajectory of state formation through centralization, at least in relation to the monitoring of lethal violence. This is not to say that this period represented a missed opportunity. The impact of the Tudor-Stuart regulatory moment was significant and real, as will be explored in Chapter 7. Although the locus of oversight had shifted from center to periphery, the long years of effective, central oversight had irrevocably wed English men and women to the idea that the adjudication of lethal violence was the exclusive preserve of the state and its courts of law. The mid-sixteenth century can therefore be seen as the era in which the English state first obtained a successful, effective monopoly of interpersonal violence, a monopoly it would never again lack.

SEVEN

A Crisis of Violence?

LOOKING AROUND AT A WORLD RIVEN by war, dearth, and factional violence, the jurist William Lambarde observed in 1582 that "all men do see, and good men do behold it with grief of mind that sin of all sorts swarmeth and that evildoers go on with license and impunity."[1] As pessimistic as Lambarde's words may seem, he was not alone in believing his era to be one of chaos and disorder, crime and violence. In a phrase that could just as easily have tripped off the tongue of a modern-day alarmist, Philip Stubbes despaired that in his era—the late sixteenth century—the traditional bonds of hierarchy were failing. "Was there ever seen," Stubbes asked, "less obedience in youth of all sorts, both menkind and womenkind, towards their superiors, parents, masters and governors?"[2] For Stubbes, the answer was clearly a resounding no. But were Stubbes and Lambarde right to despair, to castigate their contemporary society for its apparent violence and disorder? Or was the hysterical moralizing of contemporaries instead the result of greater awareness of crime as a result of improved policing and oversight of criminal justice? The answers to these questions are crucial to understanding how the English state's quest to create a monopoly of violence affected both the actual incidence of homicide and the interpretations of early modern *and* modern commentators.

The twenty-first century certainly does not lack its Lambardes, quick to decry the seemingly unprecedented level of violence in modern society. In recent years, however, social scientists of various stripes have garnered much attention by advancing the counterintuitive claim that despite our contemporary obsession with crime and the all too common hand-wringing about the pervasiveness of violence in modern society, levels of violence have in fact declined steadily in the Western world since sometime in the seventeenth century.[3] These accessible syntheses of course rely on detailed studies by various historians who have long noticed—and debated the causes and consequences of—a general European trend of rising violence in the sixteenth century, with a peak sometime between 1560 and 1630, followed by a gradual but ineluctable decline over the course of the seventeenth and eighteenth centuries and on into the present day.

In general, these national and regional studies of early modern patterns of violence, and the popular works that rely on them, cite two primary factors for the rise and fall of violence in the sixteenth and seventeenth centuries: one economic and one cultural. On the whole, the rise in rates of violence in the mid- to late sixteenth century is explained by reference to a combination of rising economic and demographic strains that fundamentally undermined social and political order. Poor harvests and rising populations combined to create a world of greater inequality and more widespread poverty than had existed before.[4] It seems intuitive that such poverty and instability would ultimately lead to growing rates of crime and violence. The subsequent decline in crime and violence in the early and mid-seventeenth century is explained in a similar manner, though with the added factor of cultural change. According to the dominant narrative, the improving economic and demographic conditions of the seventeenth century and the concomitant rise of Norbert Elias's famous "civil society," which valued restraint over aggression and placed civility at the heart of conceptions of honor, together caused a slow but continual decline in rates of violence.[5] These conceptions are not without debate or detractors, but they continue to hold both the popular and academic imagination.[6] Whatever the causes of the growth and decline of violence provided by historians, one thing remains relatively uncontroversial: early modern Europe witnessed a peak of recorded prosecutions for violent crime between roughly 1580 and 1620, followed by a noticeable decrease for the rest of the early modern period.[7] Most historians seeking to explain this phenomenon have focused on possible causes for growing rates of crime and violence. But what if the growth in recorded prosecutions was not primarily the result of growing rates of actual violence, but rather the consequence of better, more efficient methods of criminal investigation, oversight, and record keeping?

When patterns of homicide in England are examined through the lens of coroners' inquests, it becomes evident that what historians have assumed to be rising levels of violent crime between 1580 and 1620 is in fact simply a trick of the archives. Instead of evidence of rising rates of homicide, the increasingly voluminous inquest records of the period are rather a byproduct of better detection and recording of lethal violence. This greater detection and record keeping were in turn the result of intensified oversight and legal and criminal justice reforms that had their roots in the 1530s. It is possible, then, that early modern court records sometimes "reflect the process of prosecuting crime rather than crime itself," and thus that fluctuations in levels of prosecution may be a product of changes in the nature and administration of criminal justice rather than of a real change in crime rates.[8] In contrast to other types of crime, homicide indictments have long been assumed by historians to more accurately reflect the actual number of homicides committed, and thus to provide a more realistic portrait of levels and patterns of violence.[9] While it is true that homicide is unique in that it almost always led to a formal investigation in the early modern period, this was not always the case before the sixteenth century. Furthermore, even when homicide was investigated, the creation, storing, and keeping of records depend largely on official will. Local criminal investigations are only tied to the state, and thus only reach the eyes of historians, when efforts are made by the state to mandate and collect records, to create a nation bound by paper. It is my contention, therefore, that while crime in general, and property crime in particular, may have indeed fluctuated in the Tudor–Stuart period as a result of economic and demographic stress, the incidence of homicide was not as strongly bound to economic factors; instead, the fluctuations in rates of homicide noted by historians were the result of a unique strengthening of oversight of the coroner system in the sixteenth and early seventeenth centuries.

As we have seen, legal changes in the 1530s led to a "regulatory moment" in which the detection of suspicious death, and the oversight of the coroner system that was responsible for policing it, became particularly intense and effective. This regulatory moment was largely responsible for the rise in recorded prosecutions for violent crime witnessed by historians in England between 1580 and 1620. Likewise, the shift in the system of oversight in the seventeenth century in turn resulted in a decrease in the number of recorded prosecutions for violence. The early modern crisis of violence was in fact an illusion created by greater state control over the regulation of death. Given this new interpretive framework, the self-congratulatory and self-reassuring narratives that stress the relative lack of violence in the modern world are misguided in their assessments of the pre-modern world, for they ignore the possibility that early modern spikes in violence are more illusory than previously imagined. In other words, the extent of the decline of violence in the seventeenth and eighteenth centuries has been overstated. Hence we must reevaluate the chronology of decline, placing the start of the centuries-long process in the early sixteenth century, when Tudor law reform and state building first began to effectively control nonstate violence.

Early Modern English Homicide and Its Historians

Since the exponential growth of histories of crime in the 1970s and 1980s, historians charting patterns of crime have noted a spike in rates of criminal prosecutions in the late sixteenth and early seventeenth centuries. Encompassing such areas as witchcraft, theft, homicide, and other felonies, this crime wave found in the court records of the era, combined with increasingly strident contemporary outcries over the perceived growth of crime and disorder, has led some historians to term this period "the crisis of order."[10] There is some debate over the dates of this crisis, but whatever the exact chronology or the specific criminal acts included, there is general agreement among historians that the late sixteenth and early seventeenth centuries witnessed a surge in criminal prosecutions, a phenomenon of which contemporaries were certainly aware.

If there is relative consensus among historians that crime peaked in England between the late sixteenth and early seventeenth centuries, there is also a broad agreement as to the causes of this period of crisis. Peter Lawson, for instance, argues that the pattern of theft prosecutions was "in large part determined by the economic crises and changes of the period."[11]

Likewise, J. A. Sharpe states that the spike in indictments for felony was in part the result of "harvest failure and other forms of economic crisis."[12] This connection between crime rates and economic conditions in early modern England is perhaps unsurprising given the conditions that prevailed in the late sixteenth and early seventeenth centuries. According to Lawson, "by at least the 1580s the economic expansion of the sixteenth century was beginning to give way to crisis. England's society and economy suffered the combined effects of war, harvest failure, plague and industrial stagnation. Mortality and food prices rose, wages fell, employment opportunities shrank, and poverty became more pronounced."[13] Given the state of the economy, it would be logical to assume that crime rates soared between 1580 and 1620.

Several historians, most notably Lawrence Stone, J. M. Beattie, J. S. Cockburn, and J. A. Sharpe, have shown that the incidence of homicide followed the general parameters of the more general crisis of order: an upsurge in crime rates and concern about disorder around 1580, followed by a decline after about 1620.[14] Despite the difference in counties or sources, the general pattern that emerges from the studies of Sharpe, Beattie, and Cockburn is one of growing rates of homicide between roughly 1580 and 1620, followed by a slow but regular decline throughout the rest of the early modern period and perhaps beyond. Indeed, Randolph Roth, who has aggregated the available data on homicide from the figures provided by Sharpe, Cockburn, Beattie, and others, has concluded that "homicide and indictment rates, which were moderate in the 1560s and 1570s, rose sharply in the 1580s and 1590s and peaked in the 1600s and 1610s." Roth further found that "the rates receded in the 1620s and 1630s, but did not fall to the levels that had prevailed in the mid-sixteenth century until the early eighteenth century."[15]

The reasons provided for this spike in homicides in the late sixteenth and early seventeenth centuries are varied, but usually focus on a few common factors. According to Stone, the rise in homicide in Essex at the end of the sixteenth century was the result of the growth of "social anomy" and "socio-cultural crisis," which manifested itself in a rise in the frequency of disputes between neighbors and a collapse of traditional means of dispute resolution in local communities caused by growing economic and demographic pressures between 1560 and the mid-seventeenth century.[16]

Roth's recent study of patterns of homicide similarly suggests economic and demographic reasons for the growth of homicides between 1580 and 1620. Following Cockburn and Sharpe, Roth argues that "most scholars believe that demographic pressure, economic depression, crop failures, the militarization of culture, and military demobilization together caused homicide rates to soar in the late sixteenth and early seventeenth centuries."[17] As Roth tells us, there were harvest failures in 1586, 1590, 1595, 1596, and 1600, while real wages dropped. In addition, England conscripted as much as 15 percent of its adult male population for the almost continuous wars between 1585 and 1604, many of whom returned home without jobs or the skills to acquire them. As a result of these factors, Roth tells us, nondomestic homicide rates rose from 1.82 per 100,000 persons per year between 1559 and 1579 to 3.23 per 100,000 persons between 1580 and 1619.[18]

The contention put forward by Stone, Sharpe, and Roth that the dislocating effects of dearth, plague, and warfare combined with other economic factors to cause a crisis in homicide rates seems relatively intuitive. It is natural to suppose that such events would have the potential to destabilize society and undermine familiar communities and institutions. Upon closer examination, however, it is unclear whether these phenomena were in fact responsible for the growing incidence of homicide in the late sixteenth century. Dearth and plague, for example, are often thought to have a negative impact on the cohesiveness of society and thus to lead to crime and violence. However, studies of dearth by Keith Wrightson and John Walter and studies of plague by Wrightson have shown that, contrary to conventional wisdom, such catastrophic events often brought communities together, or at the very least did not cause the sort of disruption one would suspect.[19] Thus, while long-term economic collapse might well have caused a general increase in crime—as has convincingly been shown by Peter Lawson and others—it seems unlikely that short-term events such as a specific harvest failure or a plague resulted in an increase in crime, never mind homicide, over a period of 40 to 80 years.

It is true that England was at war for much of the period in question, and studies of later periods have shown the potentially disastrous consequences of the rapid demobilization of soldiers and sailors trained for war and little else.[20] However, it is unclear why the wars of the late sixteenth and early seventeenth centuries should result in a large, lasting spike in homicide, and indeed in crime more generally. Moreover, later periods of warfare did not produce an analogous rise in homicide rates. Warfare certainly continued to be a fixture of English life after the 1620s and 1630s; in fact, it became more frequent and took place on a much greater scale in the late seventeenth and eighteenth centuries. Although these later wars did on occasion lead to immediate crime waves — such as that which followed the War of Austrian Succession — these waves were of much shorter duration than the late sixteenth-century crisis, and neither levels of crime in general nor levels of homicide in particular ever rose again for any sustained period to those seen in the late sixteenth and early seventeenth centuries. It is difficult, then, to believe that warfare was the cause of, or even a significant factor in, the rise of homicide in the late sixteenth and early seventeenth centuries.

If the widely accepted explanations of the rise in recorded homicides seem flimsy on closer examination, the reasons for the seventeenth-century decline in homicides have been even more difficult for historians to pinpoint convincingly. Following the work of Norbert Elias, historians such as Stone, Beattie, and Robert Shoemaker suggest that the decline in homicides in the seventeenth and eighteenth centuries was the result of cultural changes that helped to civilize and pacify what had been a violent society.[21] For Stone, the decline in homicide was the outgrowth of an eighteenth-century "commercialization of values," which led to a "revulsion of public opinion against overt physical cruelty."[22] Beattie argues along similar lines that the decline resulted from a "developing civility, expressed perhaps in a more highly developed politeness of manner and a concern not to offend or take offense, and an enlarged sensitivity towards some forms of cruelty and pain."[23] Shoemaker likewise focuses on cultural change, although he is most concerned with conceptions of male honor, and suggests that "with the increased regulation and institutionalization of commercial credit, men became less dependent on the opinions of others for economic success. Similarly, constant geographic and social mobility and a breakdown of traditional forms of community meant the role of neighborly opinion in shaping social reputations diminished."[24] However, even if we concede that the factors cited by Stone, Beattie, and Shoemaker signal a general decline in violence, most evidence of changing attitudes toward violence relates to the mid- or late eighteenth century, a full 100 years or more after homicide rates began to decline.

The disconnect in the historical literature between the chronology of violence and the chronology of cultural change is only one of many. Another of the chief deficits of the existing narratives of early modern homicide is that none has compared the inquest records relating to homicide with inquest records overall. Thus, while historians have long viewed homicide in conjunction with other types of crime, as yet no one has thought to compare homicide with other types of death. Without knowing the contours of untimely or suspicious death of all types, it is difficult to know whether homicide was in fact increasing relative to other types of death — such as accident or suicide — or whether similar patterns were occurring in relation to untimely death as a whole. This study seeks to remedy this problem by looking at coroners' inquests as a whole, and not simply homicide in isolation, to reassess possible patterns of homicide and violent death. When inquest records are examined holistically, the connections between the incidence of homicide and economic fluctuations become even less clear.

The Central Courts, Forfeiture, and the Increased Detection of Violent Death

The period between 1580 and 1620, previously identified by historians as a period of crisis and of growing homicide rates, did indeed see an increase in the absolute numbers of homicides. If we take Sussex, a county whose extant coroners' inquests have been admirably compiled by R. F. Hunnisett, this trend seems to hold true. Thus, whereas the period 1530–1580 witnessed 96 inquests relating to homicides, the period 1580–1620 contained 143 homicide inquests, a significant rise of roughly 33 percent.

As the traditional narrative of the crisis of order would suggest, the period 1620–1660 witnessed a decline in the total number of homicide inquests, falling to 109.[25] Based on these figures, it does seem clear that the absolute numbers of inquests relating to homicide increased dramatically between 1580 and 1620 and declined slowly thereafter. The absolute numbers, however, do not tell us the whole story about the possible connection between the supposed increase in homicides and economic crisis.

If the incidence of homicide and other forms of violent death were directly tied to economic change, then we would expect to see such deaths grow as a proportion of all suspicious deaths in periods of economic decline or stagnation. As has been shown, the period 1580–1620 certainly experienced economic depression of various sorts. Thus, we should expect to see the numbers of homicides found in coroners' inquests increase relative to other types of death in this period of economic crisis. When we look at the records, however, this is not what we find. If we again take the county of Sussex as an example, it becomes clear that the proportion of inquests relating to homicide did not increase relative to other forms of death, namely suicide, natural, or accidental death. Between 1530 and 1580, the years immediately prior to those identified as the period of crisis, we find that homicides represented just over 23 percent of all inquests held in Sussex. Inquests relating to suicide accounted for about 25 percent of the total, whereas accidental deaths accounted for 38 percent. When we compare these proportions for the decades before the crisis with those of the crisis period itself, there is little noticeable change. For the period 1580–1620, homicides accounted for just under 25 percent of all Sussex coroners' inquests, with suicides accounting for 19 percent and accidental deaths for 36 percent of the total.[26] In terms of the proportion of the total number of inquests, the percentage of homicides hardly changed at all (from 23.5 percent to 24.7 percent) between the years 1530–1580 and the crisis period of 1580 to 1620. The proportion of accidental deaths also stayed relatively stable between the pre-crisis and crisis periods, moving from 38.3 percent of the total in between 1530 and 1580 to 35.8 percent between 1580 and 1620. The proportion of inquests related to suicide actually fell by over 5 percent (from 24.8 percent to 19.2 percent) between the two periods, even if the absolute number of suicide inquests rose slightly (from 101 in 1530–1580 to 111 in 1580–1620). The only significant proportional increase between the pre-crisis and crisis years was in the proportion of inquests that were classified as natural deaths, which rose from 13.2 percent of all inquests for the period 1530–1580 to 20.2 percent of inquests between 1580 and 1620 (Table 1).

What the records show, then, is not a proportional increase in the numbers of homicides between 1580 and 1620 but rather a general increase in inquests of all types. Indeed, the total number of inquests rose from 407 for the years between 1520 and 1580 to 578 between 1580 and 1620 before falling to a mere 236 for the years between 1620 and 1660.[27] Homicide, suicide, accidental death, and natural death all increased in absolute numbers between 1580 and 1620; the proportions, however, remained roughly the same.

So what does this overall rise in the number of inquests held between 1580 and 1620 tell us about patterns of homicide during this period of crisis? First and foremost, the lack of proportional change suggests that the rise in homicides was not closely related to economic change. Although I remain skeptical, an argument could be made based on modern analogies — and seeming common sense — that homicide rates fluctuate relative to the health of the economy. In this conception, as economic conditions deteriorate, more individuals in desperation turn to crime and violence to make ends meet. Economic and demographic conditions did worsen over the long sixteenth century, and this may have led to a surge in property

Table 1. Sussex Inquest Verdicts, 1485–1660

	Homicide	Suicide	Accident	Natural	Total
1485–1530	42 (61.7%)	9 (13.2%)	14 (20.5%)	3 (4.4%)	68
1530–1580	96 (23.5%)	101 (24.8%)	156 (38.3%)	54 (13.2%)	407
1580–1620	143 (24.7%)	111 (19.2%)	207 (35.8%)	117 (20.2%)	578
1620–1660	109 (46.1%)	21 (8.8%)	70 (29.6%)	36 (15.2%)	236

Source: *Sussex Coroners' Inquests.*

crime of various sorts. I am not convinced, however, that violent crime, and especially homicide, were so closely tied to economic fluctuations in the early modern period.[28] In the modern world such a connection between economics and violent crime seems reasonable, especially in a world of organized crime, where violence is often tied up in disputes over control of drugs and their sale. In sixteenth- and seventeenth-century England, however, most violent crime was not the result of economic interest, but rather the consequence of spur-of-the-moment disputes resulting from drunkenness, insult, and slights of honor.

For instance, in 1588 John Slywright, a gentleman from London, and Gervase Carter, a local tailor, were drinking together at Wartling in Sussex. At about 5 o'clock that evening the gathering became heated and "insulting words rose between them." As so often happened, insult was followed by violence, and Slywright stabbed Carter with a rapier, giving a wound that caused the hapless tailor's death the next day.[29] Although the weapon used was somewhat rare (knives, staves, and farm implements being more common), the crime itself was not. Homicides arising from similar disputes between individuals were the most usual type of homicide in the period. The state of medical knowledge and provisioning in the early modern period meant that many more brawls resulted in deaths than is the case in the modern world. Most homicides were a byproduct of interpersonal disputes in the "heat of the moment," rather than of such planned activities as robbery, turf wars or organized crime. Given this, it is difficult to see just how or why economic crisis or an economically induced "social anomy" would cause an increase in homicides of this immediate and personal variety. If institutions of order were not being undermined, as most historians now accept, and if most homicides were spontaneous acts involving no pecuniary interest, it is hard to see why homicides should rise so dramatically in this period.[30]

If spontaneous homicides such as these were relatively commonplace, the Sussex records for the period of heightened prosecutions, 1580–1620, show no noticeable increase in homicides related to robbery or other illicit economic activities. In fact, such deaths remained a rare exception throughout the early modern period, both before and after the crisis period. Thus, homicide specifically and violent crime in general were unlikely to have been greatly affected by economic or demographic fluctuations.[31] It seems evident, then, that if we are seeking to explain the rise in prosecutions for violent crime, we have to look beyond economic factors.

The fact that the proportions of homicides relative to accidental deaths, suicides, and other deaths held at the same rates across the period 1520–1620 suggests that the absolute rise in homicide witnessed between 1580 and 1620 was not directly connected to economic changes. If the increase in homicides between 1580 and 1620 was related to economic change, why did other types of death, deaths not at all related to economic stagnation, increase as well and at similar rates? As we have seen, while the absolute number of homicide inquests rose between 1580 and 1620, so too did those associated with other types of death. Most significant for evaluating the possible connections between homicide and economic decline, the absolute number of accidental deaths recorded in the coroners' records of Sussex also increased between 1580 and 1620, and at a rate similar to that of homicide inquests.

Most accidental deaths in this period involved such domestic or work-related accidents as drowning in a pond or river while fetching water or washing clothes, falling from a horse or cart, or being trampled by the same. This was the fate of William Emes of Hastings, who died in 1603 when he "accidentally fell" from a bridge and "was drowned in the water flowing under it." In 1604, Thomas Trymlet fell to his death from a plum tree that he had climbed to pick fruit. Christopher Cook met his untimely demise in 1605 when he fell under the cart he was driving and "was pulled violently by a horse and 2 oxen, and was wounded in his right legg which was run over by the wheel."[32] Deaths such as these were not the result of crime or deprivation, and as such should have been immune to fluctuations relating to economic change. There is no reason to suspect that when economic conditions became more difficult in the late sixteenth and early seventeenth centuries, more people fell from horses or drowned while fetching water. Accidental deaths provide a kind of controlled data set in the criminal justice records, immune from the influence of economic stagnation. Therefore, the fact that the number of accidental deaths in Sussex increased at a rate similar to that of homicide between 1580 and 1620 suggests that neither one was directly tied to economic change.

One of the usual methods of connecting crime rates to economic conditions has been the comparison of changing levels of crime and changing economic indicators. In his work on the connections between property crime and economic conditions, Peter Lawson has compared rates of indictment with price levels for the period 1560–1624 to show that levels of indictment closely followed fluctuations in prices, a standard measure of the health of the economy.[33] Although year-by-year numbers for coroners' inquests are not available for most counties, it is possible to use the records of Sussex to see whether this correlation between the number of indictments, homicide inquests, or accidental deaths on the one hand and prices on the other holds true.[34] If homicide and accidental deaths were both tied to economic fluctuations, then we would expect to see both types of death rise with rises in prices. If homicide, but not accidental death, was tied to economic patterns, we would expect the number of homicides to rise and fall with prices and the number of accidental deaths to follow no discernible pattern in relation to prices. If instead patterns of neither homicide nor accidental death were tied to economic conditions, but rather were the result of better record keeping and oversight, then we would expect random patterns of homicide and accidental death not correlated with price levels.

When we examine the data for Sussex and compare coroners' inquests for homicide and accident with average prices (Fig. 5), it seems clear that there was no discernible connection between prices and patterns of total inquests, homicides, or accidental deaths. Nor does there seem to be any connection between years of harvest failure—1586, 1594–1597, 1608, 1613, and 1617, according to Hoskins—and spikes in inquests, homicides, or accidental deaths.[35] This suggests that, unlike property offenses or crime in general, these types of death presented no logical patterns. They were instead events that were the result of various and contingent circumstances. Homicides occurred when individuals quarreled over honor, insults, and drink. Similarly, accidental deaths resulted from the seemingly trivial dan-

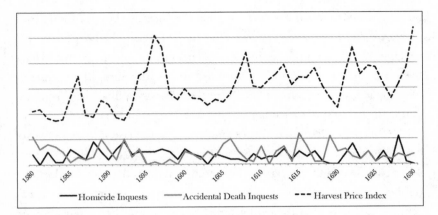

Figure 5. Comparison of price index (price of wheat in shillings per quarter) and number of inquests held.

gers of everyday life: washing, bathing, traveling, and working. It should come as no surprise that these random, chaotic events did not adhere to the economic conditions that pushed people into actual crimes of necessity such as robbery, theft, and vagrancy.

Suicide, a type of death that could possibly be linked to economic change, did increase slightly in the period 1580–1620 in terms of absolute numbers. However, while the absolute number of suicides increased, the proportion of suicides actually decreased by a small amount, again suggesting that the relationship between economic stress and violent death was not as straightforward as has been suggested by modern historians.

The supposed spike in homicides in the late sixteenth century is no more evident in contemporary writings than it is in the available data. While writers of the period frequently complained about disorder in general, it appears that they were more concerned with theft than with homicide.[36] William Harrison (1534–1593) for one thought murder was rare in the England of his day and saved his contempt and concern for property offenses. According to Harrison, "we doo not often heare of horrible, merciless, and wilfull murthers." If Harrison thought murder was rare, however, he was in no doubt that "[c]ertes there is no gretare mischeefe done in England than by robberies."[37] Harrison was far from alone among early modern Englishmen and women in placing concerns about property over concerns about violence. It seems likely that if England had experienced a precipitous rise in homicides in the late sixteenth century, there would have been a greater contemporary outcry. Instead of lamenting the frequency of homicide, however, more contemporary ink was spilled castigating vagrants, decrying property offenses, and worrying about disorder.

Coroners' records for Sussex suggest that the rise in the number of homicide inquests between 1580 and 1620 was not directly, or at least primarily, related to the very real economic changes that occurred in that period. If the deterioration of economic conditions in the late sixteenth century did not lead to a growth in lethal violence, how then can we explain the overall increase in homicides and indeed other types of death in this time of perceived crisis? The answer to this question lies not in searching for reasons why crime might have increased in these years, but rather in asking whether more crimes were simply detected and recorded. Changes in the coroner system and its oversight created the conditions necessary for the growth in investigation and record keeping that in turn resulted in a new proliferation of recorded homicides. State growth rather than economic contraction produced the illusion of homicide run rampant.

The Sussex inquest records for the period 1485–1530 are patchy; however, they are still in many ways revealing. Examining the inquest data for this period side by side with the inquests of the pre-crisis and crisis periods creates a picture that undermines the causal links between economic decline and growing rates of homicide in early modern England. As Table 1 demonstrates, there were a total of 42 known homicides in Sussex in the years 1485–1530, as well as 9 suicides, 14 accidental deaths, and 3 natural deaths. Thus, in this period, inquests relating to homicide accounted for 61.7 percent of all inquests, while those relating to suicide and accidental death made up 13.2 and 20.5 percent of the total, respectively.[38] It is difficult to believe that homicide inquests represented a much larger percentage of the total number of inquests in the period before 1530 than they did thereafter. Given that the years before 1530 preceded the economic decline usually associated with the crisis of order and the growth in homicide rates, one would expect homicide to represent a smaller proportion of total inquests than in the period 1580–1620. Instead, homicide represented a much greater proportion of inquests in the early sixteenth century than in the late sixteenth century. These numbers suggest that both the absolute growth in the number of coroners' inquests and the proportional decline of homicide occurred in the years around 1530 rather than in the late sixteenth century. Therefore, the real moment of change occurred in the 1530s. In this period, the total number of coroners' inquests began to grow at a remarkable rate. As the number of inquests grew across the sixteenth century, the proportion of inquests related to homicide steadily declined. Thus, while historians have seen a rise in homicide inquests as evidence of a rise in the actual incidence of homicide, what was actually occurring was a general rise in the number of inquest records of all types. Rather than an era of crisis, the late sixteenth and early seventeenth centuries were in fact a period of growing state monopolization of violence.

That the rise in total inquests should begin in the mid-sixteenth century is both curious and telling. As early as 1487, a statute entitled "An Act Against Murderers" made the registration of all coroners' inquests at the next assize and the subsequent filing of all inquests at King's Bench mandatory.[39] Despite this new legal obligation that should have ensured that all inquests were filed at either the assize or King's Bench, it was not until the mid-sixteenth century that coroners' inquests are found consistently in either court in significant numbers. The failure to register and preserve coroners' inquests as the law of 1487 required has been mainly ascribed to the incompetence or laziness of individual coroners in both drawing up inquests and delivering them to the courts.[40] If this contention is indeed true, as seems likely, the question remains, why did the more regular recording and preservation of coroners' inquests begin in the mid-sixteenth century? The answer, I will argue, lies in the growth in oversight of the coroner system from the 1530s.

As was discussed at greater length in Chapter 5, the royal almoner acquired the right to sue in Star Chamber in the 1530s. From the 1550s, this newfound ability to sue in the central courts coincided with a general rise in central court litigation brought about by declining real costs of litigation and official encouragement of the use of the central courts.[41] As a result of this combination, litigation involving the almoner in both Star Chamber and King's Bench rose significantly from the middle of Elizabeth's reign, and reached a peak between 1560 and 1630.[42] With few exceptions, this central court litigation concerned disputes over forfeit property. As we have seen, the law of forfeiture mandated that the property of felons and suicides, as well as those goods or property that were the proximate cause of an accidental death, were forfeit to the crown. In practice, the property thus forfeited was granted to the high almoner and other royal patent holders such as lords of liberties or urban corporations. As a result of the practice of forfeiture, most violent deaths involved the potential for property to be forfeit, and thus the potential for disputes and disagreements over the proper redistribution of the goods and lands of the deceased or those held responsible for the death.

The centrally appointed almoner was not the only one with claims on forfeit property, as other franchisees, and the heirs and creditors of the deceased or felon, also vigorously pursued forfeit property. These competing economic interests led in turn to regular central court litigation over the proper distribution of forfeit goods. Because the outcome of these forfeiture disputes depended on the records and verdicts of individual coroners, the competing economic claims of creditors, franchisees, heirs, and almoner provided a considerable and unprecedented level of oversight of the coroner and his records in the late sixteenth and early seventeenth centuries. Indeed, the distribution of forfeit goods often depended directly on the verdict reached by the coroner's inquest, as when Henry Carant was found drowned in a well in Wiltshire. The almoner and his agents argued that Carant's death was an obvious suicide. As evidence they claimed that he had tried to kill himself before on numerous occasions and that the well in which he drowned was too narrow for a man unless the man first removed his gown, which Carant had done, suggesting that his death was no accident. Carant's property was valued at £500 — a sum that would be forfeit to the almoner if the coroner's inquest returned a suicide verdict. Given the amount of money at stake, it is unsurprising that his wife Elizabeth contested the scenario given by the almoner, instead proclaimed that the death was accidental. The coroner and his jury agreed with Carant's widow and returned a verdict of accidental death. The almoner, having been informed that the coroner was bribed and witnesses favorable to the crown suppressed, was not satisfied with the outcome and began a suit in Star Chamber to recover the goods he believed rightfully belonged to him.[43]

This case is fairly typical, but it nicely illustrates what was at stake in forfeiture disputes. The difference between £500 being forfeit to the almoner and £500 remaining with the widow of the deceased hinged on whether the coroner's inquest returned a verdict of suicide or accidental death. Given the precarious nature of the redistribution of the property of the deceased in cases such as these, it would clearly have behooved almoner, heir, creditor, and franchisee to closely monitor the actions of the coroner, his records, and his jury for signs of corruption, incompetence, or inaccuracy. With the advent of a relatively cheap and effective venue to try such cases, these economically motivated litigants and litigation provided a level of oversight of the coroner system that was unique to the period between roughly 1550 and 1640.

The intensified oversight in the late sixteenth and early seventeenth centuries led in turn to an insistence by the central courts—and in particular by King's Bench—on more accurate and consistent record keeping of coroners' inquests. During this period coroners were frequently summoned to King's Bench to answer for defects in inquests or for failing to register inquest verdicts with the assize or King's Bench. For example, in 1593 Magnus Fowle, a long-standing and diligent county coroner in Sussex, was summoned to King's Bench to answer for a defect in the inquest relating to the death of 11-year-old Thomas Whyttur, who had fallen from a plough cart and been crushed by its wheel. Fowle had neglected to record the name of the person who possessed the deodand and instead left a blank space. The process against Fowle seems to have ceased when the name of the woman in possession of the deodand was later added.[44] In fact, coroners were more likely to be summoned to King's Bench for defects between roughly 1550 and 1630 than at any other time in the early modern period. Between 1554 and 1625, legal processes were initiated against coroners for defects in their

inquests in almost 7 percent of all inquests in Sussex, more than double
the proportion of inquests that resulted in such litigation against coroners
between 1625 and 1650.[45] The stricter monitoring of coroners and their inquests and the concomitant demand for better record keeping that resulted
from the competing economic interests of central court litigants led in turn
to a rise in the total number of inquests returned. Thus, it seems clear that
the growth in litigation, and thus oversight, led to a rise in the number of
both homicide inquests and overall inquests.

If we compare the patterns of central court litigation, coroners' inquests, and homicides, a plausible explanation for the seeming rise in
homicides at the end of the sixteenth century emerges. By the late sixteenth
and early seventeenth centuries, the amount of central court litigation resulting from coroners' inquests in Sussex more than doubled, growing from
77 cases in 1530–1570 to 168 in 1570–1620.[46] Similarly, the total number of
inquests in Sussex rose from 238 in 1530–1570 to 735 in 1570–1620.[47] These
two figures for inquests and litigation relating to inquests map on almost
exactly to the pattern of homicides noticed in Sussex and other counties: a
precipitous rise between 1580 and 1620. Just as Sussex forfeiture litigation
peaked at King's Bench between 1570 and 1620, Star Chamber forfeiture
litigation also reached its zenith between about 1560 and 1625. The nature
of Star Chamber record survival makes it difficult to draw firm conclusions
about the period after 1625; however, it is clear that the amount of forfeiture
litigation reached its peak in the reign of Elizabeth and slowly declined under James I before Star Chamber was abolished in 1641.[48]

Based on this confluence of patterns of central court litigation, coroners' inquests, and homicides, we can form a clear picture of a potential
cause of the late sixteenth-century spike in homicides. Legal reforms in the
1530s, combined with easier access to the central courts in the mid-sixteenth
century, resulted in a massive increase in litigation over the forfeit property
of the deceased. Because these cases often hinged on the records and outcomes of coroners' inquests, the increase in litigation caused a regulatory
moment in which the activities and records of coroners were more heavily
scrutinized than before or after. This intensified monitoring of coroners
and their records in turn led to better and more accurate record keeping,

and thus to a general increase in the number of inquests registered with the assize or King's Bench. This rise in inquests concerned not only homicide, but also other types of violent death such as suicide, natural death, and accidental death. By failing to examine the rise in homicides in the context of coroners' inquests more generally, historians of homicide have mistaken this general rise in coroners' inquests—a rise that resulted from increased oversight rather than from a surge in violent deaths—for a rise in homicides in particular. Therefore, what seems on the surface to be a surge in homicides in the late sixteenth and early seventeenth centuries is likely in large part the result of increased oversight and better record keeping.

The Decline in Oversight and the Decrease of Homicide

As Table 1 above demonstrates, the rise in total inquests between 1580 and 1620 was followed by a decline between 1620 and 1660, a pattern that would persist through the rest of the seventeenth century and beyond. The total number of recorded inquests in Sussex dropped dramatically after 1620, from a peak of 1,578 between 1580 and 1620 to a mere 236 between 1620 and 1660. Absolute numbers of all types of death fell rapidly in the immediate postcrisis period: homicides from 143 to 109, suicides from 111 to 21, and accidental deaths from 207 to 70. In terms of a proportion of the total number of inquests, inquests relating to homicide actually rose from 24.7 to 46.1 percent between 1620 and 1660, while the proportion of suicides declined sharply from 19.2 percent to 8.8 percent. Inquests concerning accidental deaths also declined proportionally, from 35.8 percent of all inquests between 1580 and 1620 to 29.6 percent of all inquests in 1620–1660.[49]

These numbers again fly in the face of economic determinist models of early modern English homicide rates. The period 1620–1660 saw slow but steady improvement of economic conditions in England, pulling the country out of its previous period of depression.[50] If the incidence of homicide was in fact closely tied to changing economic conditions, the period after 1620, which saw the beginning of economic recovery in England, should have seen a gradual decline in the number of homicides. Indeed, on the surface this is exactly what we see, with the total number of homicides declining by roughly 24 percent from 1620 to 1660. However, just as for the period of crisis, what was really happening during this period of decline may be disguised by the absolute numbers. The years between 1620 and 1660 saw a general decline in every variety of recorded death. The number of inquests related to suicides fell by 81 percent between 1620 and 1660, while the number of accidental deaths fell by over 66 percent in the same years. Thus, though the absolute number of homicides was falling, the proportional number of homicide inquests was growing rapidly. Indeed, in the years 1620–1660, homicide came to represent a greater proportion of all inquests than had been the case since the early sixteenth century — despite the economic recovery of these years. Again, it is evident that the explanation for the decline in the number of homicides, like the explanation for the rise in the late sixteenth century, is not to be found in measures of economic decline or growth.

The records of coroners' inquests for Cheshire reveal a similar, if slightly delayed and less dramatic, pattern of declining inquests. As we have seen, the overall number of coroners' inquests fell drastically in Sussex in the mid-seventeenth century. Cheshire inquests also fell significantly in this period. Whereas Cheshire held 720 inquests between 1580 and 1620, by the end of the seventeenth and the beginning of the eighteenth centuries the number began to decline rapidly, from 619 inquests between 1700 and 1750 to only 507 between 1750 and 1800.[51] As in Sussex, this later decline in Cheshire inquests was the result of across-the-board reductions in the numbers of accidental deaths, suicides, and homicides rather than of homicides alone. While the evidence from Cheshire may complicate the precise chronology of the rise and fall of homicide rates, it does reinforce the notion that the numbers of all types of inquests were declining in the seventeenth and eighteenth centuries, a fact that suggests that the decline in all types of violent death was the result of similar factors that went beyond simple economic change.

If the coroners' inquests of Cheshire provide evidence of a rough pattern of declining inquests in the seventeenth and eighteenth centuries, the records of Kent seem to coincide more exactly with the pattern witnessed for Sussex. According to Cockburn, whose study of homicide in Kent relied on both the assize and inquest records for that county, coroners' inquests began to be recorded with regularity from about 1560. However, as Cockburn notes, after the 1620s "the practice of returning inquests to King's Bench seems to have gradually lapsed."[52] As a result of this lack of consistent evidence from coroners' inquests, Cockburn's study of homicide relies entirely on assize indictments for the period after 1660. The slow but remarkable decline in the return of inquests to King's Bench from the mid-seventeenth century in Kent coincides almost exactly with a similar decline in the return of inquests in Sussex.

The rise in the number of homicides between 1580 and 1620 was in large part the result of increased detection and oversight of coroners, as well as the more regular recording of their inquests. The explanation for the decline in homicides after 1620, therefore, must been sought in similar phenomena. Just as the rise in homicides coincided with both a rise in central court forfeiture litigation and an increase in overall coroners' inquests, the slow decline in homicides also matches similar declines in central court forfeiture litigation and total inquests. I have suggested above that the rise in homicides in the late sixteenth century was the result of a general rise in inquests caused by greater oversight of coroners and their records, and that this greater surveillance was a product of the competing interests of growing numbers of forfeiture litigants. If this was indeed the case, it follows that the decline in the incidence of homicide that occurred after the mid-seventeenth century may have been the result of a shift in the nature of the oversight of coroners. Thus, poorer record keeping caused by a decline in central court oversight caused a similar decline in central court forfeiture litigation.

As argued in the previous chapter, the decline in central forfeiture litigation began with attacks on Star Chamber that led to its being dissolved in 1641. With this central venue for forfeiture litigation, and thus oversight of coroners, gone, the burden of resolving such disputes and of monitoring coroners and their records fell to King's Bench, which, unsurprisingly, slowed under the weight of business. Additionally, without the threat of Star Chamber and with the rise in both court costs and the average duration of cases, it seems likely that heirs, creditors, and royal patent holders turned to locally mediated settlements for the resolution of forfeiture disputes.[53] The final blow to the system of oversight provided by central court forfeiture litigation came in the 1690s, when legislation made it easier for such disputes to be settled without reference to the courts in Westminster.[54] Just as homicides, total inquests, and central court forfeiture litigation all rose sharply at roughly the same time, homicides seem to have declined at roughly the same time as the total number of coroners' inquests and forfeiture litigation. The total number of inquests fell from a high of 735 between 1570 and 1620 to only 232 between 1620 and 1660. Similarly, central court litigation declined in terms of overall numbers, from 162 to 27 cases in the same period. In terms of the proportion of all inquests, the number that resulted in litigation declined from 22 percent of inquests in the earlier period to 12 percent between 1620 and 1660.[55] Again, if the decline in inquests caused the decline in litigation rather than vice versa, we would expect to see a proportional decline of litigation and total inquests. However, instead of a proportional decline, the proportion of inquests resulting in litigation decreased as well. The explanation for the decline in homicides from the mid-seventeenth century, then, is similar to the cause of the rise in homicides in the late sixteenth century in that declining forfeiture litigation led to a decrease in oversight of coroners and their duties. As a result of this more lax monitoring of coroners, record keeping became poorer and the consistency with which inquests were registered at the assize, and especially at King's Bench, decrease markedly. Once again, historians seem to have mistaken changes in record keeping and oversight with fluctuations in the incidence of homicide.

In their study of Cheshire inquests, Sharpe and Dickinson also acknowledge that the decline in Cheshire inquests in the late seventeenth and especially the eighteenth centuries was the result of a failure to record certain types of verdicts. "The crucial issue here, in all probability, is a failure to note inquests in the Crown Books. . . . In particular, there was a failure to note accidental deaths."[56] Thus, while the number of homicides in this period of declining inquests decreased slowly, the number of suicides and accidental deaths dropped significantly.[57] As was the case in Sussex, when coroners' inquests began to decline overall, the reason was not a rapid decline in lethal violence, but rather a decline in the numbers of accidental deaths and suicides as well as homicides. That accidental death was a main factor in the decline in Cheshire inquests further underscores the point that changing economic conditions were not the cause of declining homicide rates; if economic factors were paramount, we would expect homicide to decline at a much faster rate than accidental death, which was in no way tied to economic fluctuations.

The question remains, why did the decline in coroners' inquests occur decades earlier in Sussex than in Cheshire? Although the possible reasons for this divergence must remain speculative, a simple but plausible hypothesis can be offered. The proximity of Sussex to the central courts in Westminster may have made the use of those courts more attractive to potential litigants in Sussex than to those in Cheshire. If this was indeed the case and fewer Cheshire litigants made use of the central courts, the impact of the dissolution of Star Chamber in 1641 may have had a greater, and earlier, impact on Sussex than on Cheshire. Thus, it is possible that the dissolution of Star Chamber affected oversight and record keeping in Sussex more dramatically than in Cheshire, leading to an earlier decline in inquest returns. The early eighteenth-century decline in inquest returns in Cheshire, on the other hand, may have been more a result of the legislation enacted in the 1690s, which made forfeiture disputes easier to resolve without reference to the central courts. These tentative suggestions may help to explain why Cheshire court records seem to diverge so radically from the records of other areas and reconcile them to a more general pattern.

The general picture that emerges from the coroners' records of Sussex is rather different from the traditional narrative of the crisis-of-order literature, which focuses on the years roughly between 1580 and 1620. Instead of a brief period in the late sixteenth and early seventeenth centuries in which economic pressures led to a growth in crime in general and homicide in particular, my research suggests that the true anomalous period occurred between about 1530 and the 1620s. Instead of a period that witnessed a rapid growth in violence or criminality, I contend that this period saw a rise in the absolute numbers of all types of death investigated by coroners, but a decline in the proportion of deaths that were attributed to homicide. The periods both before (1485–1530) and after (1620–1660) this era contained fewer inquests overall, as well as higher proportions of homicides relative to the total number of inquests. The general pattern that emerges thus contradicts attempts to explicitly tie the growth of homicide between 1580 and 1620 to economic change. In place of this economic determinism, I have suggested another model to explain the changes that historians of crime have observed in the sixteenth and early seventeenth centuries. Rather than a crime wave resulting from economic stress, the years between the 1530s and the 1620s saw a growth in regulation, detection, oversight, and recording of crime. This regulatory moment was the result of a system of forfeiture that incentivized central court litigation, litigation which in turn created increased oversight of the coroner system. Increased oversight of coroners and their records led to a more regular and consistent regime of record keeping, which was in large part responsible for the rise in the number of homicides that historians have observed in the late sixteenth and early seventeenth centuries. In a society dependent on amateur local officers and local private initiative for the detection and prosecution of crime, oversight is essential for the consistent, effective enforcement of the law and the containment of violence. When the system of central oversight began to erode in the mid-seventeenth century, the number of inquests recorded began to decline as well. Thus, both the rise of homicide rates in England after 1580 and the rapid decline after 1620 can be explained by the existence in those years of a system of oversight that led to better detection and record keeping, and thus to the greater visibility of homicide.

As previous historians of homicide—and of patterns of crime more generally—have noted, one must be wary of overreliance on monocausal explanations for fluctuations in crime rates. The hypotheses put forward by Peter Lawson and others for an economically induced overall rise in crime in the late sixteenth and early seventeenth centuries are convincing, and it seems likely that economic changes and economic stress had some impact on the incidence of homicide in the Tudor-Stuart period. With harvest failures, price increases, frequent warfare, and demographic growth, the conditions of the period probably left some Englishmen and women feeling alienated from society and community, without hope and seemingly with no stake in society. These marginal and marginalized people must have felt that they had little to lose and thus small disincentive to avoid a life of crime. This was perhaps especially the case among the growing numbers of young and landless people. Given what we know about the resiliency of early modern English society and the strength of its local and national institutions, however, it seems unlikely that even economic and demographic crises—which were all too familiar in the premodern world—are sufficient to explain the near doubling of homicide rates as a proportion of the nation's growing population.

An overall growth in population—or even a growth of the population most likely to commit acts of violence—was not, however, the cause of the spike in homicides witnessed between 1580 and 1620. First, the rate of population growth was not nearly large enough to match the growth in homicides, let alone accidental deaths. Second, if population growth caused the rise in homicides, we would expect the numbers to hold relatively steady across the 1620s rather than declining sharply, as they did. Fluctuations in population, therefore, were not wholly responsible for changes in the incidence of homicide or suspicious death.[58]

While I am less convinced by the cultural arguments for the seventeenth- and eighteenth-century decline in homicides made by those following in the footsteps of Norbert Elias, it must be acknowledged that homicide was likely declining across the early modern period. As with the rise in homicides in the sixteenth century, it is plausible that the later decline was partly a result of a combination of economic improvement and cultural change. And yet, cultural explanations for the long-term decline of violence have failed to address the fact that the rise of a culture of civility and politeness did not occur until the late seventeenth and eighteenth centuries, long after violence first began to decline. The growth of civility also followed directly on the heels of the regulatory moment that characterized the period between 1530 and 1640. Culture, therefore, must be seen not as the cause of the decline of violence, but instead as a product of the state monopolization of violence.

Even if an overall trend of declining homicide rates did exist, as seems plausible, it seems equally evident that more intense oversight of the coroner system and more consistent record keeping between 1580 and 1620 were responsible for a large proportion of the seeming increase in homicides. This greater oversight has given historians a false and distorted impression of the level of lethal violence in the late sixteenth and early seventeenth centuries, as well as an inaccurate impression of the significance of the seventeenth-century decline. While homicide may have been declining over the course of the early modern period, it seems clear that the magnitude of this decline has been masked by a failure to recognize that more rigorous oversight of the coroner system between 1580 and 1620 resulted in better detection of homicide and more evidence of homicides being recorded and registered at the assize and King's Bench. Thus, rather than being a particularly violent and crime-ridden era, the late sixteenth and early seventeenth centuries in fact represented a zenith of early modern governance and criminal justice.

Instead of a period of crisis and violence, the years between 1530 and 1640 marked the growth of the monopolization of violence when, for the first time, the English state began to effectively regulate the violence of nonstate actors. This new control over violence was accomplished in an amateur society, with relatively few formal institutions, by means of a centralized adjudication of private economic interests. When this centralization was challenged in the mid-seventeenth century, oversight shifted to the localities and to regional representatives of state authority. This shift, as we will see, did not fatally weaken the state monopoly of violence. Instead, a new system of oversight was created that again pitted local, individual economic interests against each other in the name of regulation. Decentralization did not mean a decline in state power over violence, but merely a reorganization of the means of control.

Legislation, Incentivization, and a New System of Oversight

FROM THE MIDDLE DECADES OF THE seventeenth century, the primary responsibility for the oversight of the coroner system devolved back to the counties and localities. As in the Middle Ages, the justices of the peace and assize judges—sitting at quarter sessions, assize, and often more informally—bore the brunt of the supervisory role. As we have seen, this shift in the locus of oversight did not necessarily entail a decline in the efficacy of surveillance. It is likewise important to remember that justices and judges were centrally appointed officers whose primary responsibility was to enforce the laws as dictated by the center. The decline in central court litigation was therefore not simply a matter of decentralization, but of shifting the focus of oversight from one aspect of central control to another. However, as the reorientation of supervision did lead to a decline in the number and quality of records created and centrally stored and reviewed, it is difficult to make more than an approximate judgment of the quality of oversight in the years between the mid-seventeenth century and the mid-eighteenth century. The relative haze of this century, however, would be lifted in the years after 1752, when new legislation once again provided the financial incentives necessary to spark coroners, communities, and central authorities to hold inquests, create records, and scrutinize both. As a result, this legislation ushered in a new era of oversight that was more robust, responsive, and effective than the informal system that had prevailed in the preceding century.

This chapter will demonstrate that this creation of a new system of surveillance was the direct result of the decision in 1752 to restructure the manner in which coroners were compensated for their labor. As we saw in Chapter 2, in this year legislation was enacted that allowed coroners to be paid per inquest and per mile traveled instead of simply for inquests that led to indictments for homicide. The effect this change in the nature of payment had on the method and nature of oversight will be the central concern of this chapter. I will argue that this seemingly simple change led to a reinvigoration of central oversight. As in the sixteenth and early seventeenth centuries, this new system of oversight was the result of competing financial interests and incentives on the part of coroners, communities, and central authorities. In the wake of attacks on the perceived instruments of arbitrary power — the prerogative courts in Westminster — a new system of oversight was created that once again made up for the deficit of formal institutions by leveraging the power of self-interest.

On the surface, the change in remuneration may seem a straightforward, logical reform of an outdated system, a fix that had been a long time coming. However, such a reformulation meant that the wholly amateur nature of the office of coroner was perhaps compromised in the eyes of contemporaries — not a consideration to be taken lightly. It would take the immense pressure of a perceived crisis of order in the middle of the eighteenth century to eventually create the impetus for reforming the coroner system. An examination of the details of this crisis, debates over solutions, and the government's response is another aim of this chapter. I will show that the perceived crisis of violence of the mid-eighteenth century led to debates and discussions about ways to prevent and deter crime, which in turn led to a series of legal reforms that fundamentally changed the criminal justice system of England. The reform of the coroner system is perhaps the most overlooked of the midcentury reforms, but its importance for the history crime and policing was profound. The Coroner Act of 1752 provided both incentives to spur the nation's coroners to greater action and new opportunities for oversight of the coroner system. This new era of oversight reversed the trends of the previous century and established a level of efficiency and accountability not seen since the early seventeenth century.

An Eighteenth-Century Crisis of Order

The Treaty of Aix-la-Chapelle, which put an end to the War of Austrian Succession, may have brought some measure of peace to the European stage, but the domestic tranquility of England was rudely shattered in its wake. The years following the cessation of hostilities in 1748 were characterized by contemporaries as an era of rising violence, crime, and disorder, a period of chaos and mob rule. There is some debate among historians as to whether the mid-eighteenth-century crime wave was more perception than reality. However, the consensus now seems to be that the years between 1748 and 1753 did in fact witness a dramatic surge of crime, violence, and disorder that reverberated in the echo chamber that was the popular press and in the corridors of power in Parliament.[1]

Historians may quibble, but contemporaries were in no doubt that they lived in especially dire times. In his treatise *An Enquiry into the Causes of the Late Increase of Robbers,* the writer and magistrate Henry Fielding made manifest the concerns of the propertied classes about levels of crime when he stated that "I make no doubt, but that the Roads . . . will shortly be Impassable without the utmost hazard; nor are we threatened with seeing less dangerous gangs among us, than those which the Italians call Banditi."[2] For Fielding "the great increase of robberies within these few years" was real enough and "an evil" that deserved "some attention" from the government.[3]

Fielding was not simply an alarmist, nor was he alone in perceiving an increase in crime and violence in the years after 1748. In 1750, the *Whitehall Evening Post* complained that "the streets of this city [London], and the suburbs thereof are greatly infested with a Number of Villains confederating in small companies to rob, and on the smallest Opposition, to maim and murder the passengers."[4] Newspapers, especially in London, the acknowledged epicenter of the crisis, reported on crime with increasing regularity in the five years after 1748, reflecting the level of popular concern about disorder.[5] Fears of violence and crime were enough to make Horace Walpole lament in 1750 that "robbing is the only thing that goes on with any vivacity."[6]

The available criminal records for the mid-eighteenth century paint much the same picture as that so stridently portrayed by the popular press and contemporary chroniclers. In London, the records of the city's primary criminal court, the Old Bailey, indicate that the total number of offenses grew rapidly in 1748 and continued to remain at a high level until the mid-1750s. The number of indictments for theft rose by over 30 percent from 1747 to 1748, and the number of violent thefts rose by an incredible 350 percent in the years between 1749 and 1751.[7] The general increase in crime hit Surrey as well, with indictments for felonies against property reaching a peak in 1751.[8]

Both the criminal records and the contemporary literature seem to agree that there was in fact a significant rise in crime and violence in the years after 1748. The causes of this crime wave are complicated and not completely clear, but it has been suggested by both modern historians and eighteenth-century commentators that the blame for the emergent disorder could be placed squarely on the shoulders of the men coming home from war after the Peace of Aix-la-Chapelle. According to Nicholas Rogers, "the demobilization of some 80,000 soldiers and sailors, most of them in their twenties and most of them unable to find work, sparked a rise in property crime and particularly robberies that carried with them the threat of violence."[9] Men trained to fight, survive, and little else, soldiers and sailors returned to England without employment or the means of getting it. Often these men were still awaiting back pay from the government, and as such had little to live on and little incentive to leave London.

Perhaps unsurprisingly, these men, familiar as they were with weapons, violence, and plundering, turned to crime with alarming frequency.[10] The dangers of demobilization were not lost on contemporaries. The *Gentleman's Magazine,* for instance, recognized that "the approach of peace has raised not only compassion, but terror in many private gentlemen . . . who consider well the consequences of discharging so many men from their occupations in the army, the fleet and the yards for building and repairing the navy. As half of these poor men will not be able to get employment there is great, and just apprehension, that necessity will compel them to seize by violence what they can see no method to obtain by honest labour."[11] The mass demobilizations of the eighteenth century were of a much greater order of magnitude than those of the late sixteenth century discussed in Chapter 7. Hence, it is more likely that demobilization contributed to a spike in crime in the 1740s and 1750s than in the earlier period. In any case, any crime spike caused by demobilization would have been short in duration and thus not likely to cause such a long-term crisis as that which occurred in the years between 1580 and 1620.

The Murder Act of 1752

Faced with what appeared to be an epidemic of crime and violence, as well as cries from all corners to take action to address the disorder, Parliament finally acted in 1751 by creating a committee charged with providing recommendations for solving the crisis. The task of the House of Commons Committee on the Criminal Laws was to "revise and consider the laws in being, which relate to felonies, and other offences against the peace; and to report their opinion thereupon from time to time, to the House, as to the defects, the repeal, or amendment of the said laws."[12] The expansive remit given the committee was unusual in a period when most revisions of the law were considered on an ad hoc basis rather than holistically, a sign of the level of concern created by the post-1748 crime wave.[13]

The committee consisted of members who represented the pinnacle of power as well as the interests of London, which was seen as the epicenter of the crime crisis. Included among the committee members were all the members of Parliament representing London, Surrey, and Middlesex, as well as Henry Fox, William Pitt, and the prime minister himself, Henry Pelham. The committee considered numerous matters relating to crime, including methods of encouraging prosecutions and ways of controlling a population that was increasingly seen as a threat to law and order.[14]

Contemporary social commentators did not hesitate to provide their own suggestions and solutions. Primary among the concerns of the commentators was the belief that the punishments stipulated by the law were no longer sufficient to cow potential criminals into submission. They looked at the bacchanalian nature of public executions at Tyburn and elsewhere—and the cavalier attitude adopted by the condemned—and concluded that the law had become impotent in the face of an ever more callous criminal class. Some worried that executions failed to inspire fear or awe, but instead "accustom the populace to look on violent death with indifference, and instead of rendering the punishment terrible, insensibly render it familiar."[15]

The committee made a number of recommendations and introduced bills that addressed such themes as disorderly public houses and the punishment of some felons with imprisonment and hard labor rather than execution.[16] Perhaps most famously, in February 1752 Parliament passed into law the so-called Murder Act of 1752.[17] The "Act for the better preventing the horrid crime of Murder" followed the suggestions made by many in the period and mandated that the bodies of murderers were to be given to surgeons for the purpose of dissection, a punishment that the populace in general seemed to dread. Furthermore, the act stipulated that the punishment was to be meted out within two days of the sentence being passed. The intended effect of these new regulations was to "impress a just horror in the mind of the offender, and on the mind of such as shall be present, of the heinous crime of murder."[18]

Historians have long characterized the legal reforms of 1752 as a failure, a desperate act by desperate men. Although fear of dissection was common, and riots often broke out when surgeons attempted to claim the corpses that belonged to them by law, the new, swifter punishments for murder seem to have had little impact on the incidence of crime. If the Murder Act was indeed an act of desperation, doomed to fail, other pieces of legislation enacted in 1752 had a significant impact on the way violence was dealt with by the criminal justice system. In fact, a seemingly simple act that merely reorganized the system of payment for coroners was to have momentous consequences for the investigation of violence in England.

Coroner Legislation of 1752

Lost in the plethora of legal reforms enacted in the 1750s was a piece of legislation entitled "An Act for the Better Ordering of the Office of Coroner."[19] First introduced into Parliament as a bill in 1749, this legislation sought to reform the payment system for the office of coroner in hopes of incentivizing those officers into greater action. Although this legislation is often overlooked in discussions of mid-eighteenth-century legal reform, likely because it seems unrelated to the punishment-centered reforms of the more famous Murder Act, the Coroner Act is in fact inseparable from the other reform legislation. Like the Murder Act, the Coroner Act was a direct result of the context of the 1750s. Contemporaries feared that crime and violence were rampant and insisted that steps be taken to rein in the disorder. This seems odd given that if concerns about violence and murder were to be addressed, the office of coroner was perhaps the most significant tool of law enforcement.

As discussed in Chapter 2, from 1487 to 1752 the coroner was eligible to receive a fee of 13s 4d only in cases that led to a verdict of homicide.[20] In cases other than homicide, the coroner received no fee. Because the vast majority of violent deaths in the early modern world were the result of suicide, natural causes, and especially accident, the coroner was rarely eligible for compensation and most of his work went unremunerated. When inflation is factored in, coroners operating in the seventeenth and eighteenth centuries were even less well compensated. Considering the substantial outlay of time and the expense of travel to and from the inquest site, service as coroner was clearly not a money-making venture, and coroners were unlikely to break even. Still, the position of coroner was eagerly sought and elections contested, but the lack of payment meant that those who aspired to the office must have had a significant private income.[21]

This all changed with the reforms of 1752. This legislation, which went into effect on June 24, mandated that coroners were henceforth to be paid £1 for every inquest they held, in addition to the 13s 4d they were allowed in cases of homicide. In recognition of the significant distances traveled by coroners in the course of their duties, the act also stipulated that coroners were to be reimbursed 9d for every mile traveled between their usual place of residence and the site of the inquest. These new fees were to be paid out of the county tax revenue at quarter sessions by order of the justices of the peace. There were, however, some exceptions to the new legislation. Inquests held on the bodies of those who died in jail were exempt, and the fees were further restricted to inquests held in areas that contributed to the county rate. This meant that coroners operating in boroughs were not eligible to receive the new fees and continued to be reimbursed on the basis of arrangements particular to the borough in question.[22] This new system of payment remained unchanged until 1835, when the system of payment for the counties was extended to include boroughs.[23] The fees instituted in 1752 then remained in place until 1861, when coroners were at last given a salary.[24]

The 1752 reforms were designed to perform two primary functions: the elimination of corruption and inducement to action. In terms of corruption, there had long been concerns that as unsalaried amateurs, coroners were, like most unpaid officeholders of the day, susceptible to corruption. The level of corruption should not be overstated, and the coroner was certainly no more likely to stray than other officers, but complaints about corruption, especially in the late seventeenth and early eighteenth centuries, certainly existed. The erosion of the supervision provided by the central courts likely resulted in a growth in accusations of corruption and lassitude. For example, on November 4, 1734, it was brought to the attention of Adam Williamson, lieutenant general of the Tower of London, that a body had been found in the Tower ditch. The coroner was called and the inquest revealed that the deceased was "a man whose name was Noel from the West Indies" who "being a lunatic drowned himself in the Tower ditch."[25] Under pre-1752 law, as the death was ruled to be a suicide, the coroner was not eligible to receive a fee. The coroner, however, was either ignorant of the law or ignored it and "insisted on a fee of 13s 4d," the standard fee in cases of homicide.[26] Despite the law, the coroner was given his fee, "but a prosecution being intended against him on the stat. I of H 8 [1 Henry 8, c. 7], he returned the money, and promised to insist on his fee when the Person came by his Death without Murder no more."[27] In this case, the threat of litigation forced the coroner to give up his ill-gotten fee, but there are more examples of the potentially corrupting nature of the pre-1752 system of remuneration.

A little over a decade earlier, the diarist John Cannon would confront the potentially corrupting nature of unpaid officeholding when he considered standing for coroner of Somerset in 1723. After deciding to run for the post after the death of Joshua Beach, one of the previous county coroners, Cannon spent two weeks canvassing for votes and gauging local opinion.

During this time he sought the help of a number of influential local figures, including Thomas Uphill of Stone. Uphill promised to use his influence in Cannon's favor, but he offered some advice about the dangers of the office as well. According to Cannon, Uphill pledged his support for Cannon's candidacy, "but at the same time desired me to decline the office for a particular reason viz. that he thought me of honest family and well knowing my father and relations, and that he feared that should I obtain the post I sought after I would degenerate and fall from my primitive original."[28]

At first glance, Uphill's warning may seem to suggest that he thought the position of coroner was beneath Cannon given his family's position and status. However, Cannon records that Uphill's hesitancy about the office was instead the result of previous experiences with coroners' elections. At an earlier election for coroner of Somerset, Uphill had backed the candidacy of an upstanding lawyer by the name of Querce. Despite his past honesty and good character, however, once in office as coroner Querce became "a notorious villain."[29] It was not that Uphill doubted the prestige of the office or that men of status and character sought the position, but rather that he had experienced its potential to corrupt. The formally respectable Mr. Querce had become a villain after gaining the office, and Uphill feared that the same fate "will be your case when obtained."[30]

Cannon persevered in his quest for the coronership notwithstanding Uphill's warning, only withdrawing when support for his candidacy was found wanting. This episode, however, aptly illustrates the concern that many people in the period had over corruption. The story of the honest man who became a villain once in office—and the use of the words "honest" and 'villain" in particular—suggest that the problem with office-holding was not that the office of coroner attracted men predisposed to impropriety, but that it turned good men bad. As monetary irregularities were the only real outlet for coronial corruption, it seems safe to assume that the reason for Querce's fall from grace, and thus Cannon's potential fate, was greed for payments, bribes, or fees to which the coroner had no legitimate claim.

Again, the level of corruption should not be overstated, and in the sixteenth and early seventeenth centuries much of the attempted corruption

was effectively monitored and punished by the central courts. Real or perceived, complaints about corrupt officeholders were not limited to coroners. It could even be said that the late seventeenth and early eighteenth
centuries constituted a general crisis of officeholding corruption, at least in
the popular imagination. The preamble to the bill aptly describes popular
attitudes toward coroners in the mid-eighteenth century. According to the
bill, of late "many Abuses have been suffered and done by them [coroners],
as well to the injury of His Majesty, as to his Liege Subjects, owing to the
ignorance of such coroners."[31] As the bill suggests, it was thought that one
reason for this negligent behavior was the lack of payment for coroners,
which led to a situation in which "many Crimes have never been inquired
into at all; and Coroners have, under pretence of Fees very often wrongfully
taken diverse Sums of Money for their own use."[32]

In addition to allaying fears of corruption, the 1752 reform sought to
spur coroners to greater action. It had long been recognized that the office
of the coroner was the key to increasing the efficiency of criminal investigations into sudden or violent deaths. In 1700, in his *Essay Concerning
Self-Murther,* John Adams had argued that the outcome of a coroner's inquest "depends very much upon the coroner, and tis his fault chiefly if the
laws which provide against self-murther are eluded."[33] Although Adams
was specifically addressing the issue of suicide, his claim for the central
responsibility of the coroner holds for other forms of violent death. If the
coroner was seen to be the figure of central importance in the detection of
violent death, ensuring that the coroner was motivated to act was critical to
the success of the criminal justice system.

The need to prod coroners into fulfilling their duties was reinforced
by complaints of inaction on their part. For instance, in 1693 a coroner's
jury in Cheshire complained that while the coroner had summoned them
to hold an inquest, on the day they were to meet the coroner failed to arrive. When the coroner failed to appear at a second scheduled meeting, the
jurors came to a verdict on their own.[34] Such concrete examples of coronial
neglect are few and far between, even in the lax regulatory years of the late
seventeenth and early eighteenth centuries, but they were frequent enough
that when combined with fears over a general rise in violence in the mid-

eighteenth century, such complaints helped convince those in power that reforms were needed.

It must be stressed once again that the records do not allow a definitive answer to the question of whether coroners and other officials were more corrupt in the late seventeenth and early eighteenth centuries than in the centuries preceding this period.[35] Certainly, fewer inquests were filed in King's Bench than in the sixteenth and early seventeenth centuries, but the mere fact of uneven record keeping does not necessarily entail a decline in standards. Instead, as I have argued, the low number of records may in fact simply signal a shift in the nature of oversight from formal to informal and the locus of oversight from the central courts to the counties and justices of the peace. It is clear, however, that both record keeping and central oversight of coroners did decline from the mid-seventeenth century, and it thus seems reasonable to conclude that without the robust central oversight that existed in the sixteenth and early seventeenth centuries, the standards of efficiency for coroners declined as well.

Whether or not the coroner had in fact become less efficient and more corrupt in the late seventeenth and early eighteenth centuries, by the mid-eighteenth century perceptions of growing corruption among officeholders in general had combined with fears over a midcentury explosion of crime and violence to provide the context in which reform seemed necessary. As a result of these concerns, in 1752 Parliament passed a series of acts to address the problems facing the nation. Although scholarly attention has focused on the Murder Act and the new punishments it mandated, the restructuring of the payment system for coroners had perhaps the greatest impact of any of the mid-eighteenth-century crime legislation. On the surface, the Coroner Act merely changed the system of payment for coroners, but however mundane this change might seem, the effects of the act were significant and long-lasting.

The Effects of Legislation or a New System of Oversight

The effects of the decision to pay coroners by mile and inquest rather than simply for cases that led to indictments for homicide were immediate and impressive. To fully understand the impact of the new system of payment, it is crucial to take a holistic view of coroners' records for a county both before and after 1752, as it at first appears that the change in method of remuneration had very little, if any, impact. When the number of inquests returned for East Sussex is tabulated, for instance, the raw data remains unimpressive. Overall, the county coroners of East Sussex held 31 extant inquests between 1689 and 1751, a paltry figure that averages out to about one inquest for every two years.[36] The number of extant inquests for East Sussex taken between 1752 and 1810—a period of roughly the same duration—is strikingly similar to the number for the period preceding 1752. Coroners undertook a total of 34 inquests between 1752 and 1810, almost exactly the same number for the earlier period (Table 2).[37]

A similar situation seems to have prevailed in Cheshire in the years before and after 1752. The records of the Court of Great Sessions, the principal court for the palatinate of Cheshire, indicate a fairly stable number of inquests throughout the eighteenth century. For instance, a total of 619 inquests were taken in the 50 years between 1701 and 1750, and 507 in the 50 years after 1750.[38] On the surface, at least, the inquest records of East Sussex and Cheshire seem to indicate that the reforms of 1752 had little impact on the output of coroners.

If we are to get an accurate picture of the impact of the reforms of 1752, however, we must look beyond coroners' inquests and examine a new type of record: the coroner's bill, an innovation that sprang directly from the legislation of 1752. The coroner's bill was a list of all the inquests undertaken by a coroner since the last quarter sessions. The bills included such information as the date, location, and subject of the inquest, the number of

Table 2. East Sussex Coroners' Inquests, 1689–1810

	Homicide	Suicide	Accident	Natural	Total
1689–1751	27	1	2	1	31
1752–1810	33	0	0	1	34

Source: *East Sussex Coroners' Records, 1688–1838.*

miles traveled, and the amount of money claimed by the coroner for each inquest, as well as a tally of the total fees due. The bills were submitted for review and approval to the justices of the peace at quarter sessions. Once approved, the fees owed to the coroner were to be paid out of the county rate.

When we compare the number of inquests taken in East Sussex before and after 1752 with the number of coroners' bills submitted after 1752, we get a fuller appreciation of the effects of the change in the system of remuneration. As we have seen, East Sussex coroners submitted just 31 inquests between 1689 and 1752, and 34 between 1752 and 1810. The number of coroners' bills submitted at quarter sessions, however, provides a clearer picture of the true number of inquests held after 1752. In the first ten years after the midcentury reforms alone, East Sussex coroners submitted bills representing a total of 112 inquests, almost four times the number of inquests submitted in the 60 years before or after 1752.[39] Thus, the information obtained from coroners' bills demonstrates that the number of *recorded* inquests (those listed in the records of the assize) were far lower than the number actually *held* (those listed in the coroners' bills).

The coroners' bills for Wiltshire suggest that the growth in known coroners' inquests that occurred after 1752 was not limited to East Sussex. In the first ten years after 1752, Wiltshire coroners submitted bills representing a massive 465 inquests.[40] Like Sussex, Wiltshire was divided into two jurisdictions, North and South, with one coroner operating in each district at any given time. As a point of comparison with East Sussex, South Wiltshire coroners tallied 128 inquests in their bills between 1752 and 1762, while North Wiltshire coroners tallied 344 inquests in the same period.[41] As we can see, the numbers for South Wiltshire and East Sussex are almost identical, suggesting a similar expansion of recorded inquests after 1752. North Wiltshire also seems to have witnessed significant expansion, but on a much larger scale; the North Wiltshire jurisdiction was both much larger than its southern counterpart and contained a greater number of areas of high population density, a fact that naturally resulted in a greater number of inquests in the North.[42] Despite the differences in absolute numbers of inquests created by the disparate geography and demography of various jurisdictions, it is clear that most areas experienced a growth in total inquests after 1752, at least when the evidence of coroners' bills is taken into account (Table 3).

The similarities between the East Sussex coroners' records made before and after 1752 are not, however, limited to the number of inquests. If we break down the inquests by verdict, the same pattern seems to prevail before and after 1752. In both periods, the overwhelming majority of inquests relate to various forms of homicide. Between 1689 and 1752, 27 of the 31 inquests (87 percent) involve homicide, with only two relating to accidental deaths (6 percent), and one each involving suicide and natural death (3 percent).[43] Once again, the breakdown is almost identical for the period 1752–1810. In these years, 33 of the 34 total inquests involved homicide (97 percent), while the only nonhomicide case involved a natural death (3 percent).[44] James Sharpe and J. R. Dickinson have likewise found that the number of accidental deaths in the Cheshire records of the eighteenth century have been underrecorded in relation to homicide, if not on anything like the same scale as occurred in Sussex.[45]

At first glance this pattern of inquest verdicts is rather surprising given what we know about inquests in the sixteenth and seventeenth centuries. The records from these centuries indicate that throughout the early modern period the number of accidental deaths, suicides, and natural deaths investigated by coroners far outweighed the number of homicides, often by a factor of ten to one or more. There are several possible explanations for the steady preponderance of homicide inquests in relation to other types of death between 1689 and 1810. There is the possibility that the paltry num-

Table 3. Coroners' Bills, 1752–1762

	Homicide	Suicide	Accident	Natural	Total
East Sussex	4 (3.5%)	30 (26.7%)	66 (58.9%)	12 (10.7%)	112
South Wiltshire	6 (4.6%)	14 (10.9%)	72 (56.2%)	29 (22.6%)	128*
North Wiltshire	26 (7.5%)	41 (11.9%)	187 (54.3%)	90 (26.1%)	344

* Seven of the 128 South Wiltshire inquests have unknown or unlisted verdicts.

Source: *East Sussex Coroners' Records*, 1–21; *Wiltshire Coroners' Bills*, 138–145.

ber of inquests relating to accident, suicide, and natural death in this period reflected a real decline in the number of people who died by these means. This hypothesis seems highly unlikely given that accidental deaths alone numbered in the hundreds in the sixteenth and early seventeenth centuries. There is no reason to suspect such a precipitous decline in accidental deaths, from hundreds in the sixteenth and early seventeenth centuries to a total of two between 1689 and 1810.[46]

The second possible explanation for the differential between homicide and other types of inquests is that because homicide inquests were the only cases for which coroners received payment before 1752, they generally only held inquests when the death seemed likely to lead to a homicide verdict. It is certainly possible that in the absence of both incentives to hold nonhomicide inquests and central oversight, coroners simply ceased holding inquests for which there was no monetary benefit.

The third possibility for the scarcity of nonhomicide inquests is that coroners simply failed to return inquests to the assizes and King's Bench other than those relating to homicide. If this was the case, it is not clear whether a decline in the practice of returning nonhomicide inquests to the assizes and King's Bench as the law required was the result of the coroners' lassitude or of the indifference of superior judicial officials.

The answer to this puzzle can be found in an examination of the verdicts recorded in coroners' bills after 1752, which demonstrates the hidden patterns of coroners' inquests in Sussex. While the inquest records for the periods 1689–1752 and 1752–1810 show a very high proportion of homicide verdicts, the coroners' bills of East Sussex provide a picture closer to what one would expect. In the ten years after 1752, East Sussex coroners' bills recorded 4 verdicts of homicide (3.5 percent), 30 suicide verdicts (26.7 percent), 66 verdicts of accidental death (58.9 percent), and 12 verdicts of natural death (10.7 percent).[47] These figures indicate that large numbers of nonhomicide inquests were in fact held in the years after 1752, but that these inquests were not submitted with regularity to either the assizes or King's Bench. Thus, while it is possible that in the pre-1752 period coroners failed to hold inquests relating to verdicts other than homicide, a much likelier explanation for the seemingly disproportionate number of homicides was, at least in part, a failure to submit the required documents.

Once again, the coroners' bills for Wiltshire back up the evidence gleaned from the East Sussex coroners' bills. Between 1752 and 1762, Wiltshire coroners' bills record a total of 32 homicide verdicts (7 percent), 55 suicide verdicts (11.8 percent), 259 verdicts of accidental death (55.6 percent), and 119 natural deaths (25.5 percent).[48] Although there is some variation in the proportions of various verdicts recorded in East Sussex and Wiltshire—East Sussex had a higher proportion of suicide verdicts and Wiltshire a higher proportion of natural deaths—in general, the figures for the two areas coincide. Of especial importance is the fact that East Sussex and Wiltshire had very similar proportions of homicide and nonhomicides verdicts. This suggests that the high proportion of homicide verdicts seen in the Sussex inquest records does not in fact reflect the actual verdict patterns. Instead, the numbers provided by the Sussex inquest records are an illusion created by a combination of lax central oversight and a failure to submit nonhomicide inquests to the proper repositories. These figures also demonstrate that while the oversight provided by the central courts may have diminished after the mid-seventeenth century, the invention of coroners' bills allowed a new locus for monitoring the office and work of the coroner.

Whether the preponderance of homicide inquests noted above was the result of coroners failing to hold inquests where they were unlikely to be eligible for a fee or simply failing to return nonhomicide inquests to the proper courts, the lack of nonhomicide inquests and the relatively low number of inquests overall could only be tolerated in an era in which oversight of the coroner system was weak. It is striking that both the total number of inquests and the breakdown of inquests by verdict for the years between 1689 and 1752 bear a remarkable similarity to those of the late fifteenth and early sixteenth centuries. For instance, between 1485 and 1530, nearly 62 percent of all Sussex inquests (46) related to homicide, while 13 percent related to suicide, 20 percent to accidental death, and 4 percent to death by natural causes.[49] Although the inquests for East Sussex in the late seventeenth and early eighteenth centuries are weighted even more toward homicide cases, the period between 1485 and 1530 witnessed a similar, if less extreme, preponderance of homicide verdicts.

It is important to note that the figures for the years before 1530 represent the known inquests for a period before the expansion of central oversight detailed in Chapter 5. The inquest figures for the years between 1689 and 1752, on the other hand, represent the known inquests for an era in which the central oversight of the sixteenth and early seventeenth centuries had gradually broken down. Thus, it seems reasonable to surmise that the lack of oversight of the coroner system in both periods—1485–1530 and 1689–1752—resulted in both a focus on inquests relating to homicide and fewer total inquests. Given what we know about actual patterns of death in the early modern world, this lack of oversight in the periods 1485–1530 and 1689–1752 seems to have led to similar levels of coronorial lassitude, or at least to similar failures in record keeping.

As with the periods of lax oversight, the years of robust oversight —1530–1620 and 1752–1810—also share common characteristics. While the proportion of homicide inquests had declined even further by the post-1752 period, the years between 1530 and 1620 and those after 1752 both saw greater proportions of nonhomicide inquests. North Wiltshire between 1752 and 1762 saw 7.5 percent of inquests relating to homicide, while 12 percent related to suicide, 54 percent to accident, and 26 percent to natural death. Similarly, between 1580 and 1620, Sussex saw 24.7 percent of inquests relating to homicide, 19 percent to suicide, 36 percent to accident, and 20 percent to natural death.[50] The figures are not exactly the same, but both periods—1530–1620 and the years after 1752—saw similar proportional declines in homicide verdicts and proportional increases in inquests resulting in verdicts of accidental death and natural death. These similarities suggest that the higher number and greater diversity of inquests in these periods were a result of the more rigorous oversight that prevailed. It seems safe to say, then, that the periods roughly between 1485 and 1530 and between 1640 and 1752 were characterized by lax oversight and poor record-keeping practices, while those periods between 1530 and 1640 and between 1752 and 1810 witnessed robust oversight and better record keeping.

The strong oversight of these periods was no accident. In both periods conscious government action created systems that incentivized the
supervision of lethal violence. In an age before widespread bureaucratic
institutions, the fostering of private, competing economic interest served
as a means of regulating the coroner system on the cheap. The systems
produced by these policies were surprisingly effective and had a dramatic
impact on both the operation of the coroner and the creation and keeping
of legal records. With new incentives to act and to record, late eighteenth-
century coroners went to great lengths to perform their duties: investigating and recording suspicious death.

Distances Traveled after 1752

Not only were coroners holding more inquests relating to a wider variety of
types of death after 1752 than before, but they were also traveling significant
distances to do so. For instance, between May and September 1753 John
Clare, one of the county coroners for North Wiltshire, held 11 separate inquests. With the perhaps painful exception of the inquest of Joseph Green,
who died when he accidentally fell into a well in the coroner's hometown
of Devizes, Clare was required to travel a substantial amount in discharging his office. On May 9 Clare traveled 25 miles from Devizes to South
Marston to investigate the drowning of Margaret Wells. Two days later, he
journeyed 20 miles to Brinkworth to examine the body of William Selman
before turning around the next day and traveling 15 miles to Norton Bavant,
where William Feltham had been crushed by a mill wheel.[51]

Between May and September our weary coroner traveled distances
of as little as three miles and as much as 30 miles in order to hold inquests,
often staying on the road for several days in succession. In total John Clare
traveled 187 miles in five months and averaged 17 miles per inquest.[52] Over
the first three years of his career, this Wiltshire coroner traveled an impressive total of 1,354 miles in the pursuit of 106 separate inquests, an average of
nearly 13 miles per inquest.[53]

John Clare was clearly committed to his office, but the distances
he traveled were not at all unusual for mid-eighteenth-century coroners.

Thomas Attree, coroner for East Sussex, for example, traveled distances of 14, 24, 13, 8, 5, and 12 miles between October 1756 and June 1757, a total of 76 miles, or an average of nearly 13 miles per inquest.[54] Although the average distance traveled by Attree was slightly less than that of Clare, it must be remembered that Sussex's coroners were divided into two districts, East and West, and numerous liberties and boroughs. This subdivision meant that Attree was likely operating in a smaller geographical jurisdiction than Clare was in North Wiltshire, which while a division of Wiltshire, was much larger than East Sussex. It is surely true that the amount of ground covered by an individual coroner differed with the size of his jurisdiction, and the time invested in travel was likely affected by the time of year and the difficulty of the terrain. Even so, the distances traveled by the average county coroner were substantial and the investment in time significant (Table 4).

Obviously, the distances traveled by any coroner were a direct reflection of the size of his jurisdiction as well as the location of his place of residence within the county. Hence it is difficult to make a simple comparison between the distances traveled by various coroners. However, Table 4 shows that coroners of various jurisdictions were regularly making trips of quite significant distances to hold inquests. Furthermore, there are no clear patterns to the data, suggesting that the mileages reflect the distances actually traveled and not the coroners' travel preferences. That is to say, a breakdown of the miles traveled per inquest does not support the contention that coroners generally held more inquests closer to their places of residence—a sign of laziness, lack of commitment, or poor communication. Nor does

Table 4. Distances Traveled by Coroners to Sites of Inquests, 1752–1762

	0–5 Miles	6–10 Miles	11–19 Miles	20 or More Miles
East Sussex	16 (15%)	27 (26%)	54 (51%)	8 (8%)
South Wiltshire	48 (35%)	48 (35%)	27 (21%)	4 (3%)
North Wiltshire	60 (17%)	69 (20%)	142 (41%)	78 (22%)

Source: *East Sussex Coroners' Records*, 1–21; *Wiltshire Coroners' Bills*, 138–145.

the data support the argument that coroners either preferred to travel longer distances, or at least claimed to in their bills, as a method of obtaining greater reimbursement from the quarter sessions. Instead, the numbers suggest that coroners simply traveled whatever distance was required to hold actual inquests rather than favoring cases near to home or far away.

Although the lack of coroners' bills for the years before 1752 makes it difficult to calculate the miles traveled by coroners in the sixteenth and seventeenth centuries, a comparison between the distances traveled by coroners before and after 1752 will help create a clearer picture of coroner travel patterns. Between 1689 and 1736, 61 percent of inquests held were within ten miles of the coroner's residence, and on only two occasions did East Sussex coroners make journeys of 20 miles or more.[55] These percentages are not too far off those for the post-1752 period, and given the small size of most jurisdictions it would be dangerous to make too much of the differences between the pre- and post-1752 periods. However, it does seem that before the reforms of 1752 East Sussex coroners were less likely to travel more than 15 miles to hold an inquest.

One of the characteristic criticisms of the early modern coroner was that he was less likely to hold inquests in remote locations or "off the beaten track."[56] Obviously, it stands to reason that remote areas with smaller populations would have produced fewer violent deaths and thus fewer inquests; however, any claim that coroners were unwilling or less willing to hold inquests in distant locations is not borne out by the evidence.[57] The period before the introduction of coroners' bills in 1752 is more difficult to measure, but certainly after 1752 there is no reason to suspect that coroners favored inquests closer to home. The evidence of North Wiltshire alone demonstrates that coroners for that jurisdiction traveled over 20 miles to hold inquests on 78 separate occasions in the ten years after 1752. That these coroners traveled such distances for nearly a quarter of their inquests suggests that any reluctance to hold such remote inquests had disappeared in the wake of the 1752 reforms.

R. F. Hunnisett has further suggested that there was plenty of corruption to be found in the coroners' bills of the mid- and late eighteenth century, or at the very least that individual coroners "successfully manipulated

the statute 25 George 2, c. 29 to their financial advantage."[58] This financial malpractice could involve claiming longer journeys than were actually
made, claiming multiple journeys when several inquests were held in the
same place, and requesting reimbursement for travel that did not result in
an inquest, all of which was technically illegal.[59] Corruption and financial
manipulation most certainly occurred, and it is nearly impossible to know
which bills and inquests, or how many, involved such practices. However,
a closer look at the distances claimed in the Wiltshire coroners' bills reveals
patterns that suggest corruption was limited.

If the legislation of 1752 had created a system of widespread corruption, with coroners regularly submitting inaccurate bills in an attempt to
gain extra remuneration for extra miles traveled, we would expect that the
distances given in the coroners' bills would be weighted toward inquests
held at significant distances from the coroners' places of residence. Coroners did regularly claim to have traveled 20 or 30 miles. However, the
distribution of distances claimed is impressively even between short and
long journeys. If we assume that sudden, violent deaths were rather ran-
domly spread throughout a given county, we would expect to see relatively
even numbers of inquests taken near and far from the coroners' place of
residence.[60] This relatively even distribution is exactly what we see in the
East Sussex and Wiltshire coroners' bills.[61] Even if coroners did occasionally cook the books, safeguards were put in place to limit the possibility of
corruption.

As we will see below, after the coroners' bills had been registered at
quarter sessions, the justices tasked with reviewing the documents and
granting payment often altered bills in order to correct the number of miles
recorded by the coroner, and thus the money claimed. To take the example
of John Clare once again, at the quarter sessions of April 1754, six of the
entries for the coroner's 16 total inquests were altered by the court to reflect the true number of miles. The small difference in the numbers of miles
between the coroner's claim and the corrected bill suggests that in John
Clare's case, the change was likely to have been to correct errors rather than
intentional acts of corruption. In all, the justices reduced the number of
miles Clare could claim by just 13 (out of 185), and as a result the amount of

money he was entitled to by 9s 9d.[62] As this example illustrates, the justices of the peace sitting at quarter sessions were not content to simply accept the coroner's word when it came to counting miles traveled and money due. Instead, the justices were fairly regular in their altering of coroners' bills in order to rein in the mistakes or excesses of the coroners' claims. Thus, while corruption and manipulation were certainly a fact of early modern officeholding, such practices do not seem to have been particularly rife in the context of coroners' bills.

Remuneration after 1752

The reason for the growth in reported inquests after 1752 and the concomitant expansion of nonhomicide inquests seems clear. Given the expansion of inquests and the distances traveled noted in coroners' bills for East Sussex and Wiltshire, the most obvious explanation for the renewed vigor of England's coroners was that, for the first time in English history, coroners were being paid for every inquest they held, regardless of the verdict. The impact of the new system of remuneration is not surprising. The amount of money coroners could earn after 1752 was impressive, especially when compared to the amount of money they received in the sixteenth and seventeenth centuries. As we have seen, William Playfere, one of the most active and longest-serving coroners in sixteenth-century Sussex, earned a total of a little over £9 over the course of roughly 30 years in office, an average of only about 6s per year. Playfere held a total of 127 inquests, and thus he earned about 1s 6d per inquest on average.[63]

The prospects for financial compensation did not improve by the end of the seventeenth century. John Neville, another conscientious coroner with many years of service, this time in Lincolnshire, received only £5 5s 8d for his services in the late seventeenth century, during which time he held 42 inquests.[64] When one compares this paltry sum with those made by coroners after the legislation of 1752, the difference wrought in the life of the coroner becomes clear. For instance, John Clare, who served as one of the county coroners for Wiltshire between 1752 and 1771, made a grand total of £972 4s 5d over the course of his career, or about £51 per year. In

19 years as coroner, Clare held 687 inquests grouped into 29 separate bills. Thus, on average, he made nearly £34 per bill, or about £1.5 per inquest.[65]

The comparison between the money earned by John Clare and John Neville or William Playfere is astounding, and yet the sums Clare received were not at all unusual for the years after 1752. In the 25 years after the reform of the payment structure, North Wiltshire coroners earned a total of £1,547 16s 11d, or approximately £62 per year. Between 1752 and 1777, Wiltshire coroners held 1,071 inquests grouped into 43 bills submitted to quarter sessions. On average, then, they earned about £36 per bill and somewhere in the neighborhood of £1.45 per inquest, figures that largely tally with those earned by John Clare.[66]

East Sussex coroners made a bit less than their North Wiltshire counterparts, but this is largely explained by the fact that they held slightly fewer inquests and traveled shorter distances on average, a result of the fractured nature of Sussex coroner jurisdictions. Between 1752 and 1762, East Sussex coroners submitted 16 bills to quarter sessions and earned a total of £150 3s 9d, or an average of a little over £9 per bill.[67] On a per year basis, East Sussex coroners could expect to receive about £15 for their work, not an insignificant sum.

Coroners for East Sussex may have made less than coroners for North Wiltshire, but their figures largely match those for the coroners of South Wiltshire. In the same ten-year period after 1752, South Wiltshire coroners submitted ten bills claiming £169 7s 3d.[68] On average, then, South Wiltshire coroners earned about £17 per year and per bill, an amount very close to that earned in East Sussex. As with distances traveled, the amount of money earned by a coroner was greatly circumscribed by the size of his jurisdiction both geographically (because coroners earned money for every mile traveled) and demographically (because a greater number of people meant a greater number of deaths and inquests). Although somewhat restricted, the amounts coroners made after 1752 dwarfed those earned by coroners in the sixteenth and seventeenth centuries.

The Wiltshire bills fluctuate from a low of £16 to a high of £61. However, it is interesting to note that the amounts granted vary from bill to bill rather than rising or falling steadily over the course of the period.[69]

A growth in the amounts claimed might result from a growth in corruption or a relaxation of oversight, but no such rise in claims existed. This suggests that the amounts claimed by Wiltshire coroners largely followed random fluctuations in the number of deaths and distances traveled, as one would expect if corruption was minimal and the law largely followed. If the amounts of money claimed by coroners after 1752 did indeed follow the natural rhythm of deaths, the responsibility for the Wiltshire coroners' seeming probity largely lies with the justices of the peace who reviewed the coroners' bills at quarter sessions. The justices apparently took this task seriously, as they altered or revised an impressive 10 percent of all bills submitted between 1752 and 1777. The majority of these alterations, some 80 percent, involved a downward revision of the sum claimed by the coroner.[70] This is not to suggest that corruption was widespread, but rather to demonstrate that inaccuracies in coroners' claims were caught and changed regardless of whether they resulted from errors or intention.

For example, at the Devizes Quarter Sessions of April 24, 1759, John Clare submitted a bill claiming £28 4s 3d as recompense for the 20 inquests he had held since November 7, 1758. In their examination of the bill, however, the justices, John Jacob and E. Goddard, challenged the accuracy of two of Clare's items relating to one inquest each. In December 1758 Clare claimed to have traveled 16 miles from Devizes to Lyneham to examine the corpse of Thomas Norris, who had fallen into a ditch and drowned. The justices did not challenge the existence of the inquest or the veracity of the verdict, but they did alter the bill to reflect the fact that Lyneham was 15 miles from Devizes, not 16. As a result, they also altered the per mile compensation Clare was eligible to receive for the inquest from £1 12s to £1 11s 3d.[71] In a similar manner, the justices also revised Clare's mileage claim for the inquest held to view the body of Philip Hayward at Leigh in April 1753, reducing the miles traveled from 13 to 12, with a corresponding reduction in fee of 9d.[72] As a result of these alterations, the justices revised the total amount of money due to John Clare from £28 4s 3d to £28 2s 9d.[73]

Not all alterations came at the expense of the coroner. Twenty percent of alterations actually revised the sum due to the coroner upward because the coroner had failed to claim enough money in his bill.[74] At the

April 1766 Devizes Quarter Sessions, the oversight provided by the justices worked in John Clare's favor. Clare had submitted a bill for £22 13s 9d to Edward Bayntun and Edward Poore, the justices responsible for examining the coroners' bills. Bayntun and Poore found one defect with Clare's bill: Clare recorded that he had traveled 27 miles from Devizes to Oaksey to examine the body of a John Reynolds in January 1766. He claimed £2 for the inquest, but Oaksey must have been further from Devizes than Clare calculated, as the bill was altered to grant Clare £2 3s for the inquest. As a result, the total bill was increased from £22 13s 9d to £22 14s before being approved by Bayntun and Poore.[75]

The temptation to submit false or inaccurate bills must have been greater after the reforms of 1752. However, the substantial percentage of altered bills leads one to conclude that many, perhaps most, false or corrupt bills did not go without challenge. Such contestation of coroners' claims demonstrates that while the potential money to be made after 1752 likely motivated coroners to greater action, the potential for corruption that such sums might have inspired was largely tempered by the oversight provided by the justice of the peace at quarter sessions. Some financial corruption likely continued to exist throughout the period, but there is no evidence that it was widespread or that it negatively affected the operation of the coroner system. Minor errors of accounting were much more frequent than actual corruption, but both types of inaccuracy were rigorously monitored by the authorities. If the financial rewards on offer after 1752 did indeed spur the country's coroners to greater action, then a little bit of overbilling was a small price to pay for efficiency.

The mere fact of payment, however, does not explain all the changes wrought by the 1752 reforms. The manner of payment also had a substantial impact in the way coroners performed their duties. The 1752 legislation allowed coroners to receive a set fee for every inquest they held regardless of verdict, a clear inducement to hold more inquests in general and a greater variety of inquests in particular. The midcentury reforms also mandated that coroners receive a fee for every mile traveled to and from an inquest; this grant was designed as reimbursement for the cost of travel incurred by a coroner rather than simply as a reward. Paying a per mile reimbursement had two primary effects. First of all, it was meant to spur coroners to hold inquests regardless of how near or far away the death occurred. In this the legislation largely succeeded, as we have seen in the long distances traveled by coroners after 1752. Second, the reimbursement increased the opportunities for oversight by forcing coroners to submit bills at quarter sessions not only to receive a financial reward, but also to be reimbursed for the expenses they had already incurred. A relatively wealthy coroner may not have gone to the trouble of submitting a bill to receive his per inquest fee, but few would have neglected to recover the sums they had already spent out of pocket in traveling to and from the inquest site. Thus, it was the combination of per inquest payment and per mile reimbursement that provided the incentive both to hold more inquests and to submit bills with greater regularity. This practice ensured that a greater proportion of violent deaths were investigated while providing new records, the scrutiny of which allowed for an increased level of oversight.

The greater financial rewards available to coroners after 1752 may also have led to a growth in the length of time the average coroner spent in office. As we saw in Chapter 2, Sussex county coroners in the reign of Elizabeth held office for an average of about seven and a half years. By the second half of the eighteenth century, county coroners remained in office for more extended periods. William Clare, coroner for North Wiltshire, served as coroner for 25 years between his father's retirement in 1771 and 1796. Similarly, Alexander Forsyth held the position of coroner of South Wiltshire for 27 years, from 1768 to 1795.[76] William Wheeler, who like William Clare followed his father as coroner, operated as county coroner for East Sussex for 24 years between 1785 and 1809.[77] In all, the coroners for North and South Wiltshire and East Sussex who served between 1752 and 1796 held the position of coroner for an average if 20 years, almost three times the average time served by Sussex coroners between 1558 and 1603.

The most obvious explanation for the disparity in average length of service between Elizabethan coroners and their mid- to late eighteenth-century counterparts is that after 1752 coroners were paid substantial sums for the performance of the office. Given that they were only eligible to receive payment in cases of homicide and that they had to pay their own travel expenses, most coroners likely lost money as a result of their service before 1752. The only explanation for the significant lengths of time that pre-1752 coroners spent in office and the fact that elections were hotly contested even before the reform of the payment system is that the office itself held sufficient prestige to make up for the money and time spent in the execution of its obligations. The power of such an incentive should not be underestimated, but it is also reasonable to conclude that the money provided by the statute of 1752 meant that coroners were willing to hold the position for a greater portion of their working lives.

The effects of this long service were legion. The stability created by the extended length of service made individual coroners more familiar and perhaps less threatening figures in the eyes of the communities they served. Since the investigation of violent death relied so heavily on local communities to inform the coroner when a death had occurred, a familiar face or name made sending for the coroner in such difficult times a little easier. Greater length of service—and less turnover—translated to more expert and efficient coroners. Given that the office of coroner was largely learned on an ad hoc, individual basis, longer tenures meant that less time was spent getting a new coroner up to speed and fully informed of his duties and responsibilities. Finally, longer tenures in office resulted in more effective oversight. If coroners after 1752 served an average of 20 years, they would have come into contact with the justices at quarter sessions and assizes many times over the course of their careers. In practice this meant that if a coroner was reprimanded for defects in his service or his bills for inquests were altered, such chastisement would likely have had a lasting effect. For instance, John Clare's tenure as coroner for North Wiltshire lasted 19 years. In his first few years, his bills were altered with great frequency by the justices at quarter sessions, although usually by a small amount. Later in his career as coroner, however, Clare's bills were only occasionally altered.[78] This suggests not that the justices became more lax, but that Clare had learned the lessons of his earlier chastisement and submitted more accurate and more correctly written coroner's bills.

The Mechanism of Oversight after 1752

The key to the proper functioning of the post-1752 reformed coroner system was the oversight provided by the justices of the peace at quarter sessions. Prior to 1752, coroners and their records received direct supervision only twice a year when they submitted their inquests at the assizes. After 1752, the work done by coroners was monitored six times a year: twice when they submitted their inquests at the assizes and four times at quarter sessions, when they submitted their bills for payment and reimbursement. This increase in the number of times per year that a coroner and his work came under the scrutiny of more senior, centrally appointed legal officials must have had some impact on the efficiency of the office. Coming face to face with their superiors with greater frequency surely led some coroners to be more rigorous in the performance of their office and the keeping of their official records.

The changes wrought by the midcentury reforms were not simply abstract but also involved the increased scrutiny of coroners' records and thus their work more generally. The institution of payment by mile and inquest not only provided coroners with an incentive to hold more inquests at all possible locations, it also provided a new opportunity to review the records coroners created in the course of their duties. The written bills that coroners submitted to the justices at quarter sessions allowed justices a window into the coroners' performance, as well as another way to supervise their behavior.

The alterations made by the justices usually fell into one of four general categories. First, the justices could alter the number of miles the coroner claimed to have traveled from his place of residence to the site of the inquest. Between 1752 and 1777, Wiltshire justices altered the number of miles coroners claimed to have traveled in 1.4 percent of the 1,071 total inquests.[79] While the alterations usually amounted to a change of a mile or two at most, it is clear that the justices were ready to challenge the coroners' claims when they suspected that the miles given in a bill were inaccurate.

The second type of alteration regularly made to coroners' bills was the adjustment of the money claimed by the coroner as compensation. Alterations of money claims were sometimes the result of changes in the number of miles traveled, but often they were separate matters. Wiltshire justices made alterations relating to financial claims in 3.2 percent of inquests in the 25 years after 1752.[80] As with the mileage claims, the alterations relating to money were often small, representing sums of a few pence to perhaps a few shillings, but rarely in the magnitude of pounds. Once again, this suggests that the justices tasked with reviewing the bills were alive to the small differences between the claims of the coroners and the money due by statute and that such seemingly insignificant sums were not beneath their notice.

Although alterations to the claims made regarding miles and money are perhaps the most obvious targets for judicial intervention, far and away the most common type of alterations were those relating to verdicts. Coroners' bills are laconic documents, listing the date and place of the inquest, the victim's name, the verdict, the miles traveled, and money earned. Yet even the barebones verdicts were altered with some regularity. Between 1752 and 1777, Wiltshire justices altered 5.2 percent of all inquest verdicts.[81] It is surprising that so many verdicts were changed at this initial stage in the process, before they were submitted to the assize, but clearly the justices at quarter sessions were reviewing the inquests' outcomes as well as the financial implications. Interestingly, the most common type of alteration was a change in verdict from accidental death to death by natural causes. Although the reasons for these changes are unclear, the change from accidental to natural death may have been the result of a lack of evidence of violent injury or marks on the body.

The final type of alteration was the most uncommon and the most mundane, but these changes also signal that the documents submitted by the coroner were closely read for discrepancies and mistakes, another indication of substantial levels of surveillance. These alterations related to the formula of the documents themselves and usually entailed changes in the wording of the bill, the location of the death, or the date of the inquest. Only 0.4 percent of the 1,071 Wiltshire inquests taken between 1752 and 1777 were altered in this way.[82]

On its own, each type of alteration may seem insignificant, but when taken as a whole, such alterations indicate a substantial level of oversight.

Well over 10 percent of all inquests held in the 25 years after the 1752 reforms were altered in some way.[83] It is also important to note that every
coroner operating in Wiltshire after 1752 had at least one bill, and often
many bills, altered. The ubiquity of alteration is important in that it demonstrates that all coroners had firsthand experience of surveillance and thus
the certain knowledge that someone was monitoring their behavior. For
coroners, then, the submission of a relatively clean and accurate bill was the
only way to avoid the eyes of the state and the only method to ensure that
the work they had done was properly compensated.

    This system of remuneration and oversight clearly worked well in the
provincial counties of England. Some historians, however, argue that the
inquest process broke down in London in the eighteenth century and that
supervision of lethal violence declined as a result. Scholars examining bills
of mortality have suggested that homicide may have been underrecorded
in London in the eighteenth century, implying that killings went unnoticed
or at least unprosecuted.[84] While the spotty nature of London inquest records before the end of the eighteenth century makes it difficult to know for
certain whether homicide was in fact underrecorded, the existing evidence
does not suggest that London was the exception to the growing monopolization of violence in the rest of the country.

    The bills of mortality, records of burials compiled by parish clerks,
are a shaky source for the measurement of violent death for a variety of
reasons. First, the bills did not cover every parish or ward of the city, and
certainly did not include burials in Westminster or suburban Middlesex.
Nor did they include burials made outside of Church of England cemeter-
ies, making any figure of violent deaths a fraction of the actual total. Second, the bills only record burials, not deaths. Hence it would have been
impossible for the clerks to know whether any coroner's inquest had been
completed, what its verdict had been, and whether the case had been sent
to the Old Bailey. It seems probable that many deaths that were later found
to be homicides, suicides, or accidental deaths were not recorded at all, or
not recorded as such due to the potentially drawn-out process of inquest
and trial. Third, it is clear that the consistency of the bills had begun to fail
by the early decades of the eighteenth century. Some parishes seem to have

ceased reporting, or at least reporting regularly, and parish clerks who had previously made weekly tallies of burials began to compile their reports haphazardly, combining several weeks together and going months between reports. Finally, if we compare the bills of mortality with eighteenth-century London coroners' inquests, we find that the bills seem to have significantly underreported homicide. While it is not possible to make such a comparison for much of the eighteenth century, looking at 1788, a year in which the records of the City of London coroner survive, we see that the coroner's inquests detail 250 percent more homicides than are noted in the bills of mortality for the same year.[85] Thus, while an interesting measure of mortality, the bills do not provide an accurate picture of actual levels of violent death, the regulation of violence, or whether coroners and the system designed to detect and punish violent death were operating effectively in the capital. The evidence provided by coroners' inquests and the Old Bailey, however, suggest that the trend toward the monopolization of violent death was both a provincial and a metropolitan phenomenon.

In some respects, criminal justice was becoming more dispersed in the eighteenth century as powers and responsibilities were devolved to the localities. The power of the justices of the peace and of the court of quarter sessions for governance and the administration of justice was growing across the period.[86] The 1752 Coroner Act can perhaps be seen as a part of this general process, as the responsibility for examining coroners' accounts and paying their fees had been granted to the local justices at quarter sessions. This new tool of oversight rested in the hands of local elites; however, we should be careful about drawing too fine a line between the roles of local and central government in the regulation of violence. While responsibility for scrutinizing coroners' bills fell to local justices, these justices were still centrally appointed officials subject to removal from the bench by central authorities. Trials for homicide and suicide, as felonies, remained in the exclusive purview of the assize courts and their centrally appointed judges. Coroners' inquests also continued to be both submitted to and examined by the central courts. Thus, as in the sixteenth and early seventeenth centuries, we see the interplay between central and local oversight. After 1752, coroners and the communities they served had competing financial interests in the accuracy of inquest records, helping to ensure some level of local oversight at the quarter sessions. This local monitoring was supplemented by the central oversight provide by the assize and central courts. Combined, local financial interest and central concerns for order helped to continue the robust policing of lethal violence, begun in the sixteenth century, in a more dispersed manner consistent with wider contemporary judicial practice.

By creating a new venue for oversight and new documents to supervise, the legislation of 1752 provided enhanced opportunities for monitoring the office of coroner and thus the system for maintaining the monopoly of violence. As with the system of oversight that prevailed in the sixteenth and early seventeenth centuries, the central facet of this new surveillance was the creation of competing financial interests and incentives, which meant that local communities, central officials, and coroners themselves had a new stake in the proper functioning of the coroner system. For coroners, the financial interest was obvious: the more inquests they held and the further they were willing to travel, the more money they stood to earn. This new incentive could have led to corruption instead of efficiency, but because it was tempered by competing interests, the worst of the potential abuses were likely eliminated. One competing interest was that of the local communities who were charged with providing the funds to reimburse coroners for their labors. By the statute 25 George 2, c. 29, the payment of coroners was to be made out of the county rate. Thus, any inaccuracies in the coroners' bills or any attempts by the coroner to claim more than his due, directly and negatively affected the finances of the county community. As representatives of the local communities and rate payers themselves, it was in the justices' personal and official interest to ensure that the potential greed of coroners for greater fees than they were legally entitled to was stamped out through rigorous supervision of the coroners' records at quarter sessions.

For the central authorities, the incentives remained the same. First, the proper functioning of the coroner system helped to maintain the monopoly of violence, forcing disputes over violence to be resolved in government courts according to the government's rules. Second, the crown still possessed the right to any and all deodands and the goods forfeited by felons. It thus remained in the government's interest to make sure the coroner system was rigorously monitored. Although at times this aspiration was beyond the government's reach, paying coroners for all types of inquests and reimbursing them for the miles they traveled encouraged coroners to hold inquests on nonhomicides. Since the crown stood to gain from the forfeiture of the property of suicides and the deodands in cases of accidental death, encouraging coroners to hold inquests on deaths not related to homicide was in the government's financial interest.

It is clear that the change in the system of remuneration and the renewal of oversight succeeded in spurring England's coroners to greater action. The number of known inquests undertaken by coroners increased dramatically in the years after 1752 and continued to increase for the rest of the eighteenth century. By creating a new type of record, a record that had to be submitted to superior officials for scrutiny, the reforms of 1752 also offered a new opportunity for the government to monitor the coroner and the incidence of violent death. Paying the coroner per inquest and per mile out of the county rate created a new system of overlapping and competing financial interests and incentives that resulted in greater action by the coroner and a greater level of oversight than had existed since the 1640s. The surveillance of violent death remained decentralized, as it had since the mid-seventeenth century, but the level of oversight after 1752 was such that criminal detection was as robust and efficient as it was to be until modern reforms.

Conclusion

IN SEPTEMBER 1728, JOHN AND William Lennox fell ill with surprising speed and violence. By all accounts a healthy boy, young William now vomited and sweated so profusely that shirts could not be dried fast enough to keep him clothed. John eventually recovered, but despite the care of their grandmother and an emetic administered by a local apothecary, William Lennox died on the fifteenth of that month. Disease was common in the early modern world and the deaths of children heartrendingly common. And yet the suddenness of the illness aroused suspicions. Elizabeth Lennox had no doubts as to the cause of her grandchildren's illness, blaming "that wicked woman" for poisoning the boys. In fairytale fashion, the "wicked woman" decried by the distraught grandmother was William and John's stepmother. Relations between in-laws being what they ever were, Elizabeth's accusations were thin grounds for prosecution. The suspicions of family and neighbors, however, were enough to draw the notice of the county coroner.[1]

Henry Syrer, the longtime coroner for Lancashire, traveled to Warrington on September 15 to examine the body of William Lennox and inquire into the cause of his death. Suspecting poison, the coroner's first step was to call on John Browne, a local surgeon, and ask him to perform an autopsy on the boy's body. Although Browne dissected William's stomach, the surgeon was not able to reach any firm conclusion about the cause of death. Nevertheless, the inquest did not cease, for the community had been watching and were waiting for their information to be gathered, collated, and assessed by the coroner.

Poison is difficult to detect and murder by poisoning even more difficult to prove, but Henry Syrer was not at all dissuaded from his duty and set about tapping local knowledge to create a clear picture of the events that led to William's death. The assiduous coroner collected at least 13 separate depositions and likely interviewed many more people. The story, as it emerged, could have been ripped directly from the pages of the Brothers Grimm. John Warburton deposed that he had bought ratsbane on orders from William's stepmother, a story confirmed by Doris Wilson, who had helped him purchase the poison, and Samuel Humphrey, who had delivered it. Margery Wishall told the coroner that on the day the boys fell ill, their stepmother had brought some gingerbread to her (Margery's) house to be baked in her oven. Wishall's suspicions were raised when she was warned "that neither she nor her children should touch the gingerbread nor see it." Furthermore, Wishall was instructed to bake the gingerbread immediately, even though the "fire was in the oven," meaning that the cakes would be burned rather than baked. Andrew Robinson, a soldier quartered in the Lennox household, likewise found the boy's stepmother's actions to be suspicious. He deposed that though he had been sent to fetch the gingerbread from Margery Wishall's oven, when the Lennox boys fell ill, their stepmother had claimed that she had bought the gingerbread, a clear lie.[2]

The gingerbread had been delivered to John and William Lennox—then living at their grandmother's house—by John Southorne. Southorne deposed that he had been instructed to deliver the cakes by the boy's stepmother. According to Elizabeth Lennox, the grandmother, the boys fell ill immediately after eating the gingerbread. In fact, everyone who ate the cakes fell ill, but those who did not partake did not. Elizabeth, who had only taken a single bite, told the coroner that she "fell sick and fell to vomiting, although on other occasions she hath been very hard to vomit without the use of a feather put into her throat." Furthermore, Elizabeth continued, the roof of her mouth was "so hot by eating thereof that she cou'd not imagine how or after what manner such a disorder might happen." She and her grandchildren remained ill with "violent and racking pain" for two days and two nights.[3]

When Henry Lennox was informed of his children's illness, he was furious. He knew his second wife harbored ill feelings toward William, John, and their grandmother and flatly accused her of poisoning them. Not willing to let the matter rest, Henry went to the place where his wife had claimed she bought the gingerbread, bought some cakes, and took them to the apothecary, who compared the newly bought cakes to those that had poisoned the Lennox boys. The apothecary concluded they were not the same. Meanwhile, the boys continued to sicken and suspicion continued to grow, but the accused refused to see her stepchildren and even begged Andrew Robinson not to swear that she had put poison in the gingerbread.[4]

In a bittersweet ending to an unhappy tale, the information provided by the numerous deponents sealed the "wicked" stepmother's fate. She was found guilty of murder at the coroner's inquest and was tried at the next assize. As bizarre as this case is, it nicely illustrates the effective operating of the coroner system in early modern England. It demonstrates that, though rare, even the most surreptitious homicides were likely to attract the notice of coroner and community alike. Communal knowledge and community watchfulness were among the greatest strengths of the amateur system of control. The unblinking eyes of the community (of families and neighbors) were an omnipresent fact of life in early modern England. Yet this natural font of local information was worth nothing unless it could be harnessed by the state. In the coroner, the English state had found an effective method of collecting and using local repositories of knowledge in service of the judicial system.

Looking back on the early modern period from the perspective of the year 1800, it is clear that the roughly 200 years between 1530 and 1752 were crucial for the creation of a successful monopoly of violence in England. As we have seen, this period witnessed the successful regulation of private warfare, which ceased to play a significant role in the life of the country. Moreover, international competition and domestic developments ensured that the institutions necessary to extract the resources required to engage in state-sponsored warfare were largely in place by the beginning of the seventeenth century.[5] All that remained for the creation of a true monopoly was the restriction of nonjudicial interpersonal violence.

There were three fundamental requirements necessary to enforce a monopoly of interpersonal and judicial violence in England: a crown officer dedicated to the detection of lethal violence, the ability of that officer to detect a high proportion of suspicious deaths, and a system of oversight to ensure that the officer operated without sloth or corruption. Although previous attempts had been made to regulate lethal violence, it was not until the sixteenth century that all three prerequisites of an effective monopoly were in place.

The coroner, the officer charged with detecting and investigating violent death, had been operating in England since the Middle Ages. However, it is in the early modern period that the office first showed signs of nascent professionalization. While previous accounts have stressed the decline in status and responsibilities of the coroner from the late Middle Ages, the evidence shows that the prestige of the office had hardly diminished at all in the early modern period. Coroners remained respected members of the county gentry and retained many of their medieval functions, such as jurisdiction over shipwreck and treasure trove and a central role in election procedures. Rather than being an object of scorn, the office was highly sought after and the elections of coroners remained highly contested events throughout the period. Furthermore, after the reforms of 1752, coroners became officials with regular incomes and long terms of service. Although training was not mandatory or uniform until the nineteenth century, as the early modern period progressed, greater access to a wider array of printed guides complemented informal systems of education to ensure that coroners in the sixteenth, seventeenth, and eighteenth centuries were increasingly cognizant of their duties and responsibilities. Early modern coroners may have remained amateur officeholders, but the path to professionalization had been created.

The chief responsibility of the coroner, however, remained the investigation and prosecution of violent death. Sadly, most modern scholars have dismissed the investigatory potential of the office due to a perceived dearth of forensic science and medical expertise. We now know, however, that early modern forensic medicine, while rudimentary to our eyes, was usually sufficiently advanced to adequately discern the cause of death in most cases encountered by the early modern coroner. Furthermore, it is clear that, as in modern times, forensic medicine was not necessarily a prerequisite for effective criminal detection. Then as now, the vast majority of early modern deaths were investigated and explained through the use

of witness testimony and local knowledge rather than by forensic medicine. The most important feature of any system of criminal detection is the
ability to gather and process witness testimony and communal knowledge.
The coroner and his jury were well equipped to access and assess this vital
information in the service of regulating death. Thus, we can conclude that
at least by the sixteenth century, the investigatory repertoire needed to enforce a monopoly of lethal violence was present.

The existence of an officer dedicated to the detection and regulation of
violent death and the presence of the necessary techniques of investigation,
however, would have all been for naught if the state had not had a method
of monitoring the coroner system. The effects of the absence of effective
oversight can be seen in the late fifteenth and early sixteenth centuries. In
this period, coroners seem to have operated with variable efficiency, focusing primarily on inquests for which a fee was granted. Likewise, relatively
few inquests were sent to the central courts, which made monitoring the
coroner system haphazard at best. Given this lack of systematic oversight,
it was impossible for contemporary rulers to have an adequate sense of the
true number of violent deaths that occurred in the realm.

Beginning in the 1530s, however, a new, more effective system of surveillance was created, a development that would allow the state to possess
a true monopoly of interpersonal violence for the first time. Central to this
new system of oversight was the creation of overlapping financial interests
in the outcome of coroners' inquests caused by the system of forfeiture.
The goods and property of felons, including suicides, and any property
considered to have been the proximate cause of death in the case of a lethal
accident were by law forfeited to the crown. The crown in turn appointed
almoners to pursue and redistribute forfeit goods, which they did ruthlessly through the use of suits in Star Chamber and other central courts.
The crown and its agents were not the only claimants who had an interest
in the proper redistribution of a deodand or a felon's goods. Lords of liberties and royal franchise holders, such as great landed magnates and many
boroughs, also pursued the rights to forfeit property in the central courts.
Finally, the heirs and creditors of a felon or the deceased and the owners
of goods deemed to have caused accidental deaths all had a direct financial

interest in the outcome of coroners' inquests. The system of forfeiture thus created a set of competing interests adjudicated by the central courts. This process of adjudication in turn created a system of checks and balances that ensured that every coroner's inquest was scrutinized by self-interested and self-motivated parties located in both the center and the localities.

The pursuit of these competing interests, however, was difficult without an effective and affordable venue for adjudication. In the 1530s, the almoner won the right to sue in Star Chamber, and soon thereafter the cost of litigation dropped sufficiently for the central courts to become a realistic site of contestation for individual heirs and creditors. With the new availability of central court forfeiture litigation, the number of such suits rose dramatically. The effect of this rise in forfeiture litigation for the coroner system was to allow new methods and venues for surveillance by the central authorities. The competing financial interests in the outcome of coroners' inquests meant that the records created by coroners in the course of their duties were more rigorously monitored and disputed than ever before. As a result of this growing surveillance of coroners' records, the number of inquests returned by coroners expanded exponentially in the late sixteenth and early seventeenth centuries, a development that in turn allowed more opportunities for oversight.

Although we have seen that the agents of the state were perhaps more physically omnipresent than has previously been allowed, it must be stressed that the most important site of early modern oversight and the most crucial apparatus of state surveillance was written records. The explosion of written records of all sorts in the sixteenth and seventeenth centuries, such as those created by the massive rise in central court litigation surveyed here, allowed novel opportunities for oversight of local officials and private citizens alike. In our case, the growth of central court forfeiture litigation provided the central authorities with a new resource for monitoring the system responsible for the regulation of violent death. The central courts scoured coroners' inquests for errors, inaccuracies, and incompetence and ruthlessly fined or outlawed those officers whose behavior was lax or record keeping insufficient. The records created by coroners were thus collected, scrutinized, and challenged to a remarkable degree by both the central authorities and those individuals with specific personal interests in the outcome of inquests. This new substantial surveillance in turn resulted in greater action by coroners and less corruption in the inquest system. In addition, the pursuit of forfeiture in the courts as an effective means of dispute resolution effectively tied creditors, heirs, and all those with an interest in the verdict of coroners' inquests—and the verdict's effect on the redistribution of property—to the courts as the primary site of adjudication in instances of violent death.

While this system of oversight changed from the mid-seventeenth century with the abolition of Star Chamber, the monopoly of violence created in the sixteenth and early seventeenth centuries was not reversed. Even though the locus of oversight shifted from the central courts to crown officials operating in the localities, individuals and communities were already effectively tied to an understanding that violent death was regulated by the state. The formal legal system's exclusive right to adjudicate cases of violent death had been legitimated through use. That is to say, by using the courts as an affordable and effective venue for the settlement of disputes over forfeiture and for challenging the outcome of coroners' inquests, individuals not only provided new opportunities for oversight of the coroner system, but also gave to the official courts the power to settle disputes over death. Hence, even though oversight shifted and decentralized in the late seventeenth century, the state's monopoly of violence was not seriously challenged—a contention supported by the rapid disappearance or displacement of extrajudicial settlements or compensation in cases of violent death.

Oversight of Death and the Decline of Extrajudicial Settlement

The system of monopolization created in the early modern period was impressive, but the question remains, how do we measure the effectiveness of the system? The evidence for the success of the monopoly of violence is threefold: the elimination of private warfare, the eradication of extrajudicial forms of dispute resolution, and the gradual decline of violence. By each of these measures, England began to create a monopoly of violence in the early decades of the sixteenth century, a monopoly that continued to grow throughout the seventeenth and eighteenth centuries.

Attempts to restrict private warfare began in the Middle Ages, especially in the tense years after the end of the Wars of the Roses. Starting with Henry VII, the Tudor monarchs sought to consolidate royal authority by placing new limits on noble power. By limiting, and eventually eliminating, the practice of retaining the Tudors fatally weakened the ability of subjects to make war on each other or on the crown. The process was gradual, but by the end of the sixteenth century, the possibility of a noble revolt against the crown had been effectively undermined, as the failed rebellions of the century attest. By the seventeenth century, private armies were a relic of the past. The state alone now had the power to make war both within and outside of England.

It has been suggested that the late survival of traditional forms of compensation, such as blood money or wergeld, constituted a threat or an impediment to the state's attempts to monopolize lethal and judicial violence, or perhaps is a sign of its failure.[6] The evidence to support such a claim is limited, but it is safe to assume that extrajudicial forms of dispute resolution continued to occur, if rarely, in cases of violent death as they did in more mundane disputes. It would be unwise, however, to conclude from a few scattered instances of extrajudicial settlements that the practice was either widespread or a threat to the authority of the formal courts of justice.

The practice of blood feud, quite common in early medieval England, was already in decline by the beginning of our period, as more and more individuals turned to the courts to settle their disputes.[7] Obviously, there were some late survivals of these practices, especially in the more remote corners of the realm. Examples of blood feud and blood money were reported in Wales and the North of England well into the sixteenth century.[8] We should not, however, make too much of these late anomalies. It is clear that the decline in such forms of reconciliation from the thirteenth century shown by Paul Hyams continued in the sixteenth century.

Even those examples of sixteenth-century extrajudicial settlements should be handled with care. For instance, in 1589 Thomas Houghton was killed by Sir Thomas Langton at Lea Hall in Derbyshire. Two and a half years later, in 1592, the earl of Derby recommended that the legal proceedings against Langton be dropped and the matter settled out of court with a monetary compensation. Lawrence Stone sees this as evidence of the survival of an honor culture that eschewed the formal courts of law in favor of extrajudicial settlement.[9] To my mind, however, this example better illustrates the death throes of a culture rather than its continued vibrancy. The first resort of those seeking justice for the deceased Thomas Houghton was not an extrajudicial settlement, but instead the pursuit of formal legal proceedings against the accused murderer. The earl of Derby may have recommended a settlement by blood money in exchange for dropping the proceedings against Langton in court, but this was clearly a possibility that was only considered after formal charges had been brought. Furthermore, there is no evidence that the earl of Derby's recommendation was followed or that the formal proceedings against Langton were in fact dropped. Read this way, the earl of Derby, an old man in 1592, seems more like a man struggling against the tide than an embodiment of a still-vital culture of blood feud and blood money.[10]

The culture of honor represented by the earl of Derby, one that prized retaliation and extralegal reconciliation, did not entirely disappear in the early modern period. Indeed, evidence for the continued importance of such mentalities is still not difficult to find in modern Western societies. By the late sixteenth century, however, the vast majority of disputes over violent death were being resolved in the formal courts of law. The restoration of honor and the compensation for the families of the deceased remained an important cultural concept throughout the early modern period. Importantly, however, the restoration of honor was increasingly sought in the courts of law, as the popularity of defamation suits well attests. Compensation and reconciliation retained a place in English conceptions of justice, but the venue for the adjudication of such claims had changed.

In fact, almost all of our early modern evidence for nonjudicial resolutions and compensations in cases of death are to be found in the legal records of the period. It seems that in many instances disputes over nonjudicial settlements ended up being adjudicated in the formal courts of law.

In addition, the pursuit of private compensation for a death did not in any way preclude a simultaneous conviction in the formal law courts. Court action and private compensation were "both/and" rather than "either/or" propositions. Individuals convicted of manslaughter were occasionally ordered by the courts to pay compensation to the family of the deceased.[11] The fact that these deaths were pursued by the justice system and that the compensation was part of a judicial sentence demonstrates that even if some Englishmen still sought compensation, by the mid-sixteenth century the venue for such a pursuit had shifted away from a popular, extrajudicial arena and toward the apparatus of the formal legal system. If the courts occasionally ordered monetary payments in cases of lethal violence, such settlements were hardly a threat to the state's monopoly of violence. On the contrary, court-ordered compensation was not in any way extrajudicial or extralegal, but instead further evidence that authority over crime, death, and violence belonged increasingly to the state, and to the state alone. Compensation for violent death may well have continued, but the power to grant such settlements had been usurped by the state. The most convincing explanation for the fact that attempts to secure extralegal compensation in cases of violent death were increasingly pursued in the courts of law from the mid-sixteenth century is that there was relative certainty that all deaths would be investigated and pursued by the courts, and that most people had been inured to the financial benefits of the courts by the system of forfeiture in the 1530s.

By the end of the sixteenth century, extrajudicial settlements were on the wane. Likewise, the ability of nonstate actors to engage in private warfare had been fatally undermined across the century. The power of the state and its institutions—formal and informal alike—had grown to such a degree that violence in general, and lethal violence specifically, began a long decline from its medieval peak to its modern trough. By all available measures, then, the monopolization was growing apace in the early modern period. Actions taken in the early sixteenth century bore fruit, creating a system that effectively detected, prosecuted, and punished lethal violence. The advent of this system created a state monopoly of violence that would never again see serious challenge. With lethal violence firmly controlled, other forms of violence began to be targeted for regulation as well, starting a pattern of greater and greater state control, and less and less nonstate violence.

Popular Political Violence

Thus far our discussion of violence and its control has focused primarily on violence of and between individuals. We have witnessed a sharp decline in the power of elite individuals to engage in private warfare against each other or the state, as well as the state's growing control over the everyday violence of less august individuals. However, violence could be a tool or consequence of collective action as well. As we will see, the general early modern trend toward greater state control of violence was not limited to private warfare or interpersonal violence but encompassed crowd violence as well.

Although portrayed as politically stable, the eighteenth century has long been characterized as the age of the riot and the mob. As previous historians have shown, this moniker was well deserved. Robert Shoemaker has demonstrated that London experienced a massive increase in rioting and crowd violence between the Restoration in 1660 and the mid-eighteenth century, while Adrian Randall has likewise argued that Hanoverian England saw "a higher level of social disorder than any other similar period, the Civil Wars included."[12] The underlying causes of this increase in popular political violence are complex and disputed, but generally include the emergence of party politics, changes in the nature of industry and the economy, and a growing divide between the poor and better sort.

Riots may have become more frequent in the eighteenth century, but rioters' actions and tactics remained largely the same as in the sixteenth and seventeenth centuries. Eighteenth-century crowds, far from being simply chaotic, instead followed a coherent logic based on an appeal to custom, a sense of a "moral economy" based on fairness rather than mere profit, and the reciprocal obligations of rulers and ruled.[13] Thus, in the earlier years of the eighteenth century, this ordered logic resulted in a violence that was present more in threat than in action. When violence did occur, it was usually aimed at property or symbols rather than people. Crowds would demolish tollgates, destroy enclosures and machinery, throw rocks through the windows of dissenters' houses, pull down brothels, and burn effigies, but with few exceptions they spared individuals. Riots caused serious material damage and even widespread panic, but they were rarely bloodbaths. This selective violence was a conscious tactic that sought to allow for a full-throated declaration of discontent without undermining the legitimacy of the rioters' actions or eroding the sympathy of elites.[14]

As important as the causes and nature of crowd violence are, our primary concern is how the state responded to these crises and whether these responses were effective. The most important early modern innovation in the regulation of crowd violence was the Riot Act of 1714. The Riot Act had been passed in response to a series of widespread riots: anti-Hanoverian riots in the wake of George I's coronation, election riots, and attacks on dissenting chapels in the Midlands. These popular disturbances seemed to many a grave threat that sought to "raise divisions and alienate the affections of the people from His Majesty" and his administration.[15] With the country seemingly under siege, new, harsher measures were taken to ensure that rioters were treated with a firm hand.

Prior to 1714, riot—defined as "an assembly of three or more persons, gathered with intent to commit disorder"—was classed as a misdemeanor unless and until the assembly used force or violence, at which point it became a felony.[16] Because assembly with intent to commit disorder was only a misdemeanor, the authorities had to wait until violence broke out to disperse crowds rather than acting preemptively to prevent violence. Furthermore, as riot was only a felony if a specific act of criminal violence occurred, the prosecution of rioters depended on the ability to prove that such an act had occurred, a difficult proposition. The 1714 Riot Act sought to remedy these problems by redefining a riot as 12 or more people "tumultuously assembled together, to disturb the public peace."[17] This meant that the very act of unlawful assembly was a felony subject to the penalty of death. The Riot Act was to be read to the assembly by a magistrate and the crowd given an hour to depart, after which all those still assembled would be considered felons. Such a redefinition allowed authorities to violently suppress crowds—often through the use of the army—before any other criminal acts occurred. It also allowed prosecutors to charge rioters merely for their presence in the crowd rather than for any specific acts. Thus, lethal violence could now legally be used against a still peaceful but menacing crowd, and all those arrested for riot could be executed merely for being present. Such harsh measures were designed both to enforce order through the use of direct coercive force and to take the decision to punish rioters out of the hands of potentially sympathetic jurors.[18]

Despite these sweeping new powers, there was no noticeable, immediate decline in the frequency of riots or other types of violent collective action. The failure to eradicate the riot was the result of both general sympathy with rioters and the lack of an effective coercive force. As we have seen, the logic of the crowd generally dictated that violence was directed toward property and symbols rather than people. This relative restraint—combined with the often celebratory nature of rioters, the involvement of a wide range of the social order, and the use of legitimating symbols and language in the protest—meant that the population in general, and even the authorities specifically, evinced "a remarkable degree of toleration for public disorder."[19] This toleration, which often verged on sympathy, was contingent upon the minimization of violence and the depth of the appeal of the rioters' aims; nevertheless, on the whole, crowd violence was tolerated. Constables, justices of the peace, politicians, and other elites often joined in riots or organized them for their own purposes, and this wide social participation—which included the frequent participation of women—lent an air of legitimacy to the mob that made its violent suppression both difficult and potentially unpopular.[20]

Even if rioters had not been imbued with a patina of legitimacy, forcefully dispersing crowds would have been difficult given the paucity of manpower available to the authorities. As with so much else, the responsibility for controlling riots fell to the justices of the peace. Obviously, justices alone could not forcefully contain a crowd, nor did they necessarily want to, as they continued to live in close proximity to the rioters they were supposed to suppress. Furthermore, the constable, the officer employed by justices in the regulation of ordinary crime, was not effective against crowds given their communal loyalties and limited numbers. Hence, justices increasingly had to rely on the army to disperse crowds. The use of the army to control riots, however, had its own problems. First, outside of London, soldiers were rather thin on the ground. Second, a standing army in peacetime was seen as a symbol and tool of tyranny and oppression; the use of the army to combat riots thus added a sticky political dimension to the process and risked alienating rioters, local communities, and elites alike. Finally, the army itself was often hesitant to act against crowds. Military rank and file often came from the same social order as the rioters and were thus sympathetic to such crowds; army officers, feeling their orders and remit were often unclear, were likewise hesitant to use force against rioters. Thus, while the army was used against rioters with greater frequency across the eighteenth century, it was never fully effective in preventing disorder.[21]

The Riot Act may not have had an immediate impact on the incidence of riot, but by the mid-eighteenth century, the authorities, elites, and the public more generally began to withdraw their support of and sympathy with rioters. In London, where the resources and manpower necessary to combat mob violence were present, small-scale riots had already begun to decline by the 1750s, but it was the very violence of the larger riots of the 1760s and 1780s that turned the tide against the mob. According to Shoemaker, protests in support of John Wilkes and industrial disturbances in 1768–1769 were marked by a greater use of violence and weaponry by both rioters and authorities. Whereas earlier rioters had limited themselves to stones and the like, from the 1760s rioters began to use swords, guns, and other lethal weapons, with the authorities responding in kind. The violence of these newly weaponized riots and their suppression made the stakes in joining a riot much higher than they had been previously, which helped discourage all but the most committed from joining in. At the same time, the use of armed violence served to alienate a wide range of the population that had previously been sympathetic to rioters, especially elites who now viewed riots as simply a source of disorder rather than a tool of protest and negotiation. Politicians and newspapers also began to withdraw their support from mob protests. This more critical, negative opinion of riots became even harsher after the violent spasms of the anti-Catholic Gordon

Riots of 1780 and the French Revolution, when even radical politicians began to separate themselves from popular political violence. As elites withdrew their sympathy, the authorities were given a freer hand in suppressing crowds. From the 1760s, the army was increasingly used to forcefully put down riots, a fact that made participating in mob action much more dangerous. At the same time that crowd action became more costly, new forms of political action such as the public meeting, voluntary association, and the petition allowed for an alternative form of protest. These factors—public alienation, violent suppression, and new forms of nonviolent protest—all helped to ensure that crowd violence in London was a much rarer event after the late eighteenth century.[22]

Outside of London, crowd violence also declined, but at a slightly later date. As previous historians have shown, there were two main factors in the decline in provincial popular political violence. First, food riots, once perhaps the most common form of riot, began to decline as appeals to the moral economy were undermined by a growing acceptance of free market capitalism. Second, from the late eighteenth century, the ability of the state to project coercive power increased. The outbreak of the French Revolution in 1789, and perhaps especially the fears of French invasion and Irish uprising from the mid-1790s on, forced the wider populace to reassess its attitude toward the army. Dread of invasion and a radical fifth column began to convince most individuals that the potential threat of internal disorder and anarchy was greater than that of a standing army. With political opposition to the use of the army removed, the state had a freer hand to use military force against its own population. As in London, this increased use of force raised the stakes of crowd action and initiated a slow decline of crowd violence.[23]

This brief outline of the history of popular political violence helps to demonstrate the wider contours of the monopolization of violence in early modern England. While the first targets of the state were the restriction of private warfare and the regulation of interpersonal violence, the quest to control violence did not stop there. As we have seen, prior to the eighteenth century, crowd action—due to its organized, controlled, and generally nonviolent nature—was generally tolerated to some degree by the state. However, when the nature of crowd violence changed, becoming more violent and more subversive, and when the resources of the state increased, popular political violence itself began to be violently restricted. While cultural factors surely played a role in this process, it is important to note that the prime mover in the decline of crowd violence was the state and its use of military power to suppress violent popular protest. Thus, we can see the history of crowd violence as of a piece with that of private warfare and interpersonal violence. All three types of violence faced greater state control and greater regulation across the early modern period: private warfare in the fifteenth and sixteenth centuries, interpersonal violence in the sixteenth through eighteenth centuries, and popular political violence in the eighteenth and early nineteenth centuries. And yet, the monopolization of violence did not stop with the control of crowd violence, but continued with new attention paid to nonlethal violence.

The Restriction of Nonlethal Violence

The regulation and control of lethal violence—whether interpersonal, extrajudicial, or the result of private warfare—was without doubt the most vital aspect of the English state's efforts to monopolize violence. As we have seen, reforms to the coroner system meant that this effort was largely successful after the early sixteenth century. Lethal violence, however, was not the only species of violence that began to succumb to increased scrutiny and regulation in the early modern period. Indeed, by the end of the eighteenth century, violence of all stripes was subject to greater control than ever before. While measuring nonlethal violence in all its sundry forms is a difficult task, a brief discussion of the intensifying regulation of assault will help to illustrate the broader monopolization of violence that took place in the early modern period.

Recent research has shown that momentous changes were occurring in the judicial treatment of assault across the eighteenth century. Before the middle of the century, most nonlethal violence was dealt with in an informal manner. Peter King has demonstrated that in this period most assaults were resolved either through a minor fine of less than one shilling or through such means as private mediated settlements between parties or recognizances for keeping the peace in the future. Hardly any individuals charged with assault faced imprisonment or corporal punishment. The ubiquity of these types of punishment makes sense. Most people at the time viewed nonlethal violence as a private matter between the parties involved rather than a public matter in need of state intervention. When the state did intervene, it was usually to speed along the private mediated settlements or to punish the few recalcitrant individuals who refused mediation.[24] By the second half of the eighteenth century, however, changes were underway that helped to shift the regulation of assault from a private to a public concern. In this period, the proportion of those imprisoned for assault began to rise dramatically, and by the nineteenth century those convicted of assault were far more likely to be imprisoned than to face a fine or private settlement.[25]

As with the general decline in violence, historians have traditionally explained this change in attitudes toward assault by reference to broad cultural changes: the increasing revulsion toward violence and cruelty led to campaigns to reform harsh public punishments, prison conditions, and other aspects of man's inhumanity to man. As King has noted, this cultural explanation falls flat in the face of the evidence of the timing of the changes. While popular attitudes toward cruelty and violence were still in the early stages of change in the nineteenth century, the shifts in attitudes toward assault began to gain momentum from the middle of the eighteenth century, if not earlier.[26] Instead of broad cultural changes, the impetus for a more restrictive treatment of assault in the courts seems to have come from the state. It was the desire for order on the part of state officers and judicial officials rather than popular scruples that spurred change. William Blackstone's decrial of private settlements does a wonderful job of encapsulating the position of the judicial class. According to Blackstone, such private settlements in cases of assault were problematic because, "although a private citizen may dispense with satisfaction for his private injury, he cannot remove the necessity of public example. The right of punishing belongs not to any one individual in particular, but to society in general, or the sovereign who represents that society."[27] Thus, the power to regulate and punish violence, even nonlethal violence, belonged to the state, not to the individual. Once again, legitimate and illegitimate violence were to be defined by the state, not the populace. By the end of the eighteenth century, the monopoly of violence was to include all forms of violence, lethal and nonlethal alike.

The treatment of assault by the judicial system was even changing in the realm of the household, perhaps the most intractable arena for legal regulation. Popular conceptions of domestic relations, focusing as they inevitably do on the proscriptive literature of the period, have tended to portray pre-modern society as one in which domestic violence was common and accepted. Early modern English society certainly did generally tolerate a higher level of domestic violence than do modern Western societies, but such violence was not without bounds, nor were official attitudes toward it static and unchanging. Across the early modern period, judges and other judicial officials began to take an increasingly harsh view of domestic violence.

Petty treason—the killing of a husband by a wife or a master by a servant—had long been viewed as the most vile and dangerous type of murder, given that it coupled homicide with an aspect of treason by overturning the traditional social order. As a result, those convicted of the crime were sentenced to an especially horrific punishment in line with the punishments for high treason: hanging, drawing, and quartering for men and burning at the stake for women. Because petty treason was a species of treason, there were special rules concerning the trial procedure as well. The most important of these rules was that provocation and self-defense, legitimate mitigating circumstances in all other types of homicide, were not supposed to be a valid defense. As there was no excuse for treason, a woman who killed her husband in self-defense or because of a pattern of physical abuse could not use these facts in her defense. Although this harsh treatment of petty traitors seems to have been the rule in the sixteenth century, by the early decades of the seventeenth century, judges and legal experts began to change how they interpreted the laws regarding petty treason. From the mid-seventeenth century on, a husband's violence toward his wife was regularly taken into account as a mitigating circumstance when trying women accused of petty treason. The killing was not always excused, but those women who lashed out in violence to protect themselves from domestic abuse were generally treated with greater leniency than in previous centuries. This shift in judicial treatment of petty traitors demonstrates that tolerance of violence, even that which occurred between husband and wife in the privacy of their home, was beginning to decline.[28]

It was not in cases of petty treason alone that the courts began to change their perspective on domestic violence. As Elizabeth Foyster has shown, between the late seventeenth and mid-nineteenth centuries, attitudes toward domestic violence changed dramatically. Such violence was no longer tolerated by the courts, largely as a result of changes in judicial opinions rather than any change in popular attitudes. As late as the 1850s, when a new Divorce Act was being debated, "the threat, exercise and control of violence was cherished still as a male right and prerogative."[29] Despite this continuing popular conception of marital violence, legislation in 1803, 1828, and 1853 made it increasingly easy for magistrates to try and punish cases of assault, including those between husbands and wives. The reason for this change in judicial policy in the face of more slowly changing popular perceptions was that the middle- and upper-class legislators and magistrates of the period considered marital violence to be a problem of the working class. Such elites may never have dreamed of interfering in the marriages of their own class; however, they did consider restricting the violence of the lower classes to be an important priority of the state.[30]

The greater legislative and judicial regulation of domestic violence illustrates two important points. First, the attempt to control violence in the early modern world continued to expand beyond lethal violence and elite violence to encompass violence of all types, even the most culturally ingrained and private species of violence. Second, Foyster's work shows that the driving force behind the greater restriction and regulation of violence was legislative and judicial mechanisms — that is, the impetus of the state working through Parliament and the courts, rather than any broad changes in cultural attitudes. There had been critics of male violence in general and marital violence in particular since at least the seventeenth century, but by and large regular men and women continued to believe in the acceptability of a certain level of domestic violence. The state, however, continued to expand its monopolization of violence even into the inner sanctum of traditional domesticity, in the first instance by more rigorously policing the domestic violence of the lower classes. As with the monopolization of private warfare and interpersonal lethal violence, it was the state, through the mechanisms of the judicial system, that drove the shift toward an ever tighter control of nonstate violence. The restriction of lethal violence through the coroner system was the beginning of a process that continued throughout the early modern and modern eras.

Official attitudes toward the physical correction or punishment of servants were changing in the eighteenth century as well. Servants even began to go so far as to sue abusive masters in court for treatment deemed too severe, and many were winning. In one representative instance, a maid received damages of £30 after prosecuting her mistress for her ill treatment.[31] Perhaps most surprisingly, physical violence toward slaves was also beginning to be viewed with distaste by the end of the period. While visiting London to oversee his sons' education, Henry Laurens, a planter and slave trader from South Carolina, was hesitant about applying the type of "smart flogging" he thought necessary to rein in the increasingly challenging behavior of his slave Robert. Laurens feared that such physical punishments would not be viewed favorably in the capital, and he was not alone in this assumption. Writing in the *Gentleman's Magazine,* another slaveholder bemoaned that it was "impracticable" to make slaves useful in London given that the "rigor and severity" necessary to do so were frowned upon. A Virginia planter agreed with this sentiment, telling the slave he had recently taken to England that "you were very saucy while you were in England, and resisted me twice. There must be no more of that." Back in Virginia, such behavior, the planter continued threateningly, would result in the slave being "tied up and slashed severely."[32] Obviously, this does not at all excuse or even mitigate the continuing English role in slavery and the slave trade, but merely helps to demonstrate the ever-growing regulation of violence in the early modern period, public and private, lethal and nonlethal.

Violence did not need to be intentional for it to be subject to increasingly robust state control. As we have seen, coroners had long been charged with investigating accidental deaths. Most of these deaths were the mundane consequences of everyday life and work, consisting mostly of falls, traffic accidents, drownings, and accidents involving animals or fire. The logic behind investigating these types of fatalities flowed naturally from the justification for monopolizing violence. Even accidental deaths could cause disorder, dispute, and a cycle of revenge, and therefore it was in the state's interest to intervene to ensure order. In addition, as an accidental death robbed the state of a subject and thus a resource, it was crucial that the crown be reimbursed for the loss in the form of the deodand. It was thus crucial that the state intervene to categorically define what constituted an accident, investigate accidental death, and determine culpability.

As with the regulation of homicide, state control over accidental death intensified in the sixteenth century. We have seen in Chapter 7 that there was a huge rise in the number of inquests relating to accidental death in the late sixteenth and early seventeenth centuries, as central oversight of coroners increased. After the legislation of the mid-eighteenth century allowed coroners to be paid by the mile and inquest rather than for homicide inquests alone, the number of accidental deaths that reached the courts also rose significantly. Although subject to some degree of waxing and waning, it is clear that from the mid-sixteenth century the investigation and punishment of accidental death became a new priority in the state's struggle to restrict violence in all its forms.

Although coroners were the prime agents in the restriction and punishment of accidental violence, other efforts were also being made in the period to limit and control this unique species of violence. Commencing in the late seventeenth century, the City of London began to pass legislation designed to control the growing traffic of the capital. Aimed particularly at the reputedly disorderly hackney coaches, these acts established new regulations and created new officers, "streetmen" in 1692 and "warders" in the eighteenth century, to combat the chaos and disorder that was becoming an ever greater problem. In part, these new measures were designed to relieve street congestion, which threatened both order and commerce. However, such regulations were also meant to control the violence and injury that resulted from crowded streets and unregulated traffic. An act of Parliament passed in 1715 that sought to regulate wheeled traffic was specifically concerned to "prevent the maiming and wounding of pedestrians."[33] The refractory nature of hackney drivers was notorious, but even when the violence they caused was accidental, it was important that such acts were both prevented when possible and punished when not.

Although the state's first priority in the creation of a monopoly of violence was the regulation of private warfare and lethal interpersonal violence, across the early modern period the tentacles of the Leviathan began to reach into every realm of violence. From the private armies of the nobility to homicide, assault, and even accident, the English state sought to define legitimate and illegitimate violence and to reserve for itself the use of force. The process was long and varied, but over the course of the early modern period, the state first began to effectively monitor, punish, and regulate nonstate violence in all its forms.

Legal Reform and the Increase in Prosecutions in Europe

How far can the trends witnessed in early modern England be tied to patterns of monopolization of violence throughout Europe? The historical literature on crime rates in general and homicide rates specifically suggests that the continent as a whole witnessed a rise in violent crime in the late sixteenth century, followed by a gradual decline from the mid-seventeenth century similar to that witnessed in England.[34] Like their English counterparts, continental historians have generally ascribed the rise in violent crime to economic and demographic pressures, and the subsequent decline to cultural changes in attitudes toward violence. Although a full investigation of the possible explanations for the rise and fall of lethal violence is beyond the scope of the present study, it may prove worthwhile to briefly suggest some tentative connections between the causes of the rise and fall of homicide in England presented above and similar possible causes of the rise and fall of violent crime in continental Europe. I have argued that the fluctuations in the incidence of homicide noted by historians of England were in large part the result of more rigorous oversight of the system that investigated suspicious death; this in turn led to a more regular and consistent recording and holding of those documents related to homicide used by historians to measure crime rates. While there were considerable differences between English and continental criminal justice systems in the early modern period, there are tantalizing hints that sixteenth-century continental legal reforms may have had an impact on detection and record keeping similar to that which caused a perceived rise in the incidence of homicide in England.

It could be argued that the first half of the sixteenth century was characterized by a pan-European shift from the private reconciliation of homicide to the criminalization of homicide. This process involved a re-conceptualization of the nature of homicide and the way it was prosecuted. In much of Europe before the sixteenth century, homicide was a matter for reconciliation between the perpetrator and the family of the victim. Negotiated settlements such as wergeld were common throughout much of Europe, and recourse to the law was seen as unnecessary to the process.[35] Beginning in the sixteenth century, however, states throughout Europe began to monopolize violence, to move from "private to public justice," and to seize, centralize, and reserve for themselves "the power of vengeance."[36]

One aspect of the monopolization of lethal violence entailed the rationalization and codification of legal and criminal justice systems throughout Europe. In the Holy Roman Empire, the *Constitutio Criminalis Carolina* sought to standardize rules for criminal procedure and punishment relating to capital crimes.[37] In ducal Florence the Otto di Guardia was reformed and its power and jurisdiction expanded by the ascendant Medici dukes after their consolidation of power in the 1530s.[38] In Spain, the *Nueva Recopilacion,* the law code of Castile, was first published in 1567.[39]

All of these legal reforms are significant for our purposes because they increased oversight of the criminal justice system and put measures in place that improved and centralized record keeping and the scrutiny of criminal records. For instance, in the Holy Roman Empire legislation enacted in various principalities—Hesse in 1540 and Saxony a short time thereafter—and inspired by the *Carolina* required that lower or local courts send files on capital cases to higher courts.[40] In Florence, the Otto di Guardia reviewed all cases heard in lower courts until the middle of the sixteenth century, when the process was made more efficient by requiring only capital offenses to be reviewed by the Otto.[41] These innovations were important because they helped to create a centralized system of oversight that could better monitor the activities of lower courts and officeholders. They also created a more robust system for the collection and holding of criminal records.

As in England, it seems possible, even likely, that centralization and better record keeping caused the number of *recorded* criminal offenses, especially capital offenses, to skyrocket in the second half of the sixteenth century throughout Europe. Indeed, Joel Harrington has suggested just such a phenomenon for parts of the Holy Roman Empire. According to Harrington, "Within one generation of the *Carolina*'s proclamation, criminal arrests, interrogations and punishments all spike dramatically throughout the empire."[42] Given that these reforms were in general put in place long before the economic and demographic crises of the late sixteenth century, it seems unlikely that the reforms were a result of an economically induced rise in crimes. Instead, it seems probable that the spike in crime witnessed in Europe in the late sixteenth century resulted from the legal reforms of the first half of the century. Harrington, for one, argues that this was in fact the case, stating that whereas "rising unemployment and inflation" may have heightened contemporary perceptions of rising criminality, "the most powerful reason for the increase in prosecutions was, paradoxically, the *Carolina* itself."[43] While Harrington suggests that the rise in prosecutions was a result of the *Carolina* making prosecution easier and the use of torture more universal, it seems equally likely that the increased oversight provided by the *Carolina* led to both the better detection of crime, as Harrington suggests, as well as to the more regular keeping of criminal records.

It is my contention that this better detection and record keeping have fooled historians into believing that violent crime and homicide were on the rise, when in all likelihood the greater number of capital indictments was the result of better detection and recording of a similar level of crime. In this conception, levels of violent crime, and especially homicide, remained

relatively stable throughout the early modern period. What changed or fluctuated was not the actual incidence of homicide or violence, but rather the
states' ability to detect and prosecute crime and the frequency with which
the records of these investigations and prosecutions were recorded and
filed. Instead of fluctuations in levels of homicide, perhaps what changed in
the early modern period was the proportion of crime that went unnoticed,
unpunished, and unrecorded. More research remains to be done, but perhaps what historians have seen as the rise and fall of homicide is in part
simply a rise and fall in oversight, detection, and record keeping as European states sought to increase their control over the definition of legitimate
and illegitimate violence. In England, the mechanism responsible for this
greater detection, record keeping, and control was the coroner system.

The state's exclusive right to define legitimate and illegitimate violence did
not go completely unchallenged. In the wake of the 1819 Peterloo Massacre,
when government troops and local yeomanry killed 11 and wounded many
more in an attempt to disperse a crowd agitating for parliamentary reform,
radical politicians such as Henry Hunt seized on the inquest as a tool of
protest. Hunt and others used the inquest on the death of John Lees as a
forum in which to press for what they saw as fundamental liberties of open
justice. For the radicals, the inquest was supposed to be an "'open' court to
which 'the public' had a fundamental right of access."[44] The public nature
of the inquest and the press's responsibility for advertising its proceedings
to the wider national community were thus seen as an important check on
the potential despotism of the state. If inquests and their verdicts were public, the state could not hide any attempt to excuse the violence of its agents
or unduly prosecute innocent individuals.[45]

    In the years following Peterloo, radical politicians continued to use
inquests relating to violence committed by the authorities — such as in the
disturbances during the funeral procession of Queen Caroline in 1821 and
a series of prison deaths in the 1830s — as a platform from which to voice a
radical reformist agenda focused on open justice.[46] Although the agitation
and publications surrounding these inquests continued throughout the

nineteenth century, they remained a minor aspect of the reformist toolkit. The impact of the politicization of the inquest in the nineteenth century is also striking for its absence of practical effect. In the case of the inquest of John Lees, for instance, while radicals pushed for an open inquest and the coroner for a private inquest, the High Court ended the inquest's proceedings prior to its conclusion. Although radical politicians began to challenge the state's monopoly of violence through the coroner's inquest, there is little evidence that they were successful in altering the nature of the inquest or its oversight. This may have been the result of a number of factors. Despite radical protests to the contrary, most inquests were to some degree open to the public throughout the early modern period. As inquests were held at the site of death, often in open air or in a public house, there was little to restrict access except in extraordinary cases. With the exception of deaths caused by agents of the state, the interests of state and citizen in the outcome of inquests usually coincided. What was changing over the course of the nineteenth and twentieth centuries was not the acceptance of the state's monopoly of violence, but the very conception of the state. In the modern period, as the franchise and political participation expanded, definitions of the state expanded as well, becoming increasingly synonymous with the people. While the state's exclusive right to define legitimate and illegitimate violence went unchallenged, as the definition of the state expanded and changed, definitions of what constituted illegitimate violence changed apace. Thus, official attitudes toward the use of violence changed without altering the state's monopoly of violence.

How, then, do states create a monopoly of violence in an era before professional policing and widespread bureaucratic institutions? As the case of England makes clear, the process of monopolization is not always a straightforward process of centralization. In England, the monopolization of lethal violence in the sixteenth century was caused by an increase in oversight that was in turn both the result and the cause of a growing popular use of the formal courts of justice. By providing people something they valued or needed in response to death and violence, the law courts of the early modern period helped to bind the people of England to the

arbitration of the state. Thus, the English state's definition of legitimate
and illegitimate violence was itself popularly, if unknowingly, legitimated
through the use of the courts as sites of arbitration and adjudication.

It is true that the successful monopolization of lethal violence in England in the sixteenth century was the result of a new centralized system of
oversight: however, by the mid-seventeenth century the locus of oversight
had shifted away from the center and toward the localities. While this shift
in oversight created a dearth of records that makes firm conclusions about
its efficacy difficult, it is clear that after 1752 a new system of surveillance
was created that was both rigorous and decentralized. Thus, it is evident
that state formation does not necessarily require centralization. Instead, it
must be granted that a monopoly of violence can be effectively established
based on different models and various levels of centralization, even within
the same country.

Perhaps as interesting as how violence was controlled is the type of
state that was created in the process. Although the bureaucracy of English
governance grew substantially from the early sixteenth century, professional officeholders and bureaucrats remained surprisingly thin on the
ground, especially outside of London. What is truly remarkable is that
a robust regulatory regime was created, maintained, and monitored in a
world with rudimentary formal institutions of government. The state that
was built through the monopolization of violence was not the bureaucratic
behemoth of modern imagination, but rather a state made of paper and the
interconnected private interests of a wide swath of individuals, a system
that efficiently bound individual self-interest to the needs of state. This informal, largely amateur, and often diffuse state structure was remarkably
effective and thoroughly modern.

Certainly, states never gain complete control over the monopoly of
violence. Homicide, suicide, and culpable accidental deaths continue to
occur with regularity in the modern world, and not all of these instances of
illegitimate violence are either detected or punished even today. However,
a successful monopoly of violence does not require the complete absence of
acts of nonstate violence, nor does it require that punishment be certain and
universal. What is required, though, is that acts of lethal violence be regu-

lated, detected, and punished to such a degree that the state's definition of legitimate and illegitimate violence is almost universally accepted and never seriously challenged. In England, this vital prerequisite for the creation of a modern state was first established in the sixteenth and seventeenth centuries. In these centuries, the regulation of lethal interpersonal violence was sufficiently effective to tie the adjudication and arbitration of disputes over death and violence to the justice system exclusively and permanently. The central figure in this process of monopolization and legitimization was the coroner.

Notes

Abbreviations

BL   British Library
CCA   Cheshire County Archives
CRO   Cheshire Record Office
ERO   Essex Record Office
OBP   Old Bailey Sessions Papers
SRO   Shropshire Record Office
TNA   The National Archives

Introduction

1. TNA STAC 5/A2/14.
2. Ibid. The particulars of the forfeiture system and the almoner's role in it will be described in greater detail in Chapter 6.
3. Ibid.
4. Max Weber, "Politics as a Vocation," in David Owen and Tracy B. Strong, eds., *The Vocation Lectures* (Indianapolis: Hackett Publishing Company, 2004), 33.
5. Ibid.
6. Thomas Hobbes, *The Leviathan* (London, 1651), XIII, 9.
7. Ibid.
8. John Locke, *Second Treatise on Government* (London, 1689), Chapter 1, Section 3.
9. Ibid., Chapter 1, Section 7.
10. Ibid., Chapter 9, Sections 124–156.
11. Michael Mann, "State and Society, 1185–1815: An Analysis of English State Finances," in M. Zietlin, ed., *Political Power and Social Theory,* vol. 1 (Greenwich, CT: JAI Press, 1980), 166. See also Michael Mann, *The Sources of Social Power,* vol. 1, *A History of Power from the Beginning to AD 1760* (Cambridge, UK: Cambridge University Press, 1986).
12. Charles Tilly, *Coercion, Capital and European States, AD 990–1992* (Cambridge, MA: Blackwell, 1992), 1.

13. Philip S. Gorski, *The Disciplinary Revolution: Calvinism and the Rise of the State in Early Modern Europe* (Chicago: University of Chicago Press, 2003), xvi.

14. See Perry Anderson, *Lineages of the Absolutist State* (London: NLB, 1974), and Immanuel Wallerstein, *The Modern World System* (New York: Academic Press, 1976).

15. Weber, "Politics as a Vocation," 35.

16. Mann, "State and Society," 196.

17. G. R. Elton, *The Tudor Revolution in Government: Administrative Changes in the Reign of Henry VIII* (Cambridge, UK: Cambridge University Press, 1966).

18. Thomas Ertman, *Birth of the Leviathan: Building States and Regimes in Medieval and Early Modern Europe* (Cambridge, UK: Cambridge University Press, 1997), 30.

19. John Brewer, *The Sinews of Power: War, Money and the English State, 1688–1783* (Cambridge, MA: Harvard University Press, 1988).

20. Steve Hindle, *The State and Social Change in Early Modern England* (Houndmills, Basingstoke, Hampshire: Macmillan, 2000), 23.

21. Ibid.

22. Michael Braddick, *State Formation in Early Modern England, 1550–1700* (Cambridge, UK: Cambridge University Press, 2000), 9.

23. Ibid., 11–172.

24. Ibid., 164.

25. See Alan Harding, *Medieval Law and the Foundations of the State* (Oxford: Oxford University Press, 2002), 5–7.

26. Charles Davenant, as quoted in Ted McCormick, "Population: Modes of Seventeenth Century Demographic Thought," in Philip J. Stern and Carl Wennerlind, eds., *Mercantilism Reimagined: Political Economy in Early Modern Britain and Its Empire* (New York: Oxford University Press, 2014), 37.

27. Robert Powell, as quoted in McCormick, "Population," 27–28. Although Powell is speaking specifically about enclosure and rural depopulation, his argument clearly applies to those who drained the country's population through violence.

28. Charles Davenant, as quoted in McCormick, "Population," 37.

29. Jean Bodin, as quoted in McCormick, "Population," 30.

30. Paul Slack, *Poverty and Policy in Tudor and Stuart England* (London: Longman, 1988); Alison Games, *Migration and the Origins of the English Atlantic World* (Cambridge, MA: Harvard University Press, 1999), 18.

31. Norbert Elias, *The Civilizing Process: Sociogenetic and Psychogenetic Investigations* (Oxford: Blackwell, 1994).

32. T. R. Gurr, "Historical Trends in Violent Crime: A Critical Review of the Evidence," *Crime and Justice* 3 (1981): 295–353; Manuel Eisener, "Long-term Historical Trends in Violent Crime," *Crime and Justice* 30 (2003): 83–142.

33. Elias, *Civilizing Process*.

34. Tilly, *Coercion, Capital and States,* 30–31. For other prominent examples of bellicist explanations of state formation, see Geoffrey Parker, *The Military Revolution: Military Innovation and the Rise of the West 1500–1800* (Cambridge, UK: Cambridge University Press, 1988); Brian Downing, *The Military Revolution and Political Change* (Princeton: Princeton University Press, 1992); Ertman, *Birth of the Leviathan*.

35. Tilly sees the seventeenth century as the crucial period, while Downing champions the sixteenth and Brewer the eighteenth century. Tilly, *Coercion, Capital and European States*, 31; Downing, *Military Revolution*, 27; Brewer, *Sinews of Power, 3–25.*

36. Christopher Brooks, *Law, Politics and Society in Early Modern England* (Cambridge, UK: Cambridge University Press, 2008), 281–286. See also G. R. Elton, *Tudor Revolution in Government,* 81–82; Penry Williams, *The Tudor Regime* (Oxford: Clarendon Press, 1979), chapter 4; Lawrence Stone, *The Crisis of the Aristocracy, 1558–1641* (Oxford: Clarendon Press, 1965), 199–272; Tilly, *Coercion, Capital and European States,* 69.

37. Bruce Lenman and Geoffrey Parker, "The State, the Community and the Criminal Law in Early Modern Europe," in Vic Gatrell, Bruce Lenman, and Geoffrey Parker, eds., *Crime and the Law: The Social History of Crime in Western Europe since 1500* (London: Europa Publications, 1980), 11–48. See also J. A. Sharpe, *Crime in Early Modern England, 1550–1750* (London: Longman, 1984), 168–188.

38. Lenman and Parker, "State, Community and Criminal Law," 34–42.

39. See R. F. Hunnisett, *The Medieval Coroner* (Cambridge, UK: Cambridge University Press, 1961).

40. The practice of forfeiture in cases of violent death will be explained more fully below. For now it is sufficient to say that all goods and chattels of felons, including murderers and suicides, were forfeit to the crown, as was any property deemed to have been the direct cause of death in cases of accidents.

41. J. G. Bellamy, *Crime and Public Order in England in the Later Middle Ages* (London: Routledge, 1973), 1; R. A. Griffiths, *The Reign of Henry VI* (London: Ernest Benn, 1981), 129.

42. Lawrence Stone, "Interpersonal Violence in English Society 1300–1980," *Past and Present* 101 (1983): 22–33; J. R. Lander, *Government and Community: England 1450–1509* (Cambridge, MA: Harvard University Press 1980), 40.

43. Barbara Hanawalt, *Crime and Conflict in English Communities, 1300–1348* (Cambridge, UK: Cambridge University Press 1979), 261–263; J. B. Given, *Society and Homicide in Thirteenth-Century England* (Stanford, CA: Stanford University Press, 1977), 160–163, 188–189; Bellamy, *Crime and Public Order*, 25.

44. Philippa Maddern, *Violence and the Social Order: East Anglia, 1422–1442* (Oxford: Oxford University Press, 1992), 18–21. Maddern and K. B. Macfarlane have dissented from the consensus to suggest that the levels of violence in medieval society were not as great as has been imagined, or at least that the evidence available is insufficient to draw any concrete conclusions. Yet even they concede that violence was more prevalent in the medieval period than it was in the early modern and modern eras. K. B. Macfarlane, *The Nobility of Later Medieval England* (Oxford: Oxford University Press, 1973), 114–115.

45. See for instance Hunnisett, *Medieval Coroner;* J. D. J. Havard, *The Detection of Secret Homicide* (London: Macmillan, 1960); T. R. Forbes, "Crowner's Quest," *Transactions of the American Philosophical Society*, New Series 68, no. 1 (1978), and *Surgeons at the Old Bailey* (New Haven, CT: Yale University Press, 1985); Paul Knapman, "Crowner's Quest," *Journal of the Royal Society of Medicine* 86 (1993): 716–720.

46. For the decline of the medieval coroners, see Hunnisett, *Medieval Coroner.* For an account of the modern coroner, see Havard, *Detection of Secret Homicide.*

47. Havard, *Detection of Secret Homicide*, 37.

48. 1 & 2 Philip & Mary, c. 13 (1554–1555); 2 & 3 Ph. & Mar., c. 10 (1555); 25 George II, c. 29.

49. Havard, *Detection of Secret Homicide*, 37.

50. Forbes, *Surgeons at the Old Bailey*, 1–13.

51. Malcolm Gaskill, *Crime and Mentalities in Early Modern England* (Cambridge, UK: Cambridge University Press, 2000), 266.

52. Forbes, *Surgeons at the Old Bailey*, 11, and "Crowner's Quest," 5–7.

53. Anthony Fletcher, "Honor, Reputation and Local Officeholding in Elizabethan and Stuart England," in Anthony Fletcher and John Stevenson, eds., *Order and Disorder in Early Modern England* (Cambridge, UK: Cambridge University Press, 1985), 92–115.

54. Forbes, *Surgeons at the Old Bailey*, 12.

55. Havard, *Detection of Secret Homicide*, 38.
56. Gaskill, *Crime and Mentalities*, 246.
57. Ibid., 246–260.

Chapter 1. Restricting Private Warfare

1. Norman Davis, ed., *Paston Letters and Papers of the Fifteenth Century, Part I* (Oxford: Clarendon Press, 1971), 344–345.
2. Ibid.
3. Helen Castor, *Blood and Roses: The Paston Family in the Fifteenth Century* (London: Faber and Faber, 2004), 276–278, 295–330.
4. Christine Carpenter, *The Wars of the Roses: Politics and the Constitution in England, c. 1437–1509* (Cambridge, UK: Cambridge University Press, 1997); Michael Hicks, *The Wars of the Roses* (New Haven, CT: Yale University Press, 2010). Philippa Maddern and others have argued that warfare did not always lead to destabilization in the medieval period, as it could provide a legitimate outlet to lawless and violent men, removing them from the local picture. This was likely the case in some areas of the kingdom; however, the perceived threat of elite violence and military might to the stability of the crown was sufficient to increase royal efforts to erode elite power and increase central authority in the late fifteenth and sixteenth centuries. Maddern, *Violence and the Social Order*, 17–19. In 2012 the remains of Richard III were discovered in the buried remnants of Greyfriars Priory in Leicester, now the site of a car-park.
5. Michael Hicks, *Bastard Feudalism* (London: Longman, 1995).
6. Michael Hicks, "The 1468 Statute of Livery," *Historical Research* 64 (1991): 15–28.
7. 8 Edward 4, c. 2.
8. 19 Henry 7, c. 14.
9. Stanley Chrimes, *Henry VII* (New Haven, CT: Yale University Press, 1999), 69–75. Dominic Luckett, "Crown Office and Licensed Retinues in the Reign of Henry VII," in *Rulers and Ruled in Late Medieval England*, ed. R. E. Archer and Simon Walker (London, 1995), 223–238.
10. Alasdair Hawkyard, "George Neville, Third Baron Bergavenny (c. 1469–1535)," *Oxford Dictionary of National Biography*, ed. H. C. G. Matthew and Brian Harrison (Oxford: Oxford University Press, 2004), www.oxforddnb.com.
11. It has been suggested that this anecdote may be apocryphal, but even so, it demonstrates the perception that Henry VII was concerned to limit the

power of friend and foe alike. S. J. Gunn, "John de Vere, Thirteenth Earl of Oxford (1442–1513)," *Oxford Dictionary of National Biography*.

12. K. J. Kesselring, *Mercy and Authority in the Tudor State* (Cambridge, UK: Cambridge University Press, 2003), 1–23.

13. John Skelton, as quoted in Lawrence Stone, *The Crisis of the Aristocracy, 1558–1641* (Oxford: Clarendon Press, 1965), 208.

14. Stone, *Crisis of the Aristocracy*, 209.

15. Ibid., 212.

16. As quoted in Stone, *Crisis of the Aristocracy*, 213.

17. Ibid., 215.

18. Steven G. Ellis, "Tudor State Formation and the Shaping of the British Isles," in Steven Ellis and Sarah Barber, eds., *Conquest and Union: Fashioning a British State, 1485–1725* (London: Longman, 1995), 46–48.

19. S. J. Gunn, *Early Tudor Government, 1485–1558* (Houndmills, Basingstoke, Hampshire: Macmillan, 1995), 62–70.

20. Ellis, "Tudor State Formation," 48–58; Gunn, *Early Tudor Government*, 65–70.

21. Ibid.

22. Ciaran Brady, "Comparable Histories?: Tudor Reform in Wales and Ireland," in *Conquest and Union: Fashioning a British State, 1485–1725*, ed. Steven G. Ellis and Sarah Barber (London: Longman, 1995), 64–80.

23. Anthony Fletcher and Diarmaid MacColloch, *Tudor Rebellions*, 5th ed. (London: Longman, 2004), 134–135.

24. J. G. Bellamy, *Bastard Feudalism and the Law* (London: Routledge, 1989), 42–45. The manor courts had previously been dealt a serious blow by the Black Death, which led to a decline of serfdom and villain tenures. However, they remained a useful tool for the control of tenants well into the fifteenth and early sixteenth centuries.

25. Gunn, *Early Tudor Government*, 93–94.

26. Ibid., 72.

27. Penry Williams, *The Tudor Regime* (Oxford: Clarendon Press, 1979), 39–40.

28. W. J. Jones, *The Elizabethan Court of Chancery* (Oxford: Clarendon Press, 1967), 27–36.

29. Gunn, *Early Tudor Government*, 79.

30. Ibid., 77–79.

31. Ibid., 81–82.

32. Ibid.

33. As quoted in ibid.

34. Ibid.

35. Ibid., 100–102.

36. Ibid., 44–45.

37. Stone, *Crisis of the Aristocracy*, 203.

38. Ibid., 205.

39. Ibid., 204–205.

40. The unreliability of the gentry is well illustrated in Andy Wood, *Riot, Rebellion and Popular Politics in Early Modern England* (Houndmills, Basingstoke, Hampshire: Macmillan, 2002), 52–53.

41. Stone, *Crisis of the Aristocracy*, 217.

42. John Guy, *Tudor England* (Oxford: Oxford University Press, 1988), 97.

43. M. W. Thompson, *The Decline of the Castle* (Cambridge, UK: Cambridge University Press, 2008).

44. Stone, *Crisis of the Aristocracy*, 217–218.

45. Ibid., 220.

46. For more on Leicester and his noble affinity, see Simon Younger, *Leicester and the Court: Essays on Elizabethan Politics* (Manchester: Manchester University Press, 2002).

47. Stone, *Crisis of the Aristocracy*, 218–219.

48. Ibid., 219–221.

49. Ibid., 220.

50. As quoted in Stone, *Crisis of the Aristocracy*, 223.

51. Andy Wood, *The 1549 Rebellions and the Making of Early Modern England* (Cambridge, UK: Cambridge University Press, 2007), 187–208.

52. Fletcher and MacColloch, *Tudor Rebellions*, 26–51; K. J. Kesselring, *The Northern Rebellion of 1569: Faith, Politics and Protest in Elizabethan England* (Houndmills, Basingstoke, Hampshire: Macmillan, 2007).

53. Fletcher and MacColloch, *Tudor Rebellions*, 109–110.

54. John Paston III to John Paston II, September 1469. Davis, *Paston Letters and Papers*, 547.

55. Castor, *Blood and Roses*, 295–330.

Chapter 2. Coroners and Communities

1. *Charges to the Grand Jury, 1689–1803*, ed. Georges Lamoine, Camden Society, 4th Series, 43 (London: Royal Historical Society, 1992), 39.

2. R. F. Hunnisett, *The Medieval Coroner* (Cambridge, UK: Cambridge University Press, 1961), 191.

3. Ibid., 192. Abjuration of the realm was a formal oath to leave the country

within a specific timeframe in return for a temporary suspension of a legal sentence. It was usually made by individuals who had been declared outlaws.

4. Ibid., 196.

5. J. D. J. Havard, *The Detection of Secret Homicide: A Study of the Medico-legal System of Investigation of Sudden and Unexplained Deaths* (London: Macmillan, 1960), 28.

6. Hunnisett, *Medieval Coroner,* 197.

7. Literally, "of behavior and reputation." Inquisitions *de gestu et fama* were legal processes initiated on the basis of or as a result of the impeachment of an individual's reputation.

8. Hunnisett, *Medieval Coroner,* 198–199.

9. For the process and politics of outlawry, see Melissa Sartore, *Outlawry, Governance and Law in Medieval England* (New York: Peter Lang Publishing, 2013).

10. ERO Q/SR 68/71. Such outlawries were common, and often dozens of individuals were outlawed at a time.

11. William Greenwood, *Bouleuterion, or A Practical Demonstration of County Judicatures* (London, 1685), 9–10.

12. In cases of accidental death any piece of property deemed to have been the proximate cause of death was declared forfeit to the crown. For example, if a person was trampled by a horse, the horse (or its value) was forfeited to the crown. Carts, ladders, trees, minerals, animals, tools, and weapons were all regularly claimed as deodands. This provision even applied to the goods of the individual who died.

13. Edward Coke, *The Third Part of the Institutes of the Laws of England* (London, 1669), 132.

14. Ibid., 133. A liberty was a territory granted by royal franchise to an individual, organization or corporate body. The rights of and responsibilities for justice in that jurisdiction thereafter fell to the franchise holder. In practice liberties were granted to great magnates, towns, and educational or religious organizations.

15. CCA QCI/3/22.

16. See for instance TNA DL 44/23, 1052. The duchy of Lancaster is a royal duchy whose vast territory was the hereditary possession of the monarch (as distinct from the crown) from the thirteenth century on. The monarch, as duke of Lancaster, thus had the right to appoint officers, including coroners, who were to operate on duchy lands. For the duchy of Lancaster, see Helen Castor, *The King, the Crown and the Duchy of Lancaster: Public Authority and Private Power, 1399–1461* (Oxford: Oxford University Press 2000).

17. Edward Coke, *The Second Part of the Institutes of the Laws of England* (London, 1642), 166–167.

18. Ibid., 167–169. Although a year and a day was given to owners to claim their property, sheriffs were permitted to sell any goods that perished in the interim.

19. For examples of cases of shipwreck see TNA DL 44/826, 830, 950, 970.

20. *Western Circuit Assize Orders, 1629–1648: A Calendar,* ed. J. S. Cockburn, Camden Society, 4th Series, 17 (London: Royal Historical Society, 1976), 59. The inhabitants of Chew Magna had been ordered to pay one-half of the charges for the repair of the bridge at the Epiphany Quarter Sessions of 1631, but had failed to do so. As a result, the case was referred to the assize.

21. Ibid., 62.

22. ERO Q/SR 204/26.

23. Ibid.

24. Greenwood, *Bouleuterion,* 272–273.

25. ERO Q/SR 461/76.

26. The exact nature of election procedure was not explicitly stated for most of the early modern period, differing widely from place to place, although a general pattern emerged from the late seventeenth century. For election procedure, see Mark Kishlansky, *Parliamentary Selection: Social and Political Choice in Early Modern England* (Cambridge, UK: Cambridge University Press, 1986), 180–191, and Derek Hirst, *The Representative of the People?: Voters and Voting in England under the Early Stuarts* (Cambridge, UK: Cambridge University Press, 1975).

27. "House of Commons Journal Volume 10: 2 April 1689," *Journal of the House of Commons,* vol.10: *1688–1693* (1802), 75–77.

28. Ibid.

29. Ibid.

30. Ibid.

31. Ibid.

32. Ibid.

33. Greenwood, *Bouleuterion,* 271–272.

34. CCA CH/13.

35. CCA CH/32.

36. *Sussex Coroners' Inquests, 1558–1603,* ed. R. F. Hunnisett (Kew, Surrey: PRO Publications, 1996), xxiii.

37. Ibid., xxii.

38. Ibid., xviii.

39. King's College Archive KCE/307. King's College Cambridge and Eton

College both also had the right to appoint coroners for their lands in Sussex, but it seems neither chose to do so in the early modern period.

40. *Sussex Coroners' Inquests, 1558–1603*, xx–xxii.

41. Ibid.

42. Mark Goldie, "The Unacknowledged Republic: Officeholding in Early Modern England," in Tim Harris, ed., *The Politics of the Excluded, c. 1500–1850* (Houndmills, Basingstoke, Hampshire: Palgrave Macmillan, 2001), 153–194. For specific local officers see Joan Kent, *The English Village Constable, 1580–1642: A Social and Administrative Study* (Oxford: Clarendon Press, 1986), and E. Carlson, "The Origins, Function and Status of Churchwardens with Particular Reference to the Diocese of Ely," in Margaret Spufford, ed., *The World of Rural Dissenters, 1520–1725* (Cambridge, UK: Cambridge University Press, 1995), 164–207.

43. Hunnisett, *Medieval Coroner*, 148.

44. Greenwood, *Bouleuterion*, 268.

45. Ibid., 268–269.

46. Edward Coke, *The Reports of Sir Edward Coke*, vol. 2 (London, 1658), 45–47. The famous inquest into the death of Christopher Marlowe at Deptford, Kent, in 1593 was undertaken by William Dandby, the queen's coroner, who was likely also county coroner for Kent. Park Honan, *Christopher Marlowe: Poet and Spy* (Oxford: Oxford University Press, 2005), 354.

47. John Godolphin, *Sunegoros Thalassios: A View of the Admiral Jurisdiction* (London, 1661), 137–138. Godolphin, quoting Edward Coke, seems to suggest that all felonies, not simply deaths, that occur on water but within a county's jurisdiction are the responsibility of coroners. This may have been accurate; however, such nonlethal felonies do not appear in any of the coroners' records surveyed here. For other contemporary accounts of Admiralty jurisdiction see Richard Zouche, *Jurisdiction of the Admiralty Asserted* (London, 1663), and John Exton, *Sea Jurisdiction of England* (London, 1664).

48. CCA QCI/14/4–5.

49. BL ADD MS 31028, f. 53.

50. Ibid. It seems likely that the inquest fell to the Lincolnshire coroner because the body had been recovered on the Lincolnshire side of the river, despite the fact that Watson seems to have been traveling from Hull to the ship.

51. *The Official Diary of Lieutenant-General Adam Williamson: Deputy— lieutenant of the Tower of London 1722–1747*, Camden Society, 3rd Series, 22 (London: Offices of the Society, 1912), 161.

52. Ibid., 69–86.

53. Ibid., 75.

54. TNA STAC 4/7/14.

55. Ibid.

56. Ibid.

57. Ibid.

58. Ibid.

59. Ibid.

60. Ibid.

61. Steve Hindle, *On the Parish?: The Micro-Politics of Poor Relief in Rural England, c. 1550–1750* (Oxford: Oxford University Press, 2004), 300–360.

62. TNA SP 36/17, ff. 13–14.

63. Ibid.

64. Henry Fane was a younger son of the eighth earl of Westmorland and would go on to become the chief clerk of the Privy Council and a member of Parliament for Lyme Regis. Why his help in particular was sought in this instance is unclear.

65. TNA SP 36/17, ff. 13–14.

66. Ibid.

67. *Sussex Coroners' Inquests, 1558–1603*, xxxii.

68. Ibid., 23, 26, 102, 111. *Sussex Indictments, Elizabeth I*, ed. J. S. Cockburn, Calendar of Assize Records 1 (London: HMSO, 1975), No. 1547, 297.

69. *Sussex Coroners' Inquests, 1558–1603*, xxxi.

70. *Sussex Coroners' Inquests, 1485–1558*, ed. R. F. Hunnisett, Sussex Record Society 74 (Lewes: Sussex Record Society, 1985), 46–66.

71. *Sussex Indictments, Elizabeth I*, 39–297.

72. Claire Cross, "Henry Hastings, Third Earl of Huntingdon (1536–1595)," *Oxford Dictionary of National Biography*, ed. H. C. G. Matthew and Brian Harrison (Oxford: Oxford University Press, 2004), www.oxforddnb.com.

73. Hunnisett, *Sussex Coroners' Inquests, 1558–1603*, xxiii.

74. Greenwood, *Bouleuterion*, 212.

75. Robert Tittler, *The Reformation and the Towns in England: Politics and Political Culture, 1540–1640* (Oxford: Clarendon Press, 1998).

76. CRO A/B/1/63.

77. CRO ZQC1/1–19.

78. Ibid.

79. CRO A/B/1/195v–196.

80. Ibid., 80.

81. Ibid., 175, 179.

82. CRO A/B/1/138v–139. Wright eventually submitted, paid a fine, and was

readmitted as a citizen, but it was declared that henceforth anyone who connived in the elopement of an alderman's daughter would be "disfranchised."

83. *Somerset Assize Orders, 1640–1659*, ed. J. S. Cockburn, Somerset Record Society 71 (Frome: Butler & Tanner, 1971), 39.

84. Greenwood, *Bouleuterion*, 9.

85. Ibid., 9.

86. Ibid., 50.

87. *Somerset Assize Orders*, 39.

88. Ibid.

89. Ibid.

90. TNA C242/19.

91. TNA C242/21, 22.

92. TNA C202/22–122.

93. Ibid.

94. TNA C115/98.

95. John Money, ed., *The Chronicles of John Cannon, Part 2, 1734–1743* (Oxford: Oxford University Press, 2010), 432.

96. Ibid.

97. Ibid.

98. Ibid., 435. Declining the office of coroner or being forcibly removed from office due to a disqualifying conflict of interest was not uncommon. Further examples will be discussed below.

99. Ibid.

100. Ibid.

101. Ibid.

102. Ibid., 436–437.

103. Ibid., 437.

104. Ibid.

105. Ibid.

106. Ibid.

107. John Money, ed., *The Chronicles of John Cannon, Part 1, 1684–1733* (Oxford: Oxford University Press, 2010), 176.

108. Ibid.

109. Ibid., 437.

110. Ibid., 438.

111. Ibid., 496.

112. Ibid., 499.

113. Ibid.

114. Ibid., 507. Cannon does not give the specific figures for this election, but he

suggests that Rowley, had he campaigned in earnest, could have expected 900 votes, a number which suggests that the 1,300-odd votes cast in the 1739 election were the norm, if possibly on the low end.

115. W. A. Speck, "The Electorate in the First Age of Party," in Clyve James, ed., *Britain in the First Age of Party, 1680–1750: Essays Presented to Geoffrey Holmes* (London: Hambledon Press, 1987), 48–49.

116. *The Poll at the Election of a Knight of the Shire for the County of Northumberland* reprinted in *The Poll Book of the Contested Election for the Northern Division of the County of Northumberland* (Newcastle, 1841).

117. For more on elections and election practices in the eighteenth century, see Geoffrey Holmes, *The Electorate and the National Will in the First Age of Party* (Lancaster: University of Lancaster Press, 1976); J. C. D. Clark, *English Society, 1688–1832: Religion, Ideology, and Politics during the Ancien Régime* (Cambridge, UK: Cambridge University Press, 1985); John A. Phillips, *Electoral Behavior in Unreformed England: Plumpers, Splitters, and Straights* (Princeton, NJ: Princeton University Press, 1982); Julian Hoppit, *A Land of Liberty?: England 1689–1727* (Oxford: Clarendon Press, 2002), 282–311.

118. Hunnisett, *Medieval Coroner;* Havard, *Detection of Secret Homicide.*

119. Thomas Frankland, *The Annals of King James and Charles I* (London, 1681), 467.

120. John Sadler, *Rights of the Kingdom* (London, 1682), 307.

121. *Western Circuit Assize Orders,* number 1203, 287. It is not entirely clear exactly which offices either excused or disqualified a potential coroner from holding the position, and these issues were occasionally debated and discussed in contemporary sources.

122. Money, *Chronicle of John Cannon, Part 2,* 435.

123. *Somerset Assize Orders,* 37.

124. Ibid., 41.

125. *Sussex Coroners' Inquests, 1558–1603,* xx–xxi.

126. *East Sussex Coroners' Records, 1688–1838,* ed. R. F. Hunnisett, Sussex Record Society 89 (Lewes: Sussex Record Society, 2005).

127. CRO ZQCI/1–21.

128. *Sussex Coroners' Inquests, 1558–1603,* xx–xxi.

129. Ibid.

130. Ibid., xx.

131. *The Court Records of Prescot, 1640–1649,* ed. Walter J. King, Record Society of Lancashire and Cheshire 142 (Lancaster: The Society, 2008), 69, 88.

132. See, for instance, Norma Landau, *The Justices of the Peace, 1679–1760*

(Berkeley: University of California Press, 1984); Lionel K. J. Glassey, *Politics and the Appointment of Justices of the Peace, 1675–1720* (Oxford: Oxford University Press, 1979).

133. Greenwood, *Bouleuterion*, 271. See also Michael Dalton, *The Countrey Justice* (London, 1618).

134. CRO A/B/2/76.

135. *Somerset Assize Orders*, 41.

136. 3 Henry 8, c. 2.

137. *Official Diary of Lieutenant-General Adam Williamson*, 69.

138. Ibid.

139. *Sussex Coroners' Inquests.*

140. BL ADD MS 31028. The paltry sums received by coroners and the fact that accident and other nonhomicide inquests outnumbered murder and manslaughter inquests by a factor of five to one or more should put to rest any suggestions that coroners neglected those inquests not related to homicide because they did not provide the potential for monetary reward. For such a suggestion, see Malcolm Gaskill, *Crime and Mentalities in Early Modern England* (Cambridge, UK: Cambridge University Press, 2000), 246, 266.

141. 25 George 2, c. 29.

142. *Wiltshire Coroners' Bills, 1752–1796*, ed. R. F. Hunnisett, Wiltshire Record Society 26 (Devizes, Wiltshire: Wiltshire Record Society, 1981), 1–45.

143. Gaskill, *Crime and Mentalities*, 247.

144. *Charges to the Grand Jury, 1689–1803*, 237.

145. *Official Diary of Lieutenant-General Adam Williamson*, 85–86.

146. Ibid., 86.

147. On judicial corruption, see Wilfrid Prest, "Judicial Corruption in Early Modern England," *Past and Present* 133 (Nov. 1991): 67–95. Similar charges of negligence and corruption were formerly aimed at constables before their rehabilitation by Joan Kent, who argues for their relative effectiveness in carrying out their duties. Joan Kent, "The English Village Constable, 1580–1642: The Nature and Dilemmas of the Office," *Journal of British Studies* 20 (1981): 26–49, and Kent, *English Village Constable*.

148. T. R. Forbes, *Surgeons at the Bailey: Forensic Medicine to 1878* (New Haven, CT: Yale University Press, 1985), 11, and "Crowner's Quest," *Transactions of the American Philosophical Society*, New Series 68, no. 1 (1978): 5–7.

149. Anthony Fletcher, "Honor, Reputation and Local Officeholding in Elizabethan and Stuart England," in *Order and Disorder in Early Modern England*, ed. Anthony Fletcher and John Stevenson (Cambridge, UK: Cambridge University Press, 1985), 92–115.

150. Greenwood, *Bouleuterion*, 269.

151. According to Greenwood, the original qualifications were altered because in *De Coronatore Eligendo* it was stated that the original stipulations that all coroners were to be knights with 100s freehold rent were invalid because they were late editions inserted into the original statute. Ibid.

152. Coke, *Second Part of the Institutes of the Laws of England*, 174–175. The Latin term *probus homo* simply meant "a good man." *Legalis homo* meant an individual who possessed all normal legal rights—to make an oath, to offer testimony in court, to serve on a jury—and whose legal rights were not constrained by his having been declared an outlaw, excommunicated, or otherwise disqualified.

153. Greenwood, *Bouleuterion*, 270.

154. Havard, *Detection of Secret Homicide*, 37.

155. As cited in Greenwood, *Bouleuterion*, 271.

156. *Sussex Coroners' Inquests.*

157. Keith Wrightson, *English Society, 1580–1680* (London: Routledge, 2003), 31–35.

158. For gentry incomes in seventeenth-century Kent, see C. W. Chalklin, *Seventeenth-Century Kent: A Social and Economic History* (London: Longman, 1965), 191. For gentry landholding in early modern Yorkshire, see J. T. Cliffe, *The Yorkshire Gentry from the Reformation to the Civil War* (London: Athlone Press, 1969), 29.

159. Magnus Fowle, for instance, was styled "esquire" in the later part of his tenure as coroner.

160. David Cressy, *Literacy and the Social Order: Reading and Writing in Tudor and Stuart England* (Cambridge, UK: Cambridge University Press, 1980), 42–62.

161. Cressy, *Literacy and the Social Order*, 119–121. The range of percentages given by Cressy is the result of differing literacy rates between different geographical areas. For more on literacy see Wrightson, *English Society*, 192–207; W. B. Stephens, "Literacy in England, Scotland and Wales, 1500–1900," *History of Education Quarterly* 30 (1990): 555; Barry Reay, *Popular Cultures in England, 1550–1750* (London: Croom Helm, 1998), 36–70.

162. BL ADD MS 31028, 122.

163. For more on gentry education, see George C. Brauer, Jr., *Education of a Gentleman: Theories of Gentlemanly Education in England, 1660–1775* (New York: Bookman Associates, 1959), and Rosemary O'Day, *Education and Society, 1500–1800: The Social Foundations of Education in Early Modern Britain* (London: Longman, 1982).

164. TNA SP 36/67, f. 75.

165. TNA SP 36/38, f. 128.

166. *Sussex Coroners' Inquests*, 101.

167. CRO A/B/1/146.

168. Ibid., 227, 242v.

169. CRO A/B/1/214; A/b/2/86.

170. CRO A/B/1/65.

171. *Sussex Coroners' Inquests*, 119.

172. Charles Carlton, *This Seat of Mars: War and the British Isles, 1485–1746* (New Haven, CT: Yale University Press, 2011), 31.

173. As quoted in ibid., 32.

174. Christopher Brooks, *Law, Politics, and Society in Early Modern England* (Cambridge, UK: Cambridge University Press, 2008), 6–7, 20–21.

175. For the growth of print in the early modern period, see Elizabeth Eisenstein, *The Printing Revolution in Early Modern Europe*, 2nd ed. (Cambridge, UK: Cambridge University Press, 2012); Lucien Febvre and Henri-Jean Martin, *The Coming of the Book: The Impact of Printing, 1450–1800*, 3rd ed. (London: Verso Books 2010).

176. See John Rastell, *Tabula Libri Assisarum et Plactorum Corone* (London, 1514), and Anthony Fitzherbert, *LaGrande Abbregement de le Ley* (London, 1516).

177. Coke, *First Part of the Institutes of the Laws of England;* Dalton, *Countrey Justice;* Nicholas Collyn, *Laws and Statutes Concerning Justices, Sherifs etc.* (London, 1655).

178. Greenwood, *Bouleuterion,* 275–290.

179. Ibid., 284–289.

180. Ibid., 275–278.

181. Ibid., 276.

182. Ibid., 277.

183. Robert Tittler, *Townspeople and Nation: English Urban Experiences, 1540–1640* (Stanford, CA: Stanford University Press, 2001), 25–26; Wilfrid R. Prest, *The Rise of the Barristers: A Social History of the English Bar, 1590–1640* (Oxford: Clarendon Press, 1986), 240–252.

184. CRO A/B/2/109.

185. Much education in the pre-modern world was acquired through ad hoc education of makeshifts. For more on informal education see Margaret Spufford, "First Step in Literacy: The Reading and Writing Experiences of the Humblest Seventeenth-Century Spiritual Autobiographers," in Harvey J. Graff, ed., *Literacy and Historical Development: A Reader* (Carbondale: Southern Illinois University Press, 2007), 207–238.

186. Kent, *English Village Constable.*
187. *British Newspapers, 1600–1950;* find.galegroup.com/bncn (accessed February 2015).
188. *Old England or the Broadbottom Journal* 153 (April 18, 1747).
189. *Early English Books Online;* eebo.chadwyck.com (accessed March 11, 2015).
190. Ian Burney, *Bodies of Evidence: Medicine and the Politics of the English Inquest, 1830–1926* (Baltimore: Johns Hopkins University Press, 2000).

Chapter 3. Proving the Case

1. Tom R. Tyler, "Viewing *CSI* and the Threshold of Guilt: Managing Truth and Justice in Reality and Fiction," *Yale Law Journal* 115, no. 5 (March 2006): 1,052. For examples of the discussion of the CSI effect in mass media, see Paul Rincon, "*CSI* Shows Give 'Unrealistic View,'" *BBC News,* Feb. 21, 2005 (http://news.bbc.co.uk/1/hi/sci/tech/4284335.stm); Kit R. Roane, "The *CSI* Effect," *U.S. News & World Report,* Apr. 25, 2005: 48; Jamie Stockwell, "Defense Lawyers Hinge Cases on 'CSI' Savvy," *Washington Post,* May 22, 2005: A1.
2. TNA ASSI 44/1/1–45/1/2; BL ADD MS 31028; TNA PL 27/2/1–2.
3. Medical testimony was most likely to be provided by surgeons, with the occasional doctor or apothecary supplying depositions. In cases of infanticide, midwives were often called to give evidence. Unfortunately, little is known about the biographies or backgrounds of these figures, and thus some of the crucial context that surely informed and affected interactions between medical experts, coroners, and jurors remains, for the moment, unknown.
4. J. D. J. Havard, *The Detection of Secret Homicide: a Study of the Medico-legal System of Investigation of Sudden and Unexplained Deaths* (London: Macmillan, 1960), 37. Unfortunately, Havard's cursory, superficial treatment of the pre-modern coroner is frequently cited as an authority on the subject despite the almost total lack of archival materials used in his study.
5. Ibid., 38.
6. T. R. Forbes, *Surgeons at the Bailey* (New Haven, CT: Yale University Press, 1985), 1–13.
7. David Paul, Foreword, in T. R. Forbes, "Crowner's Quest," *Transactions of the American Philosophical Society* 68, no. 1 (1978): 3. Despite their age and the recent proliferation of work on crime, the works of Havard and Forbes remain influential among historians of medicine, crime, death, and policing. For example, Forbes is cited favorably or without question in J. M. Beattie, *Crime and the Courts of England, 1660–1800* (Princeton: Princeton

University Press, 1986), 111 n. 83; Malcolm Gaskill, *Crime and Mentalities in Early Modern England* (Cambridge, UK: Cambridge University Press, 2000), 254 n. 58; Vanessa MacMahon, *Murder in Shakespeare's England* (London: Hambledon Press 2004), 31 n. 3; Andrew Wear, *Knowledge and Practice in English Medicine, 1550–1680* (Cambridge, UK: Cambridge University Press, 2000), 115 n. 20; Katherine Watson, *Forensic Medicine in Western Society: A History* (London: Routledge, 2011), 39 n. 65; Ian Burney, *Bodies of Evidence: Medicine and the Politics of the English Inquest, 1830–1926* (Baltimore: Johns Hopkins University Press, 2000), 3 n. 1.

8. Watson, *Forensic Medicine in Western Society;* Catherine Crawford, "Legalizing Medicine: Early Modern Legal Systems and the Growth of Medico-legal Knowledge," in Michael Clark and Catherine Crawford, eds., *Legal Medicine in History* (Cambridge, UK: Cambridge University Press, 1994); McMahon, *Murder in Shakespeare's England* and "Reading the Body: Dissection and the 'Murder' of Sarah Stout, Hertfordshire, 1699," *Social History of Medicine* 19 (2006): 19–35; Carol Loar, "Medical Knowledge and the Early Modern English Coroner's Inquest," *Social History of Medicine* 23 (2010): 475–491.

9. Gaskill, *Crime and Mentalities,* 242–280.

10. Ibid., 266. In this conclusion, Gaskill follows Havard and Forbes almost exactly.

11. For example, none of the roughly 500 depositions from Lancashire, Lincolnshire, or the Northern Assize Circuit examined here contain any references to bleeding corpses or other types of popular magic, nor do the coroners' inquest records for Sussex between 1558 and 1603. TNA ASSI 44/1/1–45/1/2; BL ADD MS 31028; TNA PL 27/2/1-2; *Sussex Coroners' Inquests, 1558–1603,* ed. R. F. Hunnisett (Kew, Surrey: PRO Publications, 1996).

12. Tyler, "Viewing *CSI* and the Threshold of Guilt," 1071.

13. TNA ASSI 44/1/1–45/1/2; BL ADD MS 31028; TNA PL 27/2/1-2.

14. TNA ASSI 44/1/1–45/1/2; BL ADD MS 31028; TNA PL 27/2/1-2.

15. Most of these percentages seem to more or less accord with the general proportion of each group within the overall population, with a few exceptions. Laborers seem to be significantly underrepresented, while tradesmen/artisans and innkeepers seem to be significantly overrepresented as deponents.

16. Women employed to prepare bodies for burial were usually asked if they noticed any signs of violence on the body of the deceased. The women giving evidence at inquests into suspected infanticides tended to testify to the stage of development of the deceased child to ascertain whether it had been brought to term. Such deponents tended to give evidence in groups, with

sometimes three or four women giving evidence of the babies' development at one inquest.

17. TNA ASSI 44/1/1–45/1/2; BL ADD MS 31028; TNA PL 27/2/1–2.

18. TNA ASSI 44/1/1–45/1/2; BL ADD MS 31028; TNA PL 27/2/1–2.

19. TNA PL 27/2 (deposition of Thomas Orme).

20. Ibid.

21. It is also possible, given the order in which the depositions were recorded, that Derbyshire had taken the statements of four individuals before hearing that of the surgeon. This may suggest in turn that the coroner had sought the evidence of the surgeon only to confirm what other witnesses had said, rather than to provide any new or crucial evidence.

22. TNA PL 27/2 (deposition of Nicholas Whittle).

23. Ibid.

24. TNA PL 27/2 (depositions of William Park and Hugh Johnson). Presumably, Dandy sought to kill Margret Hollinhurst, or at least draw her blood, in the belief that such an act would lift the bewitchment. Such a belief was not uncommon in the early modern period. James Sharpe, *Instruments of Darkness: Witchcraft in Early Modern England* (London: Hamish Hamilton, 1996), 159–160.

25. TNA PL 27/2 (deposition of Robert Hunter).

26. TNA PL 27/2 (depositions of Ellen Gill and Janet Blackhurst).

27. TNA PL 27/2 (deposition of Jame Blooer).

28. Ibid.

29. TNA PL 27/2 (deposition of Thomas Orme).

30. BL ADD MS 31028, 43.

31. Ibid.

32. BL ADD MS 31028, 43.

33. Ibid.

34. BL ADD MSS 31028; TNA ASSI 45/1/1–4; TNA PL 27/2.

35. BL ADD MSS 31028; TNA ASSI 45/1/1–4; TNA PL 27/2.

36. BL ADD MSS 31028; TNA ASSI 45/1/1–4; TNA PL 27/2.

37. Infanticide cases were the most likely deaths to have no witnesses other than the mother, the most likely to be concealed, and thus the most likely to turn on medical evidence. That such evidence was not always up to the task does point to some shortcomings in the forensic and pathological abilities of early modern medical experts; however, these cases were an exception.

38. BL ADD MSS 31208, 68–70.

39. Of the roughly 28 percent of cases that lacked eyewitness evidence or a confession, around a third involved cases of suspected infanticide, and many

of the rest seem to have involved cases of accidental drowning. TNA ASSI
44/1/1–45/1/2; BL ADD MS 31028; TNA PL 27/2/1–2.

40. TNA ASSI 44/1/1–45/1/2; BL ADD MS 31028; TNA PL 27/2/1–2.

41. TNAASSI 45/1/4, 54.

42. Ibid.

43. BL ADD MS 31028, 12.

44. BL ADD MS 31028, 12v.

45. Ibid.

46. TNA ASSI 45/1/4, 54.

47. Ibid.

48. Ibid.

49. Ibid.

50. BL ADD MS 31028, 26.

51. BL ADD MS 31028, 3.

52. Ibid.

53. TNA PL 27/2; TNA ASSI 44/1/1–45/1/2; BL ADD MS 31028.

54. On privacy, see Lena Cowen Orlin, *Locating Privacy in Tudor London* (Oxford: Oxford University Press, 2007).

55. BL ADD MS 31028, 10–11.

56. TNA PL 27/2.

57. TNA ASSI 45/1/2 (deposition of James Barnesley).

58. Ibid.

59. TNA ASSI 45/1/2 (depositions of George Hoyland and Eleanor Bilcliffe).

60. TNA ASSi 45/1/2 (deposition of Elizabeth Creswicke).

61. TNA ASSI 45/1/2 (deposition of Katherine Barnesley.).

62. Ibid.

63. The participatory nature of the early modern English criminal justice system has been admirably described by Cynthia Herrup, and Keith Wrightson has highlighted the often divergent conceptions of justice held by judicial officials and local inhabitants. But while both see local opinion and involvement as crucial to the operation of justice, the idea that local witnesses were expert witnesses and officeholders of a sort has been overlooked. Cynthia Herrup, *The Common Peace: Participation and the Criminal Law in Seventeenth-Century England* (Cambridge, UK: Cambridge University Press, 1989); Keith Wrightson, "Two Concepts of Order: Justices, Constables and Jurymen in Seventeenth-Century England," in John Brewer and John Styles, eds., *An Ungovernable People: The English and Their Law in the Seventeenth and Eighteenth Centuries* (New Brunswick, NJ: Rutgers University Press, 1980), 21–46.

64. TNA STAC 8/2/42.

65. For the continued importance of communal policing and local knowledge for criminal justice and policing in the modern world, see Robert Trojanawicz and Bonnie Bucqueroux, *Community Policing: A Contemporary Perspective* (Cincinnati: Anderson Publishing Company, 1990).

66. Steve Hindle, "Bleeding Afreshe? The Affray and Murder at Nantwich, 19 December 1572," in Angela McShane and Garthine Walker, eds., *The Extraordinary and the Everyday in Early Modern England: Essays in Celebration of Bernard Capp* (Houndmills, Basingstoke, Hampshire: Palgrave Macmillan, 2010), 224–246.

67. Trojanawicz and Bucqeroux, *Community Policing*, 11.

68. In some boroughs the mayor was also, ex officio, coroner. Some liberties also had the right to appoint coroners. On the whole, however, coroners were elected by freeholders.

69. Also, unlike modern police officials, early modern coroners had few problems relating to ethnic or racial differences between police and community.

70. TNA SP 46/174.

71. TNA SP 46/174, 113.

72. TNA SP 46/174, 38.

73. TNA SP 46/174, 113–115.

74. TNA PL 27/2 (deposition of Robert Parkinson).

75. TNA PL 27/2 (deposition of Andrew Grayham).

76. TNA PL 27/2 (deposition of Richard Nuttall).

77. TNA PL 27/2.

78. Ibid.

79. For more on identification through clothing, see Valentine Groebner, *Who Are You?: Identification, Deception, and Surveillance in Early Modern Europe* (New York: Zone Books, 2007), 77–89; Edward Higgs, *Identifying the English: A History of Personal Identification, 1500 to the Present* (London: Continuum, 2011), 49–52.

80. Gaskill, *Crime and Mentalities*, 246.

81. TNA ASSI 44/1/1–45/1/2; BL ADD MS 31028; TNA PL 27/2/1–2.

82. *Sussex Coroners' Inquests, 1558–1603*.

83. Forbes, *Surgeons at the Old Bailey*, 11–12.

84. It is important to note that even to this day there is no universally accepted laboratory test for drowning.

85. BL ADD MS 31028, f. 10.

86. BL ADD MS 31028, f. 10.

87. BL ADD MS 31028, f. 11.

88. BL ADD MS 31208, f. 38.

89. Ibid.

90. Ibid.

91. BL ADD MS 31028, f. 21.

92. TNA ASSI 45/1/1–4.

93. BL ADD MSS 31028, passim.

94. TNA PL 27/2.

95. Loar, "Medical Knowledge," 453–456.

96. Ibid., 476.

97. Ibid., 489. Similar arguments about the growing recourse to forensic medicine have been put forward in Helen Brock and Catherine Crawford, "Forensic Medicine in Early Colonial Maryland, 1633–1683" and David Harley, "The Scope of Legal Medicine in Lancashire and Cheshire, 1660–1760," in *Legal Medicine in History*, ed. Michael Clark and Catherine Crawford (Cambridge, UK: Cambridge University Press, 1994), 25–44 and 45–63, respectively.

98. TNA PL 27/2 (deposition of James Low).

99. Ibid.

100. TNA PL 27/2 (deposition of Joseph Etough).

101. Ibid.

102. TNA SP 46/174, f. 50.

103. Ibid.

104. TNA C 4/49/57.

105. Ibid.

106. Barbara Shapiro, *A Culture of Fact: England, 1550–1720* (Ithaca, NY: Cornell University Press, 2000), 192–200. See also Steven Shapin, *A Cultural History of Truth: Civility and Science in Seventeenth-Century England* (Chicago: University of Chicago Press, 1994).

107. On the early adoption of autopsies by the gentry and nobility, see Wear, *Knowledge and Practice in English Medicine*, 146–147, and David Harley, "Political Post-Mortems and Morbid Anatomy in Seventeenth Century England," *Social History of Medicine* 7, no. 1 (1994): 1–28.

108. On the dissemination of knowledge of forensic medicine through the popular press, see Harley, "Scope of Legal Medicine," 59.

109. Ian Mortimer, *The Dying and the Doctors: The Medical Revolution in Seventeenth-Century England* (Woodbridge, Suffolk: Boydell Press, 2009).

110. B. Parker, "The status of Forensic Science in the Administration of Criminal Justice," *Revista juridica de la Universidad P.R.* 32 (1963): 405.

111. P. Greenwood, J. Chaiken, J. Petersilia, and L. Prusoff, *The Criminal Inves-*

tigation Process, vol. 3: *Observations and Analysis* (Santa Monica, CA: Rand Corporation, 1975).

112. B. Forst, J. Lucianovic, and S. Cox, *What Happens after Arrest? A Court Perspective of Police Operations in the District of Columbia* (Washington, DC: Institute for Law and Social Research, 1977).

113. Joseph Peterson, Ira Sommers, Deborah Baskin, and Donald Johnson, *The Role and Impact of Forensic Evidence in the Criminal Justice Process* (National Institute of Justice, #2006-DN-BX-0094, Sept. 2010), 11.

114. Ibid., 4.

115. Ibid., 9.

116. Simon A. Cole, "More than Zero: Accounting for Error in Latent Fingerprint Identification," *Journal of Criminal Law and Criminology* 95, no. 3 (2005).

117. Jonathan J. Koehler, "On Conveying the Probative Value of DNA Evidence: Frequencies, Likelihood Ratios, and Error Rates," *University of Colorado Law Review* 67 (1996): 865.

118. Ibid., 885.

119. Spencer S. Hsu, "Review of FBI Forensic Does Not Extend to Federally Trained State, Local Examiners," *Washington Post,* Dec. 22, 2012.

120. Campbell Robertson, "Questions Left for Mississippi over Doctor's Autopsies," *New York Times,* Jan. 7, 2013.

121. Peterson et al., *Role and Impact of Forensic Evidence,* 4.

122. Ibid.

123. Greenwood et al., *Criminal Investigation Process.*

124. Only 15.8 percent of cases in a modern study contained evidence given by the victim. Peterson et al., *Role and Impact of Forensic Evidence,* 4. Gaskill argues that the reliance of early modern criminal justice on the statements given by dying victims in homicide cases demonstrates the system's weakness. I am not convinced, however, that malice or intentionally false evidence in the testimony of dying victims would have been very likely or usual. Additionally, the evidence of dying victims would likely be used in modern criminal cases. Gaskill, *Crime and Mentalities,* 237.

Chapter 4. One Concept of Justice

1. For recent works on the early modern English jury, see T. A. Green, *Verdict According to Conscience: Perspectives on the English Criminal Trial Jury, 1200–1800* (Chicago: University of Chicago Press, 1985); J. S. Cockburn, *A History of the English Assizes, 1558–1714* (Cambridge, UK: Cambridge University Press, 1972); *Twelve Good Men and True: The Criminal Jury in*

England, 1200–1800, ed. J. S. Cockburn and T. A. Green (Princeton, NJ: Princeton University Press, 1988); *"The Dearest Birth Right of the People of England": The Jury in the History of the Common Law,* ed. John W. Cairns and Grant McLeod (Portland, OR: Hart Publishing, 2002); *Judges and Judging in the History of the Common Law and Civil Law,* ed. Paul Brand and Joshua Getzler (Cambridge, UK: Cambridge University Press, 2012); Robert Tittler, "The Sequestration of Juries in Early Modern England," *Historical Research* 61, no. 146 (October 1988), 301–305.

2. Cynthia Herrup, *The Common Peace: Participation and the Criminal Law in Seventeenth-Century England* (Cambridge, UK: Cambridge University Press, 1987), 6. See also Cynthia Herrup, "Law and Morality in Seventeenth-Century England," *Past and Present* 106 (1985): 1,002–1,123; and Joel Samaha, "Hanging for Felony: The Rule of Law in Elizabethan Colchester," *Historical Journal* 21 (1978): 763–782.

3. On the debate over whether the medieval jury was self-informing, see Daniel Klerman, "Was the Jury Ever Self-Informing?" in Maureen Mulholland and Brian Pullan, eds., *Judicial Tribunals in England and Europe, 1200–1700: The Trials in History* (Manchester: Manchester University Press, 2003), 58–80.

4. J. H. Langbein, "The Origins of Public Prosecution at Common Law," *American Journal of Legal History* 17 (1973): 314, and J. H. Langbein, *Prosecuting Crime in the Renaissance: England, Germany, France* (Cambridge, MA: Harvard University Press 1974), 22, 118–122.

5. BL ADD MS 31028, f. 2.

6. William Greenwood, *Bouleuterion, or A Practical Demonstration of County Judicatures* (London, 1685), 273.

7. *Sussex Coroners' Inquests, 1558–1603,* ed. R. F. Hunnisett (Kew, Surrey: PRO Publications, 1996), xl.

8. Ibid., 274.

9. SRO LB/1662.

10. SRO LB 1684.

11. SRO LB 1659.

12. BL ADD MS 31028. The Lincolnshire inquests are very unusual (perhaps unique) in that they not only list the coroners' jurors but also their status or occupation and their place of residence. This offers a rare glimpse of the social and geographical background of early modern coroners' jurors.

13. BL ADD MS 31028.

14. David Cressy, *Literacy and the Social Order: Reading and Writing in Tu-*

dor and Stuart England (Cambridge, UK: Cambridge University Press, 1980), 42–62.

15. Barry Reay, *Popular Culture in Seventeenth-Century England* (London: Croom Helm, 1985), 39.

16. BL ADD MS 31028.

17. Ibid. The proportion of gentlemen is likely slightly skewed by the fact that gentlemen jurors' status was often listed even when the status or occupation of the other jurors was not.

18. Ibid.

19. SRO LB 1657–1687.

20. For contemporary conceptions of hierarchy and status, see Keith Wrightson, "Sorts of People in Tudor and Stuart England," in *The Middling Sort of People: Culture, Society and Politics in England, 1550–1800,* ed. Jonathan Barry and Christopher Brooks (Houndmills, Basingstoke, Hampshire: Macmillan, 1994), 28–52.

21. *Sussex Coroners' Inquests, 1485–1558,* ed. R. F. Hunnisett, Sussex Record Society 74 (Lewes, Sussex: Sussex Record Society, 1985), 14.

22. BL ADD MS 31028, f. 10. While it is sometimes difficult to know for sure whether a juror and witness with the same name are the same person, in the case of Matthew Everatt it is certain that the Matthew Everatt who acted as a witness was the same man who served on the jury, as identical marks were used to sign the deposition and the inquest.

23. BL ADD MS 31028, ff. 16–17.

24. BL ADD MS 31028, ff. 28–30.

25. Ibid.

26. Ibid.

27. SRO LB/1687.

28. Klerman, "Was the Jury Ever Self-Informing?" 58–80.

29. Greenwood, *Bouleuterion,* 274.

30. BL ADD MS 31028.

31. Ibid., 26–27. Ulceby is rendered in the document as Houlsby, while Croxton is rendered as Crowston.

32. TNA PL 27/2 (inquest of Thomas Duckworth).

33. Ibid.

34. *Village Government and Taxation in Later Stuart Nottinghamshire: The Gedling "Town Book," 1665–1714,* ed. Edward White, Thoroton Society 45 (Bristol: Thoroton Society of Northamptonshire, 2010), 11–111.

35. Ibid.

36. SRO LB/1659.

37. *Village Government and Taxation,* 11–111.

38. Donald Woodward, "Wage Rates and Living Standards in Pre-Industrial England," *Past and Present* 91 (May 1981): 28–46.

39. BL ADD MS 31028, f. 46.

40. SRO LB/1687; Greenwood, *Bouleuterion,* 276.

41. Just as it is likely that more summoned jurors actually failed to appear than were listed by the coroner in his records, it is also safe to assume that many more fines were levied for failure to appear than were actually recorded.

42. TNA STAC 10/2/29.

43. SRO QSR 56/i/51; 67/iii/77.

44. *Western Circuit Assize Orders, 1629–1648: A Calendar,* ed. J. S. Cockburn, Camden Society, 4th Series, 17 (London: Royal Historical Society, 1976), no. 409, 94.

45. Ibid., no. 511, 116–117. Forty shillings was a common amount of money for fines. Fines were also often graduated based on the wealth or status of the person fined, so it is possible that Dryall's fine reflected his status. It is also possible that the greater fine was a result of Dryall being the jury foreman, or simply that he was held more responsible for the failure of the jury to return a verdict.

46. Ibid.

47. The idea that judicial or governmental officials and local communities had divergent concepts of justice is not new. See Keith Wrightson, "Two Concepts of Justice," in *An Ungovernable People: The English and Their Laws in the Seventeenth and Eighteenth Centuries,* ed. John Brewer and John Styles (New Brunswick, NJ: Rutgers University Press, 1980), 21–46.

48. The question of the independence of jury decision making is not restricted to coroners' juries and has been debated at length in relation to grand juries and petty juries. See, for example, J. S. Morrill, *The Cheshire Grand Jury, 1625–59: A Social and Administrative Study* (Leicester: Leicester University Press, 1976), 56–71; Thomas A. Green, *Verdict According to Conscience: Perspectives on the English Criminal Trial Jury, 1200–1800* (Chicago: University of Chicago Press, 1985); Stephen K. Roberts, "Juries and the Middling Sort: Recruitment and Performance at Devon Quarter Sessions, 1649–1670," in *Twelve Good Men and True: The Criminal Trial Jury in England, 1200–1800,* ed. J. S. Cockburn and Thomas A. Green (Princeton, NJ: Princeton University Press, 1988).

49. TNA STAC 4/8/18.

50. Edward Umfreville, *Lex Coronatoria: or the Office and Duties of Coroners* (London, 1761), 107.

51. *Old Bailey Proceedings Online* (hereafter OBP), August 1679 (o16790827–1); www.oldbaileyonline.org, version 7.2 (accessed June 29, 2015).

52. Ibid.

53. Ibid.

54. *London Lives, 1690–1800,* Middlesex Sessions Papers: Justices' Working Documents, LMSMPS500540186; www.londonlives.org, version 1.1 (accessed April 6, 2015).

55. OBP, April 1692, trial of Henry Harrison (t16920406–1).

56. Ibid.

57. Ibid.

58. Adam Fox, *Oral and Literate Culture in England, 1500–1700* (Oxford: Oxford University Press, 2000), 259–299.

59. OBP, April 1692, trial of Henry Harrison (t16920406–1).

60. Ibid.

61. Ibid.

62. OBP, May 1693, trial of D- P- (t16930531–25).

63. OBP, February 1722, trial of Isaac Ingram (t17220228–10).

64. OBP, January 1732, trial of Corbet Vezey (t17320114–12).

65. OBP, January 1720, trial of Jane Griffin (t17200115–35).

66. Ibid.

67. OBP, April 1692, trial of Henry Harrison (t16920406–1).

68. OBP, February 1733, trial of Sarah Malcolm, alias Mallcombe (t17330221–52).

69. OBP, July 1715, trial of Thomas Baker (t17150713–61).

70. OBP, April 1693, trial of Anthony George Van-Eke (t16930426–8).

71. OBP, December 1689, trial of N- C- (t16891211–41).

72. OBP, April 1786, trial of Frances Lewis (t17860426–84).

73. Herrup, *Common Peace,* 138–141; Keith Wrightson, *Poverty and Piety in an English Village: Terling, 1525–1700* (Oxford: Clarendon Press, 1995), 103–109; J. S. Cockburn, *A History of English Assizes, 1558–1714* (Cambridge, UK: Cambridge University Press, 1972), 111–113.

74. Craig Muldrew, *The Economy of Obligation: The Culture of Credit and Social Relations in Early Modern England* (Houndmills, Basingstoke, Hampshire: Macmillan, 1998).

75. Stephen White, *Sir Edward Coke and the Grievances of the Commonwealth* (Manchester: Manchester University Press, 1979), 54–56.

76. For examples of such complaints, see P. G. Lawson, "Lawless Juries?: The

Composition and Behavior of Hertfordshire Juries, 1573–1624," in Green and Cockburn, *Twelve Good Men and True*, 125.

77. Morrill, *Cheshire Grand Jury*, 41–42; Herrup, *Common Peace*, 109.

78. As quoted in White, *Sir Edward Coke*, 53.

79. Matthew Hale, *The History of the Common Law of England*, ed. Charles Gray (Chicago: University of Chicago Press, 1971), 160.

80. *Essex Quarter Sessions Order Book, 1652–1661*, ed. D. H. Allen, Essex Record Office Publications 65 (Chelmsford, Essex: Essex Record Society, 1974), 204.

81. Morrill, *Cheshire Grand Jury*, 41–42.

82. As cited in Wrightson, "Two Concepts of Order," 36.

83. *Somerset Assize Order Book, 1640–1659*, ed. J. S. Cockburn, Somerset Record Society 71 (Frome: Butler & Tanner, 1971), 63.

84. Cockburn, *History of English Assizes*, 118–123.

85. Wrightson, *Poverty and Piety*, 134–136.

86. Ibid.

87. Hale, *History of the Common Law*, 165.

88. Lawson, "Lawless Juries?" 117–157; Cockburn, *History of the English Assizes*, 119.

89. Ibid.

90. Ibid., 122–123; J. S. Cockburn, "Twelve Silly Men?: The Trial Jury at Assize, 1560–1670," in Green and Cockburn, *Twelve Good Men and True*, 159 and 173–174.

91. James Oldham, "The Origins of the Special Jury," *University of Chicago Law Review* 50, no. 1 (Winter 1983), Article 3. See also Oldham, *Trial by Jury: The Seventh Amendment and Anglo-American Special Juries* (New York: New York University Press, 2006).

92. For more on mixed juries in the early modern period and the protections they provided, see Matthew Lockwood, "'Love Ye Therefore the Strangers': Immigration and the Criminal Law in England, 1675–1750," *Continuity and Change* 29, no. 3 (December 2014): 349–371.

93. OBP, May 1727, trial of Bernard Kentye Massip (t17270517-39).

94. Oldham, "Origins," 170.

95. Cockburn, *History of the English Assizes*, 120–121.

96. John Lilly, *The Practical Register: or a General Abridgment of the Law*, vol. 2 (London, 1719), 125.

97. Marianne Constable, *The Law of the Other: The Mixed Jury and Changing Conceptions of Citizenship, Law, and Knowledge* (Chicago: University of Chicago Press, 1994), 120–127. Constable ties this change in legal interpretation

to a contemporary shift away from a jury with local knowledge toward a jury that sought fact and truth. If such a shift did occur, however, the trial evidence indicates that it did not take place until at least the second half of the eighteenth century.

98. OBP, December 1686, trial of George Nicholson (t16861208-32).

99. Jacob Selwood, *Diversity and Difference in Early Modern London* (Farnham, Surrey: Ashgate, 2010), 28. See also R. D. Gwynn, "The Number of Huguenot Immigrants in England in the Late Seventeenth Century," *Journal of Historical Geography* 9, no. 4 (1983): 393.

100. OBP, December 1686, trial of George Nicholson (t16861208-32).

101. OBP, passim.

102. Lilly, *Practical Register,* vol. 2, 125.

103. For two such examples, see OBP, September 1736, trial of John Latour (t17360908-63); and OBP, October 1740, trial of John Loppenburg (t17401015-66).

104. Morrill, *Cheshire Grand Jury,* 6; Herrup, *Common Peace,* 99-102.

105. *Charges to the Grand Jury, 1689-1805,* ed. Georges Lamoine, Camden Society, 4th Series, 43 (London: Royal Historical Society, 1992), 331.

106. Ibid., 332.

107. *Western Circuit Assize Orders, 1629-1648,* 76.

108. Ibid., 253, 254.

109. Morrill, *Cheshire Grand Jury,* 13.

110. Herrup, *Common Peace,* 96.

111. Ibid., 13.

112. Ibid., 14.

113. Ibid.

Chapter 5. Economic Interest and the Oversight of Violence

1. For a contemporary discussion of the importance of consistent detection and punishment for an effective criminal justice system, see, for example, Cesare Beccaria's pioneering work *Essay on Crimes and Punishments* (London, 1767).

2. 3 Henry 7, c. 1.

3. 1 Henry 8, c. 7. For an explanation of how the certification worked in practice, see S. J. Stevenson, "The Rise of Suicide Verdicts in South-East England, 1530-1590," *Continuity and Change* 2 (1987): 43-44.

4. 1,2 Mary, c. 13; 2,3 Mary, c. 10.

5. R. F. Hunnisett, *The Medieval Coroner* (Cambridge, UK: Cambridge University Press, 1961), 97.

6. Ibid., 120, 199.

7. 1 Henry 8, c. 7; 1,2 Mary, c. 13; 2,3 Mary, c. 10. For more on early modern justices of the peace, see J. H. Gleason, *The Justices of the Peace in England, 1558–1640: A Later Eirenarcha* (Oxford: Clarendon Press, 1969); Norma Landau, *The Justices of the Peace, 1679–1760* (Berkeley: University of California Press, 1984); Anthony Fletcher, *Reform in the Provinces: The Government of Stuart England* (New Haven, CT: Yale University Press, 1986).

8. TNA Pl 27/2, f. 2.

9. As justices of the peace likely had, on average, a better understanding of the law and criminal justice system as a whole, it would not be surprising if coroners regularly consulted with justices, especially in regard to uncommon or unusual cases or circumstances. On the legal knowledge of justices, see Landau, *Justices of the Peace*, 333–362; L. R. McInnis, "Michael Dalton: The Training of the Early Modern Justice of the Peace and the Cromwellian Reforms" and Wilfred Prest, "Lay Legal Knowledge in Early Modern England," both in *Learning the Law: Teaching and the Transmission of English Law, 1150–1900*, ed. Jonathan A. Bush and Alain Wijffels (London: Hambledon Press, 1999).

10. TNA ASSI 44/1/1.

11. TNA SP 46/174.

12. *Sussex Coroners' Inquests, 1558–1603*, ed. R. F. Hunnisett (Kew, Surrey: PRO Publications, 1996), inquest 243, 53.

13. TNA ASSI 35/22/9, mm 1, 16–19. For justices of the peace committing suspects to jail as a result of inquests, see TNA ASSI 35/14/6, mm 3, 4, 11.

14. For the justices' role in local and county government and criminal justice, see Fletcher, *Reform in the Provinces;* Steve Hindle, *State and Social Change in Early Modern England, 1550–1640* (Houndmills, Basingstoke, Hampshire: Macmillan, 2000).

15. Coroners were legally obligated to attend the biannual assizes and were fined if they failed to do so. On the assize, see J. S. Cockburn, *A History of English Assizes, 1558–1714* (Cambridge, UK: Cambridge University Press, 1972).

16. *Sussex Coroners' Inquests*, inquest 150.

17. *Calendar of Assize Records, Sussex Indictments, Elizabeth I,* ed. J. S. Cockburn (London: HMSO, 1975).

18. *Western Circuit Assize Orders, 1629–1648: A Calendar,* ed. J. S. Cockburn, Camden Society, 4th Series, 17 (London: Royal Historical Society, 1976).

19. Rab Houston, "What Did the Royal Almoner Do in Britain and Ireland, 1450–1700?," *English Historical Review* 125, no. 513 (2010): 281–282. See also Kate Mertes, *The English Noble Household, 1250–1600: Good Governance and Political Rule* (Oxford: Blackwell, 1988), 50; C. M. Woolgar, *The Great Household in Late Medieval England* (New Haven, CT: Yale University Press, 1999), 9, 18, 44, 161–163.

20. L. E. Tanner, "Lord High Almoners and Sub-Almoners, 1100–1957," *Journal of the British Archeological Association*, 3rd Series, 20–21 (1957–1958): 72–83.

21. Houston, "What Did the Royal Almoner Do in Britain and Ireland," 283.

22. Michael MacDonald and Terrence R. Murphy, *Sleepless Souls: Suicide in Early Modern England* (Oxford: Oxford University Press, 1990), 25–26. See also Houston, "What Did the Royal Almoner Do in Britain and Ireland," 279–313.

23. For the development of the Court of Star Chamber in this period, see J. A. Guy, *The Cardinal's Court: The Impact of Thomas Wolsey in Star Chamber* (Totowa, NJ: Rowman and Littlefield, 1977); Guy, *The Court of Star Chamber and Its Records to the Reign of Elizabeth* (London: HMSO, 1985). For the development of King's Bench, see Marjorie Blatcher, *The Court of King's Bench, 1450–1550: A Study in Self-Help* (London: Athlone Press, 1978).

24. Rab Houston, *Punishing the Dead?: Suicide, Lordship and Community in Britain, 1500–1830* (Oxford: Oxford University Press, 2010), 2.

25. Houston, *Punishing the Dead?* 3–4; Otto von Gierke, *Community in Historical Perspective,* trans. Mary Fischer, selected and edited by Antony Black (Cambridge, UK: Cambridge University Press, 1990).

26. For more on "negotiated communities," see Craig Muldrew, "From a 'Light Cloak' to 'the Iron Cage': An Essay on Historical Changes in the Relationship Between Community and Individualism," in A. Sheppard and P. Withington, eds., *Communities in Early Modern England* (Manchester: Manchester University Press, 2000), 161–166.

27. G. R. Elton, *The Tudor Constitution: Documents and Commentary* (Cambridge, UK: Cambridge University Press, 1960), 170–171. For more on Star Chamber procedure, see T. G. Barnes, "Due Process and Slow Process in Elizabethan–Early Stuart Star Chamber," *American Journal of Legal History* 6 (1962), 221–249; and Barnes, "Star Chamber and the Sophistication of the Criminal Law," *Criminal Law Review* 24 (1977): 316–326.

28. Elton, *Tudor Constitution,* 161.

29. For contemporary discussions of forfeiture and deodand, see Michael Dalton, *The Countrey Justice* (London, 1655), 338; William Greenwood,

Bouleuterion, or A Practical Demonstration of County Judicatures (London, 1659), 149–150, 388–389.

30 J. H. Baker, *An Introduction to English Legal History,* 2nd ed. (London: Butterworth, 1979), 206, 412–413.

31. Anna Pervukhin, "Deodands: A Study in the Creation of Common Law Rules," *American Journal of Legal History* 47, no. 3 (2005): 237–256.

32. TNA STAC 4–7.

33. MacDonald and Murphy and Houston focus solely on the 138 cases relating to suicide and thus have neglected over 20 percent of Star Chamber cases involving the almoner or forfeit property.

34. TNA STAC 8/1–8/3.

35. Ibid.

36. Ibid.

37. TNA STAC 8/3/16.

38. Ibid.

39. TNA NA STAC 8/3/7.

40. Ibid.

41. Ibid.

42. TNA STAC 5/A4/34.

43. Ibid.

44. Ibid.

45. For instance, TNA STAC 5/A2/14.

46. Paul Griffiths, *Lost Londons: Change, Crime and Control in the Capital City, 1550–1660* (Cambridge, UK: Cambridge University Press, 2008).

47. TNA STAC 8/3/4.

48. Ibid.

49. TNA STAC 5/A4/34.

50. Ibid.

51. C. W. Brooks, *Pettyfoggers and Vipers of the Commonwealth: The "Lower Branch" of the Legal Profession in Early Modern England* (Cambridge, UK: Cambridge University Press, 1986), 48–57.

52. Ibid., 96–100.

53. Ibid., 79–101. For other explanations, see F. W. Maitland, "English Law and the Renaissance," in *Select Essays in Anglo-American Legal History by Various Authors,* vol. 1 (Boston: Little, Brown, and Company, 1907), 185–195; E. W. Ives, "The Common Lawyers in Pre-Reformation England," *Transactions of the Royal Historical Society,* 5th Series, 15 (1968): 170; Ives, *The Common Lawyers of Pre-Reformation England* (Cambridge, UK: Cambridge

University Press, 1983), ch. 9; Blatcher, *Court of Kings Bench,* 20; J. H. Baker, ed., *The Reports of Sir John Spelman,* Publications of the Selden Society 94 (London: Selden Society, 1978), 23–28, 53–55, 86–88, 253–297; Baker, *Introduction to English Legal History,* 38–46; J. A. Guy, *The Public Career of Sir Thomas More* (New Haven, CT: Yale University Press, 1980), 38–49; G. R. Elton, *Tudor Constitution,* 142.

54. Brooks, *Pettyfoggers and Vipers,* 71.

55. TNA STAC 7/9/13.

56. Ibid.

57. Ibid. For another example of a case not initiated by crown officials, see TNA STAC 4/7/14.

58. 1 Henry 8, c. 7.

59. *Sussex Coroners' Inquests, 1485–1558,* ed. R. F. Hunnisett, Sussex Record Society 74 (Lewes, Sussex: Sussex Record Society, 1985); *Sussex Coroners' Inquests, 1558–1603; Sussex Coroners' Inquests, 1603–1688* (Kew, Surrey: PRO Publications, 1998); *East Sussex Coroners' Records, 1688–1838,* ed. R. F. Hunnisett, Sussex Record Society 89 (Lewes, Sussex: Sussex Record Society, 2005). I have used Hunnisett's excellent calendars of coroners' inquests for Sussex as a guide to both the total number of inquests and to King's Bench litigation relating to inquests.

60. *Sussex Coroners' Inquests, 1485–1558.*

61. *Sussex Coroners' Inquests, 1558–1603.*

62. *Sussex Coroners' Inquests, 1603–1688.*

63. *Sussex Coroners' Inquests, 1558–1603.*

64. Ibid., inquest 100, 23.

65. *Sussex Coroners' Inquests, 1558–1603,* 85; *Sussex Coroners' Inquests, 1603–1688,* inquest 340.

66. *Wentworth Papers, 1597–1628,* ed. J. P. Cooper, Camden Society, 4th Series, 12 (London: Royal Historical Society, 1973), 317.

67. Ibid.

68. Ibid.

69. MacDonald and Murphy, *Sleepless Souls;* Houston, *Punishing the Dead?*

70. MacDonald and Murphy, *Sleepless Souls,* 26.

71. See for example TNA KB 27/1174, Rex m 31; 1175, Rex m 24; KB 29/188. M. 2.

72. See for example TNA KB 9/756, mm 75, 75d; KB 29/265, m 61d; KB 9/698, mm 376, 379d; KB 29/236, mm 4–4d.

73. Houston, "What Did the Royal Almoner Do in Britain and Ireland?" 279–313.

74. Ibid.
75. Catherine Patterson, *Urban Patronage in Early Modern England: Corporate Boroughs, the Landed Elite and the Crown, 1580–1640* (Stanford, CA: Stanford University Press, 1999); Ilana Krausman Ben-Amos, *The Culture of Giving: Informal Support and Gift Exchange in Early Modern England* (Cambridge, UK: Cambridge University Press, 2008), 145–192.
76. TNA STAC 5–8; *Sussex Coroners' Inquests, 1558–1603; Sussex Coroners' Inquests, 1603–1688.*
77. Houston, *Punishing the Dead?* 285–323.
78. *Sussex Coroners' Inquests, 1558–1603,* 27.
79. Ibid., 57.
80. For a discussion of differing ideas of justice between classes and within communities, see Keith Wrightson, "Two Concepts of Order: Justices, Constables and Jurymen in Seventeenth-Century England," in John Brewer and John Styles, eds., *An Ungovernable People: The English and Their Law in the Seventeenth and Eighteenth Centuries* (New Brunswick, NJ: Rutgers University Press, 1980), 21–46.
81. Hindle, *State and Social Change,* 71.
82. TNA STAC 8/3/5.
83. Ibid.
84. *Sussex Coroners' Inquests, 1558–1603; Sussex Coroners' Inquests, 1603–1688.*
85. Houston, *Punishing the Dead?* 113–120.
86. *Sussex Coroners' Inquests, 1603–1688,* inquests 153, 155, and 156, 36–37.
87. For example, TNA KB 9/806, mm 79, 80d; KB 29/284, m 19.
88. Houston, *Punishing the Dead?* 97–98.
89. *Sussex Coroners' Inquests, 1558–1603; Sussex Coroners' Inquests, 1603–1688.*
90. Houston, *Punishing the Dead?* 134.
91. *Sussex Coroners' Inquests, 1485–1558; Sussex Coroners' Inquests, 1558–1603; Sussex Coroners' Inquests, 1603–1688.*
92. Houston, *Punishing the Dead?* 135–140.
93. TNA STAC 5/A1/21.
94. Ibid.
95. Ibid.
96. Ibid.
97. Ibid.
98. TNA STAC A2/14.
99. Ibid.

100. Ibid.

101. *Sussex Coroners' Inquests, 1558–1603*, xxxiv.

102. James Sharpe and J. R. Dickinson, "Coroners' Inquests in an English County, 1600–1800: A Preliminary Survey," *Northern History* 48, no. 2 (September 2011): 257.

103. TNA STAC 8/2/42.

104. TNA STAC 8/2/46.

105. See, for instance, TNA STAC 5/A1/15.

106. TNA STAC 5/A5/3.

107. Houston, *Punishing the Dead?* 138.

108. TNA STAC 5/A1/21.

109. TNA STAC 5/A4/34.

110. TNA STAC 5/A1/13 and STAC 5/A1/15, for example.

111. See TNA STAC 8/3/22, for example.

112. TNA STAC 5/A3/ 34.

113. Houston, *Punishing the Dead?* 138.

114. TNA STAC 8/1/7.

115. TNA STAC 5/A5/3.

Chapter 6. The Changing Nature of Control

1. For the political context of the abolition of Star Chamber, see James S. Hart, Jr., *The Rule of Law, 1603–1660: Crowns, Courts, and Judges* (Harlow: Longman, 2003), 185–187; Harold J. Berman, *Law and Revolution II: The Impact of the Protestant Reformations on the Western Legal Tradition* (Cambridge, MA: Belknap Press of Harvard University Press, 2003), 313–314; and H. E. I. Phillips, "The Last Years of Star Chamber, 1603–1641," *Transactions of the Royal Historical Society* 21 (1939): 103–131.

2. Rab Houston, "What Did the Royal Almoner Do in Britain and Ireland, c. 1450–1700?" *English Historical Review* 125, no. 513 (2010): 303.

3. Hart, *Rule of Law,* 185–187.

4. William Prynne, *Histriomastix: a Scourge of Stage-players* (London, 1632). On Prynne, see William Lamont, *Marginal Prynne, 1600–1669* (London: Routledge & Kegan Paul, 1963). On Puritan printing and censorship in the Civil Wars era, see Annabel Patterson, *Censorship and Interpretation: The Conditions of Writing and Reading in Early Modern England* (Madison: University of Wisconsin Press, 1984); Randy Robertson, *Censorship and Conflict in Seventeenth-Century England: The Subtle Art of Division* (University Park: Pennsylvania State University Press, 2009); Cyndia Susan

Clegg, "Censorship and the Courts of Star Chamber and High Commission in England to 1640," *Journal of Modern European History* 3, no.1 (2005): 50–80; Anthony B. Thompson, "Licensing the Press: The Career of G. R. Weckherlin During the Personal Rule of Charles I," *Historical Journal* 41, no. 3 (1998): 653–678.

5. William Prynne, *News from Ipswich* (Ipswich, 1636).

6. John Lilburne, *A Worke of the Beast, or A Relation of the Most Unchristian Censure executed upon John Lilburne* (London, 1638).

7. Hart, *Rule of Law*, 185–187.

8. On Pym, see John Morrill, "The Unweariableness of Mr. Pym: Influence and Eloquence in the Long Parliament," in *Political Culture and Cultural Politics in Early Modern England*, ed. Susan Amussen and Mark Kishlansky (Manchester: Manchester University Press, 1995), 19–55.

9. Conrad Russell, "The First Army Plot of 1641," *Transactions of the Royal Historical Society*, 5th Series, 38 (1988): 85–106.

10. Berman, *Law and Revolution II*, 217.

11. Ibid., 216–217; Hart, *Rule of Law*, 185.

12. Houston, "What Did the Royal Almoner Do in Britain and Ireland," 285.

13. *Calendar of State Papers, Domestic Series, of the Reign of Charles I*, ed. William Douglas Hamilton, 16: April–Aug 1640 (London: Longman, 1880).

14. There is a tantalizing hint that the office of almoner was reinstated in some form under Cromwell. An entry in the state papers from 1656 mentions that a petition from the earl of Mulgrave regarding an inquiry into the possessions of William Toomes, a recent suicide, was being referred to a Dr. Bernard, "His Highnesses almoner." The Dr. Bernard in question is likely Nicholas Bernard (1600–1661), chaplain to Oliver Cromwell. If an almoner was operating during the Interregnum, however, there is no other evidence of his activity and thus the office can, at least for now, be considered vacant. *Calendar of State Papers, Domestic Series, During the Commonwealth*, ed. Mary Anne Everett Green, vol. 10: July 1656–May 1657 (London: Longman, 1883), 114.

15. Ian Green, "Brian Duppa," *Oxford Dictionary of National Biography*, ed. H. C. G. Matthew and Brian Harrison (Oxford: Oxford University Press, 2004), www.oxforddnb.com.

16. Houston. "What Did the Royal Almoner Do in Britain and Ireland."

17. TNA STAC 4–8.

18. *Sussex Coroners' Inquests, 1603–1688.*

19. Ibid.

20. *East Sussex Coroners' Records, 1688–1838,* ed. R. F. Hunnisett, Sussex Record Society 89 (Lewes, Sussex: Sussex Record Society, 2005).

21. C. W. Brooks, *Pettyfoggers and Vipers of the Commonwealth: The "Lower Branch" of the Legal Profession in Early Modern England* (Cambridge, UK: Cambridge University Press), 48–57.

22. Ibid.

23. C. W. Brooks, "Interpersonal Conflict and Social Tension: Civil Litigation in England, 1640–1830," in A. L. Beier, D. Cannadine, and J. Rosenheim, eds., *The First Modern Society: Essays in Honour of Lawrence Stone* (Cambridge, UK: Cambridge University Press, 1989), 359–399.

24. Brooks, "Interpersonal Conflict and Social Tension," 359–399; H. Horwitz and P. Polden, "Continuity or Change in the Court of Chancery in the Seventeenth and Eighteenth Centuries?" *Journal of British Studies* 35 (1996): 24–57.

25. W. A. Champion, "Recourse to the Law and the Meaning of the Great Litigation Decline, 1650–1750: Some Clues from the Shrewsbury Local Courts," in Christopher W. Brooks and Michael Lobban, eds., *Communities and Courts in Britain, 1150–1900* (London: Hambledon Press), 184–187. See also W. A. Champion, "Litigation in the Boroughs: The Shrewsbury *Curia Parvia*, 1480–1730," *Journal of Legal History* 15 (1994): 205–211.

26. Brooks, "Interpersonal Conflict and Social Tension," 382.

27. Champion, "Recourse to the Law," 179–186.

28. Michael MacDonald and Terence J. Murphy, *Sleepless Souls: Suicide in Early Modern England* (Oxford: Oxford University Press, 1990), 114–117.

29. Ibid., 116.

30. Ibid., 116–118. The shift in suicide verdicts from *felo de se* (felon of self) to *non compos mentis* (not of sound mind) in the late seventeenth and eighteenth centuries is central to MacDonald and Murphy's argument for an early modern shift in perceptions of suicide from a form of sin to a form of illness.

31. Ibid., 118. For the midcentury attempts at forfeiture reform, see *Calendar of State Papers, Domestic Series, During the Commonwealth,* ed. Mary Anne Everett Green, 2: 1650 (London: Longman, 1882), 142.

32. Ibid., 118–119. 5 William and Mary, c. 22, and 7 & 8 William, c. 36.

33. R. A. Houston, *Punishing the Dead?: Suicide, Lordship, and Community in Britain, 1500–1830* (Oxford: Oxford University Press, 146), 2.

34. Houston, "What Did the Royal Almoner Do in Britain and Ireland," 305–313. For assumpsit, see A. W. B. Simpson, *A History of the Common Law of Contract: The Rise of the Action of Assumpsit* (Oxford: Clarendon Press,

1975); D. Ibbetson, "Assumpsit and Debt in the Early Sixteenth Century: The Origins of the Indebitatus Court," *Cambridge Law Journal* 41 (1982): 142–161.

35. Houston, "What Did the Royal Almoner Do in Britain and Ireland," 312.

36. MacDonald and Murphy, *Sleepless Souls*, 118–119.

37. TNA KB 33/25/2.

38. Brooks, *Pettyfoggers and Vipers*, 75–76.

39. On the growing power of the justices of the peace in the seventeenth and eighteenth centuries, see Keith Wrightson, *English Society, 1580–1680* (London: Routledge, 2003), 162; Anthony Fletcher, *Reform in the Provinces: The Government of Stuart England* (New Haven, CT: Yale University Press, 1986); and David Lemmings, *Law and Government in England during the Long Eighteenth Century: From Consent to Command* (Houndmills, Basingstoke, Hampshire: Palgrave Macmillan, 2011), 17–41.

40. Derek Hirst, *England in Conflict, 1603–1660: Kingdom, Community, Commonwealth* (Oxford: Oxford University Press, 1999), 228–229.

41. Local Cheshire gentry even went so far as to draw up a written agreement to remain neutral, the Bunbury Agreement, in 1642. This attempt at neutrality failed, as neither side honored its provisions.

42. John Morrill, *Revolt in the Provinces: Conservatives and Radicals in the English Civil Wars, 1630–1650* (London: Longman, 1980), 72.

43. TNA CHES 21/4, 156–162.

44. For the Civil Wars in Cheshire, see Morrill, *Revolt in the Provinces*.

45. TNA CHES 21/4, 156–162.

46. Ibid.

47. TNA CHES 21/3; 21/4, 6–162.

48. TNA CHES 21/4, 408v–424v.

49. TNA CHES 21/1–7. See also James Sharpe and J. R. Dickinson, "Coroners' Inquests in an English County, 1600–1800: A Preliminary Survey," *Northern History* 48, no. 2 (2011): 257.

50. TNA ASSI 94/862, 913.

51. East Sussex Record Office, Quarter Session Rolls, QR/E 495–536.

52. TNA ASSI 94/862, 913.

53. TNA CHES 21/1–7. See also Sharpe and Dickinson, "Coroners' Inquests in an English County," 257.

54. The passing of the Murder Act in 1752 and legislation in 1751 that instituted payment of coroners by the mile may have ushered in a new era of oversight given that such acts required coroners to present records in order to receive payment, which incentivized investigations into all types of deaths and the

filing and preservation of coroners records that could be used for the purposes of oversight. 25 George 2, c. 37; 25 George 2, c. 29, s. 1.

Chapter 7. A Crisis of Violence?

1. *William Lambarde and Local Government: His "Ephemeris" and Twenty-nine Charges to Juries and Commissions,* ed. Conyers Read (Ithaca, NY: Cornell University Press, 1962), 68.
2. Philip Stubbes, *The Anatomie of Abuses* (London, 1595).
3. The most famous example of this literature is surely Steven Pinker, *The Better Angels of Our Nature: Why Violence Has Declined* (New York: Viking, 2011). Other prominent examples include Robert Muchembled, *A History of Violence: From the End of the Middle Ages to the Present* (Cambridge, UK: Polity Press, 2012), and Pieter Spierenburg, *A History of Murder: Personal Violence in Europe from the Middle Ages to the Present* (Cambridge, UK: Polity Press, 2008).
4. Paul Slack, *Poverty and Policy in Tudor and Stuart England* (London: Longman, 1988), 8.
5. Norbert Elias, *The Civilizing Process: Sociogenetic and Psychogenetic Investigations,* rev. ed. (Oxford: Blackwell, 2000).
6. See, for example, the attention in popular media surrounding the publication of Pinker's *Better Angels of Our Nature.*
7. This is not to say that there were not other spikes in crime or violence in the early modern period; however, general levels of prosecution for violent crime declined relatively throughout the seventeenth and eighteenth centuries.
8. Bruce Lenman and Geoffrey Parker, "The State, the Community and the Criminal Law in Early Modern Europe," in *Crime and the Law: The Social History of Crime in Western Europe since 1500,* ed. V. A. C. Gatrell et al. (London: Europa Publications, 1980), 11–48.
9. J. A. Sharpe, *Crime in Early Modern England, 1550–1750* (London: Longman, 1984), 60; Keith Wrightson, *English Society, 1580–1680* (New Brunswick, NJ: Rutgers University Press, 2003), 168.
10. On the rise and fall of witchcraft prosecutions, see Alan Macfarlane, *Witchcraft in Tudor and Stuart England: A Regional and Comparative Study* (London: Routledge & Kegan Paul, 1970); Keith Thomas, *Religion and the Decline of Magic: Studies in Popular Beliefs in Sixteenth- and Seventeenth-Century England* (London: Penguin, 1991), 517–681. For the rise in property crime, see Peter Lawson, "Property Crime and Hard Times in England, 1559–1624," *Law and History Review* 4, no. 1 (1986): 95–127; Joel Samaha,

Law and Order in Historical Perspective: The Case of Elizabethan Essex (New York: Academic Press, 1973). For felony and homicide, see Sharpe, *Crime in Early Modern England,* 55–58.

11. Lawson, "Property Crime and Hard Times," 97.

12. Sharpe, *Crime in Early Modern England,* 62. Sharpe is, however, careful to note that the relationship between economics and crime is often ambiguous and rarely straightforward.

13. Lawson, "Property Crime and Hard Times," 96.

14. J. M. Beattie, *Crime and the Courts in England, 1660–1800* (Princeton, NJ: Princeton University Press, 1986); John Beattie, "Violence and Society in Early Modern England," in *Perspectives in Criminal Law: Essays in Honour of John Ll. J. Edwards,* ed. A. N. Doob and E. L. Greenspan (Ontario: Canada Law Book, 1985), 47; J. S. Cockburn, "The Nature and Incidence of Crime in England, 1559–1625: A Preliminary Survey," in *Crime in England, 1550–1800,* ed. J. S. Cockburn (Princeton, NJ: Princeton University Press, 1977), 49–71; J. S Cockburn, "Patterns of Violence in English Society: Homicide in Kent, 1560–1985," *Past and Present* 130, no. 1 (1991): 70–106; J. A. Sharpe, *Crime in Seventeenth-Century England: A County Study* (Cambridge, UK: Cambridge University Press, 1983); Sharpe, *Crime in Early Modern England,* 41–73; Lawrence Stone, "Interpersonal Violence in English Society, 1300–1980," *Past and Present* 101, no. 1 (1983): 22–33. For a good overview of the literature on early modern homicide in England and Europe, see Randolph Roth, "Homicide in Early Modern England, 1549–1800: The Need for a Quantitative Synthesis," *Crime, History and Societies* 5, no. 2 (2001): 33–67.

15. Roth, "Homicide in Early Modern England," 45.

16. Stone, "Interpersonal Violence," 31–32.

17. Roth, "Homicide in Early Modern England," 46.

18. Ibid. Those seeking a true picture of crime rates in the popular literature of the early modern period, or any period for that matter, should be extremely careful.

19. Keith Wrightson and John Walter, "Dearth and the Social Order in Early Modern England," *Past and Present* 71, no. 1 (1976): 22–42; Keith Wrightson, *Ralph Tailor's Summer: A Scrivener, His City, and the Plague* (New Haven, CT: Yale University Press, 2011).

20. Nicholas Rogers, *Mayhem: Post-War Crime and Violence in Britain, 1748–53* (New Haven, CT: Yale University Press, 2013).

21. The impact of Elias on most explanations for the decline of crime or violence has been immense. See Elias, *Civilizing Process,* passim.

22. Lawrence Stone, "A Rejoinder," *Past and Present* 108, no. 1 (1985): 220.

23. Beattie, *Crime and the Courts*, 112.

24. Robert Shoemaker, "Male Honor and the Decline of Public Violence in Eighteenth-Century London," *Social History* 26, no. 2 (2001): 207.

25. *Sussex Coroners' Inquests, 1485–1558*, ed. R. F. Hunnisett, Sussex Record Society 74 (Lewes, Sussex: Sussex Record Society, 1985); *Sussex Coroners' Inquests, 1558–1603*, ed. R. F. Hunnisett (Kew, Surrey: PRO Publications, 1996); *Sussex Coroners' Inquests, 1603–1688*, ed. R. F. Hunnisett (Kew, Surrey: PRO Publications, 1998); *East Sussex Coroners' Records, 1688–1838*, ed. R. F. Hunnisett, Sussex Record Society 89 (Lewes, Sussex: Sussex Record Society, 2005).

26. *Sussex Coroners' Inquests, 1558–1603; Sussex Coroners' Inquests, 1603–1688*.

27. *Sussex Coroners' Inquests, 1485–1558; Sussex Coroners' Inquests, 1558–1603; Sussex Coroners' Inquests, 1603–1688*.

28. Sharpe, *Crime in Early Modern England*, 59–60; Lawson, "Property Crime and Hard Times."

29. *Sussex Coroners' Inquests, 1558–1603*, 93.

30. I find the idea that a general breakdown of the norms and institutions of society in the period led to a rise in homicide to be entirely unconvincing, as well as unproven.

31. *Sussex Coroners' Inquests, 1558–1603; Sussex Coroners' Inquests, 1603–1688*. The laconic nature of both coroners' inquests and assize records often makes it difficult to ascribe economic motives to homicides, although such motives are occasionally recorded. Even so, there is no evidence either at the assize or in the coroners' records of a significant rise in robberies or thefts leading to homicides in the period in question.

32. *Sussex Coroners' Inquests, 1603–1688*, nos. 11, 18, 37.

33. Lawson, "Property Crime and Hard Times," 109–112.

34. Estimates of prices for the period 1580–1620 have been taken from W. G. Hoskins's calculations in W. G. Hoskins, "Harvest Fluctuations and English Economic History, 1480–1619," *Agricultural History Review* 12, no. 1 (1964): 46, and Hoskins, "Harvest Fluctuations and English Economic History, 1620–1759," *Agricultural History Review* 16, no. 1 (1968): 28.

35. Ibid.

36. Wrightson, *English Society*, 170.

37. William Harrison, *Description of England* (London, 1577), part 1, 229–230.

38. *Sussex Coroners' Inquests, 1485–1558*.

39. 3 Henry 7, c. 2.

40. Cockburn, "Patterns of Violence," 73.

41. C. W. Brooks, *Pettyfoggers and Vipers of the Commonwealth: The "Lower Branch" of the Legal Profession in Early Modern England* (Cambridge, UK: Cambridge University Press, 1986), 48–57.

42. Ibid.

43. TNA STAC 5/A5/3.

44. TNA KB 9/684A, mm 1d, 16; KB 29/231, mm 2d, 3.

45. *Sussex Coroners' Inquests, 1485–1558; Sussex Coroners' Inquests, 1558–1603; Sussex Coroners' Inquests, 1603–1688.*

46. *Ibid.*

47. Ibid.

48. TNA STAC 4–8. See also Chap. 5 above.

49. *Sussex Coroners' Inquests, 1603–1688.*

50. While the period up to the mid-seventeenth century saw economic improvement in Sussex, the late seventeenth century saw a brief return of economic and demographic stagnation. Mary J. Dobson, "The Last Hiccup of the Old Demographic Regime: Population Stagnation and Decline in Late Seventeenth- and Early Eighteenth-Century South-East England," *Continuity and Change* 4, no. 3 (December 1989): 395–428.

51. TNA CHES 21/1–5. For the numbers relating to the eighteenth century I have followed those provided in James Sharpe and J. R. Dickinson, "Coroners' Inquests in an English County, 1600–1800: A Preliminary Survey," *Northern History* 48, no. 2 (2011): 253–270.

52. Cockburn, "Patterns of Violence," 74.

53. Brooks, *Pettyfoggers and Vipers of the Commonwealth*, 107–111.

54. See Chap. 5.

55. *Sussex Coroners' Inquests, 1485–1558; Sussex Coroners' Inquests, 1558–1603; Sussex Coroners' Inquests, 1603–1688.*

56. Sharpe and Dickinson, "Coroners' Inquests in an English County," 257.

57. Ibid., Table 1.

58. E. A. Wrigley and R. S. Schofield, *The Population History of England, 1541–1871* (Cambridge, UK: Cambridge University Press, 1989), 157–219.

Chapter 8. Legislation, Incentivization, and a New System of Oversight

1. For a discussion of the effects of war on domestic crime levels, see J. M. Beattie, *Crime and the Courts in England, 1660–1800* (Princeton: Princeton University Press, 1986); Douglas Hay, "War, Dearth and Theft in the Eighteenth Century: The Records of the English Courts," *Past and Present* 95,

no. 1 (1982): 117–160; Nicholas Rogers, *Mayhem: Post-War Crime and Violence in Britain* (New Haven, CT: Yale University Press, 2012), 39–63.

2. Henry Fielding, *An Enquiry into the Causes of the Late Increase of Robbers* (London, 1752), 2.
3. Ibid., 1.
4. *Whitehall Evening Post,* Dec. 4, 1750.
5. Rogers, *Mayhem,* 41–44.
6. As quoted in Rogers, *Mayhem,* 45.
7. Ibid., 46–49.
8. Beattie, *Crime and the Courts in England,* 221.
9. Rogers, *Mayhem,* 5.
10. Ibid., 46–49.
11. As quoted in Rogers, *Mayhem,* 40.
12. *Journal of the House of Commons,* vol. 26, 1750–1754 (London: HMSO, 1803), 27.
13. Beattie, *Crime and the Courts in England,* 521.
14. Ibid., 251–252.
15. As quoted in Rogers, *Mayhem,* 54.
16. Beattie, *Crime and the Courts in England,* 251.
17. 25 George 2, c. 37.
18. Ibid.
19. 25 George 2, c. 29.
20. 3 Henry 7, c. 2.
21. One might think that a lack of financial incentive could lead to corruption, but the evidence suggests that when effective central oversight was in place, little corruption escaped the attentions of the authorities. For more, see Chap. 4 above.
22. 25 George 2, c. 29.
23. 5,6 William 4, c. 76, s. 62.
24. 23,24 Victoria, c. 116, s. 4.
25. *The Official Diary of Lieutenant-General Adam Williamson, Deputy-Lieutenant of the Tower of London,* ed. John Charles Fox, Camden Society, 3rd Series, 22 (London: Offices of the Society, 1912), 85–86.
26. Ibid.
27. Ibid. 1 Henry 8, c. 7 allowed coroners to collect a fee of 13s 4d for cases that led to indictments for homicide only.
28. John Money, ed., *The Chronicles of John Cannon, Part I, 1684–1733* (Oxford: Oxford University Press, 2010), 176.
29. Ibid.

30. Ibid.

31. *A Bill for Better Ordering of the Office of the Coroner* (London, 1749), 1.

32. Ibid.

33. John Adams, *An Essay Concerning Self-Murther: Wherein is Endeavor'd to Prove it is Unlawful According to Natural Principles* (London, 1700), 128. J. A. Sharpe uses this quote to suggest that coroners did not operate in the uniform way suggested by the law. I find this contention unconvincing, as the quote simply states what should have been obvious to contemporaries and modern historians alike, that the coroner was the official who was most directly responsible for the investigation of violent death and had significant influence over the outcome of inquests. This in and of itself does not imply anything one way or another about the quality of service provided by coroners in the period. J. A. Sharpe, "A History of Violence in England: Some Observations," *Past and Present* 108, no. 1 (1985): 210.

34. Ibid.

35. For the argument that coroners acted in a more arbitrary and less efficient way in the late seventeenth and early eighteenth centuries, see Sharpe, "History of Violence in England," 206–215.

36. *East Sussex Coroners' Records, 1688–1838*, ed. R. F. Hunnisett, Sussex Record Society 89 (Lewes, Sussex: Sussex Record Society, 2005), 141–153.

37. Ibid., 153–165.

38. James Sharpe and J. R. Dickinson, "Coroners' Inquests in an English County, 1600–1800: A Preliminary Survey," *Northern History* 48, no. 2 (2011): 257.

39. *East Sussex Coroners' Records, 1688–1838*, 1–14.

40. *Wiltshire Coroners' Bills, 1752–1796*, ed. R. F. Hunnisett, Wiltshire Record Society 36 (Devizes, Wiltshire: Wiltshire Record Society, 1981), 1–21, 138–145.

41. Ibid.

42. Ibid., xlv.

43. *East Sussex Coroners' Records, 1688–1838*, 141–153.

44. Ibid., 153–165.

45. Sharpe and Dickinson, "Coroners' Inquests in an English County," 257.

46. *East Sussex Coroners' Records*, 141–165.

47. Ibid., 1–14.

48. *Wiltshire Coroners' Bills*, 1–21.

49. *Sussex Coroners' Inquests, 1485–1558*.

50. Ibid.

51. *Wiltshire Coroners' Bills*, 2.

52. Ibid.

53. Ibid., 1–7.
54. *East Sussex Coroners' Records,* 2.
55. Ibid., 141–148.
56. Malcolm Gaskill, *Crime and Mentalities in Early Modern England* (Cambridge, UK: Cambridge University Press, 2000), 246.
57. Ibid. Gaskill suggests that evidence for such an unwillingness does exist, but fails to provide any himself.
58. *Wiltshire Coroners' Bills,* 1.
59. Ibid.
60. Obviously, most counties did not have a completely even population distribution; however, given that major population centers would likely have had their own borough coroners, I think such an assumption is justifiable.
61. The greater distances traveled by North Wiltshire coroners were probably a result of two geographical considerations: first, the North Wiltshire jurisdiction was especially large; and second, Devizes, the town from which the distances were measured, was located in the extreme south of the jurisdiction, necessitating longer journeys than in East Sussex or South Wiltshire.
62. *Wiltshire Coroners' Bills,* 3.
63. *Sussex Coroners' Inquests, 1558–1603.*
64. BL ADD MS 31028.
65. *Wiltshire Coroners' Bills,* 1–41.
66. Ibid., 1–66.
67. *East Sussex Coroners' Records,* 1–14.
68. *Wiltshire Coroners' Bills,* 138–145.
69. Ibid., 1–66.
70. Ibid.
71. Ibid., 14.
72. Ibid.
73. Ibid., 13.
74. Ibid., 1–66.
75. Ibid., 26–27.
76. *Wiltshire Coroners' Bills,* 149–171.
77. *East Sussex Coroners' Records,* 20–54.
78. *Wiltshire Coroners' Bills,* 1–41.
79. Ibid., 1–66.
80. Ibid.
81. Ibid.
82. Ibid.
83. Ibid.

84. P. E. H. Hair, "Deaths from Violence in Britain: A Tentative Secular Survey," *Population Studies* 25, no. 1 (1971): 5–24.

85. Middlesex Coroners' Inquests, 1750–1800, London Metropolitan Archives, Ms. MJ/SP/C/W, LL ref: LMCOIC65102; London bills of mortality as cited in James Boswell, *Scots Magazine* 50 (January 1788): 656.

86. Adrian Randall, *Riotous Assemblies: Popular Protest in Hanoverian England* (Oxford: Oxford University Press, 2006), 28–29.

Conclusion

1. TNA PL 27/2, Part II, inquest of William Lennox.

2. Ibid.

3. Ibid.

4. Ibid.

5. Charles Tilly, *Coercion, Capital and States, AD 990–1990* (Cambridge, MA: Blackwell, 1990); Geoffrey Parker, *The Military Revolution: Military Innovation and the Rise of the West, 1500–1800* (New York: Cambridge University Press, 1996); Brian Downing, *The Military Revolution and Political Change: Origins of Democracy and Autocracy in Early Modern Europe* (Princeton, NJ: Princeton University Press, 1992); Thomas Ertman, *Birth of the Leviathan: Building States and Regimes in Medieval and Early Modern Europe* (Cambridge, UK: Cambridge University Press, 1997); John Brewer, *The Sinews of Power: War, Money, and the English State, 1688–1783* (Cambridge, MA: Harvard University Press, 1990); Lawrence Stone, *The Crisis of the Aristocracy, 1558–1641* (Oxford: Clarendon Press, 1979).

6. Malcolm Gaskill, *Crime and Mentalities in Early Modern England* (Cambridge, UK: Cambridge University Press, 2000), 250–251.

7. Paul Hyams, *Rancor and Reconciliation in Medieval England* (Ithaca, NY: Cornell University Press, 2003), 242–266.

8. Stone, *Crisis of the Aristocracy*, 227–229.

9. Ibid., 215, 228–229.

10. Henry Stanley, fourth earl of Derby, would die a little over a year after these events, in 1593. The other examples of the late survival of homicide compensation cited by Gaskill derive from B. S. Phillpotts, *Kindred and Clan*, and relate solely to Denmark and Germany rather than England. Phillpotts's discussion of England is limited to the Anglo-Saxon and Conquest periods and does not provide any examples of early modern homicide compensation in England. B. S. Phillpotts, *Kindred and Clan in the Middle Ages and After:*

A Study in the Sociology of the Teutonic Races (Cambridge, UK: Cambridge University Press, 1913), 96, 124–125, 156, 168.

11. Gaskill, *Crime and Mentalities,* 251 n. 43. For examples of these types of cases, see TNA CHES 21/2, f. 122v; CHES 21/3, ff. 2v, 9. There is little evidence that there were many, if any, early modern cases in which extrajudicial compensation was sought instead of or to the exclusion of formal legal proceedings. Thus, the existence of extralegal compensation alone does not suggest a threat to the state's monopoly of violence.

12. Adrian Randall, *Riotous Assemblies: Popular Protest in Hanoverian England* (Oxford: Oxford University Press, 2006), 23–24. Robert Shoemaker, *The London Mob: Violence and Disorder in Eighteenth-Century England* (London: Hambledon Press 2004), 111–112.

13. E. P. Thompson, "The Moral Economy of the English Crowd," *Past and Present* 50 (1971): 76–136; Andy Wood, "The Place of Custom in Plebeian Political Culture: England, 1550–1800," *Social History* 22, no. 1 (January 1997): 46–60.

14. Shoemaker, *London Mob,* 130–133. Certain types of criminals and informers were sometimes subject to mob violence in the period, but these were exceptions.

15. As quoted in Randall, *Riotous Assemblies,* 25.

16. Ibid., 24.

17. Ibid., 25.

18. Ibid., 25–26.

19. Shoemaker, *London Mob,* 132–133.

20. Ibid., 136–137.

21. Randall, *Riotous Assemblies,* 35–42.

22. Shoemaker, *London Mob,* 142–152.

23. Randall, *Riotous Assemblies,* 318–325.

24. Peter King, *Crime and Law in England, 1750–1840: Remaking Justice from the Margins* (Cambridge, UK: Cambridge University Press, 2006), 232–235.

25. Ibid.

26. Ibid., 242.

27. William Blackstone, *Commentaries on the Laws of England* (London, 1769), 4: 356–357.

28. Matthew Lockwood, "From Treason to Homicide: Changing Conceptions of the Law of Petty Treason in Early Modern England," *Journal of Legal History* 34, no. 1 (2013).

29. Elizabeth Foyster, *Marital Violence: An English Family History, 1660–1857* (Cambridge, UK: Cambridge University Press, 2005), 238.

30. Ibid., 238–241.

31. J. Jean Hecht, *The Domestic Servant Class in Eighteenth-Century England* (London: Routledge & Kegan Paul, 1956), 78–80.

32. As quoted in Julie Flavell, *When London Was the Capital of America* (New Haven, CT: Yale University Press, 2010), 40–41.

33. J. M. Beattie, *Policing and Punishment in London, 1660–1750: Urban Crime and the Limits of Terror* (Oxford: Oxford University Press, 2001), 126, n. 38.

34. On patterns of crime in Europe, see n. 2 above and P. Karonen, "A Life for a Life versus Christian Reconciliation: Violence and the Process of Civilization in the Kingdom of Sweden, 1540–1700," in H. Ylikangas, P. Karonen, and M. Lehti, eds., *Five Centuries of Violence in Finland and the Baltic Area* (Columbus: Ohio State University Press, 2001), 1–83; E. Osterberg, "Criminality, Social Order and the Early Modern State: Evidence and Interpretations in Scandinavian Historiography," in E. A. Johnson and E. H. Monkkonen, eds., *The Civilization of Crime: Violence in Town and Country since the Middle Ages* (Urbana: University of Illinois Press, 1996), 35–62; Pieter Spierenburg, "Faces of Violence: Homicide Trends and Cultural Meanings: Amsterdam, 1431–1816," *Journal of Social History* 27 (1994): 701–716.

35. Pieter Spierenburg, *A History of Murder: Personal Violence in Europe from the Middle Ages to the Present* (Cambridge, UK: Polity, 2008), 44–64.

36. Malcolm Greenshields, *An Economy of Violence in Early Modern France: Crime and Justice in the Haute Auvergne, 1587–1664* (University Park: Pennsylvania State University Press, 1994), 1.

37. Harold J Berman, *Law and Revolution*, vol. 2: *The Impact of the Protestant Reformations on the Western Legal Tradition* (Cambridge, MA: Belknap Press of Harvard University Press, 2003), 137–146.

38. John K. Brackett, *Criminal Justice and Crime in Late Renaissance Florence, 1537–1603* (Cambridge, UK: Cambridge University Press, 1992)

39. James Casey, *Early Modern Spain: A Social History* (London: Routledge, 1999), 166.

40. Berman, *Impact of the Protestant Reformations*, 143. See also John Langbein, *Torture and the Law of Proof: Europe and England in the Ancien Régime* (Chicago: University of Chicago Press, 1976), 57.

41. Brackett, *Criminal Justice and Crime*, 89–90, 142.

42. Joel F. Harrington, *The Faithful Executioner: Life and Death, Honor and*

Shame in the Turbulent Sixteenth Century (New York: Farrar, Straus and Giroux, 2013), 30.

43. Ibid.

44. Ian Burney, *Bodies of Evidence: Medicine and the Politics of the English In-quest, 1830–1926* (Baltimore: Johns Hopkins University Press, 2000), 29.

45. Ibid., 28–31.

46. Ibid., 30–35.

Index

accidental deaths: contested, 326, 341–43; and corruption, 101; inquests of, 20, 88; investigation of, 17, 259; jurisdiction over, 63; litigation of, 206–7, 216–17, 223, 226–27; rates of, 122, 132, 233, 246, 258, 270–76, 281–87, 302–5, 348; verdicts, 85, 208–9, 231, 237, 279, 317–18

almoner: abolition of, 243–52; agents of, 1–2, 231–32, 243; appointment of, 277–79, 326–27; complaints of, 208–9, 230; economic interests of, 198, 219–20; oversight by, 202–10, 219–38, 258–60; role of, 203, 220–25, 229, 351

amercements, 36, 201

assizes. *See* courts of assize

assumpsit, 249

bailiffs, 30, 68–69, 98, 151, 166, 170, 183, 229

bills, 36, 45, 191–92, 240–42, 257–58, 294, 298, 300–304, 308–20

Blackstone, William, 338

boroughs: coroners of, 69–70, 81–82, 91, 295–96; and courts, 37, 326; juries of, 154; jurisdiction, 59–61, 307

bribery, 87, 90, 155, 167, 181

bribes, 21, 32, 87, 101, 188, 297

Burdett, John, 121–22, 124, 126

Cannon, John, 74–79, 296–97

Charles I, 83, 240, 253

Cheshire: during the Civil War, 253–56; coroners in, 59, 81, 230, 254; inquests in, 233, 258, 282–85, 300; juries, 191–93, 298; officials in, 71

Chester, 54, 59–62, 70–72, 81–84, 95–99, 193, 253

churchwardens, 6, 92, 128, 182

Civil Wars, 83–84, 238, 240, 243–44, 249, 253–56, 332

Coke, Edward, 54, 90, 97, 181

common law, 37, 54, 90, 181, 202–4, 214–16

compositions, 63, 148–50, 154, 168–69, 180, 189, 213, 221–27

constables: as deponents, 110; as jurors, 182; as local officeholders, 6, 92, 100, 128; as officers of the peace, 98, 151, 157–58, 161–64; popular perceptions of, 101, 103

Coroner Act, 290, 294–99, 319

coroners: contribution to the monopoly of violence, 22–23, 325–26, 342–43, 347–49; declining oversight of, 238–40, 249–52; depositions by, 110–11; distances traveled, 306–10; duties of, 53–58; education and training of, 91–100; election of, 68–85, 325; forensic investigations by, 105–10, 111–12, 134–45; historiographical views of, 18–21; and juries, 146–48, 151–52, 159–60, 165–69; jurisdictions, 59–68; medieval, 17, 51–52, 54, 58, 198; oversight of, 199–222, 236–37, 277–81, 289–90, 316–21; payment, 85–89, 299–306, 310–15; popular attitudes toward, 100–104; post–Civil War functioning, 252–61; rates of inquest, 285–88; status of, 89–91; and trial courts, 169–80; and witnesses, 112–23, 123–34. *See also* Coroner Act

Council of Wales, 33–34, 240

Court of Chancery, 36–38, 72–74, 80, 90